T0384280

Principles of Strategic Communication

Designed to support the paradigm shift in media and communication, this book presents the basic tenets of strategic communication and its foundational disciplines of advertising, public relations and marketing communications.

Drawing on the latest research in the field, the text introduces students to the theories of strategic communication while at the same time outlining how to apply them to everyday practice. To facilitate learning and tie concepts to practice, each chapter includes introductory focus questions, a contemporary global case study, a career profile of a current practitioner, end-of-chapter discussion questions and features that highlight how research methods can be applied to strategic communication practice. A glossary of terms appears at the end of the book.

Principles of Strategic Communication is ideal as a core text for undergraduate students in strategic communication courses within media, communication, marketing and advertising programs.

The accompanying online support material features chapter summaries, useful links to examples of strategic communication in action, suggested further reading and practice test questions. Instructors will find an instructor's resource manual that includes sample syllabi, class activities, lecture topics and a test bank.

Derina Holtzhausen is Professor and Dean of the College of Fine Arts & Communication at Lamar University, USA.

Jami A. Fullerton is Professor and Director of Academic Programs in the School of Global Studies and Peggy Layman Welch Chair in Strategic Communications at Oklahoma State University, USA.

Bobbi Kay Lewis is Associate Dean in the College of Arts and Sciences and Associate Professor in the School of Media & Strategic Communications at Oklahoma State University, USA.

Danny Shipka was Associate Professor in the School of Media & Strategic Communications at Oklahoma State University, USA.

Principles of Strategic Communication

Derina Holtzhausen, Jami A. Fullerton, Bobbi Kay Lewis
and Danny Shipka

Routledge
Taylor & Francis Group

NEW YORK AND LONDON

First published 2021
by Routledge

605 Third Avenue, New York, NY 10158
and by Routledge
2 Park Square, Milton Park, Abingdon, Oxon, OX14 4RN

Routledge is an imprint of the Taylor & Francis Group, an informa business

© 2021 Taylor & Francis

Library of Congress Cataloging-in-Publication Data
A catalog record for this title has been requested

ISBN: 978-0-367-43247-8 (hbk)
ISBN: 978-0-367-42631-6 (pbk)
ISBN: 978-1-003-00204-8 (ebk)

Typeset in Times New Roman
by Apex CoVantage, LLC

www.routledge.com/9780367426316

This book is dedicated to the memory of Daniel G. Shipka, Ph.D.

Contents

About the Authors

Dr. Derina Holtzhausen

Dr. Derina Holtzhausen (Ph.D., University of Johannesburg) is professor and dean of the College of Fine Arts & Communication at Lamar University, Beaumont, TX, which is a member of the Texas State University System. She joined Lamar in July 2015 after serving as professor and director of the School of Media and Strategic Communications (SMSC) at Oklahoma State University (OSU) from 2008. Holtzhausen joined OSU after serving 11 years at the University of South Florida's School of Mass Communications as, among others, graduate studies director and public relations program coordinator. She teaches courses in strategic communication management, media management, media entrepreneurship and research at undergraduate and graduate level. In her native South Africa, Holtzhausen practiced for 25 years as a journalist, a partner in an advertising and public relations agency and a communication executive in both the public and private sectors. The U.S. Institute of Public Relations recognized her with its Pathfinder Award for her original research agenda on postmodern public relations. Since moving to the United States in 1997 she has published more than 30 articles and book chapters, served as the co-editor of the *International Journal of Strategic Communication*, which she co-founded, and published an award-winning book, *Public Relations as Activism: Postmodern Approaches to Theory and Practice*. She is co-editor of *Handbook of Strategic Communication*, which was published by Routledge in November 2014.

Dr. Jami Fullerton (Ph.D., University of North Texas) is the Director of Academic Programs in the School of Global Studies at Oklahoma State University, where she is also a full professor in the School of Media and Strategic Communications and holds the Peggy Layman Welch Endowed Chair in Strategic Communication. Prior to entering academe, Dr. Fullerton worked in the advertising industry, primarily on the client-side, where she directed the marketing and advertising functions for several national retail chains.

Dr. Fullerton's research interests include mediated public diplomacy, nation branding and advertising education. She has published numerous studies on international and ethnic advertising in national and inter-

Dr. Jami Fullerton

national academic journals including *Journalism and Mass Communication Quarterly*, *Journal of Advertising Research*, *Mass Communication & Society* and *American Behavioral Scientist*. In 2003, she received a grant to study international advertising, specifically the U.S. State Department's advertising effort in the Muslim world. Research resulting from the grant was published in her book with Alice Kendrick, *Advertising's War on Terrorism: The Story of the U.S. State Department's Shared Values Initiative* (Marquette Books, 2006). Building on this line of research, she and Dr. Kendrick more recently published an edited book on public diplomacy and nation branding titled, *Shaping International Public Opinion: A Model for Nation Branding and Public Diplomacy* (Peter Lang, 2017). She served as co-editor of the *Journal of Advertising Education* from 2011–2017 and is the now the chief editor of the 75-year-old *Journalism and Mass Communication Educator*.

Dr. Fullerton's summers are often spent abroad where she teaches communications courses and conducts research. She lives in Tulsa with her husband Sam and daughter Helen.

Dr. Bobbi Kay Lewis (Ph.D., Oklahoma State University) is associate dean of outreach and communications in the College of Arts and Sciences at Oklahoma State University. She leads the college in online programs, study abroad, professional development, events, recruitment and communications. Before joining the dean's office in 2015, she was the associate director in the School of Media and Strategic Communications (SMSC), where she is an associate professor of strategic communication, and helped lead the efforts to shift the curriculum from advertising and public relations to strategic communications in 2010. She teaches courses across the curriculum in strategic communication including,

Dr. Bobbi Kay Lewis

introduction to strategic communication, campaigns, e-media advertising, copywriting, event planning and media ethics at the undergraduate and graduate level. Prior to joining academia, Lewis worked in advertising for ten years. She started her career at an ad agency and shifted to working in newspaper advertising and events. Lewis' research interests include social media, religious media, experiential learning and strategic communication education. She has published numerous articles and book chapters in these areas.

Dr. Danny Shipka

About six months before this book was completed, our co-author, dear friend and colleague, Dr. Danny Shipka passed away from Multiple System Atrophy, a disease that attacks the neurological system. As the professor for Introduction to Strategic Communication at Oklahoma State, Danny recognized that an introductory textbook in the field did not exist and therefore, rallied us to write this book. It breaks our hearts that he did not live to see it in print, and more sadly, was not able to use it to teach the students that he loved.

Danny earned a Master of Science in International Studies at Oklahoma State University in 2001. He taught at the University of Florida while attending graduate school and earned his Ph.D. in 2007. He then joined the faculty at Louisiana State University, where he taught for six years and was a very popular assistant professor. Danny then returned to his alma mater, Oklahoma State University, in the fall of 2013, where he later earned tenure in the School of Media and Strategic Communications. He was the author of a highly valued film analysis book *Perverse Titillation: The Exploitation of Films of Italy, France and Spain*, which sold to both academic and commercial audiences. He also co-edited *International Horror Film Directors: Global Fear* with Ralph Belliveau. He was author and co-author of dozens of academic journal articles and conference papers. His voice can be heard throughout this text, particularly in the chapters on ethics, diversity and careers.

Danny lived to teach and loved nothing more than being part of his college community. His lively, witty and tenacious spirit made him a fighter despite the disabling impact of the disease. He bravely fought the demise of his voice and body, eventually forcing the loss of many things he loved like playing tennis, swimming, driving, singing, travelling, writing—but most of all, teaching.

This book is dedicated to Danny's memory and his passion for the discipline of strategic communication.

Preface

My interest in strategic communication has always been guided by professional communication practice. It has never been an interest as much as a necessity driven by the needs of my clients and employers. Every bit of my experience as a communication practitioner has informed this book and my overall approach to this rather new and emerging field, from my first job as a journalist to my current position as the dean of a college that includes a department of communication and media. Therefore, you will find the threads of my communications career throughout this text.

Journalism taught me the value of writing well, the importance of honesty and transparency in reporting and storytelling, the principles of interviewing and the overarching responsibility and impact journalists have of communicating in the public sphere.

From journalism, I moved to public relations and from there to co-owner of a public relations and advertising company (HPA) with my husband Paul, a seasoned and savvy communication practitioner, who also was my first mentor in the field. We practiced the two disciplines side-by-side and integrated, depending on the needs of the client. It is from that experience that we never understood the notion of separating these disciplines into silos because they always informed each other and from where our approach to strategic communication emerged.

We must have heard the term integrated marketing somewhere (most certainly did not invent it) because around 1979 we developed a company brochure that presented this integrated approach in a model, which we called *The HPA Blueprint for Total and Integrated Marketing*. That brochure is sitting on my desk even as I am writing this preface, in all its unsophisticated glory—although we did not think so at that time.

The model focused on *The Enterprise*, which consisted of products, services, image, structure and finances. The *Target Market* was mostly segmented demographically, e.g. nationality, sex, age, status, geographics and (strangely) timing. The *HPA Promotional Programs* consisted of publicity, media, advertising, promotion, image-building, liaison, publications and program budgeting. *The Media* were segmented into a myriad of outlets, including the sales force, theatre, networks, and many more. Today we would have called that earned, owned and paid media (although leaving out the sales force). From this you can see the primitive outlines of the field of strategic communication as I envisage it today.

My understanding of the media, which in this text is referred to as the micro level of communication, was shaped during this time in my career.

I moved on from the agency business to communication management. This role fed my interests in formal organizations and organization theory became an important component of my view of strategic communication. That is why I regard organizational communication as one of the foundational disciplines of strategic communication, which encouraged me to elaborate on the concept of the meso level of strategic communication.

At each employer, I learned something and had superb mentors on the way. At the South African Tourism Board (now called South African Tourism), I had the privilege of having Dr. Ernie Heath as a mentor. From Dr. Heath, I learned the principles of strategic planning, including the importance and relevance of the vision and mission of the organization, and how to translate that into a supporting strategic communication strategy. This experience formed the basis of Chapter 3, "The Concept of Strategy." I developed the Planning Matrix in Chapter 7 during this time and refined it over the years. In fact, I still use it in strategic planning in my role as dean. In addition to the impact of organization, I also learned the importance of considering the impact of external environments on communication practice. It was during this period that South Africa went through its transition to a democracy and the political changes had very important implications for the whole tourism industry, as well as how we had to communicate about it. From this experience came my understanding of the importance of the macro environment, one of the three levels of the general theory of strategic communication.

From there, I moved to the ABSA Group, at that time the largest financial services group in Africa. My portfolio was internal communication with a specific focus on change management because the organization had to transition to a new political dispensation. Here I learned new strategic communication values, also included in this text and in the planning matrix. I added the column Person Responsible and Evaluation Technique. I added Person Responsible because it allowed me to assess if the person responsible has all the skills needed to execute the task. If not, they would be enrolled in training programs to learn the necessary skills, which also served as a valuable employee development tool. If the task was too complex or big, it would be outsourced to an external contractor with the responsible person as the organizational coordinator.

Here my supervisor and mentor was Bert Griesel, the executive director of the Human Resources Division of the ABSA Group. From him I learned valuable lessons about organization and human resources, which further informed my understanding of the meso level of the general theory of strategic communication. I just completed my doctorate in Communication Science from the University of Johannesburg when I joined ABSA. The general theory was born in my dissertation. It was informed by the work of Drs. James and Lauri Grunig, yet two more significant mentors in my career development. I studied public relations with them for a semester at the University of Maryland at College Park before returning to South Africa. At ABSA, I applied the general theory of public relations to the design of the internal communication strategy for the organization, addressing issues at the macro level such as culture and political change, the organization of the many different communication functions scattered across the organization (the meso level), and the actual implementation of the strategy at the micro level. My late friend Retha van Niekerk developed the most innovative communication training program for the organization that I have ever encountered. It was aimed at understanding the individuals with whom we worked and was rolled out in work teams to improve cultural and political understanding of people who were previously separated by *apartheid*. This was a life changing experience for me and reinforced my understanding that we all bring our own lens to life and that not one lens is more important than another.

In 1997, I left all that behind and set out on an academic career in the United States. While I was essentially, and still am, a public relations scholar, my career experiences again steered me into the realm of strategic communication. This is where I met other mentors and colleagues who contributed to my understanding of the field.

At a conference in Bled, Slovenia, I met a group of great academics who started the *International Journal of Strategic Communication* with me: Dr. Dejan Verčič from the University of Ljubljana in Slovenia; Dr. Betteke van Ruler from the University of Amsterdam in the Netherlands, Dr. Krishnamurthy Sriramesh from the University of Singapore and Dr. Kirk Hallahan form Colorado State University. At that time, I was a newly tenured associate professor at the University of South Florida. Under the guidance of Linda Bathgate, who was at that time a publisher at Routledge, we all met in New York for a weekend to discuss the new journal and its direction. It was here that the *International Journal of Strategic Communication* was born. We wanted this to be international and representative of practices and theories from all over the world, without dominance of one single country or approach.

This international team finally found it truly hard to collaborate on editorial decisions across the huge differences in time and space and the editorship finally fell on my shoulders and those of Kirk Hallahan. Nonetheless, the most cited article in strategic communication, *Defining Strategic Communication*, co-written by the five of us, appeared in the very first issue in 2007 and is to this day setting the agenda for the field and is the foundation of Chapter 1 of this book.

Dr. Hallahan was already a full professor and his workload, and the very clunky method we had to use to receive and assess submissions, necessitated him to step down as co-editor. I was determined to find a European scholar to serve in that role. Also, during this time, the ownership of Routledge changed to Taylor & Francis and we were provided with an online submissions and review platform that has now become the norm for academic journals. Fortunately, Linda Bathgate continued to be our publisher at Taylor & Francis.

Colleagues in Europe suggested that I ask Dr. Ansgar Zerfass, Professor at the University of Leipzig, to serve as co-editor. He agreed, which was one of the saving graces of my time with the journal. He is an outstanding academic with wonderful people skills and a huge network of communication scholars and practitioners. We largely shared the vision for the field and had the same academic approach focusing on academic rigor and theory building. Slowly but surely the journal became influential and an outlet for people who were interested in the field.

An up-and-coming academic, Dr. Kelly Page Werder, joined the faculty at the University of South Florida while I was still there. Although trained as a public relations scholar, like I was, she too saw the value of the field of strategic communication. We had long discussions on how theories of message strategy could be integrated into the field. Dr. Page Werder was the first to take that step by designing a research study that tested and integrated theory of public relations message strategies and the theory of reasoned action from advertising into a single study. That was the type of work I envisioned scholars should undertake in the field and this is still one of my favorite studies. It was natural for Dr. Werder to take the baton of co-editor when I decided to relinquish the position. Drs. Zerfass and Werder are still co-editors of the journal and have taken it to new heights.

When we started the journal, Linda Bathgate and I made a strategic pact. The best way, she suggested, to develop the field is to start with a journal, then move to a handbook for academics and graduate students, and then produce an introductory text. Thus, while the journal was ongoing, we set the next step in motion and Ansgar and I organized a pre-conference at the annual conference of the International Communication Association that took place in Boston in 2011. We invited scholars to submit papers with the commitment to consider well-developed papers we thought should be included in the field of strategic communication for publication in a handbook. The response was truly overwhelming, and the *International Handbook of Strategic Communication* was published by Routledge in 2015. Since then, the handbook was issued in paperback and a second edition is now underway. This cemented a further building block of the field. Since 2015 several other strategic communication publications saw the light, which further strengthened the field and its scholarship.

One important building block remained, which was the teaching of strategic communication in undergraduate programs. While there are now many strategic communication undergraduate degrees or programs in universities across the country, they are mostly still fragmented, without the integrated approach scholars have advocated for over the years. Public relations and advertising are still offered under the auspices of strategic communication, while keeping the silos intact. While a few seminal texts in aspects of the field have been published over the past few years, one that fully integrates the theoretical approaches has not been available to undergraduate students.

But to be able to provide that, it must be taught. We started that process first at the graduate level at University of South Florida. But for me the real test came when I joined the School of Journalism and Broadcasting at Oklahoma State in 2008 as its director. The school just went through an accreditation process and the faculty there knew they had to make some serious curriculum changes. These changes were purely faculty-driven, and the three different work groups started out with what students needed to know in their specific field. The faculty groups then back engineered the course work to ensure that courses provided building blocks for the necessary outcomes.

There were core courses all students had to take, and then there were specific courses filling out each program, which ended up being three different degrees, one of which was strategic communication, which completely replaced the advertising and public relations majors. Each degree had to have a writing component beyond the core requirements, as well as a relevant research course and a capstone course. There was an important emphasis on content development and portfolio building in each degree. Each work group did an outstanding job and came up with truly innovative degrees. At that same time, they agreed to change the name of the school to the School of Media and Strategic Communication.

The team leaders of the strategic communication workgroup were Dr. Jami Fullerton and Dr. Bobbi Kay Lewis, two of the co-authors of this book. Dr. Danny Shipka, now deceased, joined later. The collective experience from the program and curriculum changes from 2008 to 2010, when the new programs were rolled out, informed this book, as did the teaching experiences we all shared before and after the new degree in strategic communication was implemented. We also brought our global and international experience to this text, as you will see in case studies and examples throughout the book. It is the culmination of the collective experience of many years of teaching and research shared between us and I could not have asked for a more informed group of scholars to complete this project.

As you will hopefully see from my personal journey, academic knowledge and insights are not developed in isolation. As I always tell my students when I introduce the concept of theory—theory is not developed by a mad scientist sitting at a desk in a dark room with a single desk lamp. Theory is developed through observation, either in a laboratory setting or through fieldwork. Particularly in our field, theory is informed by practice and the many wonderful colleagues and scholars we encounter along our way. All of us together always know more than only one of us and it is important to acknowledge that others have incredible insight that will enrich our own work, in academia and practice.

Beyond us as authors, others also contributed to this book most significantly: Dr. Cynthia Nichols, our good OSU colleague who is now practicing her amazing strategic communication skills at the U.S. Department of State and Dr. Fullerton's long-time research partner and preeminent advertising professor Dr. Alice Kendrick from Southern Methodist University (SMU). Drs. Nichols and Kendrick wrote several of sections of the book and served as editors and sounding boards for the author team as the process unfolded. Many of our former students, who are now working professionals, shared their career experiences in the "Professional Profile" features that are scattered throughout the text. We also want to recognize Dr. Ken Kim, Wes Young, Mallorie Rodak, Dr. Gayle Kerr and Leigh Terry for their generous contributions. Alexandria Mangold, an OSU strategic communications student and Global Studies marketing intern created the beautiful charts and figures for us.

My own story is also reflected in how this book is organized, namely roughly in three sections. The first four chapters lay the foundation for the rest of the book. They include a theoretical overview that elaborates on the definition of strategic communication, and a chapter on the career prospects for students as broadly described. As you progress through the book, we hope you will see yourself in one or many of those professional roles. Two chapters focus on the external and meso environments respectively to orient students toward the larger issues governing strategic communication planning and execution.

The next four chapters focus on meso-level attributes that build a foundation for the practice and are necessary considerations in the planning stages of the strategy and practice. The final five chapters focus on the micro level, namely execution of the practice.

We aimed to make the field come alive for students by grounding the theory and concepts in practice. Each chapter starts with a real-life vignette that pertains to the chapter content. Throughout each chapter we present box features of *professional profiles* from working professionals across the field with advice for students on starting their careers. Box features containing *case studies* are taken from real-life situations illustrating situations that might arise in the practice of strategic communication. *Industry Insights* give students a peek into the current state of the business. Some are how-tos and others are quick tips from professionals on how to handle the work. We sprinkled *Academic Angles* throughout to highlight important theories and or academic research that help inform the practice and assist students with connecting academic work to the bigger discipline.

Each chapter ends with a summary of the most important concepts from that chapter and discussion questions that again apply the concepts to real-life examples and cases and are set to challenge your insight and critical thinking skills. We also included a full complement of online resources for students and teachers, including further reading, sample syllabi, class activities and a test bank.

We hope you will find as much joy from this text as we have in presenting it to you and wish you the best of luck in your career as a strategic communication professional.

Derina Holtzhausen

November 2020

Chapter 1

Introduction to the Theory of Strategic Communication

Learning Outcomes

By the end of this chapter, you should be able to do the following:

- Define strategic communication.
- Grasp the three levels of analysis and apply them to strategic communication.
- Understand the importance of an outside/in approach and the role of the external environment.
- Know how the foundational disciplines of strategic communication contribute to your understanding of the field.

Chapter Opening Vignette

"Now That's An Ad" …. The Australian Tourism Campaign cleverly disguised as a movie

The 1986 action movie *Crocodile Dundee*, featuring Paul Hogan as Mick Dundee, was a worldwide hit and one of the top-grossing films in the U.S. and Australia of all time. One of the most iconic scenes from the movie took place in Manhattan, when gangsters tried to rob Mick Dundee by pulling a knife on him. Mick replied, "That's not a knife." Pulling a much bigger hunting knife out of his own jacket, he added, "Now that's a knife." This phrase instantly became part of popular culture in English-speaking countries and could therefore serve as a hook in an ad at Superbowl 2017, when Tourism Australia launched an ad campaign that was bigger, more brazen, more iconically Australian and much more effective, than the average tourism ad.

Like all great ad campaigns, it began with a problem. Even though long-haul travel from the U.S. grew by 17%, visitation from the U.S. to Australia specifically was stagnant at 1.3%.[1] It was not only the 13-hour flight that reduced the desire to visit Australia, but also the fact that destinations in Asia were seen to be more fashionable, especially to High Value Travelers (HVTs), who were the target market of Tourism Australia. HVTs take long-haul trips annually, stay longer, visit more regions and already have Australia in their decision-set; just not at the top of their list.

Tourism Australia wanted to change this, reignite HVTs passion for Australia and develop a new campaign to promote Australian tourism. Tourism Australia wanted to achieve three objectives: create affinity and desire for Australia; generate word-of-mouth (WOM) and earned media; and compel HVTs to book a trip to Australia now.

Media agency Universal McCann (or UM Sydney) suggested aiming for the ultimate media event—the Superbowl. Research showed that the Superbowl delivers more impact than any other global platform[2] and about half (48%) of HVTs would never miss a Superbowl.[3]

However, the challenge was to attract viewers' attention in one of the most competitive advertising feasts on earth. Tourism Australia's creative agency, Droga5 started with the existing tagline "There's nothing like Australia" and then extended it to "There's no one like Australians." While a lot of travel destinations have incredible scenery, the fun-loving humor and laidback look-at-life is unique to Australians. Crocodile Mick Dundee was a cultural symbol of that worldview. Crocodile Dundee made Australia irresistible to Americans in the 1980s, filling their movie theatres and boosting Australian tourism. It was time to bring him back, because at that time 70% of all new films and TV products were reimaginations or extensions.

The first phase of the campaign was to create earned media around a new movie, Dundee: The Son of a Legend Returns Home. To tease the American public there were behind-the-scene leaks of beautiful Australian scenery, four blockbuster trailers featuring Chris Hemsworth, Margie Robbie and some of Australia's best-known actors, and interviews with the original Crocodile Dundee, Paul Hogan.

In the second phase the 60-second Superbowl ad revealed that this much talked-about movie was actually an ad. The tourism campaign in disguise ignited 82,909 mentions from 100 million viewers. In fact, the "Dundee" magic was already at work with the 60-second trailer being the number one, most-viewed Superbowl ad.[4]

The third phase of the campaign was about turning this interest into packed suitcases and plane tickets to Australia. This involved a video series, performance banners, paid social media and partnerships.

The results of the Tourism Australia campaign were a 50% desirability lift; an 83% intention to book; the generation of more than $85.1 million in earned media; and a reach of nearly 900 million people.

So, when people talk of great ad campaigns, remember this movie that was a tourism campaign in disguise, that got us all talking and laughing, and filled the streets of Sydney, Melbourne and Brisbane with American tourists. As Crocodile Dundee himself would have said, "Now this is an ad."

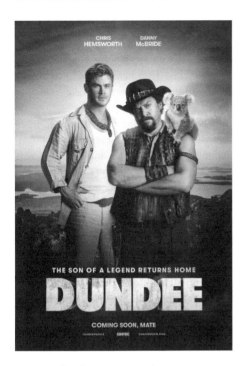

Reprinted with permission from Tourism Australia.

Leigh Terry, CEO, IPG Mediabrands, Asia-Pacific.

Gayle Kerr, Professor, Queensland University of Technology, Brisbane, Australia.

What Is Strategic Communication?

What do Tourism Australia, the Chicago Bears, the Red Cross, Apple, your local city government and sports stars such as Serena Williams and LeBron James have in common? Think about it. They all have different missions, not all their goals are to make money or save the world. So, what is the commonality they all share?

If you said they all deal with the public, you would be on the right track. Tourism Australia has a responsibility to the Australian tourism industry. The Bears have responsibilities to the community that goes beyond just winning football games and the Red Cross beyond responding to disasters. Apple does more than cutting-edge phone technology, and your local city government does more than enforce laws. Sports stars depend on their public image and personal brands to get endorsements. Each of these entities must rely on effective communication to achieve their goals in today's competitive environment. They must all utilize all forms of media and employ a variety of communication techniques. They must be purposeful and planned in the way they interact with their audiences. To be successful in their missions, they all must practice strategic communication.

Strategic communication is a new field of communication that did not exist before the turn-of-the-century. The dramatic changes in media technology that occurred at the end of the 20th century resulted in a paradigm shift—or new way of thinking—about how entities (corporations, non-profits, governments, celebrities, sport stars) communicate with their stakeholders (audiences, customers, citizens, activists). This fresh thinking came together in a new academic and professional field called strategic communication. Strategic communication incorporates traditional communication fields like advertising, public relations (PR) and integrated marketing communication (IMC) along with other disciplines such management, marketing, technical writing, branding and political communication. However, strategic communication goes beyond the simple blending of these disciplines to better address the complex communication realities and the ever-evolving media of the new millennium.

The formal study of the discipline really took off with the establishment of the International Journal of Strategic Communication in 2007. Five scholars from different continents laid down the foundation for its development in arguably the most cited article in the field.[5] This seminal article did not offer a formal definition but did lay the foundation for a definition. The definition evolved and expanded over time. The one used in this text was formalized by adding the term "public sphere" to clearly delineate it from interpersonal communication. The following is the definition that will be used in this text.

> Strategic communication is the practice of deliberate and purposive communication that a communication agent enacts in the public sphere on behalf of a communicative entity to reach set goals.[6]

For communication actions to rise to the level of strategic communication, according to the definition above, it must be purposive and deliberate and take place in the public sphere. It also must be executed by an agent.

If you return to the Tourism Australia example, it is easy to see how that campaign fits the definition of strategic communication. The strategy was purposefully designed in three stages and its execution was deliberate at every step. There was more than one communication agent—Universal McCann Sydney and Droga5, who acted on behalf of the **communicative entity** (CE), Tourism Australia, which is a government agency responsible for attracting international visitors. The campaign had set goals: create affinity and desire for Australia; generate **word-of-mouth (WOM)** and **earned media**; and compel **stake-holders**, such as High Value Travelers, to book a trip to Australia now. It also had to take place in the public sphere, in this case a variety of media and the televised Super Bowl.

It is important to remember that not all communication is strategic. According to Holtzhausen and Zerfass's definition above, strategic communication is **deliberate** and **purposive**. It involves planned messages and thoughtful, organized responses. Strategic communication involves specific messages and seeks to accomplish a specific outcome; it should be part of a larger strategy targeted to specific stakeholders and may use a broad array of media and modes of communication.

Strategic communication happens in the **public sphere,** which basically means it is open to the public and deals with concerns of society or addresses an issue that requires public support. Jürgen Habermas,[7] a German philosopher, first described the public sphere as an area in social life where people can come together to identify and discuss societal problems. Communication between friends, spouses, doctors and their patients, supervisors and their employees and many other exchanges are not considered strategic communication. Although you may be strategically arguing a point, these conversations fall outside the scope of strategic communication because they are private, somewhat spontaneous, and the public is not involved. A private discussion about a salary increase with your boss is not strategic communication even though you might communicate strategically with her. But if your company issues a statement to the media about a planned raise program, it does so for a purpose and the communication is planned. It takes place where anyone can access it and it is executed by an educated agent, somebody like you, who understands the media and can produce content professionally. For more examples of public sphere and non-public sphere communication, see Figure 1.1.

PUBLIC SPHERE COMMUNICATION	NON-PUBLIC SPHERE COMMUNICATION
Marketers to consumers Corporations to stakeholders Charities to donors Politicians to voters Governments to citizens Country to country	Friend to friend Spouse to spouse Doctor to patient Supervisor to employee Parent to child

Figure 1.1 Public Sphere Communication

In this first chapter, you will get to understand the different concepts captured in the definition. Throughout this text, you will be challenged to apply these concepts to society, organizations, public persona such as movie and sports starts, and entertainers of all sorts. This chapter will provide you with a basic understanding of the communication process, which will enable you to absorb more complex information on how to practice strategic communication later in the book.

This will serve as the foundation for a career in strategic communication and for design-ing a strategic communication campaign that will dazzle your boss, your clients and your organization because you were able to communicate strategically and effectively in the public sphere.

Why and How We Use Strategic Communication

In today's increasingly complex world, organizations, brands and individuals who have a public profile must compete for the attention, admiration and loyalty of various stakeholders including customers, employees, investors, donors, government officials, special interest group leaders and the public-at-large. Because of dramatic changes in the media landscape, earning that attention has become more difficult. It requires strategic communicators to use integrated, holistic messaging to reach fragmented audiences across multiple delivery platforms.

Furthermore, once someone has a public profile, it needs to be protected. A reputation needs to be built and maintained. If something bad happens to that public image, it will need to be restored. The media have become so pervasive that there no longer is the possibility of privacy if you are well known. For example, actor Matthew McConaughey uses the drive-through at a fast food establishment, an employee takes a video on a cell phone and the video goes viral.

We now live in a society that exists within the media—not with the media as it did for your parents. Like media scholar Mark Deuze noted, we are like fish swimming around in a fishbowl of media—sometimes without noticing that it is an essential part of our environment and even to the point that we cannot function without it.[8] For example, we carry internet connected smartphones with us everywhere, so that we can get up-to-the second news, entertainment and information. This is how we interact with friends, families, communities, corporations and governments. We even customize our media intake to meet our specific needs and interests, unlike a few decades ago, when our media choices were limited and information was restricted to a few one-way channels like newspapers, radio and TV. Because of these rapid, enormous changes in our society driven by the internet and other digital technologies, strategic communication is a dynamic mixture of the well-established practices of public relations, advertising and integrated marketing communication. Journalism and organizational communication also contribute to the theoretical foundations of strategic communication (see Figure 1.2).

Not only did the changes in media drive the need for strategic communication, but changes in the traditional sub-fields, such as **advertising** and **public relations** occurred over the last few decades as well. Many definitions of the field of public relations may lead one to believe that strategic communication and PR are synonymous. For example, the Public Relations Society of America defines public relations as "a strategic communication process that builds mutually beneficial relationships between organizations and their publics."[9]

Strategic communication, on the other hand, goes beyond the field of PR in that it takes a more holistic and all-encompassing approach to achieving organizational goals.

The ability of communicators to differentiate between traditional communications activities has been disappearing. Although integrated marketing communication (**IMC**) focuses on the coordination of various functions, it was limited to marketing and brand communication. Many of the IMC functions themselves are changing. Public relations practitioners, for example, are using paid advertising to communicate critical messages on topics ranging from corporate reputation and social issues to event sponsorships. Meanwhile, advertising executives are spearheading programs for social causes—a duty that once was the

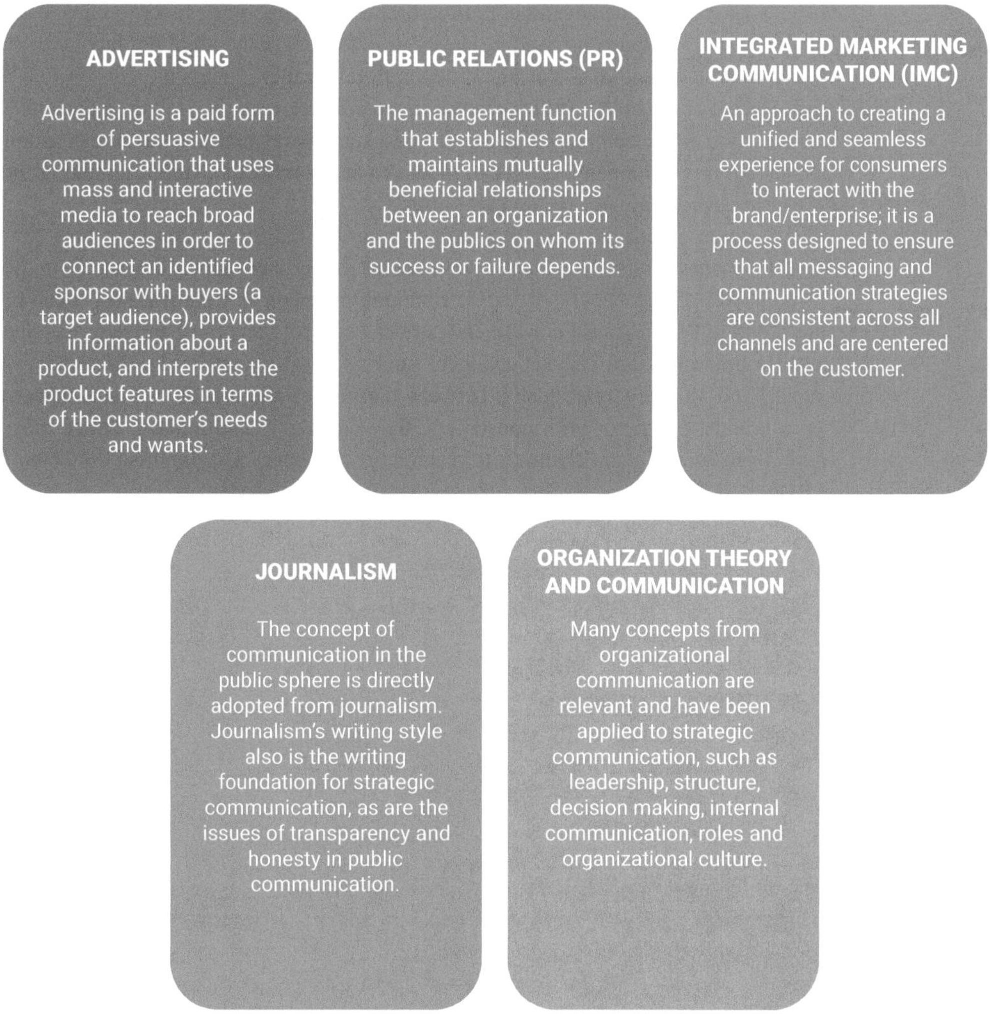

ADVERTISING

Advertising is a paid form of persuasive communication that uses mass and interactive media to reach broad audiences in order to connect an identified sponsor with buyers (a target audience), provides information about a product, and interprets the product features in terms of the customer's needs and wants.

PUBLIC RELATIONS (PR)

The management function that establishes and maintains mutually beneficial relationships between an organization and the publics on whom its success or failure depends.

INTEGRATED MARKETING COMMUNICATION (IMC)

An approach to creating a unified and seamless experience for consumers to interact with the brand/enterprise; it is a process designed to ensure that all messaging and communication strategies are consistent across all channels and are centered on the customer.

JOURNALISM

The concept of communication in the public sphere is directly adopted from journalism. Journalism's writing style also is the writing foundation for strategic communication, as are the issues of transparency and honesty in public communication.

ORGANIZATION THEORY AND COMMUNICATION

Many concepts from organizational communication are relevant and have been applied to strategic communication, such as leadership, structure, decision making, internal communication, roles and organizational culture.

Figure 1.2 **Foundational Disciplines of Strategic Communication**

exclusive job of public relations. At many organizations, claims to exclusive responsibility for different communication activities are being challenged. The management emphasis is on achieving the overall objectives of the organization, not on the communication tools and tactics. By adopting a strategic communication approach, organizations can be more efficient and effective in solving their communication problems, achieving their goals and also—importantly in today's world—accomplishing positive outcomes for society in general.

Here is one example of these changes from the field of advertising: In the 1960s and 1970s, advertising was king. New York City's Madison Avenue advertising agencies developed creative commercials that promoted products to national audiences via broadcast television. This advertising not only increased sales of the product, but the reputation of the corporation by being a nationally advertised brand. In this era, the corporation owned and controlled the brand. The consumers of the brand had little to no power to change the brand. They bought the brand and used it. If they didn't like it, they might not buy it again, but they had little influence over the brand beyond their wallet. Today, the consumer has much more control of the brand. If they don't like the product, they may tell their Facebook friends not to buy it. If the company is not acting in a socially responsible way, the consumers put pressure on the company via social media to act more responsibly by making the corporation's misdeeds known to a broader public.

The online environment has largely been the driver behind these changes in how consumers interact with brands. The internet and social media have given consumers more control, which can be both beneficial and detrimental to brands or organizations. It can be beneficial for the brand, because consumers can act positively as brand ambassadors and advocate for a brand through various channels, such as vlogs, tweets and online reviews. On the other hand, this new relationship between consumers and brands can be detrimental. When a brand loses favor with consumers, they can easily and quickly utilize those same internet and social media channels to reach large audiences and diminish the brand's reputation.

Activist consumers are empowered in this way mostly because of their access to the wider public via the internet. "The latest tendency in the social zeitgeist is '**wokeness**,' or social and political awareness. More and more people are talking about social issues like sexism, racism and inequality, and they are trying to find ways to solve them."[10] Increasingly, consumers and activists have political opinions that influence their expectations of brands. For example, after the El Paso, Texas shooting in Walmart in 2019, the company decided to limit ammunition sales and openly discouraged "Open carry" laws (people who are licensed to openly carry weapons in public).[11]

Therefore, organizations can no longer rely on one-way communication methods to interact with stakeholders. One-way television advertising is not enough and sometimes appears insensitive and out of touch when consumers are saying negative things about the brand on social media. Organizations must be planning, listening, responding and evolving on a regular basis. That's why strategic communication—this new way of thinking about an organization's stakeholders—is essential for organizations, public figures or communicative entities of any kind. They must think of all their messaging as one holistic piece. They must react immediately to consumer or public demands and they must do it in a deliberate, planned way. If organizations fail to respond to their customers in this way, negative outcomes may occur for the brand.

Journalism is yet another foundational discipline of strategic communication. Journalism is the practice of communication in the public sphere, with the emphasis on honesty and transparency in reporting and commentary on the events of the day. It is through the concept of the public sphere that journalism most closely informs strategic communication. All forms of journalism, be it in print or online media, broadcasting or radio, adhere to strict writing formats adopted for the different reporting platforms. Good writing is the foundation of journalism, which has been adopted in all forms of strategic communication.

Also, journalism increasingly uses the practice of stakeholder segmentation—most media target specific stakeholder groups whom they know are interested in their content. The fragmentation of media platforms and the proliferation of media types and content is a double-edged sword for strategic communicators. On the one hand, the many media formats and content types force strategic communicators to go beyond the traditional media and require them to have a deep understanding of how media work. On the other hand, it enables strategic communicators to very narrowly target stakeholders based on their specific interests. There is no mass audience in communications any longer. Stakeholders have splintered off into much smaller groups based on their media preferences and choice of content, which are many and varied.

Professional Profile
Gitzel Puente—Government Communications Officer

Gitzel Puente—TV-Reporter-turned-government-communications-officer.

Gitzel Puente graduated from Arizona State University with a bachelor's degree in broadcast journalism and from Oklahoma State University with a master's degree in mass communication. She has spent most of her career working in newsrooms as a TV reporter but has now made the transition to local government.

> **What did you want to do with your career?** I wanted to be a national correspondent or traveling TV host for a major channel.
>
> **Are you doing it?** No.
>
> **What are you doing now?** I am a communications officer for local government.
>
> **How did you get there?** During the COVID-19 pandemic, my reporting contract at a local NBC station was coming to an end, and I realized I needed to take a break from the deadlines and demanding work environment. The idea of transitioning into a different industry and learn a new skillset was attractive to me, so when the local mayor's office called me and offered me a job as a communications officer, I took it.
>
> **How have your dreams changed?** I think my dreams are still changing as I continue to evolve. Being on the other side of journalism has taught me that I can still make a difference in my community in the new role; I can take federal holidays off without having to rank them; I can sleep normal hours and I don't

have the daily stress and anxiety of putting a story together within a few hours, not knowing if it will pan out and deal with equipment failures. While the pay remains the same, I know that money isn't everything when it comes to my personal happiness and well-being. I also have more time to be involved in the community and be part of organizations I care about.

What has surprised you most about yourself or your career? I knew I was open-minded and flexible before when I changed cities for a new job, but now, it's clear that I can do anything I set my mind to. I am seeing how my journalism skills can be applied to this communications job and has even opened new opportunities, such as using my native Spanish to translate and write press releases in both languages. In the end, the communications field has one goal and that is to effectively disseminate information. If I ever decide to jump back into a reporting job, then I will have a different perspective to offer.

What advice would you give to someone in college now? Get hands-on experience in internships, freelancing work, organizations, study abroad, anything you are passionate about to add to your resume. I think it makes you a well-rounded person when you apply to a job and can talk about not only your skills, but your interests. If your career path happens to change along the way, that is okay! The most important thing is that you're happy doing what you do.

More information about Gitzel Puente can be found here: https://www.linkedin.com/in/gitzelpuente

The fifth discipline to serve as a foundation for strategic communication is **organization theory** and its related discipline of **organizational communication**. Organization theory focuses on all the factors that shape and affect organizations—in its broadest sense, from multinational and global organizations, to virtual organizations (organizations that are loosely structured and where employees telecommute from wherever they are in the world). It also studies leadership and decision-making styles and how different national and organizational subcultures impact how organizations operate. Chapters 3 and 4 explain more of how organization theory impacts strategic communication. Chapter 3 focuses on the concept of strategy and how organizations use it to gain competitive advantage. Chapter 4 describes how the three levels of management, which is one of the tenets of strategic communication, affect practice. Much of this work is informed by organization theory.

Agents and Domains of Practice

The definition of strategic communication also talks about agents who act on behalf of organizations. This is the person or group of people who does the communicating for the organization—the agent is you! The agent has the job of planning, managing, analyzing, implementing and evaluating the strategic communication messages that are sent by the CE. These agents, also called practitioners, might be public relations professionals, brand managers, advertising executives or corporate communications directors. They may work in various types of organizations such as corporations, non-profits, education, government, political groups, healthcare and many other fields know as domains of practice.

Domains of Practice

Below is a list of the domains of practice with each domain's specific purpose according to Holtzhausen, Hallahan and colleagues.[12] Later in this book, you will learn about how to perform duties and tasks related to strategic communication and how those jobs are practiced in the "real world."

Management Communication

Personnel: Managerial/administrative personnel throughout organization.

Purposes: To facilitate the orderly operations of the organization. Also, promote understanding of an organization's mission, vision and goals, and supply information needed in day-to-day operations, including customer and vendor transactions and customer and staff training. Facilitate open communication between management and employees or associates.

Marketing Communication

Personnel: Marketing and advertising staffs.

Purposes: To create awareness and promote sales of products and services. Also attract and retain users and customers, including intermediaries in distribution channels. Among non-government organizations and other not-for-profit organizations, marketing communications incorporates fundraising and development communications.

Public Relations

Personnel: Public relations or publicity, human resources, finance or government relations staffs.

Purpose: To establish and maintain mutually beneficial relationships with key constituencies. This includes consumers and customers, as well as investors and donors, employees and volunteers, community leaders and government officials.

Technical Communication

Personnel: Technical, engineering support and training staffs.

Purposes: To educate employees, customers and others to improve their efficiency. It involves reducing errors and promoting the effective and satisfying use of technology when performing tasks important to organization. Help with roll-outs of new technological procedures and processes such as the implementation of new software systems.

Political Communication

Personnel: Government affairs staffs as well as politicians and advocacy groups.

Purposes: To build political consensus or consent on important issues involving the exercise of political power and the allocation of resources in society. This includes efforts to influence voting in elections as well as public policy decisions by lawmakers or administrators. On the international level, this includes communications in support of public diplomacy and military stabilization.

Information/Social Marketing Campaigns

Personnel: Employees in nongovernmental, not-for-profit and governmental agencies as well as corporate staffs involved in promoting the proper use of products and services.

Purposes: To reduce the incidence of risky behaviors or to promote social causes important to the betterment of the community.

Corporate Communication

Personnel: Employees who are trained in internal and external strategic communication practice.

Purposes: Design internal and external communication campaigns to facilitate relationship and reputation building between an organization and its stakeholders. Corporations typically have a head office and regional offices or other subsidiaries.

Crisis/Risk Communication

Personnel: Communication employees across all organizational types.

Purpose: Risk and crisis communication are part of the daily practice of all strategic communicators and is most often not set up as a special component in an agency or organization. Employees identify possible risk areas and take proactive steps to prevent a crisis. In the case of a crisis, employees are tasked to communicate about the crisis to stakeholders and the media.

Financial Communication

Personnel: Employees who work in organizations that are listed on the stock exchange.

Purpose: Financial communicators are responsible for communicating the financial health of listed companies each quarter, as required by law. They also are responsible for investor relations and investor communications.

Health Communication

Personnel: Communication strategists that work for medical, pharmaceutical and governmental health organizations.

Purpose: To inform people how to deal with illness and disease and how to prevent poor health choices.

Public Diplomacy

Personnel: Government employees who can communicate on behalf of their country in different cultural settings.

Purpose: To create understanding and build relationships between countries, cultures and people.

Activism

Personnel: People who feel strongly about issues of social justice and are prepared to stand up for their principles.

Purpose: To make changes in society that will make all people have equal moral value.

To get a job in strategic communication, practitioners need skills such as excellent writing ability, understanding of research and audience analytics, and mastery of all forms of media technology. Careers in strategic communication are discussed in detail in the next chapter. Strategic communication practitioners must also be well organized, enjoy working with people and be creative—but most importantly, they must understand the communication process.

Academic Angle

Health Communication: Vaccination Messaging

Public health officials are concerned that when a COVID-19 vaccine is made available that the public may not be willing to take the shot. For a vaccine program to work, it must create herd immunity—that means almost everyone in the population needs to be vaccinated. It is the job of strategic communication professionals who work in the health care sector to get the word out about the vaccine and persuade the public to be vaccinated. These strategic communicators will likely review the vast amount of health communication research that is available to determine how to craft the most effective messages that will convince the public to be responsible and get vaccinated.

Health communication research suggests vaccination judgment is greatly affected by social influence as well as vaccine-related perceptions.[13] Research in applied health also demonstrates how individuals classify various types of vaccine for preventable diseases into two categories—relatively common or relatively contagious. For instance, seasonal influenza or human papillomavirus (HPV) may be perceived as relatively more common but highly contagious when compared to other viruses such as hepatitis and shingles. A public health message designed to focus on societal-level outcomes (e.g., "achieve herd immunity for community health," "get HPV vaccines to protect your future spouses/the health of others") may be more influential for preventing highly contagious diseases from spreading, whereas a health message stressing individual-level outcomes (e.g., "protect your immune system for your health," "get HPV vaccines to protect yourself from others") may be more effective in promoting vaccination for relative less contagious but potentially more fatal viruses.

Therefore, because COVID-19 is highly contagious and relatively common, but not necessarily fatal for young healthy adults, the best way to encourage COVID-19 vaccinations is to focus messages on the benefits for community or society. A health communication message phrased at a societal level may produce, to an extent, thoughts about others who are more vulnerable to COVID-19 rather than about individuals themselves[14] and facilitate a collective responsibility for these people. Therefore, a societal-focused health message can encourage individuals, especially healthy young adults to take action and get the vaccine.

Finally, the persuasiveness of a vaccination message phrased on a societal level may be more pronounced on social media platforms. Research suggests that individuals rely on what their peers say and are greatly influenced by word-of-mouth communication when making judgments about an uncertain choice or offering.[15] As such, further research that tests vaccination messages across various new digital media channels may help us understand what makes young adults accept or refuse vaccines.

By Dr. Ken Kim, Assistant Professor at Xavier University.

What Is Communication?

Communication is the transfer of meaning from one entity to another using mutually understood signs, symbols and language. We communicate every day. It is a natural part of the human condition. When we are babies we cannot talk to our parents, but we still communicate with them by crying if we are hungry or smiling when we feel good. Individuals communicate with each other every day through face-to-face interaction, by talking on the phone or even by text or email. This type of communication can also be called **interpersonal communication** because it happens between individuals, often spontaneously. Mostly interpersonal communication happens personally and privately among us and others in our world.

Strategic communication is different than interpersonal communication. In strategic communication there is also a transfer of meaning between entities using mutually understood symbols, signs and language, but according to the definition of strategic communication, unlike interpersonal communication, it is public, purposive and deliberate. These three traits separate strategic communication as a practice and academic discipline from other types of communication.

The Transmission Model

Many scholars have attempted to **model** how communication works. There are various models, but the most popular is the Transmission Model of Communication.[16] The

Transmission Model is very basic. It illustrates a circular movement of messages from a sender (in the top left corner of the model) to a receiver (in the top right corner of the model) and then back again from the receiver back to the original sender. The message travels through a channel (or medium) and must compete with noise that is happening during the process, which may interfere with the communication.

The Transmission Model also indicates that the sender **encodes** the message and the receiver **decodes** the message. The process of encoding simply means that the sender translates what he wishes to say into a mutually understandable system of signs, symbols and/or language before sending it out through the channel. The decoding on the part of the receiver is the opposite process—the signs, symbols and/or language are analyzed through the receiver's field of experience and (hopefully) understood. Then the receiver responds by encoding his own message and sending it back to the original sender, who will decode it. The process continues until the communication is finished between this set of senders and receivers.

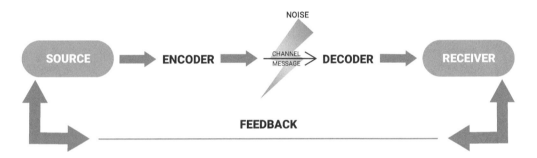

Figure 1.3 The Transmission Model of Communication

The Transmission Model applies well to interpersonal communication. Think about having a conversation with your friend. You think of something that you need to tell your friend. You quickly (sometimes without consciously thinking about it) encode the concept into spoken sentences, then you speak the message out loud and it travels across the channel of sound waves to your friend's ear. He hears the message, decodes what you said in his own mind so that he can make sense of it. If there are others in the room making noise, then sometimes the communication process is interrupted or misunderstood. Depending on how your friend decodes the message, he will think of a response, encode it into words and speak it out loud back to you in the form of feedback.

With the invention of **mass media** in the early and mid-20th century — communication happened quickly with the same messages reaching thousands of people at the same time. Mass media are media that could carry messages long distances to large audiences simultaneously, such as newspapers, magazines, books and later radio and television. Communication through mass media is known as **mass communication.** For example, when a company runs a commercial during the broadcast of the Super Bowl, millions of people see the same ad all at once, but they are limited by the amount of immediate feedback that they can provide. Traditional mass communication is very good at reaching lots of people, but it isn't interactive and does not allow for those people to provide feedback to the sender of the message.

The Transmission Model can easily be applied to mass communication with some slight adjustments. The sender who may be an advertiser, for example, identifies a message about their product that they wish to send to potential consumers. They encode the message by carefully creating a commercial on film or video with words, music and moving pictures. They send the commercial out via the television medium to thousands of consumers who are receiving the message when they watch their TV sets. Each consumer decodes the message in approximately the same way. If the TV reception is poor or the sound is turned down, then noise is created that interferes with the message. In mass communication, which is generally one-way, the feedback is not instantaneous or direct. In fact, it may not happen at all because it is impossible to send a message back through the television to the company that is advertising.

The invention of the internet at the end of the 20th century allowed for, among many other things, immediate feedback (a trait of interpersonal communication) from thousands of receivers via electronic media across large spans of space (a trait of mass communication). The opportunity for receivers (consumers, voters, donors) to provide instant feedback directed at specific senders (communicative entities) allowed for a shift in power and an upheaval in the traditional communication process. The sender was no longer in charge of the message and the receiver was no longer a passive audience who sat powerlessly decoding messages.

This transformation led to the discipline of strategic communication, which in turn revised the Transmission Model of Communication and renamed the players. What was called "senders" in strategic communication is known as communicative entities (CEs) and what were "receivers" are now called stakeholders. Communicative Entities may be individual public figures (such as celebrities, politicians or CEOs) or organizations (such as corporations, non-profits or governments). Stakeholders include any person or group that has an interest in the message, such as consumers, voters, donors, fans or investors. In the new millennium, stakeholders can also include people who are not fans of an organization or people who have a vested interest in seeing an organization fail.

When the Transmission Model is applied to strategic communication it changes considerably, particularly due to the many changes in media themselves. As mentioned before, this model was created at a time when newspapers and a few broadcast network channels dominated the media landscape. People did not have much choice in terms of which media or messages they wanted to receive. In the new media environment, there is a great **proliferation of media**—the number and types of media channels have exploded.

Virtually all media now themselves practice strategic communication. They have clearly defined stakeholders, including viewers and readers. They create content for a specific group of people. This is the case for a food or fashion blog as much as for a cable news network. People now have a wide range of content to choose from that fits their viewpoints and their interests. This leads to **media fragmentation**, which means that in contrast to the past when there were only a few newspapers or broadcast networks in a media market that featured general interest content in order to appeal to a broad audience, now there are hundreds of media options, most carrying a very narrow array of content. Because of media fragmentation people now often only consume the media that supports their interests or viewpoint. This dramatic change in how people use media has blown-up the basic linear structure of the Transmission Model, and instead puts power in the hands of stakeholders rather than media platforms.

The Constitutive Model

While the Transmission Model is still helpful to determine who our stakeholders are and to determine how and what information needs to be conveyed, the linearity of communication in this model is now thoroughly discredited. The 21st century approach to communication models rather asks: What happens to communication in the communication process and how is meaning shaped and co-created?

While there are several approaches to this question, the one commonality they share is the fact that we all hear and understand communication in a way that is shaped by our life experiences. While you might hear the same words your friend hears, your interpretation of and reaction to those words might very well be different. It is only in the interaction of communication between participants in the communication process that meaning is shaped and understanding is created. Meaning is mostly created through a process of opposing arguments in which senders and receivers exchange roles all the time. This shows how important interaction is between stakeholders and CEs. The more interaction the better the shared meaning.

Instead of the linear Transmission Model, a diagram of how communication now works, known as the **constitutive model of communication**, will more likely resemble a tornado, where opposing or supporting messages fly around randomly until it constitutes itself as a communication storm in the public sphere.

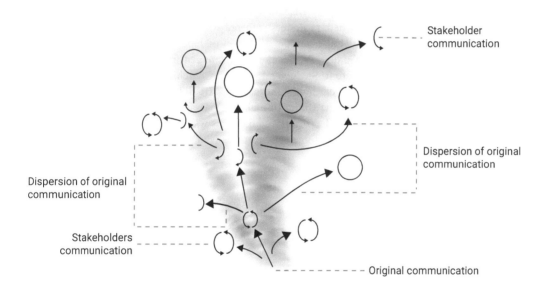

Figure 1.4 **The Constitutive Model of Communication**

Figure 1.4 explains how communication flows in the constitutive model of communication—instead of communication in the public sphere as an organized linear model, the constitutive model is non-linear and rather disorganized. It can be best envisioned as a tornado, swirling with messages, senders and receivers acting in an indirect, non-sequential manner. The larger arrows represent communication flow and dispersion of messages. The smaller black arrows represent the stakeholders participating in the communication process and show how stakeholders interact with each other, if they do at all (the closed circles reflect the end of the communication process in that instance). Through the dispersion process each stakeholder interprets the original communication in a different way, thus disrupting the linear communication flow suggested in the Transmission Model of Communication.

In this way the original communication is transformed based on the life experiences and perspectives of each individual stakeholder. A powerful example of this theory is how different stakeholders had different interpretations of what happened in Lafayette Square in Washington D.C. in June 2020, when President Trump—controversially, and using violent force—cleared a path through peaceful protestors to stage a photo-op at the St. John's Episcopal Church.

Case Study

Constitutive Communication in Action[17]

In the aftermath of the death of George Floyd at the hands of Minnesota policemen, protests broke out across the United States. Floyd, a Black man, suffocated while pleading for his life, with a white policeman kneeling on his neck. The incident was caught on camera from different views. It sparked protests from Black Lives Matter supporters, who were not only Black but also from all other race groups.

One of the places where protestors gathered was at Lafayette Square, across the street from the White House. On the afternoon of June 1, 2020, after a news conference in the Rose Garden, President Trump emerged from the White House and walked across the square to St. John's Episcopal Church. The purpose was to have a photo-op for the president holding up a Bible. He did not make a statement, but remained silent, holding the Bible. To make his passage across the square possible and safe, the protestors had to be cleared out. This was done by a variety of security personnel from many law enforcement agencies who used heavy-handed tactics.[18]

President Trump at St. John's Episcopal Church on Monday evening, June 1, 2020.
Credit: Official White House Photo by Shealah Craighead/wikicommons.

The photo-op was planned as a strategic communication event. It was devised by among others, President Trump's daughter, Ivanka Trump; Jared Kushner, the president's son-in-law and senior adviser; and Hope Hicks, a top communications adviser.

Applying this actual strategic communication event to the constitutive model of communication (see Figure 1.4), the speech in the Rose Garden, the stroll across the square and the photo-op would be viewed as the original communication message. The symbolic intent of the event was clear; the president declared himself the "law and order president." Clearing out protestors from the square and holding up a Bible in front of the church, portrayed his strength and faith.

To analyze and understand the events of June 1, 2020 at Lafayette Square, the *New York Times* used interviews, observations and experiences of a variety of eye-witnesses to understand the exact timeline of what transpired at the square.

As the constitutive model of communication (Figure 1.4) shows, however well intended the event was, different stakeholders interpreted this event in vastly different ways and communication reverberated around the globe. Rather than seeing it the way the President Trump wanted it to be seen and interpreted, various stakeholders made the event their own, by creating meaning around it in the context of their own lived experiences and belief systems.

The following table shows how differently people interpreted the whole situation, from the speech in the Rose Garden, to the clearing out of the protestors, and to the photo-op in front of the church.

Table 1.1 Reactions to President Trump's Speech in the Rose Garden

Those in support of the demonstration and against the president's photo-op	Those against the demonstration and in favor of the President's photo-op
There were so many snacks and so much love. (Protestor)	As many of the protestors became more combative … officers then employed the use of smoke cannisters and pepper balls. (U.S. Park Police)
It was peaceful, and everything was fine. (Protestor)	There was looting. There was rioting. (White House deputy press secretary)
We were there offering refreshments and just being with other people. It was really positive. (Clergyman)	His language … was strong and decisive. (White house attorney)
He sounded like he was an inch away from wanting to declare martial law. (Television viewer)	To watch my boss, the president of the United States, walk over there and tell the world, America is the greatest country on the planet and we'll protect you, is very uplifting. (Attorney)
Damn, he just declared war on the American people. (Democratic politician)	
It was the most surreal occasion that I've experienced during the White House pool. (Journalist)	For the president to recognize and validate the institution of the church against these anarchists and terrorists … was an incredible moment in American history. (Attorney)
I was outraged. My major outrage was the abuse of sacred symbols and sacred texts. … The Bible calls us to our highest aspirations, and he used it as a prop. (Bishop)	
In Australia … I've had so many messages from friends and family saying, "Just get out of there, it's too dangerous." [Referring to the United States.]	[U]pon reflection, people mostly agreed it was a good thing. (Conservative politician)

The White House strategic communicators most likely worked from the Transmission Model of Communication, thinking the message as intended would have been received as intended, without the interference of noise and different media and stakeholder interpretations. From the comments above, it is apparent that they should have adopted the constitutive model of communication, which would have allowed them to better understand the impact of their communication event in such a highly explosive environment.

Whereas the Transmission Model focuses on how to get a message from here to there, the constitutive model focuses on creating actual change, action and understanding between different entities that might start out in positions worlds apart. Strategic communicators who adopt the constitutive model of communication will understand that communication cannot be controlled, at least not in democratic societies. These communicators will understand that communication is a process that might take place over a long time and stretch over time long after a message has been transmitted.

Another important component of constitutive communication is to understand that media are no longer merely the conveyer of messages. Because there are so many media platforms and outlets, media also actively shape culture and society, particularly because they focus on select stakeholders themselves. This is an important principle for strategic communicators to understand. By understanding how media work and who their stakeholders are, strategic communicators have the power to equally shape culture and society. By giving their stakeholders the power to participate and by listening and adapting to their viewpoints and demands, media recognize that stakeholders also shape society and culture through the media. Strategic communicators thus have similar power through their knowledge of the media.

Strategic Communication Theory

The first instinct for people who are charged with a communication assignment, like the examples at the beginning of this chapter, is to think of the tools or tactics they should use. For example, should you run a commercial, host a news conference, send out direct mail or launch a social media campaign? Unfortunately, it is not that simple. The reality is that there are many factors outside and inside the organization that affect a professional's ability to communicate successfully. All these factors are important when a company or organization communicates about an issue to a specific group of people. The actual communication is almost the last step in the strategic communication process. In order to be a successful strategic communicator, you must go through the other steps that come before running ads or launching a social media campaign.

It is for this reason that this book is organized around those factors that affect our ability to communicate effectively, helping us to analyze and *understand first* and *act later* in a planned and organized way. To help you grasp the big picture of strategic communication practice and provide you with tools for communicating effectively, the first part of this book focuses on the philosophical and theoretical underpinnings of strategic communication. It provides the foundation for further in-depth discussions of the practice of strategic communication that comes later in the book.

This first section of the book provides foundational thinking in the field—the *basic principles of strategic communication*. It introduces the concepts that you will come across throughout the text. These concepts are **theoretical** in nature but are linked to a strong **professional practice**. Throughout the text you will be shown how professionals apply their theoretical knowledge to strategic communication practice. Therefore, strategic communication is called an **applied science**. While its principles are theoretical and scientifically tested, they do not exist in isolation but are based on actual practice in the professional world.

Strategic Communication as a Science

Strategic communication is a social science. Social science (like natural science) is based on **empiricism**—the idea that knowledge comes to us through our sensory experience by observation and experimentation. Scientific theories are not developed by mad scientists in laboratories, but by people in different scientific fields who observe a reality or **phenomenon** in the natural world and then use various scientific methods to test if, how and why that phenomenon occurs. This is also the case for the field of strategic communication. A diverse group of social scientists work together with strategic communication professionals throughout the world to develop an understanding of the field, what it is, how it is best practiced and what its **effects** are on the societies we live in.

Shared Meaning

Learning about the overarching theory of strategic communication will help you understand the many other concepts that are introduced later in this book. Learning these broad concepts and terms also creates **shared meaning** with other people in the strategic communication field. Shared meaning is important in all forms of communication, but it is one of the cornerstones of strategic communication. Shared meaning ensures that we are all "speaking the same language." It is important for everybody working in the same field to use the same terms, definitions and concepts. They must all agree in advance on what certain things mean. For example, in baseball, some terms are unique to the sport, like a pitcher's earned run average (ERA). Understanding what an ERA is and how that affects who will pitch in certain game situations is shared meaning for baseball fans, players, coaches and sports reporters, but may make no sense to someone who is not "inside baseball." The same applies to strategic communication and other scientific fields. The content of this book will supply you with what different terms and principles mean, so you can participate in the shared meaning of strategic communication.

Furthermore, in the field of strategic communication, the creation of shared meaning between a communicative entity and a stakeholder not only includes understanding of a single word, as would be done through a dictionary, but even more so, creating a shared understanding of what is important, acceptable and valued in the strategic communication process.

Levels of Strategic Communication

One easy way to grasp the basic principles of strategic communication is to picture it as three hierarchical levels of analysis. They are the *macro or societal* level, the *meso or organizational* level and the *micro or communication* level. As Figure 1.5 illustrates, the three levels are nested in each other and not separate levels that have nothing to do with each other.

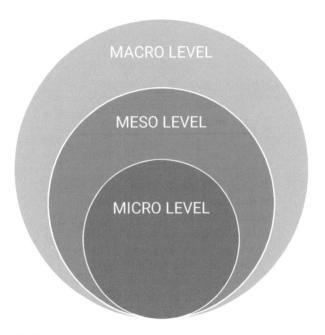

Figure 1.5 Levels of Strategic Communication

Macro Level/Societal Level

The macro level of strategic communication is the highest level and refers to the society in which a communication problem or project exists. The macro level provides the tools for an overarching, comprehensive and inclusive analysis of the external environment that affects everybody who is involved in the communication action, be it the communicative entity or the stakeholders. Analyzing the macro level helps us understand in a broad and theoretical way the societies in which we live and work. If relevant, it can also refer to international and global trends.

Meso Level/Organizational Level

Think of the middle level or the *meso* or organizational level as the peanut butter and jelly in a sandwich. Without this sticky, delicious filling two slices of bread will not adhere to each other. It is the same with strategic communication. Without the work of the strategic communication professional, the macro-level perspectives will not be interpreted effectively to enable the CE to create shared meaning with stakeholders. It is at the meso level where the work of the strategic communication professional is most important. In studying the meso level, you will also learn how organizations themselves make it possible to communicate successfully, or not.

Strategy is part of the meso level. An important function at the meso or organizational level is to plan strategically. Strategy is the cornerstone of strategic communication that sets the field apart from many other forms of communication, like interpersonal communication or journalism. The term *strategic* is associated *with thinking and planning before acting,* with the overall goal of obtaining a desired outcome. Strategic communication is all about communicating in a pre-planned, relevant way to a specific group of people with a specific message using appropriate communication channels with the purpose of persuading stake-holders to change or maintain attitudes and behaviors.

Planning and strategizing are what the communicative entity does when it has a specific message to communicate to specific stakeholders. This is where you, as the strategic communication professional, come in. You will be the one who interprets the macro-level environment for the meso or organizational level, plans the actual communication media and messages, and determines who the most important stakeholders are.

Micro Level/Communication Level

The **micro level**, also called the communication level, focuses on the actual communication functions, which, as mentioned earlier, is where many practitioners mistakenly start with planning and executing campaigns. This is the level where the communication tactics are implemented, the messages are encoded and the incoming messages are decoded on a day-to-day basis. You now already understand that such a reactive or instinctive approach cannot be successful because there are many factors affecting decisions about communication at the micro level, particularly those that are influential at the macro and meso levels. At the micro level it is important to understand how people process information, how meaning is shaped, which media people use and how they interact with those media. It is also important to understand the stakeholder's specific attitudes and behaviors. These are factors that will be discussed throughout the text but specifically beginning in Chapter 4, you will be introduced to the foundational work you as a communicator need to pay attention to that will ensure that you can communicate successfully at the micro level.

Outside-In Approach

One of the many ways the approach in this book differs from other communication disciplines and practice is the **outside-in approach** versus the typical **inside-out approach**. Traditionally, in strategic planning the organization that is doing the planning starts with an inward perspective in terms of what the organization and its leadership want from a strategic plan. What the organization wants is front and center and the rest of the world needs to be molded and shaped to fit the organization. This means that people must be cajoled, coaxed and sometimes manipulated to do what the organization wants.

However, the outside-in approach states that the most successful strategic plans— particularly strategic *communication* plans—are best done when the needs, attitudes and behaviors of the individuals and groups at whom the communication actions are directed (the stakeholders) are placed from the start at the front and center of the process. The inside-out approach asks the question, "What do we want from our stakeholders?" But the strategic communication outside-in approach asks, "What do our stakeholders want from us?" When we later discuss the process of strategic thinking and planning, you will learn how to structure a strategic plan with vision and mission statements, goals, objectives, stakeholder segmentation, tactics and budget. You will even learn how to determine the human resources you will require to execute that plan and how to work with outside resources, if you do not have those resources in your company or organization. But you will learn how to do this **outside-in**—giving preference to the ultimate stakeholders in the communication process instead of internal audiences or organizational leaders.

The outside-in approach requires the communicator to **frame** or structure a message in a way that stakeholders will understand. Framing is an essential component of strategic message design and something communication researchers have studied for decades. It basically refers to how a message is presented and what its intent is. Depending on the expected outcomes from a strategic communication campaign, the intended receivers might be people from different walks of life, perspectives and experiences. As mentioned earlier, strategic message design will be discussed extensively later in the text, so at this point, just realize that these and many other factors shape how stakeholders will react to a message and how it is framed.

It is therefore important to first understand, appreciate and acknowledge that stakeholders have unique experiences before a sender crafts the message—this is the essence of the outside-in approach. People understand messages based on their life experiences and belief systems. This leads to the challenge of creating shared meaning between CEs and diverse stakeholders. Closing the gap by improving the understanding between communicative entities and stakeholders ensures greater success, mutual satisfaction and better outcomes for all involved in the communication process. Because stakeholders have different intentions, experiences and expectations from communicative entities, it makes sense that different groups and individuals should receive messages that are framed differently in order to create mutual understanding. It also is easier to adapt the organization to the stakeholders rather than the other way around.

Communicative entities often forget, or do not even realize, that they survive because the environment in which they operate allows them to survive. The news is littered with examples of organizations, brands, celebrities and politicians whose value systems put them at odds with the social, cultural and political norms of those societies, which ultimately lead to their demise. Recent examples are actor Charlie Sheen, who lost his role, and a lot of money, in a television franchise because of his unacceptable and erratic behavior; or the executives that were fired at Uber because they consistently did not address reports of persistent sexual harassment and discrimination against female engineers in the company. In both these cases, society withdrew its support for continued success from these entities because the entities' behavior did not match society's values.

Industry Insight

United Airlines and the Mistreatment of a Passenger

Sometimes a whole company can go under or struggle to survive when stakeholder norms are not considered and applied or when a company does not keep up with technological and other changes in society. A recent example is the treatment of a passenger on United Airlines that generated such a public outcry when he was forcibly removed from his seat that the company's share price fell precipitously as a result of the event. In fact, the company was at one stage faced with the possibility that the incident might destroy the Asian arm of the company—the passenger was Asian American. While the airline was legally entitled to removing passengers, that fact did not make it right in the eyes of various societies. Understanding societal values, norms and attitudes are crucial to the survival of companies and organizations; yet another reason why the outside-in approach is so important to the success of strategic communication.

This industry insight also shows the three levels of communication at work. At the macro or societal level, there was no understanding of the cultural values of passengers, who were abhorred by the violence, and the perception of Chinese consumers that United singled them out for discrimination. At the meso or organizational level, there was clearly no coordination between the company's senior management, its strategic communicators and its flight crews on how to conduct themselves in situations such as these. At the micro or communication level, the optics of a bloodied passenger being physically dragged off the plane was the worst public communication the company could have received. All this could have been avoided if the strategic communication team at the corporate head office had anticipated such an event through strategic planning. If they did, they would have understood the social and cultural norms of its stakeholders, coordinated an approach with flight crews to prevent such incidents, and also understood that incidents such as these can no longer be covered up because of unlimited access to social media.

You now have been introduced to two very important principles in strategic communication: namely, the understanding that individual receivers of a message are very different from each other because they are influenced by many factors that exist in the environment in which they live. You also learned the importance of putting stakeholders first when planning a communication strategy or campaign. If you embrace these two principles, you have made major strides toward understanding the complexity of strategic communication as a process that takes place in an environment that is much larger than that of only one company or organization.

Summary

In this chapter you were introduced to the definition of strategic communication in considerable depth. Remembering the different components of the definition and understanding the terms will help you to explain to others what it is you are studying and planning for your career. It will also help you to understand when a situation requires strategic communication action and enable you to analyze strategic communication processes as you go through the course.

You also learned strategic communication is not only about communication but about many other factors to be considered before communication tactics are implemented. Social and cultural factors, referred to as the macro or societal level, play an important role. Similarly, issues relating to the communicative entity, its behavior and its organization—referred to as the meso or organizational level—are influential in the success of strategic communication process. Only once you have considered all these factors you can execute the actual communication tactics at the micro or communication level. You will be most successful when you use the outside-in approach, which means that you consider your stakeholders as the most important part of the communication process.

This chapter also introduced you to the different academic disciplines that form the foundation of strategic communication and to different areas of practice. You will be introduced to all these principles in greater depth as you continue studying the book.

Discussion Questions

1   Revisit the definition of strategic communication and then review the vignette at the beginning of the chapter. Match the different terms in the definition to the different entities in the vignette.

2   In this chapter you were introduced to different fields of practice. In which of these fields would you like to practice your strategic communication skills and why are you interested in those? Do you think you have specific skills and personality traits that will help you in that practice? What are they?

3   Find two celebrities from sports or entertainment; one whom you admire and one you are critical of. Write down what you like and dislike of them respectively and discuss the extent to which their communication in the public affects your impressions.

4   Reflect on the two communication theories presented in this chapter and write down which one best reflect your approach to communication and why.

 Check out the online support material, including chapter summaries, useful links and further reading, at www.routledge.com/9780367426316

Notes

1   Tourism Australia, "Consumer Demand Project," 2017. http://www.tourism.australia.com/en/markets-and-stats/consumer-research.html.

2   CMO, "15 mind-blowing states about the Super Bowl," 2017, https://www.cmo.com/adobe-digital-insights/articles/2017/1/25/adi-super-bowl-2017-analysis.html.

3   Magna Global, "Tourism Australia 2018 Super Bowl Initial Opportunity Analysis" 2017. https://magnaglobal.com.

4   *Advertising Age*, "In online views, Tourism Australia snatches Super Bowl crown from Doritos", 5 February 2018. https://adage.com/article/special-report-supr-bowl/viral-video-super-bowl-tourism-australia/3122263.

5   Hallahan, K., Holtzhausen, D. R., Van Ruler, B., Vercic, D., & Sriramesh, K. (2007). Defining strategic communication. *International Journal of Strategic Communication*, *1*(1), 3–35.

6   Holtzhausen, D. R., & Zerfass, A. (2013). Strategic Communication—Pillars and Perspectives of an Alternative Paradigm. In A. Zerfass, L. Rademacher, and S. Wehmeier (Eds.), *Organisationskommunikation und Public Relations. Forschungsparadigmen und neue Perspektiven* (pp. 73–94). Wiesbaden, Germany: Springer VS.

7   Habermas, J. (1989). The Structural Transformation of the Public Sphere: An Inquiry into a Category of Bourgeois Society. Cambridge, MA: The MIT Press, p. 30. Translation from the original German, published 1962.

8   Deuze, Mark (2012). *Media Life*. Cambridge, UK: Polity Press.

9   http://prdefinition.prsa.org/index.php/2012/03/01/new-definition-of-public-relations/; last accessed on March 1, 2021.

10 https://awario.com/blog/social-issues-marketing/, last accessed on October 23, 2019.

11 https://corporate.walmart.com/newsroom/2019/09/03/mcmillon-to-associates-our-next-steps-in-response-to-the-tragedies-in-el-paso-and-southaven, last accessed October 23, 2019.

12 Hallahan, K., Holtzhausen, D., van Ruler, B., Veri, D., and Sriramesh, K. (2007). Defining Strategic Communication. *International Journal of Strategic Communication*, *1*(1), 3–35. DOI: 10.1080/1553118070 1285244 URL: http://dx.doi.org/10.1080/1553118070 1285244.

13 Su, Z., Chengbo, Z., & Mackert, M. (2019). Understanding the influenza vaccine as a consumer health technology: A structural equation model of motivation, behavioral expectation, and vaccine adoption. *Journal of Communication in Healthcare*, *12*(3–4), 170–179.

14 Nan, X. (2007). Social distance, framing, and judgment: A construal level perspective. *Human Communication Research*, *33*(4), 489–514

15 Lim, B. C., & Chung, C. M. Y. (2011). The impact of word-of-mouth communication on attribute evaluation. *Journal of Business Research, 64*(1), 18–23.

16 Shannon, C. E. &, Weaver, W. (1949). *A Mathematical Model of Communication.* Urbana, IL: University of Illinois Press.

17 https://www.washingtonpost.com/lifestyle/style/this-cant-be-happening-an-oral-history-of-48-surreal-violent-biblical-minutes-in-washington/2020/06/02/6683d36e-a4e3–11ea-b619–3f9133bbb482_story.html, last accessed June 4, 2020.

18 https://www.nytimes.com/2020/06/02/us/politics/trump-walk-lafayette-square.html, last accessed June 5, 2020.

Chapter 2

Careers in Strategic Communication

Learning Outcomes

By the end of this chapter, you should be able to do the following:

- Understand the career options you might have with strategic communication.
- Know what skills you'll need to master for a successful career.
- Learn how to get a job and find a mentor.

Chapter Opening Vignette

A Career Path in Strategic Communication

When Cynthia Nichols first went to college, she wanted to be a meteorologist. She loved science and talking to people about the weather. She then changed her mind and wanted to be an actress. She loved being on stage and telling a story to a captive audience. Then, she changed to education. She loved sharing her knowledge and providing guidance. After changing majors four times, she finally realized the thing that she loved about each of them—strategic communication. So, she changed her major one last time and found all the things she loved about her previous majors rolled into one. She loved looking at data to find the patterns and forecast market trends. She loved creating persuasive messages for target audiences. She loved designing materials that had aesthetic appeal. She loved strategic communication.

Since getting her degree, she has changed careers several times too. Her first job out of college was as a data analyst. It was fine, but after a while, she wanted something a little more challenging. So, while in graduate school, she worked at a local television station as a producer. After graduate school, she ran the marketing department of a manufacturing company, was a college professor, worked as a communications consultant, and is now at the U.S. State Department. Cynthia didn't find her major on her first try ... or her second. Instead, she took the time to figure out where her talents lay, determined what made her happy and then found a major that suited her best. And her career path? Well, it's about the same. Cynthia realized a long time ago that her first job was not going to be her last, nor does the company that hires you expect you to stay with them forever. She learned it was okay to change your career (and your major) to build the life you want.

Cynthia Nichols, PhD.

"So, What Are You Going to Major In?"

You've probably been asked that question a few thousand times since you graduated high school. It's a big question—one you've probably thought about a lot. Perhaps you thought about becoming a doctor, but the thought of taking chemistry changed your mind faster than a firework exploding on the 4th of July (i.e. a very fast chemical reaction). Maybe you wanted to be a theater major, but when you got on stage you froze harder than Anna of Arendelle (hey there *Frozen* fans). Or perhaps you thought about being an archeologist like Indiana Jones but have a dust allergy (and a serious revulsion to snakes). Deciding a major can be hard. After all, what you major in impacts the path your life takes and who you become ... which can be a scary thought.

The beauty of college is that you can figure out exactly where you want that path to go. You don't have to decide who or what you want to be for the rest of your life right now. You just must decide a major. So, what happens after taking a variety of courses, you finally figure out that you like strategic communication? First, congratulations and welcome! But … now you must tell your family and friends.

Maybe this happened to you. You tell your people that you've decided to embark on a career in strategic communication. You're thrilled about declaring your major and finding your path, but instead of congratulating you immediately, you get a blank stare that is a mixed bit of concern and confusion. The reason you might get "the look" is that a lot of people don't understand what a strategic communicator is. You may start hearing new questions after you've declared your major. Legitimate questions like:

- What is that?
- What kind of job can you get with that?
- What exactly do you do in strategic communication?
- How is it different than public relations, advertising and marketing?
- Can you make a living in it?
- Are there any jobs out there?

Fortunately, you can tell your family and friends the truth—there are a lot of diverse, well-paying jobs available to you in a field that is consistently growing. In fact, when you get asked what kinds of business you wish to go into you can honestly tell them, "Every one of them." Think about it—what organization or company doesn't depend on successful communication to achieve its goals? None. Whether it is energy or entertainment, politics or technology, sports or medicine, no company can survive without effective strategic communication.

However, the field of strategic communication is highly competitive. Jobs may be plentiful, but without the skills needed to do the job successfully you might not even get the interview. It is not just about being creative or "good with people" anymore. Today's strategic communicators must be critical thinkers, write well, understand media systems, embrace social and cultural diversity, and understand business concepts as well as technology.

In Chapter 1 you learned the definition of strategic communication. Now, look at the job market and the exciting careers available in the field. It will give you a good idea of the functions you'll be performing on the job as well as the skills needed to get that dream job. You'll also learn some strategies of landing that job and the importance of finding a good mentor. This chapter is designed to be a practical guide to help you in your career. By the end of it you should be able to successfully erase any concerns your family and friends might have about strategic communication. Honestly, it's a great major and you're going to love your career.

Career Paths, Specializations and Skills

In Chapter 4, you will learn more about how workplaces are organized and about the concept of **division of labor**, which refers to the roles that employees perform and the skills required for those roles. Division of labor is one of the basic principles of modern organizations because it helps them to identify the work that needs to be performed to reach the CE's goals and objectives, identify the skill set required for a position and hire the right person for the job.

Roles theory in strategic communication is the study of the roles required to work in the field and the skill sets to execute them. You will immediately understand that this is of the utmost importance to strategic communication educators because we need to make sure that the degrees and programs that we teach include all the knowledge that will prepare you for a successful career. This has been an important driver in the development of the field of strategic communication. In the past, careers in communication were very isolated from each other in what could be described as professional "silos." Students had to choose between studying advertising, public relations, marketing, speech communication, journalism and more. In many ways there were, and still are, conflicts between these different jobs in terms of which is the best, the most glamorous, the highest-earning, the most ethical, and on and on.

In the past, the education of communication practitioners has strongly focused on skills, such as, can you write properly (media relations), can you think creatively (creative director), do you have the necessary people skills to direct a campaign (client liaison), and so forth. Unfortunately, this has created an environment that is so fragmented and specialized in terms of roles that it no longer serves students such as you. It is no longer beneficial to teach you how to do only one thing. You need to know and perform all the roles needed to execute all the tasks and have all the knowledge that better serves CEs in a society consisting of fragmented audiences and multiple message delivery platforms. Also, by teaching you numerous roles, you possess the knowledge and skills that will help you make changes and transitions in your future career, which will require you to be a lifelong learner.

In strategic communication, siloed divisions of roles disappear because strategic communication practice approaches roles theory very differently, arguing that students and practitioners need to understand the principles and practices of all these fields of practice. Strategic communicators must be able to **multi-skill**, that is at least understand all the skills that would go into a strategic communication campaign. As you will see from the list of possible jobs in the field later in this chapter, there are far too many jobs types to know how to do them all and you will specialize in areas that interest you. But if you do not at least understand where these jobs fit into strategic communication practice, you will not be able to coordinate or participate in a strategic communication campaign.

Practitioner Roles

It is hard to overemphasize how the changes in society affected traditional theories of organizations. The purpose of division of labor is to divide up the work that people do into very specific roles. The division of labor has concerned scholars and practitioners alike for many years. It begs the question of what it is students in the discipline should be taught and what practitioners are expected to do in the work environment.

This is not such a difficult task if one thinks differently about the roles and knowledge strategic communicators perform. Roles are traditionally defined by **tasks**. Roles set apart individuals in organizations and they define the expectations organizations have of their employees. In strategic communication practice, this task-oriented approach results in the unnecessary fragmentation of functions where marketing communicators work with consumers, public relations practitioners work with communities and the media, financial communicators work with investors, and so forth. The keyword here is traditional. To understand what strategic communication practitioners do, it is necessary to defy the notion of tradition and approach the topic from a different angle, which is necessitated by the many changes at the societal level, particularly changes in the economy that require new skill sets, one of which is critical thinking.

By applying theories used in traditionally parallel fields of communication practice, e.g. public relations, to other areas of communication practice, e.g. advertising, one can start to determine the extent to which theoretical approaches are shared across fields of practice. The question becomes: "What are the common roles communication practitioners perform whether they are in public relations, advertising, political, health or government communication, or any of the other fields of practice you are exposed to in this book?"

Roles theory is the most researched in public relations. As one of the foundational disciplines of strategic communication, public relations provides a useful basis for the comparison and integration of roles in other strategic communication disciplines.

One of the most overlooked attributes of strategic communication work is its collective and collaborative nature. The collective, shared production of advertising or other marketing-related products, which would include the functions and responsibilities of different roles, is typically ignored in most marketing and advertising research. This is also true for public relations practice, which views roles as individual rather than collaborative.

There are of course good reasons why roles are so specifically defined. It is still important to know the expectations of your position. However, it also is important to understand that you are not a prisoner of your current role. You can only move ahead if you understand all roles and, as a manager and leader, understand how to coordinate it all.

Industry Insight

A Hollywood Creative Agency

Helen Greene, Owner of Greenhaus GFX.

Helen Greene is the owner of Greenhaus GFX located in Los Angeles, California. Greenhaus is a motion graphics company that focuses on providing services to movie studios in the marketing and postproduction stages of the movie. This can involve crafting movie trailers, providing special effects and creating a title sequence.

Because she has a small team, she had to learn early-on to multi-skill. She tells the story of how her team had to create a title scene for the movie *Entourage*. The creative idea was to shoot well-known Los Angeles buildings that had neon signs and then replace the names of the buildings with the names of the cast members. They rented a convertible and for three days drove around Los Angeles photographing the buildings. They then had to use a variety of software to create the images they needed. Because of the highly specialized nature of the software different team members completed different parts of the project, which finally came together as a single product. All team members participated in the creative process. As a small team they had to be very collaborative, which they love, feeding off each other's creativity. When Greene needs more staff for a project, she will strengthen the team with freelancers. This is a great example of many of the concepts mentioned at the meso level, namely, the many roles strategic communicators must fulfill, the importance of teamwork, the role of a collaborative leader and how a network structure works.

Roles in Advertising and Marketing

Advertising campaigns for clients are typically developed in the agency environment. In advertising agencies, practitioners cluster around five core tasks: account management or account services, creative services, media, research and account planning. The account management or account services function maintains the client-agency relationship and helps client organizations determine what and if a brand will benefit from specific promotions.

Working closely with the client, practitioners working in account management have a very strategic function in terms of identifying the stakeholders, developing the unique selling proposition and developing a strategic campaign that includes a creative concept and content for the brand. Although the account executive does not do all by herself, her role is to be the communication channel between the client and the agency.

The account manager must understand what the client wants and must provide guidance to the creative and other agency teams on what the client's objectives and desired outcomes are. Depending on seniority, practitioners in account management have titles such as account manager, account supervisor or account executive. In some industries the **creative** director also serves as the account executive, such as in companies that produce marketing products for the film and television industry.

There are several roles associated with creative work. Practitioners can be copywriters, creative directors and producers. These are typically highly specialized positions and these days require knowledge of complex creative software. **Media planning** is a specialized function that, along with estimating the costs of media, develops a strategy for purchasing or utilizing media that will disseminate the client's message effectively and efficiently. The media planner, the media buyer and the media researcher carry out this function in either a specialized media agency or in an advertising agency.

The research function coordinates and compiles secondary and primary strategic research for a client's advertising goals and objectives. Along with the execution and collection of research, the researcher also interprets the research findings for the client and distills the research to other members of the advertising agency who will need the information to create the campaign. The account planner is responsible for coordinating research and ensuring that research is used in the development of materials. The account planner, too, has a very strategic role in providing input into the targeting of the campaign and in the creation of the strategy.

Roles in Public Relations

As mentioned, there is a long history of research on roles in public relations practice. For many years, though, public relations roles were described as either that of a manager or a technician with only managers making strategic decisions. This notion has been debunked in later years and it is now assumed that technicians (if one can even call content developers that) also make strategic decisions daily.

The manager and technician roles have since been explained and expanded in public relations research and practice and have increasingly focused on the inclusion of strategic thinking and intent. Managers need to act as strategists, particularly when dealing with executives and clients. Practitioners who can strategically use information from the web or add web and social media content can become information specialists. In line with the outside-in approach, public relations practitioners are also viewed as **boundary spanners** who help the organization align with its stakeholders while also representing the interests of the institution to stakeholders. In this discussion you can already see what the skills sets are you will need to acquire to be a successful strategic communicator. But remember, you can never know everything; therefore, teamwork and collaboration have become essential skills that will carry you through life.

In highly diverse environments and in international settings public relations practitioners often have the role of **cultural interpreter**, who translates local cultural practices for managers of these organizations. Personal influencers are part of an influential class and then hired to influence the elite and powerful members of society. While this practice is deemed unethical in many countries, some argue that personal influencers are like public relations' lobbying function in the United States.

Roles in Strategic Communication

The strategic planning process is similar for all strategic communication practice, with the only difference being the context. To execute a strategic communication plan might differ in terms of stakeholders, messages and media but the process remains the same. To advance strategic communication roles theory, three studies were conducted in South Africa, Europe and the United States respectively.[1]

The **strategist role** emerged as the most commonly performed role in communication practice. In this role practitioners are deemed experts in identifying and solving communication problems, they participate in strategic planning and change management, and scan the environment for stakeholder and societal trends. The South African study tested the extent to which roles overlap among public relations, advertising and government practitioners. The strategist role was performed in all settings, with advertising practitioners performing this role slightly more than public relations practitioners.

In both South African and U.S. practice a **media specialist** role was identified. This role combined the previously mentioned technician role with the media relations role. This is indeed a new development and indicates that the traditional media relations role and the technician role have become much more complex due to the many and widespread changes in the media environment. Practitioners now must be experts in media of all kinds and have moved beyond churning out media releases.

Another role identified in these studies was that of **communication liaison**. Advertising and public relations practitioners performed this role equally. This is a strategic role uniquely focused on the outside-in approach in terms of its emphasis on stakeholder relations and providing the institution with stakeholder perspectives.

As expected, the South African study confirmed the **cultural interpreter role**. This is not surprising considering that the country exhibits all the attribute of environments that are conducive to the performance of this role: high cultural diversity, political instability and a complex combination of developed and developing infrastructure.

Where in the past, roles theory suggested practitioners are either managers or technicians, the above-mentioned and several other studies found that all strategic communicators perform all roles. While at the early stages of a career in strategic communication the media expert role might be performed more than the other roles, entry-level practitioners perform all the roles. As careers progress, the liaison and strategist roles are performed more, but media expertise remains an important requirement even at the most senior level.

You will remember that the concept of the differentiation of roles were discussed earlier. The more differentiated roles are, the higher the need for coordination. The good news here is that the roles of strategic communicators are no longer so differentiated or specialized. Looking at roles theory as knowledge work rather than a specific set of skills gives one another perspective on what it is strategic communicators should know to enable them to fulfill their different roles. It is also important to note that this career requires a set of roles that need to be mastered and executed equally well.

Careers Paths

The beauty of strategic communication is that you can choose to go into any industry or area. If you're a space nerd, you can work for NASA. If you're a fashionista, you can work for *Vogue* magazine or a fashion company. If you're a political wonk, you can work at the White House. It doesn't matter—everyone needs people who can communicate effectively. As a communicator, there are five main career paths you can be in (and switch between)— agency, corporate, non-profit and government. The fifth is working for individuals in the entertainment and sports industries, as has been mentioned before. The next section will explore the roles you could take in each of these areas.

Agency

For a lot of strategic communication majors, agency life is the life for them. Think *MadMen*—you're constantly trying to win new clients, create new ideas and design innovative work. It's fast-paced, incredibly difficult and beyond rewarding. And for some, it's everything they've ever dreamed.

There are different areas about agencies that you need to explore before you dive in. Do you want to be on the account or creative side? Do you see yourself as the art director, account executive, copywriter, media buyer, creative director or one of dozens of other roles? Are you willing to work directly with clients, do project management, pitch, develop strategies and make sure the client is happy? The money in agency life can be good, the traditional 9 to 5 schedule is rare with agency life and demands are high. Satisfying the client could take long hours, bruised egos and a whole lot of rejections. But, the reward could be a satisfying and incredibly creative career.

If you want to go into an agency after graduation, start on that path now by joining local student chapters of professional organizations. This already gives you entry to your career and exposes you to many professionals. They visit student chapters as speakers or chapter members visit them on field trips. Some of these are

- Public Relations Student Society of America (PRSSA), which is affiliated with the Public Relations Society of America (PRSA);
- Ad Club, which is the student arm of the American Advertising Federation (AAF);
- Association for Women in Communication (AWC), which is a professional club that invites students to be student members;
- Society of Professional Journalists (SPJ), which has student members of local chapters and regional and national journalism competitions; and
- American Marketing Association (AMA), which has student members of local chapters.

Often major cities have their own regional professional organizations. Public relations and advertising student organizations, as do other professional student organizations, offer competitive programs, like the AAF's National Student Advertising Competition and PRSSA Bateman Case Study Competition. These strategic communication competitions will offer you invaluable tools and opportunities while you're in school and introduce you to how professionals in the industry think and what they value in future professionals. You should also strive to create solid work while you're in school. The materials and portfolio you create now can help you stand out later. Finally, figure out your passions and talents, and get an internship in that area.

Oh, and be able to write well. That's huge in agency world, no matter what your passion or specialty is.

Corporate

In every organization, there will be a need for strategic communicators. We are the group of people that can translate the jargon of any organization into strategic key messages for target audiences. Organizations need us. Fortunately, there are opportunities everywhere. Unlike agencies, where people have specialties that they tend to stick with, people who work in corporate environments are often seen as jack-of-all-trades. They are people who have a multitude of skills—writing, designing, creative, editing, strategy and more—and use all of them throughout their careers. In addition, they are typically serving one client— the organization—as opposed to many. Although people who work at agencies have a breadth of knowledge on a variety of topics, people who work in corporations have a depth of knowledge on their industry. For example, if you work for an agency you might work with clients that sell dog food, shoes, cars, cereal and more. So, you'd have some knowledge on all those topics. But, if you work in the communications department of a bathtub manufacturer, you'll know more about bathtubs (or whatever product is being sold) that you'd ever dream.

Non-Profit

If you aren't driven by money, but rather serving others, non-profits might be the way for you to go. After all, profit is not the measurement of success here. Although resources can be limited, the impact of your work goes much further. Plus, you'll gain invaluable skills through networking, fundraising, communication development and more. Much like a corporate job, there's the potential to wear a ton of hats. Your skills will diversify by working at non-profits or NGOs (non-governmental organizations), and it's a great way to get actively involved in a topic that you're passionate about.

If you want to get into the non-profit world while you're still in college, consider volunteering. The more you volunteer with the organization you want to work for, the more likely they are to notice you and be interested in offering you a job. Also, get an internship with a non-profit you love and make your mark. If you do, they might extend you a better offer.

Government

When you've caught the public servant bug and you know you want to help shape and mold the policies of your community and nation, it's a fantastic thing. But, the question remains—where do you get in? If you don't know where to start, have no fear, there are some simple things that you can do to get you in the door. If you do well, you never know where your career could go.

- *Apply for fellowships and internships within the government.* There are a lot of opportunities available to recent graduates. Programs like Pickering Fellows, Presidential Management Fellows and the Pathways Recent Graduates Program all offer young grads opportunities for growth. These will provide you the opportunity to network and build your experience with government entities.
- *Volunteer with a local campaign.* Your candidate may or may not win, and it may or may not land you a job. However, what you'll learn from volunteering your time— canvasing, crafting message strategy, getting donations—will be invaluable for your resume. Often, if you want a job on Capitol Hill, you won't even be considered without campaign experience.
- *Learn about a policy area.* Perhaps you're passionate about education reform. Maybe you think LGBTQ+ rights are something you want to fight for. Maybe you want to make the Equal Right Amendment a permanent part of the constitution. Or maybe you want to bring serious environmental policy changes to congress. Whatever it is, become actively involved and knowledgeable about what you want to do.
- *Find a consulting company.* Many people who work for the government are actually employed by contracting companies. Search the job boards of companies like Deloitte, Accenture or even the Cherokee Nation—they all have contracts with the government to provide skilled workers.

Whatever your career path, you need to determine what you want out of your career. Do you want to be the CEO or someone in the back supporting the show? Do you want high stress or low? Whatever it is, think about who you are and what you want. Then, don't be afraid to take advantage of opportunities that are presented to you. Remember, you don't always have to rush to the next thing. Be willing to create goals for yourself while you sit and learn the ropes.

Entertainment

As mentioned, celebrities in entertainment and sports often need strategic communicators. These practitioners are typically referred to in the industry as publicists because their main role is to navigate the media for these individuals. While celebrities carefully build their image in conjunction with their publicist, they can land in a crisis quicker than most due to some poorly thought-out statement, misstep or personal transgression. Thus, the work of publicists often involves crisis communication, which in turn requires a deep knowledge of media and crisis management strategies. Many strategic communication programs will have a special course in crisis communication.

Professional Profile

Ashley Wilemon—Senior Level Agency Management

Ashley Wilemon—Senior-Level Agency Management.

We asked senior-level agency manager Ashley Wilemon to answer a few questions about her career path in strategic communication and here's what she said.

What did you wish you had known? I wish I had known … gosh. So much. I wish I had understood the power of networking earlier and used that in a better way. I wish I had understood the power of a personal brand. I wish I had known how important soft skills are and developed them more in college. I wish I had known that careers are a jungle gym and not a ladder. I wish I had known that money and titles will not make you happy with your work. It is much more important to like the work you do and the people you do it with than to like that title or paycheck.

What has surprised you most about yourself or your career? How little external validation matters, and how much internal satisfaction matters. I've been surprised that I can find goodness and stories worth telling in organizations that I don't agree with personally. Everyone deserves to have their side of the story represented, so that has given me a lot of perspective on the media … and not all of that is good.

What advice would you give to someone in college now? If you're wanting to get an advanced degree, don't wait to go for it. Get it now and never stop learning. Develop soft skills and be willing to take feedback. Ask for feedback, listen to what is said and be willing to grow. How you react to feedback will be part of your personal brand/reputation, so understand how to be professional. Pay attention to the culture and social cues of your organization ... and make a new pot of coffee when the last one is done.

What do you wish young professionals working at your agency knew? Make a new pot of coffee when the last one is empty. Be resourceful. If you come up to me and say, "I can't find X," but I can find it in a five-second Google search, I'm going to be annoyed and disappointed in you. Remember: We're running a business, so this is not about you. Find the balance between being an advocate for yourself and being professional. Don't take things personally. In the course of doing business, we sometimes forget that this is supposed to be a learning and growing experience for young interns. Respectfully communicate what you need to get out of the experience ... and work those networks.

More information about Ashley Wilemon can be found here: https://www.linkedin.com/in/ashley-wilemon/.

Specializations

The beauty of strategic communication is that there are many areas you can explore. You could become an expert in advertising or public relations or marketing or design or research or digital or strategy development, or a dozen other things. Strategic communication is constantly changing because the macro, meso and micro environments are changing more rapidly than any other time in history. There will always be the need to have experts in a variety of specializations. Let's look at one full-service agency's list of specializations. According to their promotional materials, they are experts in:

- Stakeholder engagement and outreach
- Strategy development and execution
- Research analysis and insights
- Public, community and media relations
- Crisis planning and communications
- Issue advocacy and influence
- Public and political affairs
- Corporate social responsibility
- Identity development and branding
- Video/TV/Radio/Photo Production
- Website, app and intranet development
- Print (B2B/B2C) and outdoor production
- Direct mail and email marketing
- Digital marketing; content marketing
- Social media strategy
- Content, management monitoring and reporting
- Media planning, placing, training, monitoring and reporting
- Paid (SEM) and Organic (SEO) Search.

That's a lot of different areas that they consider themselves experts in. But, it goes to show you how much opportunity there is for you to find your niche in strategic communication.

Consider just one of those niche areas, namely, advertising. Advertising is an area of specialization that deals with paying for media space in order to get the attention of stakeholders (in this case consumers), generates interest, and persuades people to purchase a product or adopt an idea. Think about a Nike advertisement of Serena Williams selling a new line of work-out clothes in a *People* or *Sports Illustrated*. Before you ever pick up that magazine, there is a network of advertising professionals behind the ad working to make it happen. There might be account executives working with the client, creative directors and graphic designers coming up with the ad, media buyers purchasing the ad space and photographers working with Serena Williams. But, there are also many other people working behind the scenes to make this ad happen. Let's take a minute and explore a few of the job titles you might encounter in strategic communication.

Industry Insight

Jobs in Strategic Communication

- Account Director
- Account Executive
- Account Manager
- Account Supervisor
- Advertising Buyer
- Advertising Coordinator
- Advertising Specialist
- Advertising Traffic Manager
- Art Director
- Brand Manager
- Brand Ambassador
- Broadcast Account Manager
- Client Strategist
- Client Support Specialist
- Communications Coordinator
- Communications Director
- Communications Editor
- Communications Representative
- Communications Specialist
- Corporate Communications Specialist
- Content Manager
- Content Strategist
- Copy Associate
- Copyeditor
- Copywriter
- Creative Director
- Creative Technologist
- Crisis Communications Consultant
- Development Director
- Development Officer
- Digital Advertising Manager
- Digital Advertising Specialist
- Digital Media Planner
- Diplomat
- Director of Development
- Director of Public Affairs
- Director of Public Relations
- eCommerce Editor
- eCommerce Coordinator
- eCommerce Marketing Manager
- eCommerce Marketing Specialist
- eCommerce Merchandising Coordinator
- eCommerce Merchandising Specialist
- eCommerce Production Assistant
- Editorial Photographer
- Event Coordinator
- Event Manager
- Financial Public Relations Associate

- Fundraising Manager
- Insights Analyst
- Major Gifts Officer
- Marketing Analyst
- Marketing Assistant
- Marketing Associate
- Marketing Data Analyst
- Market Research Analyst
- Marketing Assistant
- Marketing Promotions Specialist
- Marketing Specialist
- Graphic Artist
- Graphic Designer
- Illustrator
- Lobbyist
- Marketing Associate
- Marketing Communications Director
- Marketing Communications Manager
- Marketing Coordinator
- Marketing Director
- Media Account Director
- Media Buyer
- Media Coordinator
- Media Director
- Media Planner
- Media Relations Manager
- Media Research Analyst
- Motion Graphics Designer
- Online Advertising Director
- Online Advertising Manager
- Online Product Manager
- Photographer
- Print Traffic Coordinator
- Print Traffic Director
- Print Traffic Manager
- Production Artist
- Producer
- Promotions Manager
- Public Affairs Manager
- Public Affairs Specialist
- Public Information Assistant
- Public Information Officer
- Public Information Specialist
- Public Relations Coordinator
- Public Relations Director
- Public Relations Manager
- Public Relations Specialist
- Publicist
- Researcher
- Senior Account Director
- Social Media Advertising Manager
- Social Media Analyst
- Social Media Manager
- Social Media Specialist
- Target Marketing Strategist
- Technical Writer
- Traffic Manager
- Web Designer
- Web Analytics Consultant.

This list may make your head spin, but you will soon find your passion and interest. If you are passionate and interested, your niche will find you. However, you do need to understand where you will fit into the bigger picture—that is why this course in strategic communication is so important. Perhaps the following specialization categories will make it easier for you to determine the broader area you are interested in:

- Client liaison and strategy execution
- Management and planning
- Creative
- Content creation and management
- Media liaison and strategy
- Conceptualization
- Organizing and coordination

- Stakeholder liaison
- Editorial
- Administrative
- Research.

Skills Needed for a Successful Career

Think back to the list of jobs that you just read. As you can see, there are a lot of opportunities and options out there. You can do anything you want—from public relations to graphic design to marketing to corporate communications. However, whatever path you choose, you're going to need to be nimble and capable. Gone are the days when you were expected to have one skillset. Now? You need them all; or a least some semblance of them. You may not be able to master them all, but you should at least be competent in several areas. So, what are these areas? Well, there are two big types that we're going to discuss—hard skills and soft skills.

Hard Skills

Hard skills are teachable things (i.e. the abilities that you will learn in your strategic communication program). This includes skills like writing, media production or social media planning. Perhaps you'll learn how to edit a video. Perhaps you'll be taught how to become a prolific writer. Perhaps you have a knack for business communications. Perhaps your creative side will be sparked in a graphic design class. Whatever the unique skill is, you'll likely take classes during your program to help you gain mastery. These hard skills are highly specialized to your area of expertise and they have value.

When you apply for a job, you'll want to communicate these hard skills through your resume and a portfolio. Let your skills shine and be proud of what you've learned. Any organization that you apply to will want to utilize those hard skills. And, if they are a good organization, they'll allow you opportunity to gain more hard skills.

Soft Skills

Soft Skills, on the other hand, are qualities or traits that impact how you interact with others. These skills are not necessarily going to be taught in your Introduction to Strategic Communication class or learned during your time at the university. However, they are just as important. Many of these skills come naturally to you, while others do not. Although it would be wonderful to say that you've mastered them all, it's simply impossible. No one can master them all. However, it helps to know what you're good at. Just remember, companies interviewing you are looking for more than just a degree or the ability to make a video clip go viral—they are looking for people with the qualities and skills that they would enjoy working with or would suit their team, generally referred as a "matter of fit" (whether you are a good match or not).

Soft skills can be anything from proper email communication habits to knowing how to network. Many of these skills will be inherent to you, while others are not. What's key is to find the ones you know you're good at, and when you're interviewing for a job, emphasize those. Here are just a few that you may master during your career or have already mastered in your different leadership positions in the past:

- Ability to Contextualize
- Adaptability
- Agility
- Analysis

- Authenticity
- Attention to Detail
- Brainstorming
- Calmness
- Collaboration
- Communicating with others
- Confidence
- Conflict Management
- Constructive Feedback
- Cooperation
- Coordination
- Coping
- Courage to Make Recommendations
- Creativity
- Critical Thinking
- Cultural Intelligence
- Curiosity
- Decision-making
- Delegation
- Dependability
- Diplomacy
- Discipline
- Divergent thinking
- Emotional Intelligence
- Empathy
- Experimenting
- Focus
- Forward Thinking
- Friendliness
- Generosity
- Goal Setting
- Humility
- Humor
- Idea Exchange
- Imagination
- Initiative
- Innovation
- Insight
- Inspiration
- Integrity

- Leadership
- Listening Skills
- Mediation
- Mentoring
- Motivation
- Negotiating
- Networking
- Non-verbal Communication
- Observation
- Open-mindedness
- Optimism
- Organization
- Patience
- Persistence
- Persuasion
- Planning
- Positivity
- Prioritizing
- Professionalism
- Project Management
- Public Speaking
- Questioning
- Reframing
- Resilience
- Responsibility
- Self-Awareness
- Self-Confidence
- Self-Management
- Self-Starter
- Selflessness
- Sensitivity
- Situational Awareness
- Strategic Thinking
- Stress Management
- Teamwork
- Time Management
- Tolerance
- Trust
- Versatility
- Woo
- Work Ethic.

Utilizing Both Hard and Soft Skills

There are some key differences between hard and soft skills. Soft skills can typically be used in every industry, whereas hard skills might be industry specific. For example, you may be able to care for someone who isn't feeling well and show empathy, but you wouldn't want to operate unless you were a trained surgeon. Soft skills would be the natural empathetic response you have toward that person who is ill whereas surgery comes from years of training. Soft skills relate to emotional intelligence, not technical knowledge.

Any organization you work for is going to expect you to know how communication works and use your hard and soft skills. But, what, exactly does that mean? Simply put, it means you must be able to think about *all* the ways that you'll tell your story. You must utilize your hard and soft skills to make connections and tell the story of your client. You'll do that through all the hard skills that you develop while you're in college and all the soft skills that you innately have—because they all work together to tell a story.

Let's take the prism concept and apply it to the story of Little Red Riding Hood. If you were to develop a strategic communication campaign using the tragic and dramatic story of a little girl about to be eaten by a wolf as the conceptual idea, you need to think of all the ways you could reach your stakeholders. Just like a prism, one beam of light will refract into a rainbow of ideas and media possibilities. So, you must utilize your hard and soft skills to connect the dots and tell the story. So, let's put that prism up to the story of Little Red. How would you tell it? More than likely, you would use your writing, multimedia and social media skills to get the story to the world. You'd write news releases, post social media, maybe edit a video of her first-hand account. All of these are hard skills.

Before you pitch Red's survival story to national morning news shows, you'd want to think about all the angles and ways that you could tell the story. Think about it telling the story of Little Red through all the media opportunities that are out there—local, national, regional, trade, broadcast, print and online media will all want a piece of this story. A girl was eaten by a wolf and survived—this story will go viral. But, what's the angle? Are you thinking about it from a perspective of fashion, elder care, travel routes, picnic supplies, forest safety, child welfare, identity theft, stranger danger, woodsman heroics or escape stories? Or, are you just telling one story? Coming up with a solid communication strategy is more than just putting words on paper, you need to be able to use your perspective and words to tell the whole story. Because, at the heart of it, that's what strategic communicators are—storytellers. We use our hard and soft skills together to tell a story with more depth and interest.

Getting the Job

If you followed the suggestion of joining the student chapter of a professional organization, you are already well on the way to finding a job. One of the most important strategies is to find ways in which you can expose yourself to professional environments where you can get exposed to professional practice and to professionals themselves. You can accomplish this while you are still a student. This section will discuss the different avenues open to you, so that you can start thinking about your career while still studying.

Networking and Internships

Most degree programs in strategic communication give course credit for internships.

Students in strategic communication often have opportunities to do internships, or even work, on campus because of their writing and planning skills and their ability to create media content. These are great opportunities to practice your craft while getting paid. Don't be shy to ask around or check your campus job boards for opportunities. That way, your job also will not interfere with your class schedule. Many students also work while putting

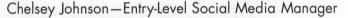

themselves through college. This might make it impossible to get a paid internship. In that case, find volunteer opportunities where you can practice your craft.

Do not hesitate to join the student newspaper or other campus media outlct. The writing skills you will practice there will be invaluable to your future career and will give you the opportunity to have reporting and writing examples for your portfolio. That will add a great deal to your credibility as a strategic communication practitioner. Not only do you get writing experience, but also get to know how media work and how news is gathered. This experience will be of great value in your future position. Yet another facet of student news outlets is that most of them now have multiple news platforms, i.e. there might be a printed product, a website and social media. For these you will need multimedia skills, which most likely will include news writing and videography. This will greatly enhance your ability and performance in your writing and media-related courses and will look great on your resume and to your future employers.

Summer breaks are typically the time when you can do an internship abroad or in a major U.S. media market. This will expose you to environments that are outside of your comfort zone and will make it easier to apply for and accept that job you want when it is in a city or town where you know nobody. The following industry insight is an example of a graduate who dared to do just that.

Professional Profile

Chelsey Johnson—Entry-Level Social Media Manager

Chelsey Johnson—Entry-Level Social Media Manager.

Chelsey Johnson is a recent graduate from Oklahoma State University. She has degrees in Strategic Communication and Political Science and is only a few years post-graduation. After graduation, she spent a year overseas working in communications and is now on the job hunt in Washington, DC.

Did you have any internships in college? Yes. I did a campus communication campaign internship, interned with an international non-profit in Belgium and I did a social media internship with the political science department.

How important do you think those internships were? I gained a lot of transferrable skills from internships as well as campus involvement, both of which exposed me to different types of organizations and informed the direction I want to go in communication. It's such a large, versatile field that being involved was an important layer on top of the skills I was gaining from class.

What do you want to do with your career? Good question. I'm figuring out new pieces of that every day. When I was at graduation, I wanted a career that was deeply rooted in communication; but with the more experience I gain, I see communication as a way to leverage myself into leadership positions. I was interested in non-profit communications and knew I was drawn towards cause-driven work, but I didn't realize the potential that a communication degree would have in relation to what I wanted to do with my life. I didn't know how high I wanted to aim my future. With a communication degree, I can really do anything.

Are you doing it? Kind of! I'm still actively exploring how my passions and abilities translate into a career. In my first year after graduation, I worked alongside an international development organization in Cambodia where I coordinated online content and social platforms, as well as produced written content for donor relations. I've been able to use skills from my communications background to open doors with organizations I'm passionate about.

How have your dreams changed? I've realized I not only want to communicate what an organization is doing and how it is changing lives, but I also want to be a part of the planning and program development. I want to have a seat at the table and be a driving force in the decision-making process for transformative non-profit organizations.

How have you changed? Having been in school for 17 years and receiving immediate, structured feedback on projects and grades, I'm now rewiring my brain on how to evaluate success. Benchmarks are different between me, my friends and classmates. I'm learning that comparison doesn't bring me closer to my own goals. I've also gained a deeper appreciation for downtime and work/life balance. College was busy for me, so learning how to be still and take a break—while still hustling professionally—have been valuable lessons!

What did you wish you knew? I wish I would have known how to professionally network. I was always so intimidated by professionals and didn't think they would be willing to take the time to invest in an up-and-comer in their industry. Turns out, many *are* up for it. Sometimes this investment is a five-minute phone call or coffee meeting, sometimes it's more intentional mentorship, but regardless, there are adults in the world who are willing (and flattered) to share their experiences and knowledge. Just ask!

What advice would you give to someone in college now? Put yourself out there! Try new things. Be curious. If you want to do something on your campus, make it happen. There is a wealth of resources in college, including communal knowledge, adults who want to see students succeed, and funding for student research and innovation. Now is the time to try, to work hard and to have fun! Give your education 100%, but make time for life and community and friendship, too.

More information about Chelsey Johnson can be found here: https://www.linkedin.com/in/chelseyjjohnson1/.

You should start networking activities while at college already so that you have established contacts when you start job hunting. It might be helpful if you already have an idea in which industry or which area of practice you are most interested. If not, use a first position as a steppingstone to explore those interests. No experience is ever wasted. Every professional will tell you that all experiences become opportunities or knowledge you will need in the future.

However, your path might not be as clearly laid out as you would have wished, and you need to prepare to land in a place where you have no contacts at all. This often happens to recent graduates who did not anticipate moving back to their families after college, or who have a life partner who relocated to a different town or city for work. If a job is not immediately forthcoming, the professional organization and volunteer routes are a great solution and will offer you many **networking** opportunities. "Networking is about establishing and nurturing long-term, mutually beneficial relationships with the people you meet, whether you're waiting to order your morning coffee, participating in an intramural sports league, or attending a work conference," says Amanda Augustine.[2]

Networking does not come easy to all people. The fact that you are interested in becoming a communication professional does not mean you are extraverted and love talking to strangers. Professional communicators are often shy and have learned the behavior required for networking. You will become more adept at it as your experiences grows. "It can be time-consuming, downright awkward on occasion, and—depending on your personality—incredibly draining," Augustine says. But she insists that networking opportunities are not only those that are offered through professional organizations. It can be work-related events or more diverse organizations such as a Rotary club that will expose you to business owners or members who work at organizations you never thought of.

There are many guides for networking on the internet such as the one from Hobart & William Smith Colleges that even provides you with a networking worksheet.[3]

Finding and Applying for the Right Job

If you have done your homework as mentioned above, have a well-designed and diverse online portfolio that displays your skills and experience, and a succinct and well-written resume, you are set to start looking for a position, if you do not already have one when you graduate. Yes, it is possible to have a job waiting for you when you graduate. This might happen if you have done internships, volunteered and networked with professionals. There might be many positions out there but make sure you are a good fit for the job. For instance, if you are not prepared to promote the products of a tobacco company, do not apply. Do not apply for a position that presents ethical conflicts or asks you to do work that would make you uncomfortable.

You will most likely not stay in your first job forever. Most people are expected to change positions at least five times in their lifetime. If you feel you get stuck and there are no opportunities for promotion or professional growth, promote yourself. After a few years in a position you should be ready for bigger challenges. If you are not promoted in a position, promote yourself by applying for more senior positions elsewhere and touting your experience. While you are in college, use the opportunity to visit your career center. Ask them if they have any an aptitude test, career assessment test or career personality test that you can take to learn more about yourself and which career choices suit you.

Psychologists develop tests all the time based on the latest scientific knowledge. Do these tests early in your student career and again later, because one's personality changes with experience and age. You will likely find it interesting to see how you have changed and grown over three to four years.

These tests will be able to guide you toward areas that interest you and help you to determine if a position is a good fit for you. The most common aspects to evaluate the potential of a position are the following:[4]

- Passion: Do you have passion for the job and is it something you can get excited about when you tell people what you do?
- Overlap: "What you're good at, what companies need and what you like to do might all be different, but it's important to try to find the overlap between the three. That's how you find your optimal career path. Rather than looking at job titles, consider your interests, hobbies, and skills, and then work out how those translate," says Ashley Stahl from *Forbes*.[5] It is important that your whole personality fits your new job, not just your skills. You will spend a great deal of time at your workplace. If you do not fit, you will be unhappy most of the time.
- Office culture: Make sure you can see yourself working at the company long-term. Depending on your personality type you might prefer an office culture that is supportive and affirming, patting you on the back frequently. Or you might prefer an office that leaves you to do your work but is supportive when you ask for guidance and advice. On the other hand, you might prefer a very controlled environment that has precise policies and procedures and that leaves the guesswork out of the job. Assess these attributes when you go for an interview or do an online search that will tell you how employees feel about the organization.
- Team culture: Different teams in an organization form a subculture that might be different from the rest of the organization. Think about how the team is structured, what the different positions are and if it requires teamwork to get assignments done. In those cases, team culture is even more important than organizational culture.
- Growth opportunities: Ask if the organization supports personal development opportunities, membership of professional organizations, conference attendance or even higher education opportunities. Some organizations will pay for or partly pay for starting graduate school.
- Hours and work–life balance: You will notice from the industry insights in this chapter that practitioners invariably refer to the importance of work–life balance. Strategic communication practitioners can easily work 80-hour days if you are so inclined. That

is the nature of the job: many events and social functions, deadlines and a great deal of multiskilling. Make sure that your organization is respectful of your time, even if you work 80 hours for a couple of weeks. There needs to be an agreement that you can take time off to recharge before the next project starts. That is one of the main problems people working in this industry face, namely, having to start on a new project immediately after the completion of a very stressful job that had a tight deadline. They complain that they do not have time to recharge and that affects their creative thinking and abilities.

- Job title: A job title might not be important to you but at the same time it should describe what you are doing or be an indication of your seniority. When applying for another position the first thing screeners look at is the current job title.
- Location: Make sure your place of work is accessible. In big cities such as Los Angeles, San Francisco, Seattle and Washington DC you can spend three hours per day on a commute—one and a half hours each way. It is not only strenuous to sit in the traffic if there is no public transport, but it is costly and takes time away from your job. If necessary, you need to consider moving closer to your workplace.
- Company history: If you are not adventurous, do not accept a position at a start-up. There might be many reasons why you would like to do that, but if not, look at the stability and history of the organization to make sure that your job will not vanish overnight.
- Salary, benefits and recognition: Do your homework and find out what the type of job pays in the type of organization you are applying to. Agencies, for instance, are different from companies, non-profits, government agencies, and so forth. Be prepared to negotiate for your salary, even if you do not get what you want. Kenya McCullum writes that 59% of workers do not negotiate for a better salary. Of these 52% are men and 68% are women.[6]

Unless you have a private income or somebody else finances your lifestyle, the salary from your job will pay for your home, food, and everything else. As such, it's vital to ensure that your job salary meets the minimum expectations for your job role and title, caters to your basic needs, and can sustain your lifestyle.[7]

- Other aspects of the job to consider are benefits and recognition such as bonuses or salary increases. Benefits such as health care and retirement contributions are very important, even if you are young and just starting out. Medical costs can cripple you for the rest of your life if something unfortunate happens to you.

Personal Branding

Creating yourself as a personal brand is important in today's highly competitive job market. Personal branding is a way for you to build your reputation and to become known for specific knowledge, skills and personality attributes. Highlighting what is unique about you, like any other brand, is called your unique selling proposition (USP). However, you cannot portray yourself as something you are not. Like any brand, reputation, trust and integrity are crucial to brand success. This is also the case for personal branding. Oprah Winfrey is an example of a successful personal brand.[8]

A personal brand has other benefits. You must first be reflexive, determine who you are as a human being and how you wish to portray your attributes. In that sense, it is a guide for your behavior: the things you value, the special knowledge you bring to the table, your ability to communicate and work with others, and many more. It also is aspirational because it will force you to continue developing your soft and hard skills and will help you to always strive for the better you. Your personal brand will not survive if it is not honest. You need to be who you are and live the life that determines your brand.

There is a difference between personal branding and a personal brand.[9] A personal brand "is a widely-recognized and largely-uniform perception or impression of an individual based on their experience, expertise, competencies, actions and/or achievements within a community, industry, or the marketplace at large." Personal branding, on the other hand, is described as

> the conscious and intentional effort to create and influence public perception of an individual by positioning them as an authority in their industry, elevating their credibility and differentiating themselves from the competition, to ultimately advance their career, increase their circle of influence, and have a larger impact.

As mentioned, an online presence has become crucial to building an online brand. However, there is a downside to social media. While you are a teenager and now a student, you might feel freer to post personal information online, showing how you are having fun with your friends or exhibit the kind of behavior future employers might frown upon. You can be sure that you will be Googled, searched and your social media scrutinized by any future employer. But before you delete your social media presence, be aware that a lack of a social media presence is also detrimental. Fortunately, there are ways in which you can clean up your social media. The online space is full of suggestions on what to remove and how to curate your social media accounts.[10] Before you apply for your first job, make sure that there is nothing online that you will be ashamed of and also make sure that your social media support your brand.

Adulting After College

Adulting is hard. After you graduate, you must successfully navigate your career, pay your bills, put money into savings and somehow have a work–life balance. It can get a bit intense—especially for new graduates. Life is expensive, new jobs are hard and figuring it all out isn't easy. Be gentle with yourself along the way—it will take a little bit to get used to all your new roles and responsibilities.

Mentors

One of the most important things to learn in college is to never stop learning. When you get out into the world, it's no different. You must go out there with your degree in hand with an open mind and a willingness to learn. Fortunately, there will be people to help you along the way—mentors.

A mentor is someone who will take you under their wing and who will share information about their own career path, as well as provide guidance, motivation, emotional support and role modeling. A mentor may help with exploring careers, setting goals, developing contacts and identifying resources. Sometimes finding a mentor is as easy as connecting with someone who is older and wiser than you. Other times, it can be a bit more difficult. The person you really want to mentor you may be unavailable, unattainable or just too busy.

Mentors can be formal or informal; they can be in your life for six days or six decades. No matters the style of relationship or length of time you have with them, there are certain things you should consider when choosing a mentor.

1   *Look for someone you want to be like when you grow up*. This may sound a bit silly, but it's an adage that's true. Much like Peter Pan, people never really grow up. It doesn't matter what age you are, there's always something new to discover about life. Along the way you'll meet people who are 10, 20 or 30 years older than you that have qualities and successes you admire. Figure out how to connect with those people and utilize their knowledge, skills and work to be like them.

2   *Connect with people you know*. There are mentors all around you. Start by getting to know people who are more experienced than you. Ask them questions about their life and career—people *love* to talk about themselves. If there's someone you know who you admire and enjoy, then ask them to be a mentor. The person you ask may not even realize that you admire their work and career and take it as a major compliment that you would like their guidance.

3   *Sometimes the mentor chooses you*. You may not realize it, but people see themselves in you. Mentors can often see your potential and want to help you along the way, because (more than likely) someone did the same thing for them. If you're lucky, they'll take you under their wing and before you know it, you'll have a mentor.

4   *Let the relationship evolve naturally*. You must remember, mentorships are relationships. And just like any relationship, you must let it evolve naturally. These are people who will check in on you and guide you through your career. But, don't assume that your mentors will go to the wall for you when they first agree to work with you. Give it time and invest in them as much as they invest in you.

5   *It's okay to have more than one mentor*. Different stages of your life and your career will demand the need for different types of guidance and mentorship. You aren't betraying one mentor by finding another. Find the people along the way that can offer you the tools you need to succeed.

6   *You can find a mentor anywhere*. Get out there and network, you never know who you might meet. Industry meetups, volunteer events, coffee meetings and random encounters can all produce mentorships.

Before you know it, you'll build connections with people, establish a career and eventually become an expert in your field. Then, it's your turn to pass your knowledge along and become a mentor for someone else. It's the circle of life.

Work–Life Balance

The importance of work–life balance was already touched on as something to consider when you are looking for a job. But there is more to it. When you first get out there, you're probably going to want to prove yourself. You'll have no problem working the long hours and paying your dues and that's great, but you also need to put emphasis on your work–life balance. A work–life balance is knowing when to invest in your work, and when to invest in yourself. After all, why do all that work if you don't have a life to enjoy it?

What's important to realize is that your life is going to change through the years. Things like age, children, working conditions, new technology and how you manage all of these can influence how important you find work–life balance. There may be times when you want to put in the hours and pay your dues, but there will also be times when you want to draw the line in the sand and be clear on your expectations for your job.

Companies realize that happy employees are more productive employees, so good ones will encourage a healthy work–life balance. Many office buildings offer benefits like on-site gyms, extra time or time to work out or a discount on their insurance for adopting a healthy lifestyle. Doing this creates healthier, happier employees and has been found to reduce healthcare costs for organizations.

Since life doesn't stop when you walk through the doors at work, some companies offer on-site professional perks to make life a little easier. For example, the State Department offers employees an on-site gym, post-office, hair salon, dry cleaners, a full-service cafeteria, a Starbucks and a Dunkin Donuts. But a work–life balance goes beyond just tangible offerings. When you are on the job hunt, look for things like designated quiet spaces, community engagement opportunities, flexible hours, telecommuting, training and good health benefits. These can make a huge difference in how much you enjoy your job.

Burn out can be real, so it's important to find a company that is invested in creating a healthy environment for employees. Employing healthy boundaries and habits at work and at home can help you succeed. When you're at work, fight off stress by setting manageable goals for yourself, taking breaks, listening to music and communicating your needs effectively. If you need five minutes to breathe, go take them. If you're offered flex time, take it. There will be times that you feel burned out and overworked. When you get that way, consider leaving a little early. Or, better yet, take a vacation—you have those days for a reason. Stay active, learn how to say no and get help if you need it. You can't be productive for your job if you aren't a whole, happy person. Any company that doesn't respect that, doesn't deserve your time. You're investing in them, be sure that they are investing in you.

Summary

In this chapter you found out the breadth and scope of strategic communication practice. You were introduced to the concept of roles, the different organizational types in which strategic communicators can find work and how that affects the roles you will perform. You were also introduced to what you can already do as a student to get ready for your future career through internships, networking and membership of professional organizations. You were provided with tips on finding the best career and job fit for you, the importance of negotiating compensation and the importance of having a career–life balance.

This chapter most likely made you realize that the career you enter at 22 is not going to decide who you are for the rest of your life. That's up to you. Find a team of mentors who will encourage you when you fail, help you figure out the tricky parts and cheer you along when you succeed. Become a mentor yourself.

Discussion Questions

1   Several professional roles were identified in the chapter. Identify five and reflect on why you would like or not like to perform that role in strategic communication practice.

2   Review the list of soft skills and evaluate yourself on each on a scale of 1–10 where one represents Poor and 10 represents Outstanding. Then focus on the five soft skills you feel you are most deficient in and work on strategies to improve those skills.

3   Make a list of professionals, professors, alumni, family members, friends and others you know who might become part of your network.
4   Design a strategy to use these people to help you network for a future position.
5   Write a short essay on what you would like your personal brand to be.

Check out the online support material, including chapter summaries, useful links and further reading, at www.routledge.com/9780367426316.

Notes

1   *International Journal of Strategic Communication*, 5(2), 2011.
2   https://www.topresume.com/career-advice/importance-of-networking-for-career-success, last accessed on July 30, 2019.
3   https://www.hws.edu/academics/career/pdfs/networking_guide.pdf, last accessed on July 31, 2020.
4   https://www.theladders.com/career-advice/better-than-money-the-top-10-things-we-look-for-in-a-new-job; https://www.forbes.com/sites/ashleystahl/2018/09/27/5-steps-to-finding-the-right-career-for-you/#2948d25f5abb, last accessed on July 31, 2020.
5   https://www.forbes.com/sites/ashleystahl/2018/09/27/5-steps-to-finding-the-right-career-for-you/#2948d25f5abb, last accessed on July 31, 2020.
6   https://www.learnhowtobecome.org/career-resource-center/negotiate-job-offer/, last accessed on July 31, 2020.
7   http://mentalfloss.com/article/71617/8-things-consider-when-looking-new-job, last accessed on July 31, 2020.
8   https://www.forbes.com/sites/goldiechan/2018/11/08/10-golden-rules-personal-branding/#f0f152158a7b, last accessed July 31, 2020.
9   https://personalbrand.com/definition/, last accessed July 31, 2020.
10 https://www.mcafee.com/blogs/consumer/family-safety/10-easy-ways-to-clean-up-curate-your-social-media/, last accessed on July 31, 2020.

Chapter 3

The Concept of Strategy

Learning Outcomes

By the end of this chapter, you should be able to do the following:

- Understand the concept of strategy and why it is important to managing communication.
- Identify the different concepts and steps in the strategic planning process.
- Understand the importance of participative communication practices from leadership levels to structuring a strategic planning session and implementing your strategy.

Chapter Opening Vignette

Strategy in Action

A big financial services organization in South Africa was challenged to change its management strategies after a merger of four banks and their affiliated organizations. This occurred while the transition to a democratic political system in that country was in full swing. This new organization was spread out geographically across the nine provinces of the country. The implementation process fell to the executive consultant responsible for internal communication, who decided that a truly participative strategic planning process was the only way to involve all employees, understand their concerns and give them an opportunity to provide solutions. The communication executive understood that there are different interpretations of the concept of strategy and knew that she had to create shared meaning of strategic planning such as goals, objectives, stakeholders and tactics. Furthermore, the internal communication strategy had to support the organization's vision, mission and value statement. Finally, the plan had to be one that provided for stakeholder input and could be realistically implemented.

The executive designed a communication strategy that involved every level of the organization. First, she presented her strategy to the executive committee of the organization, then to each divisional and regional executive leadership team to get buy-in and acceptance of the strategy. These sessions were interactive and allowed free discussion of the strategy and its possible impact on the different units because it directly impacted every business unit in the organization. The next step was to create a communication infrastructure throughout the organization. With the buy-in of leadership and management at every level of the whole organization, a network of communication champions was established. These were not full-time communication practitioners, but employees who were elected by their colleagues to serve in that role. It was yet another part of the strategy to create trust and not force down the communication strategy from the top.

The role of the champions was not to issue newsletters or press releases, but to create monthly forums where employees could openly discuss their concerns about the changes in the country and organization, invite suggestions for dealing with issues and improving the communication climate. Because the champions could be on the agenda of all management meetings and present the concerns of employees, as well as understand the concerns and practicalities of day-to-day management practices, the champions facilitated communication between all employees. This was the aim of the strategy.

Within one year the organization had more than 800 communication champions who were involved in the communication process and after three years the communication climate in the organization improved by about 20%.[1]

Understanding the Concept of Strategy

Everybody has a strategy or strategies for aspects of their lives. If you are in college, for instance, taking the course, for which you are reading this book, is likely part of a long-term strategy for your future career. Part of that strategy might be to go to graduate school or obtain a professional certification in your chosen field. Or you might decide that a better strategy will be to immediately find a job after graduation as part of a plan to see what is out there and what might excite you before furthering your education. This is a rather basic example of the use of strategy, but it nonetheless explains the use of **strategy** as a thoughtful, logical and deliberate process.

The Evolving Meaning of *Strategy*

The term *strategy* has its origin in Greek and means, literally, *generalship*. In its modern context, its meaning was largely shaped by the Prussian general and military theorist, Carl von Clausewitz. Living at the time of the Napoleonic wars, he was an influential scholar on strategic warfare. As a result, strategy has always been associated with war, conflict and conquering.

However, two German scholars, Howard Notthaft and Hagen Schölzel, recently made a study of von Clausewitz's original work in German[2] and concluded that there is a great deal still to be learned from the use of strategy in warfare that can be applied to strategic communication in the 21st century. They equated the principles of guerrilla warfare to modern-day guerrilla communication strategies made possible by technological developments, social media and online communication platforms. The aim of **guerrilla communication** is not to win but to introduce irregular ways to communicate to change the rules and norms of communication.

Case Study

What Are Guerrilla Communication Strategies and How Did Donald Trump Use Them to Break the Rules?

President Donald Trump's use of Twitter, both before and after the 2016 election, is an excellent example of strategic rule-breaking with the purpose of creating new rules. Rather than using the traditional way in which U.S. presidents have communicated, President Trump used very informal communication through the Twitter online platform. Traditionally, presidents' communication is quite formal. They would use formal news conferences, official statements and news releases, and other forms of highly controlled media and messages to communicate in a typical two-step approach to communication. In the two-step approach, the different media outlets and journalists are used to either set up communication events or to relay the president's messages. President Trump is known for not using such an approach. When he did media interviews, they were seldom structured. He would take journalists' questions while getting on board Air Force 1 or his helicopter. He is well known for going "off script" while delivering formal speeches and he is famous for his use of Twitter. In this way, he directly communicated with nearly 82 million followers without any interference from journalists or others who interpret his words. He issued close to 53,000 tweets relaying his thoughts directly. If the purpose of guerilla communication is to change the rules and norms of how presidents communicate, President Trump was highly successful.[3]

In business the term "*strategy*" started being used in the 1950s and described how organizations compete in the marketplace, obtain market share and realize competitive advantage. The business community adopted the term to mean winning, prevailing or surviving in the marketplace. Management and leadership styles are shaped by cultural and historical context. It is thus not surprising that businesses adopted the concept of strategy following World War II. Many soldiers who had leadership training during the war returned and entered business and commerce, bringing their war experience with strategy with them. This understanding contributed to the inside-out approach to strategic planning and strategic communication—CEs use strategy to create and control their environment much like armies during warfare. Likewise, leadership controls strategy without consideration of stakeholders.

A Changing Workforce

As society has changed in the 21st century, largely due to the shifts in communication technology, stakeholders have come to expect their opinions to be heard and considered. As explained in Chapter 1, stakeholders now realize that they have considerable power over and within communicative entities (CEs). When the strategic plan of the organization is determined by management alone, and then pushed out to employees and other stakeholders, this is an inside-out approach, which is a rather old-fashioned and ineffective way of approaching management and communication. In this approach, employees do not have a say in formulating the vision and mission of the organization and as a result do not buy into the strategy, because they never had an opportunity to even think about it. Without employee and other stakeholder buy-in, the organization risks unsuccessful implementation of the strategic plan, a negative reputation and potential failure.

A CE's strategies are often the result of power struggles among the individuals in charge. While some executives might argue that their organization's strategies are objective and neutral, the strategies are often created to benefit executives and managers at the top. Ideally, strategy should be participatory and include all stakeholders, including employees at all levels, investors, and even customers. An organization's strategy shouldn't only reflect the top executive's personality and desire, but rather be an expression of the entire organization's character, purpose and culture.

There are other problems with the inside-out approach, including how power can be used in organizations. Because strategy is often reflective of those in power, it is important for boards and executive teams to be as diverse as the organization's stakeholders. If not, different stakeholders' viewpoints will not be considered, and organizations will miss out on innovative ideas, talent and varying perspectives that input from diverse groups can bring.

Academic Angle

Few Women in Corporate Leadership

It is no secret that men, mostly white, dominate executive suites all over the world. Research shows that women and people of color are severely under-represented in corporations, government and other organizations around the world.

- A 2019 analysis in the United States showed that[4] in the S&P 500 there are fewer women in leadership positions than there are men named John.
- Women currently hold 5% of CEO positions at S&P 500 companies.
- The changes in leadership numbers for women drop dramatically as positions become more senior, which indicates that men are much more likely to be promoted than women. While there are 36.9% first or mid-level officials and managers in these companies, the number drops to 26.5% at executive and senior level, to 21% of board members, and 11% of top earners.
- Of the 40% off management positions in the United States, white women held 32.6% of all management positions, Latinas 6.2%, Black women 3.8% and Asian women 2.4%.

These data hold up across the globe and, in many instances, are much worse. A similar study in the United Kingdom determined that only 25% of the board members of all companies listed on the FTSE-350 stock index were women, which is one of the reasons that men are paid more than women. In Canada, men hold 90% of the highest executive roles. In 2019 only 17.6% of executives and 6.9% of CEOs were women. According to the European Union, women's labor force participation rate decreased globally from 52.4% to 49.6% between 1995 and 2015. Over 60% of the world's employed women work in the service sector. Women face a gender wage gap globally, earning 77% of what men earn. Women held only 12% of the world's board seats in 2015.[5]

The low number of women in executive positions not only hurts women, but it can be a detriment to the organization. Strategic communicators should be advocates for diversity and the advancement of women throughout their organizations, as it will not only benefit their company, but society in general.

Emergent Strategy

Most strategies in an organization's strategic plan are intended strategies—they are described in detail with intention on being carried out in the future with little fear of being disrupted by the outside environment. However, sometimes—and it seems that now more often than ever—situations change suddenly and drastically requiring the need for emergent strategy. An emergent strategy is an unplanned strategy that arises in response to unexpected opportunities and challenges. Emergent strategy places strategic communication professionals at the center of the strategic process, whether it involves strategic planning, strategy implementation or making sure new ideas are adopted in the communication plan.

In Chapter 1, you were introduced to the concept of constitutive communication. Emergent strategy is the result of constitutive communication. Unlike the traditional, functional strategic planning process that is more linear, constitutive communication is messy, risky and chaotic, but also provides the best opportunity for participation. Strategic planning processes that are constitutive are more realistic and truer to the people involved because they had an opportunity to shape the strategy. The notion of strategy as control is largely abandoned in the emergent approach.

Emergent strategy becomes a tool for all stakeholders to bond and sets a path for the institution or entity to move forward together. Essentially, emergent strategy is an alternative way of looking at strategic planning namely, formulating strategy based on the daily practices and experiences of all employees.

Of course, for employee experiences to be considered, they need to participate in the strategic planning process. But strategy is not only associated with planning and participation in the communication process; it also is associated with the practices and tactics used to implement the strategy. A strategy is useless if it cannot be implemented. Also, it is important to determine if your strategy was successful. In strategic terms, objectives and tactics must be measurable, which means there needs to be a way to determine the extent to which they succeeded. In Chapter 7, you will be provided with the tools to create measurable goals and will ultimately be able to design a strategy matrix that is a very helpful tool for practice.

For practical purposes, the intentional and emergent approaches to strategy are best combined. Once the strategy has been formulated through participative communication and continues to be shaped by continuous and inclusive communication, the actual strategic plan can take on an intentional approach for the purposes of implementation and assessment as the strategy matrix will show.

Finally, it is important to know that all phases of strategy, from planning to implementation and evaluation, are always embedded in a specific context. It is important to understand the business of the business, which means one cannot strategize or implement strategy without a comprehensive understanding of the business, organization or entity you are representing. Each context is different and the skill of formulating a good communication strategy lies in the understanding the agent has of the entity and the environment in which the entity operates. If you are representing a performer, you need to understand the context of the industry and its audiences, be it movies or music. If you represent a sport star, you surely need to understand the sport, how it is managed and who the fans are. Similarly, you must understand the industry in which the manufacturer or corporation operates, be it energy, food or cosmetics, to mention but a few. When starting a new job, give yourself at least six months to learn the basic business of your business before you start with your communication strategy. Daily practice will of course help a lot, but nonetheless, make it your goal to become an expert on the topic at hand. This is equally important if you work in a large organization, government or a small non-profit.

Ultimately, the term strategy is one of the communalities of practice that contributed to the creation of the discipline of strategic communication. Chapter 1 mentioned a long list of domains of practice. Strategy and communication are the two words they all share.

Professional Profile

Mary Cano Longoria—Global Agency Account Director

Mary Cano Longoria—Account Director at a global advertising agency.

Mary Cano Longoria graduated from Southern Methodist University with a bachelor's degree in communications. She has spent most of her career working at a full-service advertising agency supporting National and Regional accounts with experience in both Hispanic and General Market advertising. Most of her experience has been in marketing for the automotive industry.

> **What did you want to do with your career?** I wanted to work at a big adverting agency in New York and travel the world.
>
> **Are you doing it?** Yes and no, I do work for a big advertising agency in New York, but I work out of the Dallas office. While I have not traveled the world, I have traveled to 23 different U.S. states.

What are you doing now? I am an Account Director at TBWA working on the Nissan account.

How did you get there? I am here because of all of the relationships I built throughout my career. Every new job started with a referral from someone I worked with or met years prior. I now have come full circle. I started my career working at a Hispanic ad agency on the Nissan National account. I then moved to a few different agencies early in my career and worked on other business such as Levi's, Budweiser, Sherwin Williams and Toyota but now I have spent the last ten years back on the Nissan business.

How have your dreams changed? My dreams changed quite a bit, from wanting to be part of the hustle and bustle of New York City agency life and being 100% consumed by career growth and the next big account. I am now focused on my life in Dallas with my family and while I still have passion for advertising and growing my career, I have learned to better balance work and family time. I still love working in the ad world but I also love being a mom and wife. It *is* possible to do both!

What has surprised you most about yourself or your career? I was most surprised at how much I still had to learn once out of college. I was very fortunate to have great mentors early in my career that helped me navigate the ad world and helped me meet my career growth. I was also so surprised at how much fun I have had throughout my career; I truly love what I do.

What advice would you give to someone in college now? My advice to someone in college now is to network, network, network. The people you meet now and build relationships with will certainly help you once you are ready to start your career, relationships are everything. Also, set goals and visualize yourself achieving them but do not lose sight of them as you will certainly meet obstacles along the way of achieving that goal. Also, do not be afraid to fail, there are many lessons to be learned through failure.

What do you wish young professionals working at your agency knew? I would like them to know that their career path will change and evolve, and so will their personal goals and they should embrace the change. If they are lucky, they will come across a great mentor who they can learn from, so it is important not only to listen but to also ask questions. Enjoy the craziness of your early career because one day you will move on, but you will take away many valuable lessons. Enjoy every day and be open to change.

More information about Mary Cano Longoria can be found here:https://www.linkedin.com/in/mary-longoria-618a525/.

Steps in the Strategic Planning Process

This part of the chapter will deal with the different steps in strategic planning. One step builds on the other and there is a rationale for doing strategic planning in this way. Figure 3.1 explains the different stages.

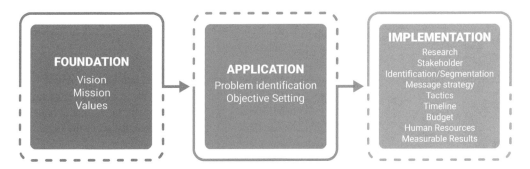

Figure 3.1 The Stages of Strategic Planning and Execution

The Foundation

As you can see from Figure 3.1, there are three components of the foundational stage. This is called foundational because it creates a stable, strong base for the strategic plan. Each component is quite permanent and not subject to regular change. If the content of any of these components is altered, it means major changes for the organization. They are foundational because the rest of the strategy is firmly built on these components and should reflect the basic assumptions inherent in them. No manner or amount of planning can be done for an organization without vision, mission and values statements.

The Vision Statement

A **vision statement** is aspirational and future oriented. It is an expression of where the CE is going rather than a description of its current situation. It is aspirational in the sense of claiming its place in the world and reflects what the entity's approach is to its environment, its employees and products. It is a statement of the reason for its existence.

Typically, vision statements are brief and to the point. They are not taglines or logos. Here are a few examples of great vision statements:

- Habitat for Humanity: "A world where everyone has a decent place to live."[6]
- Alzheimer's Association: "A world without Alzheimer's disease."[7]
- Patagonia combines its vision and mission statement: "Build the best product, cause no unnecessary harm, use business to inspire, and implement solutions to the environmental crisis."[8]
- Teach for America: "One day, all children in this nation will have the opportunity to attain an excellent education."[9]
- Amazon: "Our vision is to be earth's most customer-centric company; to build a place where people can come to find and discover anything they might want to buy online."[10]
- Apple: "We believe that we are on the face of the earth to make great products and that's not changing."[11]

PepsiCo has quite a long vision statement:

Our vision is put into action through programs and a focus on environmental stewardship, activities to benefit society, and a commitment to build shareholder value by making PepsiCo a truly sustainable company. At PepsiCo, we're committed to achieving business and financial success while leaving a positive imprint on society – delivering what we call Performance with Purpose.[12]

Typically, a vision statement does not change often. Steve Jobs, late CEO of Apple Inc., said in a 2010 interview that he cannot imagine the vision statement would change much in the next ten years and that is indeed true for the vision statement the company is using now.[13] From these examples you can see that these statements describe what the organizations want to be, who they are and what their belief system is.

The Mission Statement

While a vision statement answers "the what and why" of an institution or individual, the **mission statement** articulates how the vision will be accomplished. Mission statements are typically focused on the stakeholders, how stakeholders will be served and what the purpose of the organization is. For example, what products or services does the organization provide and what is its pricing structure? Let us compare the vision statements of the companies we discussed, with their mission statements:

Habitat for Humanity: "Seeking to put God's love into action, Habitat for Humanity brings people together to build homes, communities and hope."

Alzheimer's Association: "To eliminate Alzheimer's disease through the advancement of research; to provide and enhance care for all affected; and to reduce the risk of dementia through the promotion of brain health."

Teach For America: "Teach For America finds, develops, and supports a diverse network of leaders, working together to end educational inequity. Our alumni, corps members, and staff work in schools and in every sector and field that helps shape educational opportunity in America."[14]

Amazon: "Our mission is to be Earth's most customer-centric company. This is what unites Amazonians across teams and geographies as we are all striving to delight our customers and make their lives easier, one innovative product, service, and idea at a time."

Apple: "Apple designs Macs, the best personal computers in the world, along with OS X, iLife, iWork, and professional software. Apple leads the digital music revolution with its iPods and iTunes online store. Apple has reinvented the mobile phone with its revolutionary iPhone and App Store and is defining the future of mobile media and computing devices with iPad."

PepsiCo: "to provide consumers around the world with delicious, affordable, convenient and complementary foods and beverages from wholesome breakfasts to healthy and fun daytime snacks and beverages to evening treats."[15]

Mission statements are often criticized for being too vague and generic, e.g., "To provide the best service possible in the insurance industry." One can question what *best service* and *possible* mean—they are equally vague. Is the only possibility mediocre service? What sector of the insurance industry does it serve? Who are the stakeholders and what is the pricing philosophy? These are but a few questions that a vague mission statement raises.

A good mission statement clearly articulates the goal of the institution, provides guidance to employees on expectations of their work, and serves as a daily motivational tool.

So, remember, while both vision and mission statements are aspirational the vision state-ment says what the entity wishes to become and how it will contribute to the greater good. A mission statement is more practical in telling stakeholders how it intends to get to the place the vision articulated.

Values Statement

Another important part of a strategy is to mention the **value system** that supports the organization. The nature of the organization will also determine the value statement. For example, an energy company might specifically name a commitment to clean power and the environment as one of its value systems, in addition to a commitment to safeguard the community in which it operates. Other values might be entrepreneurial thinking, equality, social justice, integrity, innovation, and so forth.

Typically, a value statement would emphasize no more than five or six core values. Values are not meant to be measurable but are expectations for the belief systems and behavior of employees when they think of their organization.

For instance, PepsiCo's value system is described thus: PepsiCo's core values include "sustained growth, empowering people, trust, and responsibility." PepsiCo is a company that aspires to be the best both socially and economically, and therefore, these values show exactly what the company wants to be. They guide the entire organization and create a culture that drives the company towards its vision.[16]

The Application Stage

Once the vision, mission and value statements have been formulated the next strategy steps become much more practical and applied to the CE. At this stage of the process the CE is being analyzed to determine where and how it already supports the vision, mission and values. It also aims to determine what the obstacles are in reaching the goals set out in the mission. The objectives determine the actual steps the organization will take to fulfill its vision and mission and live its value system. In the case of your role as the strategic com-municator, you need to be part of the application stage, looking for communication solutions to the problems the entity faces. Typically, the strategic communication plan supports the overall strategic plan for the entity and enhances its implementation through specific actions.

The Problem Statement

The first step in the application stage is to identify the problems the entity faces to live its vision and reach the goals set out in its mission. To identify these problems organizations typically do a SWOT analysis. SWOT is an acronym for strengths, weaknesses, opportu-nities and threats. This analysis is explained in more detail and in a more applied way in Chapter 7. The purpose here is to introduce you to the concept that there needs to be an analysis of the problems the CE faces in terms of the execution of its mission.

Doing a SWOT analysis can be demanding but also exhilarating if you invite broad participation in the process. To ensure inclusiveness and buy-in for your strategy, it is best to enlist participation from the start. These techniques will become important tools in your strategic communication toolbox.

A SWOT analysis provides a better understanding of the problem or problems you need to address strategically and offers a starting point to your strategic plan. This will allow you to understand the reasons for your problems and help you to find solutions. It also provides a handy framework for brainstorming the problems with your colleagues and other stakeholders you need to involve in the planning process.

Figure 3.2 shows how the SWOT analysis considers both the internal and external environment of your organization.

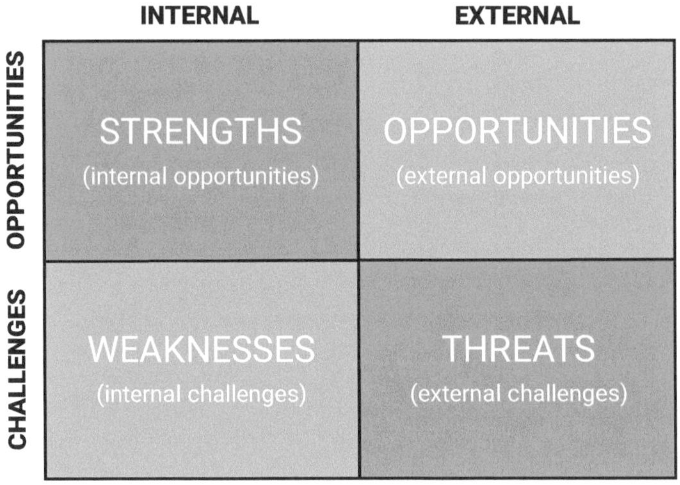

Figure 3.2 **SWOT Analysis**

In terms of strengths ask your participants to identify the positive attributes of the entity, i.e. those that can be built on and offer future opportunities. The weaknesses are those areas where the entity is not doing so well and should be improved if the mission is to be accomplished. In strengths and weaknesses, the focus is internal, i.e. on the entity itself. You also ask your participants to look at the opportunities the external environment offers and what threats there are in the external environment that can be obstacles (challenges) to overcome. At the same time the external environment might offer new opportunities that has not been considered before. In identifying opportunities and threats the focus is external to the entity. In Chapter 4 you will be provided with an easy way to analyze the entity's external environment to determine opportunities and threats.

From the information garnered in the SWOT analysis, problem statements can now be formulated. It is important to measure the problem statements you have formulated at the hand of the mission statement. Here you need to ask yourself if the problem statements enhance the mission, i.e. if this problem is solved, will it improve your ability to execute the mission?

Writing the Objectives for the Strategic Plan

Objectives are generally viewed as a top priority in organizations because they provide the direction in which the institution, department or individual will be moving, typically over a period of three to five years. Although the time period is stretched over several years, it is important to review the objectives on an annual basis to determine progress toward execution and possible adjustment. The societies we live in are fast- and ever-changing and a strategic plan needs to continually keep pace with changes. A single catastrophic event or crisis might seriously affect the ability to implement a strategic plan. Certain regions of the world are subject to weather events, such as tornados, hurricanes and flooding. In 2020, the world suffered from a pandemic of the novel COVID-19 virus. A single catastrophic event can derange the most well-laid plans and force a CE back to the drawing board in terms of its objectives.

Nonetheless, the goal is for the objective(s) to negate the problem. Say for instance one of the problems the SWOT analysis identifies is a lack of brand awareness of a product, then the objective statement can be stated as such: To create brand awareness of product XYZ among consumers who have never used the product. A problem statement can have several objective statements because it might be a multi-faceted problem. Having several objectives help to break down the problem into manageable chunks. Thus, another objective might be to reinforce brand awareness among existing consumers. Each of these objectives will require different implementation strategies.

Implementation Stage

In Chapter 7, you will become more familiar with each of the terms and steps in the implementation stage. In this chapter, you are merely introduced to the different facets of the implementation stage to help you understand throughout the text that there is a very rational and logical process attached to strategic communication. By the time you are getting ready to design a strategic plan for your client or organization, you will have all the tools you will need to do that. Each of the following steps is dealt with in this text.

Step 1. Research: You will learn how to conduct scientific research to understand your stakeholders, their attitudes and knowledge (Chapter 6).

Step 2. Stakeholder segmentation: Research will enable you to determine the *groups* of people you need to target with your communication strategy (Chapter 8).

Step 3. Message strategy: Research will guide you to understand what your stakeholders know, what they believe and how they act. This will allow you to design messages aimed at getting specific outcomes in your communication strategy (Chapter 11).

Step 4. Tactics: Tactics are the specific ways you wish to convey your messages. This would include the full range of communication techniques at your disposal, from media to other forms of communication (Chapters 9 and 10 among others).

Step 5. Timeline: In the timeline you break down when you wish to execute your specific tactics. The typical timeline for a communication strategy is three years with annual review and revision. It can be shorter, for instance one year in a political campaign that has a very specific deadline, such as an election or the promotion of new policy (Chapter 13).

Step 6. Budget: Although not all tactics cost money, buying media or producing media content can be extremely expensive. The budget for executing your strategy should be well-planned and included in your departmental or agency budget. Agencies are often expected to make big investments in campaign development before clients reimburse them (Chapter 13).

Step 7. Human resources: This helps you to determine if a strategy can be executed in-house, if employees have the necessary skills, if you need to develop skills in certain employees, or need to make use of agency services or freelancers (Chapter 13).

Step 8. Measurable results: You need to provide evidence that your campaign will deliver the results you intended. You can use the results of your benchmark research to determine the results you want or other indirect measures such as other research conducted in organizations (Chapter 13).

From this section you can now see how important your education is for being a successful strategic communicator and manager. Your education will provide you with a wide range of knowledge across academic disciplines.

The Role of Communication in Strategic Planning

Previously, we discussed the role of the communication practitioner as an agent who represents someone else. It is already important to understand at these beginning stages of your career that as an agent you are not merely a slave for the person you represent. You have the responsibility to stand up for the values and norms of society and your own. You will be the expert in strategic communication. Be careful that your skills are not used or abused to the detriment of society.

Never in the history of modern society have media and communication been as pervasive and central to the functioning of society, and in many cases in a very destructive way. Public communication is often driven by strategic communicators, as you will be. It is therefore important that you understand your role as agent in both formulating and executing strategy. You need to uphold the highest ethical standards in this role because you are the defender of communication in the public sphere, i.e. communication that will reach millions of people over your lifetime. Chapter 5 discusses ethics in more detail.

The above analysis of the importance of the foundational and application stages of the strategic planning process, including the communication strategy, emphasizes strategic communication as a management practice, but not the kind of management practice that exerts power over others. If you are a thoughtful, considerate practitioner you will consider the views, values, norms and aspirations of your stakeholders and you will be more successful as a result.

Leadership Styles and Communication

Management and leadership should not be confused. If you are a manager, you are in control of people or processes. Leadership refers to how you lead your team or others. Strategic communication is viewed as a management level function, as in strategic communication management. You cannot manage well if you do not know how to lead because leaders set the standards of behavior for the team. Thus, the concept of leadership is very important because leadership styles are directly related to how leaders communicate. In fact, some scholars believe the ability to communicate effectively is what makes it possible for organizations to thrive and survive.

Previous studies have shown that different kinds of leadership of the communication function itself have different outcomes and can determine which communication strategies the communication manager implements.[17] It is important that you take note of four kinds of leadership styles that have been studied in the context of strategic communication: transactional, transformational, inclusive and situational.

Transactional Leadership

As the name suggests, the transactional leader compensates people for following the rules. Also called an authoritative leader, this type of manager rewards employees for doing what she/he wants and punishes employees for poor results. At face value, you might well say all managers do this to some degree. The transactional leader, however, uses policies, procedures rules and authority to communicate with and direct employees, which is a very impersonal way to communicate and dampens relationship building in the workplace. This discourages employees to be entrepreneurial and use their initiative to make decisions because they fear being punished. Transactional leaders often are influential because they are feared. The problem with this leadership style is that it only works in highly routinized environments where employees know exactly what to do, such as manufacturing plants. In environments where employees must make individual decisions to execute their tasks, this kind of manager will not survive.

That is likely why a study conducted among communication practitioners in the United States showed no evidence that this leadership style exists in communication practice in the country. The very nature of communication work, in whichever environment it is practiced, is its unpredictability and the need for communicators to make daily decisions on their own.

Inclusive Leadership

Inclusive leaders emphasize collaboration, shared decision-making, relationship building and shared control. Some argue that the very nature of communication work encourages inclusive leadership. Creative work also is often done in groups through brainstorming sessions and collaboration. Inclusive leadership in these environments is a natural outflow of the type and nature of the work.

Some question the ability of inclusive leaders to make decisions and move organizations forward. In an age where everything is moving fast, first consulting with the group to gain consensus might not always be viable, which shows how important it is to have close relationships with your colleagues so that you know what their thoughts and needs are.

Transformational Leadership

Due to the tremendous amounts of change in modern societies and their resultant impact on the communication environment, transformational leaders are sought after because they can manage change. They are also called visionary leaders because they can set a vision for themselves or their institution. Transformational leaders are values-driven and appeal to employees,' collaborators' and other stakeholders' moral values and aspirations.

Other characteristics of transformational leaders are their ability to motivate others to perform for the greater good and not only seek their own self-interest. They have self-confidence and will stand up for what they believe is right. Their communication style is open, direct and informal, and focused on careful listening and consideration of the views of others. One of the reasons transformational leaders are sought after is because of their ability to communicate well, which in our current society is seen as required for change.

Transformational leaders are not pushovers, however. The aforementioned study found that these leaders have attributes of transactional leaders in that they believe in clearly set policies and procedures to ensure people know what is expected of them, without having an overwhelming number of rules. Policies and procedures usually are set collaboratively, so that it is not the leader who alone decides on what these should be. That enables them to ensure compliance without enforcement because people have participated in setting policy.

Situational Leadership

Many argue that good managers adopt aspects of different leadership styles dependent on the situation at hand. For instance, the need for policies and procedures is an attribute of both transactional and transformational leaders, while policy making is collaborative, which is an attribute of both transformational and inclusive leadership. Therefore, it is important for you to understand all the options managers and leaders have when making communication decisions in the workplace.

Attributes of both transformational and inclusive leadership are important to communication during the strategic planning process. At the same time, both leadership styles are important to the final communication strategy, which should emphasize the vision, mission and values of the entity but should also consider all stakeholders in the actual implementation stage of the communication strategy.

The Role of Stakeholder Communication in the Strategic Planning Process

The question might well be asked, why it is so important to include *all* stakeholder groups in the strategic planning process. Including external stakeholders can be very cumbersome and uncomfortable because they will bring ideas and make suggestions that might be very strange to the institution or the entity and might indeed be impractical to implement.

This process, however, is of the highest importance and the very foundation of the outside-in approach. If you wish to shape the entity to represent the highest values of the social and cultural environment and assure that the CE provides the needs for services and products its stakeholders require, guessing what those are will not get the job done.

There are different ways of including stakeholders in the strategic planning process. This can be done by inviting representatives from stakeholder groups to directly participate in the strategic planning process or by asking for input into the plan when the plan is in a draft stage. The first is the preferred option. Brainstorming sessions are important, and you will find that opinions are shaped through the very interaction process. People seldom leave these sessions with the same ideas they started out with because people's ideas and opinions change through the communication process.

The Importance of Diversity in Stakeholder Representation

One of the biggest challenges for communicators is to ensure external stakeholder diversity in terms of gender, ethnicity, income, socio-economic status, sex, political persuasion, geography, and so forth. Just as it is important to include internal stakeholders from all operational and functional levels, it is also important that the same approach to diversity for external stakeholders is followed.

The importance of diversity in internal stakeholders was again demonstrated in the case of Roseanne Barr, explained in the industry insight below. Channing Dungey was the executive most people viewed as crucial to the quick response and decision to Roseanne's tweet. Dungey, who became president of ABC Entertainment—the first Black and female executive to run a major network—was the person who made the announcement. Because she is Black, she understood the depth and extent of the insult Barr made.

Industry Insight

How Roseanne Barr Lost Her Television Show[18]

In 2018 the ABC show *Roseanne* was cancelled after the show's star, comedian Roseanne Barr, made racist remarks in a night-time tweet. She, among others, described a previous Obama aide, Valerie Jarrett, as an offspring of the "Muslim Brotherhood & Planet of the Apes." What was remarkable was that *Roseanne* was cancelled despite its popularity. The first season was a revival from an earlier show, and it ended "as the number one scripted primetime television show in the 18–49 age range," which is an important viewership demographic. It was renewed for a new season but was cancelled after Barr's tweets.

As mentioned, Channing Dungey, ABC president, announced the decision immediately and the show's consulting producer, Wanda Sykes, a famous African American comedian, confirmed it in a tweet. The fact that two such important leaders were in place to make these decisions most likely hastened Barr's departure while protecting the reputation of the ABC network. This demonstrates how important representation and diversity are at all levels of an organization.

When there is no diversity in organizations, decisions made in the strategic planning process and in the actual communication strategy will reflect the values of the dominant person or group of people in the entity, which in Western society still are largely white males. All people, not only white males, have a problem living other people's experiences of discrimination and hurtful practices, which is why it is important to bring as many voices as possible into the strategic planning process. The concepts of **implicit bias** and racial bias are now accepted concepts in discussions on dealing with people different from us. All people, even people of color, have stereotypes about different people. "It often operates at a subconscious level and can be seen in ways large and small, like where your mind goes when I say the word 'doctor' or 'convict.'"[19] The challenge is for all people to acknowledge these implicit biases and deal with them in a rational and unemotional way, thinking through where they originated.

The Importance of Stakeholder Relationships

A successful strategic communication program will determine the success of relationships with key stakeholders because a relationship emphasis replaces a short-term focus with a long-term strategy. Relationships with everyone are not possible, but it is important with stakeholders. Building relationships takes years but can be shattered in an instant.

Conflict is reduced when there is agreement on goals between CEs and key stakeholders, which is why it is so important to communicate with stakeholders and include them in the strategic planning process. Organizations make better decisions when they listen to and collaborate with stakeholders before decision-making, rather than trying to persuade stakeholders to accept goals after decisions were made. This is another attribute of the outside-in approach.

It also is important to remember that internal stakeholders are as important (if not more so) than external stakeholders. An unfriendly or aggressive security guard at the front desk can quickly shatter a relationship with a stakeholder that took years to build. If the security guard is not trained to understand how important relationships are, it can have serious repercussions for an organization. An organization's reputation or image consists of how the organization and its members behave toward stakeholders. Also, relationships are never static—they come and go and change as situations change. It is therefore important to keep in touch with the status of relationships with key stakeholders.

Case Study

Starbucks Employees and the Role of Implicit Bias

Two incidents involving Starbucks employees show how implicit bias manifests in practice and the devastating effects it can have for employees, consumers and organizations.

The first incident happened in April 2018 when two Black men, waiting in a Starbucks for someone to join them for a business meeting, asked if they could use the restroom. Their request was declined because they just sat there and did not buy anything. While they were waiting for the third party to join them (a white man) the police were called and they were handcuffed and arrested just as the third man arrived, corroborating their story. They were nonetheless led off to the police station, where it was determined that there was not enough evidence that they had committed a crime and were let go. Starbucks did not want to press charges, but the incident received national coverage, which was very harmful to the Starbucks brand. The employee was fired, and all Starbucks locations eventually closed for a whole day to ensure that all employees receive training on issues of race.[20]

In another incident in July of the same year, a Starbucks employee was fired for mocking a client who stuttered. The man's friend posted the incident on Facebook—again a major embarrassment for Starbucks. They offered the offended customer a $5 gift card, which even the organization had to admit was inadequate. The employee was subsequently fired but the incident was widely related in the media and the arrest of the two Black customers was highlighted again as an example that this was not the first incident of its kind in a Starbucks.

Who Should Be Considered for Participation?

Of course, it is important to think of the entity itself when deciding on stakeholders you wish to include. Each CE is different, and its stakeholders will therefore also be different. There is no need to mindlessly invite people who do not represent stakeholder groups, just to have a wide array of participants. With tight communication budgets, it is important the stakeholders are carefully selected. Here are some groups to be considered.

- *Geographics.* **Geographics** provide gross indications of where to find those involved or affected, but geographics do not provide information about other important differences. Nonetheless, it is often the starting point for planning a campaign. In organizations, geographics would refer to head office location, regional offices, plants, consumer outlets and so forth.

- *Demographics.* Some of the most common demographic variables are age, sex, ethnicity, education, income, marital status and religion. In organizations, additional demographics could be job level, years of tenure, years of work experience, day versus night shift or other information specific to the workplace. This is the most popular way of describing people, but, on its own, this technique offers little understanding of why or how people are involved or affected. **Demographics** are typically used with other segmentation categories to get a more comprehensive handle on the target audience.

- *Psychographics.* These are psychological and life-style characteristics of individuals. The most common is VALS™ (an acronym of SRI International's values and lifestyles psychographic research program). **Psychographics** are used to determine people's attitudes and habits that might help you to target your messages more effectively. Psychographics always are used in conjunction with other segmentation techniques, like geographics and demographics, to narrow down your target audiences.

- *Position.* Here positions held by individuals, and not the attributes of the individuals themselves, are considered. Typically, the type of work would determine position, such as journalists, doctors, computer analysts, human resources specialists, marketers, lobbyists, activists and politicians. People in specific positions, both inside and outside the organization, can be very influential for an organization. In organizations, positions often can be helpful determining obstructions to communication flow. Examples are senior executives, personal assistants to executives, managers and supervisors, computer specialists and content providers, to mention a few.

- *Role in the decision-making process.* In organizations, this is an important segmentation technique. Not only individuals are important decision-makers but also committees of some form or another. While the CEO might be an important decision-maker, the executive committee as a group might vote on your proposal. Cross-functional project teams or divisional or departmental management teams also might be important groups to target. These stakeholder groups are generally small but very influential, and your ability to continue with a campaign or project might well depend on their approval.

- *Covert power.* There are people who exert power over situations beyond their own direct sphere of influence. This type of power is hidden or covert. These people are hard to pinpoint but nonetheless remain influential. Some people might have covert power because of their trust relationships with leaders, sometimes outside the workplace. Covert power is not easily observed, but, in organizations, people often have an intuitive understanding of who these people are.

- *Reputation.* This helps identify people who are knowledgeable or influential based on others' perceptions of them. They also are called opinion leaders. They might not have institutional power, but their endorsement of a project will speed up its acceptance. In the workplace, we often refer to them as informal leaders.

- *Membership.* Sometimes membership or affiliation can be important determinants of influence. It can be membership in professional associations, clubs or trade unions.

- *Activists.* Activists are people who might never buy your product or service but have great potential to affect your organization's reputation. Think, for instance, of activists for the Prevention of Cruelty to Animals who might decide to boycott your cosmetics brand because it uses animals in experiments. There is hardly any industry that does not have activists who actively oppose certain organizational or political outcomes.

Summary

This chapter introduced you the to the meaning of strategy, how it evolved and how it is currently interpreted. You were introduced to the concept of emergent strategy, which is a strategic process that relies on the daily experiences of members of the CE and of its stakeholders to understand what issues a strategy needs to address. This also supports the outside-in approach you learned about in Chapter 1. The outside-in approach was mentioned often in this chapter, which shows its importance to the strategic planning process as well as the actual communication strategy that leads from the application stage. You also learned about the three stages of the strategic planning process, namely the foundational stage, the application stage and the implementation stage. Each of these stages has very specific attributes and steps you need to understand. Finally, the importance of communication to strategic planning was addressed. You were reminded of the importance of ritualistic rather than linear communication. You also learned about the importance of leadership communication, how different leadership types communicate and what the impact of those styles are on strategic planning. Finally, you were reminded of the concept of stakeholders and the 360-degree process of stakeholder participation in the strategic planning process. You were given tools to think about stakeholders, who they might be and how to judge their impact on the CE.

Discussion Questions

1   Review the section on vision statements and discuss the following:
   - Which of the vision statements presented in the chapter, do you like best and why?
   - Do you think length of the statement matters? Why or why not?
   - Think of a small local company and write a vision statement for it.
   - Find three vision statements online and critique them in terms of how aspirational they are.
2   Find three mission statements online and analyze if they provide direction and motivation and address stakeholders.
3   Analyze two mission statements to see if you can determine the value system that supports the vision and mission.
4   How would you define your own leadership style? Do you have examples you can share with others on how you lead when called on?
5   Think of a leader to whom you have reported or is reporting. How would you define this person's leadership style and how does it affect your performance?
6   Find five different industries that have activist groups opposing them. What do the activists stand for and how do their actions affect the different industries?

Check out the online support material, including chapter summaries, useful links and further reading, at www.routledge.com/9780367426316.

Notes

1   Holtzhausen, D. R. The effects of a divisionalised and decentralised organisational structure on a formal internal communication function in a South African organization. *Journal of Communication Management*, 6(4), 323–339.
2   Nothhaft, H., & Schölzel, H. (2015). (Re-)Reading Clausewitz: The strategy discourse and its implications for strategic communication. In D. R. Holtzhausen & A. Zerfass (Eds.), *The Routledge Handbook of Strategic Communication* (pp. 18–33). New York: Routledge.
3   https://www.socialbakers.com/statistics/twitter/profiles/detail/25073877-realdonaldtrump, last accessed June 10, 2020.
4   https://www.catalyst.org/research/women-in-management/, last accessed June 11, 2020.
5   Catalyst, Quick Take: Statistical Overview of Women in the Workplace (August 11, 2017). Last accessed on June 13, 2018 from http://www.catalyst.org/knowledge/statistical-overview-women-workforce.
6   https://www.habitat.org/about/mission-and-vision, last accessed June 11, 2020.
7   https://www.alz.org/getattachment/seva/About_Us/Annual_Reviews/1386_ALZ_2010_Annual_Report_Web.pdf, last accessed June 11, 2020.
8   https://www.oberlo.com/blog/inspiring-mission-vision-statement-examples, last accessed on June 11, 2020.
9   https://blog.hubspot.com/marketing/inspiring-company-mission-statements, last accessed June 11, 2020.
10   https://www.thebalanceeveryday.com/amazon-mission-statement-4068548, accessed June 11, 2020.
11   https://www.investopedia.com/ask/answers/042315/what-apples-current-mission-statement-and-how-does-it-differ-steve-jobs-original-ideals.asp, last accessed on June 11, 2020.
12   https://www.pepsico.com/about/mission-and-vision, last accessed June 18, 2020.
13   https://www.youtube.com/watch?v=5mKxekNhMqY, last accessed June 11, 2020.
14   https://www.teachforamerica.org/what-we-do/values, last accessed June 11, 2020.
15   https://mission-statement.com/pepsico/, last accessed June 11, 2020.
16   https://mission-statement.com/pepsico/, last accessed on June 11, 2020.
17   Werder, K., & Holtzhausen, D. (2009). An Analysis of the Influence of Public Relations Department Leadership Style on Public Relations Strategy Use and Effectiveness. *Journal of Public Relations Research*, 21(4), 404–427.
18   https://variety.com/video/roseanne-canceled-racist-tweets/, last accessed June 11, 2020.; https://www.usatoday.com/story/life/people/2019/03/12/roseanne-barr-blames-michelle-obama-getting-her-fired-roseanne-abc/3138703002/, last accessed June 11, 2020.
19   https://www.washingtonpost.com/opinions/2020/06/18/were-finally-talking-about-structural-racism-republicans-are-freaking-out/, last accessed on June 18, 2020.
20   https://www.nytimes.com/2018/04/15/us/starbucks-philadelphia-black-men-arrest.html, last accessed on June 18, 2020.

Chapter 4

The Three Management Levels of Strategic Communication

Learning Outcomes

After reading this chapter, you should be able to do the following:

▪ Articulate the role and functions of the macro (societal) environment that shapes strategic communication practice.

▪ Understand how to use the meso (organizational) environment to best manage a strategic communication function for your specific institution.

▪ Apply different approaches to set the stage for successful communication with stakeholders at the micro (communication) level.

Chapter Opening Vignette

The Political Environment and Strategic Communication

If an organization's environment is unsettled or unstable, communication practitioners must become even more strategic in their communication. This is particularly true if the political environment is the source of the instability. A 21st-century research study about the impact of a country's political environment on strategic communication practice showed how important this external factor is.

A 2011 issue of *International Journal of Strategic Communication* covering 48 countries found that the political environment influenced how strategic communication was practiced.[1]

In Western European countries the high levels of similarity among the population fostered high levels of agreement among issues raised in public. There is a greater tendency for organizations and the population to agree on issues, referred to in strategic communication as consensus. In countries that have higher levels of political instability and disagreement (called dissensus), such as Eastern Europe and South

Africa, practitioners must work harder at strategy. In South Africa, for instance, the political situation favors the population over organizations, which are often viewed very unfavorably. In those instances, the outside-in approach is even more important, and practitioners must truly understand the impact of the political system and the traits and belief systems of their stakeholders on their respective organizations. In the United States capitalism favors corporations and businesses big and small over worker rights; yet another example of how the environment affects communication entities (CEs).

The above example of the impact of the external environment also shows how the external environment (the macro level) impacts the organizational (meso) level. The external environment, in this instance, through its legal-political, socio-cultural and technology infrastructure, also affects how organizations are structured, what they can and can't do legally, what the roles are of strategic communicators and how important the function of strategic communication is.

Similarly, macro- and meso-level factors affect how CEs communicate at the micro level. Here the public sphere is yet another example of how a country's political system can affect strategic communication. You will remember that in Chapter 1 the public sphere is included in the definition of strategic communication. The public sphere is where the actual communication between a communicative entity and its stakeholders takes place. It refers to issues of freedom of speech and the extent to which governments regulate, control and censor media content. In most Western societies these are not issues of great concern, even if practitioners often think so. However, scholars believe in countries where the public sphere is tightly controlled, such as in China, or countries with autocratic regimes such as Poland, Turkey or Kazakhstan, strategic communication can only exist in its marketing context. There are many countries around the world where the government tightly controls, monitors or even owns the media, and exerts control over social media. In these places, if stakeholders cannot meaningfully participate in discussions pertaining to them, or force government change through advocacy, the democratic nature of strategic communication is lost, and it becomes mere government propaganda.

The Three Levels of Strategic Communication

In Chapter 1 you were briefly introduced to the three levels of analysis that enable successful strategic communication: macro (societal), meso (organizational) and micro (communication). In Chapter 4, you will learn how to use these levels in your practice and what are the important elements of each level. It is important to remember that the levels might change. For instance, if your strategic communication campaign was successful and you reached your goals, it would have changed the environment at both macro and micro levels. It might even have brought about changes at the meso level. Therefore, continuous assessment is very important in strategic communication practice.

The Impact of Macro-Level Sectors on Strategic Communication

The macro level refers to the external environment in which the communicative entity operates at a societal level and affects the communicative entity's ability to create shared meaning with stakeholders. Therefore, the macro level is called the external or societal environment, because it represents the overarching attributes and trends of specific societies. It is important for strategic communicators to understand the environment in which their stakeholders live and work, even if they are not part of that group. Fortunately, there are systematic methods and tools available for analyzing the environment in which people live and work.

Doing a macro-level analysis from the perspective of stakeholders rather than from the viewpoint of the communicative entity is another benefit of the outside-in approach. Traditionally, a macro-level analysis is focused on the communicative entity and is used to understand the competitiveness of the organization in the larger environment, to see where it needs to improve, where the challenges are, and so forth. This inside-out perspective allows the institution to be reflexive and improve its competitiveness and success. Therefore, the inside-out approach remains a very viable way of self-analysis. However, in the strategic communication context, the process is reversed so that the communicative entity first focuses on its stakeholders and then becomes reflexive and thoughtful by comparing its attitudes and practices with the expectations of stakeholders. Doing the analysis from a stakeholder perspective allows the entity to view itself as others do and demonstrates the importance the entity gives to its stakeholders.

Macro-Level Sectors

The external environment is always complex and includes the following sectors: social, cultural, legal, political, economic, technological, physical and media. The sectors interact with each other and are often overlapping. It is important to understand the interrelationship between the different sectors and how these relationships shape each sector. For instance, lifestyle (social sector) might be strongly affected by cultural norms (cultural sector). Wealthy people are expected to behave in certain ways in a specific community. Another example is how laws (legal sector) are usually strongly influenced by the political party in control (political sector). Although the sectors intersect and overlap, exploring each sector individually is a good place to start. The better you understand the external environment and can analyze it by sector, the more successful you will be as a strategic communication practitioner.

Social Sector

The *social sector* refers to societal and population trends. The social sector includes demographic and psychographic characteristics of people and groups of people within the population. *Demographics* are statistical data relating to populations and groups within populations, such as income, age, social class and education. Demographics are objective, but not necessarily static. They might change over time. The demographic analysis will also depend on the situation under investigation. Perhaps you were recently asked to participate in a survey that asked what your classification is, i.e. freshman, sophomore, junior or senior. It also might have asked in which college your degree program is located. These are very typical of demographic questions asked of college students, but they might be excluded from other surveys targeted at working adults.

Psychographics refer to lifestyle, opinions and attitudes and generally to the ways people prefer to live their lives. If you work for a tourism organization you might want to know if your stakeholders prefer luxury cruises and resorts, are outdoorsy people who prefer camping and hiking, or simply prefer to stay home. These are examples of psychographics. Returning to the example of the student survey, you might have been asked if you participate in the marching band, which student organizations you belong to, if you are in a sorority or fraternity, whether you play intramural sports, and so forth. These are all questions asked to determine your lifestyle preferences or your psychographic profile.

Demographics, psychographics and other variables for understanding stakeholders are discussed in more detail in Chapter 8.

Academic Angle

Geert Hofstede's Research on National Culture and the Workplace

In one of the earliest studies on the impact of a country's culture on business organizations, the Dutch researcher Geert Hofstede studied the impact of a society's culture on the values of its members and how these values related to their behavior. Hofstede gathered the data for his study by conducting a worldwide survey of employees of IBM, a large multi-national company.[2] In the original study, which took place in the late 1960s and early 1970s, Hofstede used statistical analysis to identify four distinct national cultural dimensions that influenced the way IBM employees behaved in specific cultures. The four dimensions included individualism–collectivism; uncertainty avoidance; power distance (strength of social hierarchy) and masculinity–femininity (task-orientation versus person-orientation). In later studies, he added long-term orientation and indulgence-restraint. Hofstede's work has been critiqued often, but generally his characteristics of national cultures hold true and have endured over time. Hofstede's research has been applied to many disciplines from management to psychology, especially in a cross-culture context.

To effectively use Hofstede's cultural dimension framework, it is important to understand the context of Hofstede's typology and how the indices of each dimension are measured. This chapter does not elaborate on his work. But if you are truly interested, you may read the text referenced at the end of the chapter to gain a deeper understanding. It is important to realize that cultural values, perspectives and orientations affect meso- and micro-level practices in strategic communication. Even an organization as strong and prominent as IBM in the 1970s was not able to determine one way of doing business across the globe and through Hofstede's work understood that it must adjust its management approach and practices to adapt to the local culture in which its offices operated around the world.

Cultural Sector

The cultural sector is often confused with the social sector and even sometimes combined, as in socio-cultural sector. Treating the cultural sector as separate from the social sector provides for a more thorough analysis of environmental factors shaping strategic communication that goes beyond demographics and psychographics. Cultural factors often are less obvious than social factors and pertain to belief systems, traditions, values and norms, historical interpretation and even traditions such as the foods people eat, rituals around hospitality and relaxation. Cultural-specific festivals and celebrations are very important elements of the cultural sector because they are often used in strategic communication when events are planned. For instance, Americans have a unique holiday called Thanksgiving that is very specific to its history. In China and many other Asian countries, Chinese New Year is a very special celebration where gifts are exchanged like during Christmas in Christian countries. Most countries have a holiday like the U.S. Independence Day, celebrating its independence or a new direction in its history, such as Bastille Day in France. South Africans celebrate Freedom Day and Nelson Mandela Day.

While national cultures can be quite homogenous, it is also important to understand the unique local and regional cultures that influence stakeholders. For example, Creole and Cajun are very important sub-cultures in southeast Texas and southwest Louisiana. This is reflected in regional foods, often referred to as Cajun or Creole cuisine, and festivals, such as Mardi Gras, which is celebrated in many cities in the region. Language is yet another example of the impact of culture. Last names with a French origin are pervasive in this region and it affects how they are pronounced. Sometimes these regional characteristics are humorous. When the New Orleans Saints allegedly lost a football game because of a poor call, a New Orleans billboard read, "The NFL bleaux it," a clear reference to the region's Creole heritage.[3] Each region within a country has forms of colloquial speech that is distinctive of that area or even town. Cultural analysis is one of the most enjoyable exercises a strategic communicator can conduct, particularly if it is done from a perspective of respect and appreciation for the differences that make up the population in a specific country or geographic region.

Legal Sector

The **legal sector** pertains to the constitution and laws of a country, states or provinces, and cities. CEs often face legal challenges that require them to communicate strategically about their role in a crisis. How laws are interpreted add an additional layer of complexity to the legal sector. Freedom of the press, for example, is not strongly protected in all countries, as it is in the United States and Western Europe and while the U.S. First Amendment protects our rights to a free speech, some restrictions apply to commercial speech, such as advertising. Most countries also have regulatory bodies that govern media, such as the U.S. Federal Communication Commission (FCC) that regulates the broadcast industry.

It also is important for strategic communicators to be aware of the kinds of laws that pertain to a communicative entity. For example, corporations must consider antitrust and tax laws, among many others. People in the entertainment industry can face copyright infringement challenges or challenges to free speech. In the United States, "fair use" is an important component of copyright law. You cannot merely copy a photo, music or article from the internet and use it at will. The chances are good that you will be sued. Understanding copyright law is very important to strategic communicators, as the case study below shows. Almost all organizations are governed by laws of the country, state and city in which they operate.

Case Study

Copyright and Fair Use

"In *Philpot v. Media Research Center*, Media Research Center used two of Philpot's photos without permission in two separate online articles: a photo of Kenny Chesney in an article about pro-life celebrities; and a photo of Kid Rock in an article about his rumored U.S. Senate campaign. On summary judgment, the district court held both uses to be fair use on the basis that (1) defendant's use was transformative because the purpose in using the photos—"to identify the celebrities as pro-life advocates or conservative Senate candidates"—was different from plaintiff's purpose in taking the photos; (2) the use was not commercial because, while defendant collected display advertising revenues from its articles, it "does not charge readers for access to its articles, nor did it sell the Chesney and Kid Rock photographs to other parties" (the court also gave weight to the defendant's status as a non-profit organization); and (3) the fourth fair use factor weighed in favor of fair use because "Defendant's use of the Chesney and Kid Rock Photographs cannot impair the marketability of plaintiff's works where, as here, plaintiff has not actually contemplated marketing those works" (because plaintiff had uploaded the photos to Wikimedia under a nonexclusive Creative Commons license)."[4]

Photo Credit: Larry Philpot of www.soundstagephotography.com
This work is licensed under the Creative Commons BY-SA 3.0 License:
https://creativecommons.org/licenses/by-sa/3.0/
Larry Philpot sued users of his work for minor attribution errors. Keep the attribution intact.

Political Sector

The **political sector** is often combined with the legal sector, as in legal-political sector. As is the case with the socio-cultural sector, separating these two sectors for purposes of analysis provides a much richer understanding of how and why laws are made and even to anticipate which laws might be made in the future. For instance, understanding cultural values and norms can provide a better understanding of how and why constituents vote a particular way and how political parties will act. The type of political system is part of this sector, for example whether a country has a constitutional democracy, a parliamentary system, an autocratic political system or even a dictatorship, as discussed in the opening vignette to this chapter. Political environments invariably impact issues of free speech, which are of course of primary importance to strategic communicators.

In democracies the political system is always in flux and it is important for strategic communicators to stay up-to-date on national and international developments. Understanding political developments and movements is important because they often are indicators of cultural and social shifts in societies. For instance, the #MeToo movement that started in the United States and has now spread globally, brought a political revolution to the United States Congress. While many view women's movements as cultural, this movement has now turned political, encouraging more women to become politically involved, vote and run for office.

Economic Sector

The **economic sector** points to the kind of economic structure a country has. In the United States, free market capitalism dictates many aspects in other sectors, even value systems and individual behavior. One of the outflows of this system is the debate in the U.S. on how best to deliver healthcare to citizens, with some believing individuals are responsible for their own care and that government has no role. The economic system in Western Europe often is referred to as market socialism, because these countries have free markets like the United States but believe government should provide universal healthcare and other social services to its people. In China, for instance, the government has moved toward a more market-based economy, but still centrally controls all industries and the political actions of its citizens.

Another aspect of the economic sector is the strength and stability of its financial institutions. However, financial institutions are no longer isolated from global trends and events. A financial crisis in one country might very well have a ripple effect on the economy of another. Thus, the economic and financial governance system of a country is of extreme importance. Countries, particularly those with free market systems, generally have a national agency that analyzes, interprets and addresses issues of economic importance. In the United States, the Federal Reserve serves this function and is the central bank of the United States. Its general purpose is to oversee the performance of the economy and protect the public interest.[5] In South Africa, this function is performed by the South African Reserve Bank and in the European Union by the European Central Bank (ECB). Strategic communication operates within an economic system that often shape the strategies of an organization. Therefore, understanding the economic sector of the CE is an important macro-level analysis.

Technology Sector

The **technology sector** refers not only to computers and the internet, as is one's first instinct to think, but also includes the adoption of technology in virtually every aspect of society, such as production processes, the skills consultants and professionals are required to bring to their work, the ability for advances in medicine and healthcare, and of course the ability to communicate. Social media have become pervasive and very influential in driving cultural, social and political movements. These are but a few examples of how the technology sector has infiltrated every aspect of societies' and individuals' lives. The adoption of technological advances is often based on the ability of a society to innovate and think differently about how to solve problems.

The advent of the **Big Data** movement was facilitated by the ability of different kinds of technology to gather unlimited amounts of information on people. Big data is made possible through the process of **datafication**, which refers to putting information into manageable databases. Data are collected through a wide array of embedded sensors that are linked through wired and wireless networks. These can be sensors in streetlights that track your car movements, internet transactions that monitor your spending, email, video, click streams or even a pill you swallow that tracks the health of your body. This idea is called **The Internet of Things** because all the sensors can communicate with each other and the data that are collected in this way are available digitally. The Internet of Things allows people and organizations to collect vast quantities of data that often are seemingly unrelated, using statistical algorithms. It is important to note that the main purpose of big data is strategic communication, particularly for stakeholder identification and segmentation, and then targeted communication. Businesses, political parties, government agencies and even criminal enterprises can and do buy the data for both benign and nefarious purposes. Big data can be used to simultaneously communicate persuasive messages, sell items to consumers and follow up to determine if behavior has changed or a purchase has been made. As the next case study shows, it depends on the intent of the entity whether the data are obtained legally and used for good or harmful purposes.

Industry Insight

Cambridge Analytica

The infamous end of Cambridge Analytica, a strategic communication firm in Britain, was a direct result of its abuse of illegally obtained data from Facebook before the 2016 Presidential Election. The researcher, Alesandr Kogan, worked at the University of Cambridge. He created a Facebook app in the form of a quiz, which many Facebook members took. Kogan found a loophole in Facebook that allowed Cambridge Analytica to also collect data from the Facebook friends of those members who took the quiz. The result was that the personal information of 87 million Facebook members was ultimately breached and collected for political purposes without the individual's or Facebook's consent. It was subsequently sold to the Trump presidential campaign. Steve Bannon, a senior advisor to President Trump until 2017, found funding to create Cambridge Analytica and became a vice president of the firm, which was merely a shell company for the British public relations firm, SCL Group, that had government clients worldwide. Because of the scandal that resulted from stealing the Facebook data and the negative publicity that ensued, Cambridge Analytica lost many major clients and was closed.[6]

Physical Sector

The **physical sector** of a country refers to its infrastructure. Infrastructure is deemed one of the indispensable engines of economic development in every country. The transport system includes roads, bridges, railway systems, airports and public transport and is indispensable to the movement of people and products. Other elements of infrastructure include electricity and energy grids, sanitation and water management systems, housing and even the ability of households to have access to high speed internet. One is often inclined to take infrastructure for granted until it collapses, such as during natural disasters. In the aftermath of Hurricane Harvey, many of the infrastructure elements of the city of Houston and nearby communities collapsed. The implications of infrastructure loss, up to the inability to deliver services at the local level such as garbage removal, water management and electrical systems, became evident during and after this disaster when it took weeks for communities to become accessible again.

Infrastructure is critical to the distribution of strategic communication. For example, in countries with limited internet access, strategic communication tactics, such as email blasts, may have to take the form of outdoor posters or handbills.

Media Sector

The **media sector** is not generally included in an environmental analysis, but rather viewed as a factor in other sectors, such as its role in shaping culture, society, technology, and so forth. However, the media sector has changed so dramatically and its influence on strategic communication practice is so profound that it now deserves its own sector analysis. One can now argue that media in all their various formats have become a central organizing principle in most societies, even in those where free speech is restricted. In other words, media are no longer only the transmitters of information but also of opinions, social and political actions, attitudes and belief systems, interpersonal relationships, and much more. Media use itself has become a cultural phenomenon, such as news headlines, rumors, memes or other tidbits that trend every day into millions of views on the internet through any or all the social media platforms.

Media use has become news itself, as when national leaders use Twitter to communicate their messages to the public or even to each other. Another way in which the media is shaping our environment is through a technique that is a strong component of strategic communication, namely, audience segmentation. Media platforms have proliferated so much it now necessitates media to target specific audiences and deliver specific messages to those audiences in order to be profitable and create unique audience profiles that will attract advertisers.

In the past, newspapers and television networks dominated news delivery. This meant that readers and viewers received a limited number of viewpoints on issues of local and national significance as deemed important by editors and news directors in those media. One of the major changes in the media in the 21st century is the proliferation of media outlets and news sources. This phenomenon is known as **media fragmentation.** Because of the enormous number of media sources now available via the internet, the mass media audience has splintered into much smaller groups or segments, which are typically like-minded and psychographically similar.

Media fragmentation has a very important effect on cultural and political movements, and now allows previously marginalized people to organize and join political movements.

For example, with social and other media platforms, women made gender a political issue, which has resulted in various resistance movements in societies worldwide. For instance, on January 1, 2019, 5 million women in the state of Kerala in southern India formed a women's wall of 385 miles (620 km) lining up shoulder to shoulder to make a statement about gender equality and a call to end violence against women. The women's movement in India gained momentum after the gang rape of a female student in 2012 made worldwide headlines and put India on the radar as one of the most dangerous countries for women to live. The event of January 1, 2019 would not have been made possible without new online media platforms.[7]

In a more negative context, in countries such as the United States, media fragmentation has deepened the ideological and cultural divides because people only use those media that reinforce their own belief systems, thus hardening attitudes and behaviors toward people who do not agree with their own opinions. On the other hand, the enormous variety of media platforms serves special interests for people who are interested in topics from food, to fashion, beauty, ancestry, sport, finding a dating partner, and many, many more.

Yet another aspect of the media sector is **media infrastructure**, which refers to the ability of the general population to have access to media and communication devices. This again shows how different sectors can overlap in a macro-level analysis. In most countries in the world the use of mobile phones has made access to information and online services available even to remote rural areas. Africa is a prime example of how the adoption of mobile technology in rural areas has made a tremendous difference in the quality of life of rural people. On that continent, solar energy powers cell towers and mobile phones, which means that mobiles can be used even if there is no electricity. This is an indication of how media sophistication, i.e. the ability to use media technology, has become pervasive across the globe.

The Role of Strategic Communicators in Macro-Level Analysis

As your expertise in strategic communication grows, the more adept you will become at macro-level analysis. The first step in conducting the analysis is understanding the business of your business. You cannot communicate strategically and effectively if you do not understand everything about the CE you serve, either as an employee or an agency. Working in a strategic communication agency might require you to understand the business of several, diverse clients and will require a quick and steep learning curve, which can be very exciting and a lot of fun.

One way of understanding your CE is to be involved in a macro-level analysis. In large organizations this is usually a team effort. Depending on the size of the organization, the Information Technology department will lead an analysis of the technological sector, the Finance department will lead on the economy, and so forth. Strategic communicators are typically the leaders on an analysis of the social, cultural, political and media sectors. That means you will need to stay up-to-date on these issues by following reputable news sources daily. Because you are working with media, your organization will expect you to follow the media on a broad spectrum of topics. This is a habit you can start developing immediately because you have your mobile device at your fingertips.

Macro-level factors typically vary from industry to industry. In some industries, such as entertainment and sports, cultural and social factors are dominant, although these also have major economic impact. In fact, these industries often drive social and cultural movements. Working in these sectors require strategic communicators to be leaders in macro-level analysis of the social and cultural sectors and understand how the CE adheres to social norms or shape cultural movements. This is particularly relevant to individual performers and sport stars.

In a smaller organization, such as a non-profit, you will wear many hats and will be challenged to be an expert on the impact of all the macro-level sectors on your CE. Each type of CE presents its own challenges when analyzing the macro environment. But the better you are at thinking broadly about your entity's environment the better you will be as a practitioner.

Professional Profile

Andres Giraldo—Managing Partner at The Skyline Agency.

Andres Giraldo graduated from Southern Methodist University with an Advertising Management degree with a specialization in creative writing. He went to work in the consumer package goods (CPG) sectors, as well as the field of finance, before starting his own advertising agency 11 years ago.

What did you want to do with your career? I actually wanted to be an international business lawyer.

Are you doing it? No, I'm not. Life took me in a different direction.

What are you doing now? I own and manage an international advertising agency that helps promote numerous CPG clients across the planet. We work with industry giants, as well as smaller startups, and even develop our own products and technology from time to time.

How did you get there? Working hard and never giving up. A big priority for was to form a small, but very strong team that I could depend on to create smart, high-quality work on a regular basis.

How have your dreams changed? Not at all. From the very beginning I've wanted to impact other people's lives in a positive way and to change the perception of advertising and consumer marketing in the world.

What has surprised you most about yourself or your career? My ability to evolve and adapt. It's what helped us grow and advance in these new societal norms, as well as any other challenges we've faced in the last decade.

What advice would you give to someone in college now? Soak in as much as you can from different mentors and teachers. Your foundation is so important, but in the future, being able to adapt is absolutely key to being successful.

More information about Andres Giraldo can be found here: http://linkedin.com/in/andres-g-0285b8166.

Organizational (Meso-) Level Factors

As is the case with the macro environment, meso level factors are not easily isolated and affect each other as much as macro-level factors affect the organization. The word *meso* means middle. The reason why the meso level pertains to the organization is because the organization is in the middle, between society and stakeholders. Without the organization (and you as the strategic communicator), there will be no macro-level analysis and also no micro-level communication. It is at the organizational level where processes, strategies and tactics are put into place.

In this section the way organizations are structured and the impact of those structures on strategic communication are discussed. You will also learn some more about how decisions are made and what roles practitioners perform.

The Impact of Organizational Structures on Strategic Communication Practice

Organizational structure does not refer to the structure of buildings, but to the way organization organize themselves. This doesn't mean that building architecture does not have an influence on organizational structure—ever wonder why the boss gets the great corner office? Think, for instance, of a campus where there are many buildings housing different departments and colleges that are dispersed over a large area. It might be that during your time as a student you do not even visit each of these buildings. Now imagine what the impact of such a dispersed network of buildings has for the university's communication climate. Professors, administrators and employees will find it hard to get to know each other and communicate about common issues. Online communication has broken down many of the physical structures that impeded communication. Can you imagine how campus functioned before email or even telephones?

Organizational structure also refers to the roles people perform, the rules employees must adhere to, the different departments that are tasked to fulfill different functions, the reporting lines and how people interact and communicate with each other. It is important to understand what a strategic communication function is, what roles strategic communicators fulfill, who they report to and how different ways of organizing affect performance expectations of strategic communicators.

It might be difficult to fully grasp how complex an organizational structure can be, if you have not worked in one. However, most young people have worked in the food service industry and would understand how restaurants function. Although it might not appear so, a restaurant owned and operated by a local family is much less complex than one that is part of a national fast-food chain. In the family-owned eatery, everybody knows who is in charge and employees do what the owner wants. The owner decides what is on the menu, what the operating hours are and how the restaurant looks. In this instance, the operation is not highly formalized or very complex.

An outlet of a fast-food chain on the other hand has a very rigid and strictly controlled menu. Its food should, after all, be available anywhere in the country or world. Its layout and design must strictly adhere to brand guidelines and is probably designed in a corporate headquarters. For example, it does not matter where in the world a McDonald's is located, when a customer walks in, the menu and design is immediately recognizable. The number of employees, the roles they have, and the skills required will all be determined by the corporate office. To always deliver the same product in the same environment and at the speed required, with employees exhibiting the same level of customer service, every part of the business must be formalized. It is complex to ensure that every standard is adhered to, no matter where in the world the operation is located. It also must be very centralized, that is, most decisions are made at the corporate office and executed regionally and locally. Thus, labor is not only divided into individual roles, but is also grouped together into departments, divisions and other operational units. These are typically called **multidivisional structures**.

It does not take long to understand that if you are the strategic communicator for a local restaurant your role will be very different from being a strategic communicator for a multidivisional organization. In fact, for the local eatery you might find that your skills are more tested than at a multidivisional structure. You will be required to market the establishment; work with designers or even design menus yourself; plan, design and run the website and social media and have a strategic plan that includes sponsorships of local high school or college sports events; take care of merchandizing, and many more. You will be required to be a part of the local community and will be expected to represent the establishment in the community.

This will be quite different from working in a multidivisional organization where you will be a member of a large team, probably in the marketing department, and likely assigned to a single function, such as internal communication that will require a great deal of coordination with other departments. You will be required to understand complex external environments with different social structures, cultures and political systems. It is important to understand that the one job is not inferior to the other. They are just very different from each other because of their unique organizational structures.

Communication technology has also changed organizational structures and how people work. This has opened many opportunities for strategic communicators, particularly if you have your own small agency and are working from home. This is a great option for practitioners with an entrepreneurial spirit or for people who have family or societal obligations that require them to have flexible schedules. Technology now allows you to become part of a **network organization** of practitioners who all bring their different skills sets together to complete complicated projects. These networks change notions of space and time since people can work together on complex problems and projects without being physically close or despite time differences.

Practitioners can provide all necessary client services in-house by creating contact points with other independent firms that provide auxiliary services clients might need. Consequently, independent practitioners become part of a network that can utilize their services when necessary, thus extending the service network of the practitioner. Increasingly, these networks form alliances when pitching for large projects, and it is not uncommon for nodal points consisting of a business consultant, a small graphic design house, a media placement agency, a media relations practitioner, an event organizer, a communication strategist and others to collectively vie for projects. Networks are organized informally. Members in a network organization typically do not have long-term contracts with other network participants and can benefit from being introduced to the participants in the networks of individual members, thus expanding business opportunities.

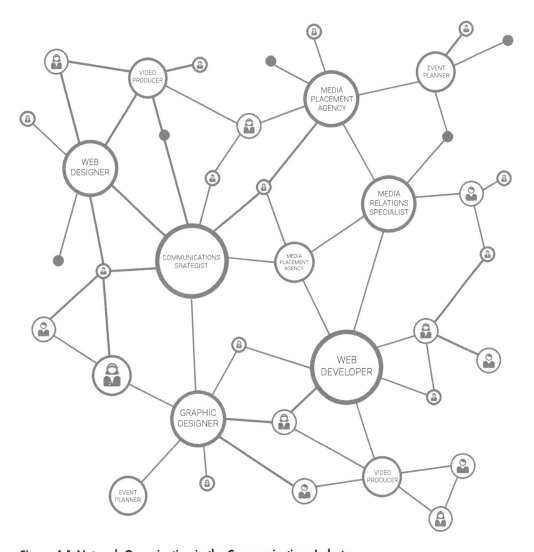

Figure 4.1 **Network Organization in the Communications Industry**

A recent study in the United States found network structures are the most prevalent in communication practice. This is directly related to the rise of the independent communication practitioner. Even in multidivisional structures, practitioners use a network of independent contractors who supply various services. This is also typically the reason why strategic communication departments in multidivisional organizations are often relatively small and more focused on strategic planning, coordination and execution.

Network organizations are often used in conjunction with **virtual organizations**. Typically, virtual organizations, such as eBay or Amazon, do not have brick-and-mortar outlets, although most have large corporate offices, warehouses and distribution centers. This is changing, though. The online interior decorating company, Wayfair, has announced it will open a store in Natick, Massachusetts, where shoppers can purchase items they can take home immediately.[8] Virtual organizations often have virtual employees (i.e., employees who only exist at a remote computer point and never enter a physical building except their own home). These employees often telecommute and can be located anywhere in the world. They are allowed autonomy and flexibility if they produce what the employer requires of them. Virtual organizations are held together by a shared vision and goal, and clearly formulated operational protocols. Other characteristics vital to virtual organizations include a learning and developmental environment, and an infrastructure that promotes communication, information and job sharing. Virtual organizations may provide an ideal working environment for women with children or single parents due to their flexibility. Working virtually became the norm during the COVID-19 global pandemic.

Research has found that organizations now use multiple structural forms simultaneously, often facilitated by technology, which led to the concept of **hybrid organizations**. For instance, multidivisional organizations might make use of virtual structuring by having employees with specially required skills to telecommute. Thus, organizations can choose which structure serves them best under what conditions.

One of the reasons why organizational structures are important is because it determines how many and what kind of departments or units an institution has, and what positions the organization requires to execute its vision and mission. Departments or units are created because they divide labor into related responsibilities and work tasks. Thinking about the earlier example of the privately owned restaurant versus the fast-food chain, you will immediately realize that even there a division of labor exists. Food servers are not line cooks. Managers order stock and oversee finances. This is what is meant by the division of labor.

This is no different in strategic communication practice. In smaller, privately owned organizations as in the local restaurant example, everybody, including the communication practitioner, reports to the owner. This means there is not much of a hierarchy of authority. However, in the fast-food example, there will be many levels of authority. Even while in an outlet such as Starbucks the baristas sometimes also serve as cashiers, there will be more formalized positions than in the restaurant example. A fast-food outlet will most likely report to a regional office, which will report to a national or corporate office. The regional office will be a smaller version of the corporate office because it will need to be divided into tasks that can support head office units and departments. If the institution is a global or international organization there will be a corporate head office somewhere and corporate offices in different countries or possibly geographical regions. Each of these structures will have its own **hierarchy of authority**.

The hierarchy of authority will have an impact on the role, function and reporting lines of the strategic communication practitioner, which is why it is important for you to understand how structures work, how labor is divided and what the reporting lines are. One of the reasons for the birth and growth of strategic communication is that in the past communication labor in large and complex organizations and even agencies was divided by the different stakeholder groups. This is called the **differentiation of labor**. The more differentiated labor is, the higher is the need for coordination. There would be an investor relations function reporting to the finance department, a media relations unit reporting to one of the executives, an internal communication department might report to human resources, a marketing communication specialist reporting to the marketing department, and so forth. If it is a multidivisional or global organization these specialists must coordinate their strategies and messages with a multitude of practitioners.

Instead of such a fragmented reporting structure, strategic communicators realized that the level of differentiation in this model is unnecessary. All communicators should think strategically about the organization and should be educated enough to serve all stakeholders. This also means that all communicators should report into a single unit to ensure that communication about the vision and mission is coordinated continuously and that every practitioner ensures that strategies, messages and tactics should be consistent and coordinated in all stakeholder communication. This approach also creates more job opportunities for practitioners because they have multiple skills and can communicate with any number of stakeholders.

How an organization is structured will affect the role, function and reporting lines of strategic communicators. The role of the practitioner in a virtual or hybrid organization will most likely differ a great deal from that in a centralized or multidivisional structure. Furthermore, structure is dependent on decision-making, leadership and other attributes of organizational participants. Of all of these, leadership style, as discussed in Chapter 3, is likely the most important.

Decision-Making Behavior

Employees at all levels make decisions. This also is true for strategic communication practitioners. It is easy to think that decision-making in professional communication environments will always be collaborative and based on consultation. However, we also know that specific situations might affect how decisions are made, particularly when practitioners are under pressure from deadlines or during crises.

The discussion of leadership styles in Chapter 3 already introduced you to the link between leadership and decision-making. Here you will be introduced to a more in-depth discussion of decision-making behavior. For the purposes of strategic communication, three ways of decision-making are relevant: rational, group and garbage-can. These behaviors have been studied and confirmed through research on decision-making in communication practice.

Sometimes decision-making is easy because there are rules and procedures in place to determine the outcome without question. But mostly, decision-making is not guided by rules and procedures. Most people assume that decision-making in work environments is always rational and based on facts. This is a very pervasive approach to strategic planning, particularly in strategic communication practice. We want to understand our stakeholders, be they consumers, customers, employees, constituents, patients or whatever the context of the situation.

Rational decision-making is understood to have three attributes: fact finding, risk-taking and technology use. Strategic communicators know that all strategic planning starts out with fact finding through research. But even with research one can never know all the facts of a situation. As a result, there is a level of guessing and risk-taking in decision-making. Previous research has shown that men are more likely than women to take risks when making decision. While new technologies can help immensely with decision-making through data provision, it can also exacerbate uncertainty because new technology requires continuous training and skills acquisition and can provide overwhelming amounts of data. Previous studies confirmed information gathering is the most important factor guiding practitioners when they make decisions, even when time is a constraint.

Generally, **group decision-making** is viewed as more effective than individual decision-making if the practitioners have the necessary skills, training and leadership to be successful at teamwork. Not only does it generate multiple ideas, but also allows more expertise in the discussion. Group decision-making is particularly prominent these days in different communication and creative environments because of new technologies. Employees, practitioners and consultants all bring different levels of expertise to meetings. It is impossible for one person to have all the skills and knowledge now required in communication practice.

Previous research showed that women were more likely to make group decisions than men. Scholars suggest group decision-making is most conducive to organizational consensus, and women appear to be more suited to this type of decision-making than men. In terms of position, group decision-making decreases with seniority, with entry-level practitioners more likely and senior managers least likely to use it.[9]

Studying decision-making behavior is not easy because people often make decisions based on choices at hand. The randomness and unpredictability of decision-making has prompted some scholars to identify a **garbage-can decision** process. It has become acceptable to acknowledge that decision-making processes are seldom perfect and are much more situational and impulsive than we would acknowledge.

Communication (Micro-) Level Factors

You might think, "Communication! Finally!" But while the communication level of the theory is indeed about stakeholder communication, this section is not yet about communication tactics. There will be multiple opportunities in future chapters to study and practice your communication tactics. This section will focus on laying the groundwork for successful stakeholder communication.

It is important that CEs should exhibit certain values and norms that are important to stakeholders, otherwise communication from or about them will be met with skepticism. The outside-in philosophy of communication is therefore very important. CEs who appear to wish to control their environment while pretending that they respect their stakeholders, will not be successful in the long run. CEs are successful and survive when their environment allows them to exist and flourish. This is as true for individuals as it is for institutions. You will remember the discussion earlier on how the actors Charlie Sheen and Roseanne Barr ruined their acting careers and lost valuable television franchises when they acted against the norms of society. Even celebrities cannot get away with so much misbehavior.

Fortunately, there are ways to monitor the extent to which CEs are viewed as reliable and trusted. There are also steps entities can take to ensure that employees live the value system needed to build a strong organization. All these internal and external conditions come about through the communication practices of CEs.

Organizational Culture

In the final analysis, there is nothing in our theory of strategic communication that does not affect the outcomes of communication. Every sector at the macro level affects issues at the meso and micro levels. It will therefore not surprise you that leadership styles, how decisions are made and how entities organize themselves will affect your ability to successfully communicate at the micro level.

You might wonder why a discussion of organizational culture is not included in the meso level of our theory. There is indeed overlap, but the micro level is where stakeholder communication takes place and one of your most important stakeholder groups is employees. Employees also are unique in their relationship to the CE. They are dependent on their relationship with the CE in terms of earning a living and might be more vested in their interests than other stakeholders. However, if the culture and climate is not conducive to that relationship, it is not only the employee who suffers but also the CE. Production, loyalty, courtesy and many more attributes are affected by workplace culture. Thus, if the CE you work for has employees, you will need to understand the relationship between organizational culture, communication and employee relations.

Organizational culture focuses on the language of the workplace, the performances of managers and employees, the formal and informal practices that mark an organization's character, such as rites and rituals, and the display of meaningful artifacts like architecture, interior design, posters, and furniture.[10]

Case Study
The Importance of Organizational Culture

Glassdoor, Inc. is a company that provides an online platform for employees and former employees to anonymously evaluate their company and management.[11] Based on these evaluations, it annually produces a Best Places to Work Award and also provides a list of the worst places to work. An analysis of comments from employees from both lists show how important corporate culture is to employee satisfaction. In an interview with Scott Dobroski, Glassdoor's director of corporate communication, he asserted, "The three top drivers of long-term employee satisfaction are company culture, career opportunities, and trust in senior leadership." Most of the comments cited from the Best Companies list indicated a strong, positive, communication culture that makes employees feel valued and supported. One of the most important vehicles for accomplishing this is the communication and relationship abilities of senior managers, who set the stage for an open, honest and above all, a supportive company culture.

An analysis of the worst companies to work for indicates a direct relationship between employee dissatisfaction and a lack of trust in the CEO. Dobroski said:

> Employees need to feel valued and that their work is important to the company. Company executives play a key role in ensuring workers know how valued their work is. It is also imperative that executives communicate to employees how the business is doing and what the plans are in the short and long term.

Other factors that contribute to employee satisfaction Dobroski mentioned are related to job and advancement opportunities and work-life balance. Fairness seems to be an important factor. For instance, the Texas supermarket chain H.E.B. (one of the best companies to work for) is lauded for the flexibility with which it allocates work time to employees. On the other hand, RGIS, a worst company, does not provide employees with enough hours to work while depending on hourly workers.

The problem with a poor organizational culture is that it not only impacts your ability to communicate with employees but also with other stakeholders who meet dissatisfied and dispirited employees. This in turn affects the company's profitability. Indeed, many of the worst companies to work for see a downturn in income and profits.

The important fact to remember here is that a strategic communicator cannot set right the negative results of the poor communication and relationship behavior of managers through formal communication. Transparency, honesty and trust in employees can only be translated through the real behavior of management and not through writing platitudes or projecting images that employees do not experience and do not see as truthful. That will only harm your reputation as a strategic communication professional.

Reputation Building

Another piece of the canvas that will help you as a strategic communicator to execute your micro-level duties is the CE's reputation. While branding is often linked to reputation, **reputation building** is essential to successful branding, while branding alone cannot determine reputation. One of the reasons is that many factors determine reputation, not only how the brand is perceived. However, the impact of communication attributes is what concerns strategic communicators.

Some of the groundwork for a discussion of communication and reputation has already been laid in our previous section on organizational culture. The communication behavior of executives, managers and employees at all levels affects a CE's reputation. Some of this behavior has already been discussed within organizational context, such as integrity, transparency and honesty.

Whereas the major impact of organizational culture is on the perceptions and experiences of employees, reputation impacts all stakeholders and, in some cases, whole societies. An example is the reputation loss Facebook suffered because of its inability to control fake news. In this case, Facebook's reputation loss cast a shadow over the legitimacy of the Brexit referendum in 2016 and the 2016 presidential election in the United States. Facebook's damaged reputation had a big political, social and economic impact on the societies involved. It also had an impact on its stock price when its role in in the U.S. election came to light late in 2018.[12]

In the past, when media could be controlled to some extent, a reputation could be managed, but the new media environment has changed everything. You surely have checked on the online customer comments when you wish to visit a restaurant, stay in a hotel or decide which airline to use. This is true for products and services as well. There is virtually nothing that escapes the online ire or satisfaction of consumers any longer. As in the case of Glassdoor or RateMyProfessor, everything is now fair game.

CEs are in the news daily because of social media posts that trend and eventually reach the mass media. Customers tape videos of all kinds of instances and events that do not benefit CEs. Pictures and materials from 40 years ago now are posted to social media and ruin reputations. As a result, it has become increasingly difficult to manage reputations. Furthermore, we know from the outside-in approach that entities do not shape stakeholders' understanding of a situation. Meaning is shaped within the frame of reference of the receiver of the message, which means each moment of communication shapes meaning and therefore reputation. It can be as simple as the ease of navigating a website or the way a security guard treats a customer, to more complex issues such as perceptions of transparency and the availability of information.

Thus, it is important to understand that an entity's reputation is based on many attributes, among others the everyday practice of employees and others related to those entities. Reputation will not be determined by a brand image or another institutional strategy. For instance, a telecommunications giant might portray itself as innovative and service-oriented, but the behavior of salespeople and their service levels at local practices will make customers skeptical if they do not support the institutional strategy. At every level of the institution, reputation will be determined locally and situationally, based on the responsible and moral behavior of its employees. This requires institutional representatives to ensure equal treatment of others and respect for the diversity of their stakeholders.

One example of loss of reputation when diversity is not considered, is the example of Fox News host Tucker Carlson. While one might be supportive of Carlson's political views, even those can become outraged when the diversity of stakeholders is not respected. In a recent survey 55% of adults say they're less likely to watch *Tucker Carlson Tonight* after hearing recently unearthed audio of Tucker Carlson's commentary on a range of sensitive topics. Carlson originally made the comments on the *Bubba the Love Sponge* radio show between 2006 and 2011.[13] Past behavior is also not easily forgiven, as in the case of the Virginia Governor Northam, who came under the spotlight when a photo of him in blackface, which is viewed as extremely racist, from a 1980s medical school yearbook page, surfaced.[14]

Despite all the things that can go wrong in reputation building, it is important to strive for a good reputation every day. To help you build your organization's reputation, it is important to understand what goes into the whole process. A handy way of looking at how reputation is established, how it can be measured and what the expected outcomes can be is a process view of reputation.[15] As you will notice in Figure 4.2, and if you remember the constitutive communication model discussed in Chapter 1, effective two-way communication is of the utmost importance. The outside-in approach requires that you give preference to the voices and perspectives of stakeholders. You can see that also is the first requirement in establishing the basis for reputation. In this model, communication behavior, perceptions and opinions are mutually changed, instead of only one side shaping the communication and its outcome.

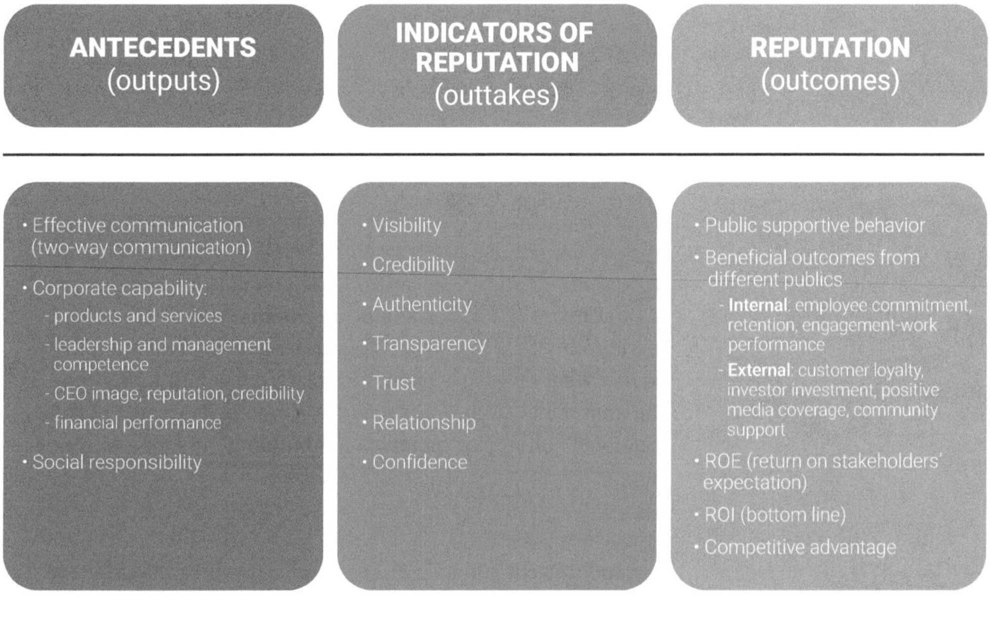

Figure 4.2 A Process View of Reputation

Another organizational output is the ability of the CE to display leadership and competent management, have outstanding products and/or services, and perform well financially. The image and credibility of the leader, be it a CEO or a sport superstar, performer or musician, is another foundation of reputation. All these qualities are also relevant to organizational culture, as discussed before. Previously, in the discussion of worst companies to work with, you saw the relationship between employee satisfaction and CEO likeability and credibility. This is also true for stakeholder satisfaction.

Social responsibility is yet another requirement for CEs to build their reputation because it is a clear indication of its value system. Increasingly sports stars are judged on their willingness to stand up for justice. Recent examples of socially responsible approaches to advertising, for instance, is the case of Nike, which used contentious football star Colin Kaepernick in a social justice campaign. Reports indicate that the campaign did not harm the company, despite extensive critique. In fact, it "added billions to its bottom line."[16]

Similarly, Gillette launched a new "We Believe" ad campaign, which is meant to show what it means to be a good man in today's culture.[17] The focus is on showing men of all ages being role models by stepping in to stop bullying and harassment and demonstrating how to treat people with respect. It has gotten nearly 100 million views on social media. Mark Pritchard, chief brand officer at Proctor & Gamble, Gillette's parent company, admitted not everybody agreed with the message. However, while Gillette appreciates different viewpoints and pays attention to them all, they distinguished "between actual consumer sentiment and some of the social media reaction that does not represent the majority opinion," Pritchard said. Several independent studies showed that consumer confidence in the brand increased among men and women.

Both these examples show how stakeholders appreciate a well-articulated, honest and transparent value system, even if they might not agree with it in every aspect. Both examples also show the results (or outtakes, as Figure 4.2 shows) for entities that lay the necessary groundwork for its reputation. Results showed increased visibility for both these organizations, and even though the value systems they expressed were not universally liked, they still came out strong. Also, they came out financially stronger and increased their competitive advantage in their respective market segments.

Summary

In this chapter you learned of the three levels of management of strategic communication analysis and practice. This is called a *general theory* of the discipline because it can be used as an instrument of analysis to see how your CE performs at each level. The factors described here are not exhaustive and you can come up with other factors at each level. But by now you should be familiar not only with the three levels of management, but also with how each level impacts your practice. The macro level you now know gives you the opportunity to look at the various sectors in society that are external to your CE. The meso-level factors provide you with tools to see how well the strategic communication function is organized and managed and what the roles communicators are required to perform. The micro level emphasizes the importance of the CE's reputation among its various stakeholders and the impact organizational culture has on reputation building.

Discussion Questions

1   Find an example of a current event and do a macro-level analysis of the different sectors that might have influenced the situation.

2   Identify the media you use and determine how you might be able to use them strategically in communication practice.

3   Identify an organization or institution you are familiar with and identify the kind or kinds of structure it uses. Describe the structural attributes you have identified.

4   Analyze your favorite brand at the hand of the reputational factors mentioned above. What do you most admire about it and are there areas that can be improved?

Check out the online support material, including chapter summaries, useful links and further reading, at www.routledge.com/9780367426316.

Notes

1   *International Journal of Strategic Communication, 5*(2), 2011.

2   Hofstede, G. (2001). *Culture's Consequences: Comparing Values, Behaviors, Institutions, and Organizations across Nations* (2nd ed.). Thousand Oaks, CA: Sage.

3   https://www.latimes.com/sports/nfl/la-sp-saints-billboard-atlanta-20190122-story.html, last accessed June 22, 2020.

4   http://www.copyright.com/blog/copyright-law-in-2018-top-10-court-cases, last accessed on March 25, 2019.

5   For more information on the U.S. Federal Reserve visit federalreserve.gov/aboutthefed. htm.

6   https://www.vox.com/policy-and-politics/2018/3/23/17151916/facebook-cambridge-analytica-trump-diagram, last accessed March 26, 2019.

7   https://www.upworthy.com/5-million-indian-women-just-made-a-385-mile-human-chain-for-equality, last accessed June 22, 2020.

8   https://adage.com/article/cmo-strategy/wayfair-bets-brick-mortar-store/317127/; accessed March 29, 2019.

9   Werder, K. G. Page, & Holtzhausen, D. R. (2009). An analysis of the influence of public relations department leadership style on public relations strategy use and effectiveness. *Journal of Public Relations Research, 21*(4), 404–427.

10 Eisenberg, E. M., Goodall Jr., H. L., & Trethewey, A. (2007). *Organizational Communication: Balancing Creativity and Constraint* (5th ed.). Boston, MA: Bedford/St. Martin's.

11 https://www.ktvb.com/article/news/nation-now/what-are-the-worst-companies-to-work-for-new-report-analyzes-employee-reviews/465–3564c612–5fed-4960-ab3d-cef81c22dd7f, last accessed on April 2, 2019.

12 https://www.macrotrends.net/stocks/charts/FB/facebook/stock-price-history, last accessed on April 3, 2019.

13 https://morningconsult.com/2019/03/15/55-of-adults-sour-on-tucker-carlson-show-after-hearing-radio-show-remarks/, last accessed on April 2, 2019.

14 https://www.nytimes.com/2019/02/07/us/virginia-governor-northam.html, last accessed on April 2, 2019.

15 Stacks, D. W., Dodd, M. D., & Men, L. F. (2013). Corporate Reputation, Measurement and Evaluation. In C. E. Carroll (Ed.), *The Handbook of Communication and Corporate Reputation* (pp. 561–573). Malden, MA: Wiley-Blackwell.

16 https://www.cnbc.com/2018/09/19/nike-colin-kaepernick-ads-national-anthem-protest-controversy.html, last accessed on June 23, 2020.

17 https://www.cnn.com/2019/02/05/perspectives/gillette-we-believe-ad-pg/index.html, last accessed June 23, 2020.

Chapter 5

Ethics and Societal Issues in Strategic Communication

Learning Outcomes

At the end of this chapter, you should be able to do the following:

- Explain the differences between ethics, morals and values.
- Identify the leading philosophers and their philosophical approaches.
- Understand the role of professional codes of ethics in strategic communication practice.
- Identify issues in strategic communication that can negatively influence society.
- Understand how strategic communication is regulated.
- Be familiar with ethical dilemmas that arise in the practice of strategic communication.

Chapter Opening Vignette

Real-World Dilemmas

Imagine the following situations that are likely to happen in the strategic communication workplace.

- In reviewing the agency's account billing, the account supervisor notices that she has accidentally overbilled one client by $10,000. However, payment has already been received from the client. She ignores the mistake.
- A recruiting brochure for a company is to feature the company's employees and facilities. The company has no disabled employees, so the photographer asks one of the employees to sit in a wheelchair for one of the photographs.
- A large petroleum company showcases its environmental initiatives in an ad campaign, even though it has been the subject of complaints by environmental groups about its negative impact on the environment.
- At the agency where he works, an employee participates in a fantasy football league. During work hours, he and coworkers spend a significant amount of

time making picks, corresponding via email with update scores, standings, offers for trades and sarcastic congratulations to the week's winner.

Do you consider these scenarios ethical? How likely would you be to engage in these behaviors? These are not easy questions and they do not have easy asnwers. Each of them represents an instance where you must apply your own personal and professional code of ethics.

Here's what other students thought. In response to a large national survey,[1] strategic communication college students said that overbilling a client was clearly unethical and 95% agreed that they would not engage in such behavior. About 80% said that posing a non-disabled person in a wheelchair for the convenience of a photo shoot was not right. However, more than half of the students considered it okay to highlight the environmental achievements of an oil company that had been criticized for environmental misdeeds. The majority of students thought they would do the same, if given the opportunity in their job as a strategic communication professional.

When asked about playing fantasy football at work, the findings were more interesting. Most students studying strategic communication agreed that it was not the ethical thing to do, but they admitted that they might likely do so, despite their awareness that it was wrong. When probed, the students admitted to the researchers that they knew that playing games on your employer's time was not ethically correct, but it is something that everyone does anyway. It became clear to the researchers that social norms influenced how one acts in the workplace, and may explain why our attitudes (what we think and feel) don't always align with our behaviors (what we do). Sometimes we do things that we know aren't right, but justify our actions because "everyone else is doing it."

Using ethical scenarios such as these help soon-to-be professionals prepare for the real world of strategic communication practice. Thinking about and discussing questionably ethical situations that may arise in the workplace makes it easier to exercise your own ethical principles when confronted with these and other real-life situations. Here are a couple more ethical dilemmas to consider. These situations are typical of what you might experience in your first job as a professional strategic communicator.

- The agency is producing a television ad for a dog food manufacturer. Several hours have been spent trying to get the star, a Labrador retriever, to eat the dog food. Since the production is costing $12,000 per hour, someone places a steak in the bottom of the dog food bowl. Though the dog never eats one bite of the dog food, the camera angle makes it appear that the dog is devouring the manufacturer's product.
- Focus group results are to be included in a marketing brochure for a client's product. The first set of focus group results is disappointing. An employee discards the first set and includes in the brochure a second set of results that are more favorable to the client's product.

Think about these situations and put yourself in the scenario. Consider how your personal code of ethics would guide you and how it would conflict with professional norms. Think of what the right thing is to do.

A Challenging Balance

A major challenge facing strategic communication practitioners is the knowledge and ability to engage in ethical reasoning. Strategic communication professionals must balance client advocacy with the public's right to know, making money with personal values, and corporate profits with societal good. The strategic communication professional fields of advertising, marketing and public relations suffer from a bad reputation because of the industry's perceived lack of ethics. Many people consider public relations a euphemism for lying, deceiving, spinning or propaganda generating. The familiar cliché "advertising ethics is an oxymoron," reveals that some consider the field inherently unethical, mostly because the goal of advertising is to persuade people to buy something, whether they want it or not. Gallup polls over the decades have asked thousands of U.S. citizens which professions they consider to be the most and least ethical. Typically, advertising executives and PR practitioners are near the bottom of the ethical ranking, along with car salesmen and members of Congress.[2]

This chapter will challenge you to consider your own personal ethics, as well as explore professional codes of ethics for the strategic communication industry. An important aspect of professional ethics is understanding how strategic communication tactics, such as advertising, promotions and advocacy, affect the larger society and how the industry regulates itself to insure that the practice remains ethical and does not harm individuals and society in general. Although the advertising and public relations professions have suffered from public image problems in the past, there are many ways that strategic communication can be used for good, including shining light on the plight of the environment and raising awareness (and dollars) for important charities. As strategic communicators, we have the powerful ability and obligation to leave the world better than we found it.

Ethics and Why They Matter

Ethics are a system of morals (a moral code) employed by a person, group or organization that dictate standards of conduct. Ethics tell us how we should behave based on what is right and what is wrong, as we do our jobs and live our lives. Ethics and morals are used interchangeably sometimes; however, there is a slight difference. Ethics refer to the rules, such as professional codes of conduct, while **morals** are our own personal principles that help us determine right from wrong. **Values** refer to the principles and ideals that a person, organization or culture believes to be important and therefore help guide ethical decision-making. Ethics determine what is right, while values determine what is important. If you value honesty then you probably would not cheat on a test under any circumstances. But if you valued achievement and success more, then you might cheat on an exam occasionly to achieve a desired outcome. In this case, you value success over honesty.

Ethics and values may differ from person to person and from culture to culture. Also, values may change as we age, based on situations that occur during our lifetimes. In a basic sense, most of us develop our moral code from our parents, our church and the culture in which we are raised. In the United States, we are generally driven by Judeo-Christian ethics, which are a moral code derived from the Ten Commandments. Other cultures have other moral frameworks, such as Buddhists' Eightfold Path.

The challenge of ethics in strategic communication comes in balancing your own set of values and sense of right and wrong against what is best for the client and society at large. The desire to make money for your agency and your client sometimes can conflict with your personal ethical standards. To make the situation more difficult, everyone has their own set of values to guide their judgments, which may or may not be compatible with yours. For example, imagine you are the account executive for a new client that is an up-and-coming rock group. To enhance the band's appeal, someone on the agency team suggests that you develop a massive list of fake names to populate the group's Twitter page and make it appear the group is more popular than it actually is. Knowing that potential fans are more apt to want to join groups that are perceived as popular, do you add the fake names to inflate the group's perceived audience following, or do you build the Twitter group from the bottom up and only include the names of actual fans? Some strategic communication professionals may see no harm in fabricating the list for the purposes of getting the band off to a quick start, while others may object on the grounds that inflating a client's perceived social media popularity amounts to deception. The point is that as a professional, you must deal with clients, stakeholders, organizations and bosses that have differing values. You also must be true to your own ethical principles. How you handle ethically questionable issues that arise in the business of strategic communication will be an indicator of your success in the field and in life.

The Importance of Ethics

Developing a sense of ethical judgment in strategic communication is critical for professional success. After all, no one wants to work with a company or person that doesn't know right from wrong. In fact, when the same strategic communication students mentioned in the chapter opener were asked how important it was for them to work for a company or agency that has high ethical standards, almost all agreed that it was extremely important. Without a good ethical base to guide our decisions and conduct, no one will trust us personally or professionally. Ethics are important because they decide our course of action. Without them, we would be aimless in our decision-making. We wouldn't know right from wrong and we would do things that only enhance ourselves, not the public. This behavior would be a personal career disaster and add to the negative impression of the profession as a whole.

A critical aspect of strategic communication is the concept of public trust. If the public does not trust strategic communicators, the profession cannot be effective and will cease to exist. For example, marketers need consumers to believe in their advertising messages. If the products fail to perform "as seen on TV," then customers will not trust the advertising claims and stop buying the product. This is why the advertising industry has a formal and stringent system of self-regulation, which will be discussed later in this chapter. Likewise, if a PR spokesperson lies to the media about their client in an effort to cover up a scandalous act, which is eventually exposed, the journalists and therefore the public will not trust that spokesperson in the future. If the spokesperson is not trusted, they cannot be effective in their role as a representative for that client and may lose their job.

On the other hand, consistent ethical behavior can create trust and help to build relationships. Think of your best relationships and what makes them so good. It might be good communication, mutual understanding and common interest. But we do know all good relationships are rooted in trust, because without trust, you cannot have a successful bond with other humans. In good relationships, you don't lie, cheat or steal, because if you did the relationship would suffer. Good and consistent ethical conduct is the way we enhance and strengthen the relationships we have with others. If you have ever lied to a loved one you might recoil at the very thought of the reaction when they found out about your deception. Chances are the relationship suffered. Depending on the scale of the deception, the outcome could be minor or it could permanently sever the relationship. Dishonesty can ruin personal relationships and in terms of professional dealings, lying can cause irrevocable damage to your professional reputation. That's why having a strong ethical code is important.

This isn't to say that behaving in an ethical manner is easy. In fact, it's difficult. Deception is often the easiest way out of a crisis situation in the short term. But it is never conducive to long-term success. Think of the last big lie you told. The outcome would undoubtedly have been better if you told the truth in the first place. Sure, the initial dust up may have been dramatic but in the long run (you should always think in the long run), the energy you expend trying to cover up or evade the truth is always more exhausting than dealing with the original problem.

Ethical Approaches

Your personal ethics are nothing more than your philosophy on life. You may not think you have a philosophy, but you do because no decision you make in your life comes without you thinking about it in terms of right and wrong. It has to come from you. The 'filter' you run it through is your own personal philosophy.

We usually arrive at a decision by first assigning a value orientation to it. There are three ethical approaches:

1   **Absolutist:** The decision is either completely right or completely wrong. There is no gray. This ethical approach is rare because seldom are decisions clear. People with too many of these are extremely rigid in their belief system. The orientation is difficult to maintain because of differing viewpoints. Think of the world. How many examples can you name of commonly held absolutist views we all share? Murder being a bad thing comes to mind, but that could be reasoned away in the case of self-defense. Probably the negative view of sexual relationships with children is a universal absolutist view.

2   **Existentialist:** Existentialists try to balance between the two extremes and make decisions that are based on immediate rational choice. They are not made from any single overriding value system. For example, you have just received a job offer from an agency offering you a substantial raise that would help pay off your student loans. You like the job, but you're not unhappy where you are currently employed. Do you take the job? If the answer is yes, congratulations you just made an existentialist decision.

3   **Situationalist:** These decisions are based on causing the least amount of harm to the most people. These can be tricky. Your boyfriend/girlfriend of one month buys you a gift that you absolutely hate. You can either refuse the gift outright or accept it with a smile. If you're smiling, you're employing a situational approach.

On the other hand, consider whether you are a situationalist or more of an absolutist in your decision-making. The truth, as you may have guessed, is you're a composite of all of these philosophical approaches. An important point to remember is, that everyone is making those same decisions, but may feel completely different than you do. Depending on the situation, you are in total control of how you act. No two people have the exact same ethical code. As mentioned earlier, conflicts can arise when one person's ethical orientation doesn't match up with another's.

Using Ethical Principles

Making ethical decisions isn't always easy. Sometimes you need a little guidance. That's where studying the great philosophers can be helpful. You may think that the dilemma you are struggling with is unique and special, and it may be true, but the ethical principle guiding your decision has been thought through and discussed over millenia. From Aristotle in ancient Greece to the 20th century work of Noddings, these philosophers have laid the groundwork to understand how people think and act in an ethical way. These guidelines are not meant to be the final answer, but they are a framework on which to build ethical decision-making in strategic communication and in life.

Aristotle and the "Golden Mean"

Aristotle's (384–322 BCE) philosophies, though complex, can be boiled down to the concept of everything in moderation. For Aristotle, it was important to find a middle ground between two extremes. We know in math that the mean represents the average of a group of numbers. Aristotle's "golden mean" represents human reaction and behaviors. Aristotle's moral virtue is a middle state determined by practical wisdom. Aristotle thought that people should use moderation in dealing with ethical dilemmas throughout their life. For Aristotle, having too much of something is just as bad as not having enough. He saw wisdom as the state between extreme caution and unreflective spontaneity. He said courage is the middle ground between cowardice and temerity.

Aristotle stressed the importance of having a strong moral character and learning from that character throughout your life. To him, it is not enough to think about doing good deeds, you must actually do them too. Doing the right thing should always be second nature. He believed that the harder you worked at being an ethical person, the more you would reap benefits such as building trust, gaining credibility and establishing a good reputation.

It is important to remember that striving for the mean, does not imply looking for a middle-of-the-road compromise. Aristotle is very clear that there are some instances where there is no middle ground. According to Aristotle, murder, spite and theft, for example, are never considered options and therefore can never be justified.

Aristotle's philosophies can be best used in strategic communication in the area of resolving disputes. His philosophies cut through ambiguity and uncertainty. For example, you represent a school district in the midst of a teachers strike. Since one side cannot exist without the other, you're going to have to come up with a communication plan that presents both sides. The only way to effectively deal with the situation is to establish a middle ground that both sides can support. The strategies and tactics you employ would be best be served by Aristotle's approach to resolve the dispute.

Kant's Categorical Imperative

Immanuel Kant (1724–1804) differed from Aristotle in respect to character. Aristotle believed that morals and ethics are ingrained in a person's personality. Kant believed it wasn't the person, but the rules that everyone follows that promote ethical behavior. He came up with his "categorical imperative" which states that we should "Act on that maxim which you will to become a universal law." Basically, it means, if you do something, everyone else should be able to do it too. Now, that sounds fine, but think about it. In practice, this means that if you have ever run a yellow light in busy traffic, or downloaded music or movies that you didn't exactly pay for, it may have worked for you when you needed it, but it would not feel so good or workable if everybody did it.

You have probably rationalized downloading music or other entertainment products is okay because one person taking it isn't going to make much difference in terms of the artist's profits. You may even rationalize that Beyoncé makes enough money as it is, so no harm done. But if you apply Kant's categorical imperative, you'll see it isn't just one person getting away with it, it's everyone. If this were the case, then no one would produce a product for anything but artistic reasons. I guarantee you that you would not be so eager to steal a product if you were the one producing it.

To have a successful career in strategic communication, you have to be perceived as honest and trustworthy. Being honest and keeping your promises are two of the best ways to achieve trust. We trust things we can believe in. When someone makes a promise to us, we instinctively want to believe them. If they fulfill that promise, then the level of trust solidifies and/or deepens. Breaking a promise has the opposite effect. It destroys trust. No one wants to work with a person they cannot trust. Imagine a world where no one kept their promises. We wouldn't trust anyone or anything and that would be a scary world. The next time you need to make an ethical decision ask yourself if you would you be happy if everyone else made the same decision. If the answer is no, then you need to rethink your course of action.

Mill's Principle of Utility

John Stuart Mill (1806–1873) came up with a philosophy that can be easily understood. Do the greatest amount of good for the greatest number of people possible. While that sounds good, it's not as easy as you might think. Mill believed that the right decisions produce the greatest balance of good over evil. It's a nice concept, but in strategic communication it can be a little more difficult to implement.

Strategic communication audiences represent diverse groups and viewpoints. These audiences may be in the majority or in the minority. They may be segmented by their race, gender, sexual orientation, and so forth. Sometimes your audience represents the smallest number of people and by making them happy, you risk alienating the majority. If this happens, does it mean you should change your plan because it's unethical? It is important to remember that Mill advocated for the greatest good for the greatest number of people possible, not what the majority thinks is the greatest good for them. Just because a particular audience population is large, doesn't mean they know what's best for them. Take for example, giving women the right to vote or allowing gay marriage. Both of these issues were extremely controversial when laws were enacted. The majority of Americans did not support either when they were initially proposed, yet now we know both work to the benefit of society.

Working with products or services that are designed to make audiences feel good can lead to other ethical issues in which Mill might be helpful. For decades the tobacco industry produced and marketed cigarettes as a luxury items, designed to make you feel good. The campaigns for cigarettes were so successful that by the mid-1950s more than half of the adult population smoked. By the end of the decade, studies began to show that smoking causes great health risks and that the tobacco companies knew this horrible fact long before it became public knowledge. Mill would argue this is unethical because it causes harm to the greatest number of people even though the majority of people like to smoke.

In Chapter 2, the concept of fit with a potential employer was discussed. One of the examples provided was if you could work for and promote the products of a tobacco company. There is no right or wrong answer, it depends entirely on your ethics. You can make the argument that working in the tobacco industry does not cause harm because people now know the facts about smoking and they can make their own decisions. Or you can simply choose to not work there because of the harm you believe these companies cause. The ethical choice is yours.

Both of these examples showed that the majority could be wrong and people were helped by strategic communication that persuaded and changed the majority opinion on the matter, both for and against. Being a strategic communication professional, you frequently come across situations where you'll be asked to advocate, promote or market from a minority standpoint. If you believe you're advocating for something that will be in the public good even though the majority may not like it, you're putting Mill to the right use.

Noddings: Love and Relational Ethics

The previous guidelines have provided a good path toward ethical behavior. What they all have in common is they are logical in nature. According to Nel Noddings (1929–), and emotional approach may also be needed. Relationships are at the heart of all good strategic communication practices. To successfully persuade, market and/or advocate, you have to establish some kind of relationship. Noddings believes there are two parties in any relationship, the "one-caring" and the "cared-for." The one-caring is invested in attending to the cared-for in deeds as well as thoughts. It's not a one-sided relationship though and the cared-for gives back promoting a true sense of stewardship. Think of your relationship with your best friend and the work and effort that went into the friendship. Good communication, being there when they needed you, being an advocate for them and supporting them all contributed to the relationship you have now. You don't lie, cheat, or tell half-truths to them on a regular basis because if you did you probably would not have the relationship you do.

Noddings believes you have to actually care about the organization you're working with. Whether it is a movement, product or an organization, it is important to "love" what they represent. By doing so, Noddings believes, it will ensure that you behave ethically toward them as you do with the people you love.

Professional Codes of Ethics

Up to this point, ethics has been discussed from an individual basis. How you behave personally, as an individual, is important because it is the individual whose ethics form the basis of our professional and organizational behavior. The ethical principles that organizations employ are reflections of the founders and the people who work there. Organizations and the individuals that work within them are expected to conduct themselves according to high ethical standards, operate with a sense of social responsibility and strive for good outcomes, not only for their organization, but for society as a whole.

Most professions—from accounting to zoo-keeping—use written codes of ethics to guide practitioners toward ethical behavior. Ethical codes help establish and maintain trustworthy relationships with clients. A good code of ethics fosters trust and sets expectations for professional relationships.

A **code of ethics** is a document in which an organization or even entire profession detail their core values and standards. It is one of the most important documents in an organization, because it outlines what a company believes in and how employees are expected to perform. Codes of ethics set forth the values of the organization, outline appropriate conduct when faced with ethical problems, as well as any punishment or action that may be taken, if the code is broken. Professional codes of ethics should be reviewed on a regular basis. A five-year review is not uncommon because situations may arise that the code does not cover or changes in laws may make a change necessary.

The various professional organizations in the field of strategic communication (as discussed in Chapter 2) provide written standards and codes of ethics to their membership to help professionals make good decisions when faced with ethical dilemmas. The basic tenets of each group's codes are similar:

1   **Tell the truth/Do not lie**. This may seem like a no-brainer, but actually it's one of the hardest ideals to adhere to. Lying is the single biggest destroyer of trust. This is especially true during a crisis. You may be tempted to lie in order to give your client a competitive advantage, but this would be a mistake. Also, in today's hypermedia environment, where every cell phone has a video and audio device, the chance of getting caught in that lie are great. If you have to lie in order to succeed, you may want to ask yourself if the client you're advocating for or the products you are promoting are worth ruining your professional reputation. This advice also goes for half-truths, where you tell people some of the truth and intentionally leave out other information that will help them make a rational decision. Half-truths operates much like a lie. Audiences are suspicious of half-truths. This is especially so when they find out the other information that's being kept from them. They always do, so try not to imply half-truths in your messaging.

2   **Don't misrepresent**. Similar to lying, misrepresenting yourself and/or a client is a definite no-no. Exaggerated claims, false or misleading information—both visual and verbal—are forms of misrepresentation that a professional communicator should avoid. Think about it; you're launching a new strategic communication agency and a prospective employee comes in telling you that they can do all the things you want them to do. You hire them, then you find out they can only do half of what they said. In the end, it costs the company time, money and resources to deal with the misrepresentation. Remember, telling the whole truth is the best way to save your personal and professional reputations.

3   **Balance loyalty to the client with loyalty to the public**. Even though the client is paying for your services, remember you are as beholden to the public as you are to your client. You would never try to sell something harmful to your friends, would you? So why would you sell it to the public? Your client and the public both depend on you to protect them from harm. It's a balancing act, but operating with good stewardship for both parties is the best way to go.

4   **Promote transparency**. It is important to open yourself and/or your client to public scrutiny in order for to public to gain a better and clearer understanding. Can you back up your claims about the product in the ad or about the politician's record? Opening up one's self is never easy, but it's an important component to developing trust with those around you and creating credibility as a professional communicator.

The Public Relations Society of America (PRSA) and the American Advertising Federation's Institute for Advertising Ethics (IAE) are two important professional associations that provide standards of practice and codes of conduct for their members. Parts of the PRSA and IAE codes are shown in the Industry Insights box on this page. You also find their full codes of ethics on their websites.

Industry Insight

PRSA Member Statement of Professional Values[3]

This statement presents the core values of PRSA members and, more broadly, of the public relations profession. These values provide the foundation for the Member Code of Ethics and set the industry standard for the professional practice of public relations. These values are the fundamental beliefs that guide our behaviors and decision-making process. We believe our professional values are vital to the integrity of the profession as a whole.

Advocacy

We serve the public interest by acting as responsible advocates for those we represent. We provide a voice in the marketplace of ideas, facts and viewpoints to aid informed public debate.

Honesty

We adhere to the highest standards of accuracy and truth in advancing the interests of those we represent and in communicating with the public.

Expertise

We acquire and responsibly use specialized knowledge and experience. We advance the profession through continued professional development, research and education. We build mutual understanding, credibility and relationships among a wide array of institutions and audiences.

Independence

We provide objective counsel to those we represent. We are accountable for our actions.

We are faithful to those we represent, while honoring our obligation to serve the public interest.

Fairness

We deal fairly with clients, employers, competitors, peers, vendors, the media and the general public. We respect all opinions and support the right of free expression.

Industry Insight

Advertising Ethics

Administered by the American Advertising Federation (AAF) in partnership with the Reynolds Journalism Institute (RJI) and the Missouri School of Journalism, the IAE was built upon the following eight principles and practices that convey how all forms of communication should do what is right for consumers, which in turn is right for business.[4]

▨ **Principle 1**—*Advertising, public relations, marketing communications, news and editorial all share a common objective of truth and high ethical standards in serving the public.* Research shows that consumers place high value in honest and ethical advertising. While the industry has long been committed to the highest standards of truth and accuracy, professionals must further enhance their advertising ethics in order to build and maintain consumer trust.

▨ **Principle 2**—*Advertising, public relations and all marketing communications professionals have an obligation to exercise the highest personal ethics in the creation and dissemination of commercial information to consumers.* The first mission of the IAE is to educate industry professionals about the importance of truthful, ethical advertising. The goal is to convey their responsibility to demonstrate professionalism at all times.

▨ **Principle 3**—*Advertisers should clearly distinguish advertising, public relations and corporate communications from news and editorial content and entertainment, both online and offline.* As we continue to blur the line between commercial communications and editorial content, consumers are increasingly being misled and treated unethically. To avoid consumer confusion and mistrust, the industry must strive to clearly separate paid advertising from actual news.

▨ **Principle 4**—*Advertisers should clearly disclose all material conditions, such as payment or receipt of a free product, affecting endorsements in social and traditional channels, as well as the identity of endorsers, all in the interest of full disclosure and transparency.* The popularity of social media and word-of-mouth marketing raises questions about the credibility of content. Advertisers must be transparent about whether bloggers are expressing their own opinions or are being compensated by a brand. There must also be full disclosure regarding the authenticity of comments on Facebook, Twitter and other social media platform.

▨ **Principle 5**—*Advertisers should treat consumers fairly based on the nature of the audience to whom the ads are directed and the nature of the product or service advertised.* Extra care must be used when advertising to children and other vulnerable audiences to avoid misleading or mistreating them. Advertisers should also use discretion based on the nature of the product or service, especially alcohol and prescription drugs.

▨ **Principle 6**—*Advertisers should never compromise consumers' personal privacy in marketing communications, and their choices as to whether to participate in providing their information should be transparent and easily made.* As marketers develop increasingly advanced means of online behavioral targeting, consumers worry about their privacy. In response to consumer concerns and government warnings, marketing and media trade associations are launching an online self-regulatory initiative to give consumers greater control over the collection and use of online viewing data.

▨ **Principle 7**—*Advertisers should follow federal, state and local advertising laws, and cooperate with industry self-regulatory programs for the resolution of advertising practices.* The Federal Trade Commission, Better Business Bureau and Food & Drug Administration are just a few of the regulatory bodies that advertisers can look to for guidance regarding ethical practices. The advertising industry has also created an exceptional self-regulatory program called the National Advertising Review Council (NARC) that covers both adult and children's advertising.

■ **Principle 8**—*Advertisers and their agencies, and online and offline media, should discuss privately potential ethical concerns, and members of the team creating ads should be given permission to express internally their ethical concerns.* Taking the time to discuss and resolve ethical dilemmas is essential to practicing the highest ethical standards. The industry must maintain an open environment where professionals feel free to express their opinions, both positive and negative. The main consideration behind all advertising should be what is best for the consumer, and this will lead to the best plan of action.

Social Impact of Strategic Communication

As mentioned at the beginning of this chapter, strategic communication can have both positive and negative effects on society. That is why understanding ethics, professional standards and codes of conduct for the profession are important. This section will explore the social impact of strategic communication, including positive activities as well as the potential negative impacts of the practice.

Professional Profile

Corey Bryant—Communications Director in the Non-Profit Sector

Corey Bryant—Communications Director in the Non-Profit Sector.

Corey Bryant graduated from the University of Alabama in 2009 with a degree in public relations, and now has experience working in several different industries— including healthcare, non-profits and entertainment.

Did you have any internships in college? My internship experience actually started very early in my college career. As a freshman, I started on the Disney College Program, which was an eight-month front-line work experience at the Walt Disney World Resort where I was able to earn college credit. That internship expanded my opportunities to serve as the Disney Internships Campus Representative at the University of Alabama, and later, serve in Professional Internship capacities for Disney Parks and Resorts Communications and Disney Parks and Resorts Services for Guests with Disabilities.

How important do you think those internships were? They were critically important for me, as they provided me with unparalleled experience in communicating with internal and external stakeholders, operational efficiency, workplace decorum and critical soft skills that can't always be learned in a classroom setting—all from the expertise of a Fortune 100 Company. It was also a foot in the door with a company that I had known I wanted to work for from an early age. Also, something I would discover a little further down the road is that a company like Disney is a tremendous "wow" factor on a resume! I can't tell you how many times people ask me what it was like, ask me to share stories from my time there, or want to pick my brain on Disney's innovations and processes.

What did you want to do with your career? I wanted to be a public relations or public affairs executive for Disney Parks or Disney Theatrical Productions.

Are you doing it? No.

What are you doing now? I'm the Director of Communications for a national non-profit that serves the organ donation and transplantation professional community of practice.

How did you get there? After a few years of networking and positioning myself for the right career path, I landed a full-time position on the Disney Cruise Line public relations team. I got to assist with the launch of two world-class cruise ships, and coordinated vacations and media opportunities for thousands of special VIP guests, including celebrities, dignitaries, heads of state, influencers, company executives and guest media. After eight years of incredible experiences, I was feeling somewhat burnt out by the travel and tourism industry and the lack of growth opportunities that seemed to be available. (The economy was still very much recovering from the economic recession, so advancement opportunities were few and far between, especially for coveted positions.) I received a call from a recruiter from a local health system, asking if I would be interested in interviewing for an in-house public relations manager position. After meeting with them, I learned that the position was dedicated to the region's organ donation program, and was responsible for government relations related to donor registration, as well as public and media relations with regard to organ, eye and tissue donation. It seemed like a different and fascinating challenge. I was offered the position, and after a few days of soul-searching and asking myself the hard questions, I willingly accepted the challenge. Over the next several years, I fell in love with the cause and became grateful for the change of pace and the literal life-saving impact that my work was carrying. After a few years, I was offered the opportunity to design and build the communications department for a national non-profit serving the organ donation and transplantation professional community of practice. How often do you get the chance to literally build your own program from the ground up? It was a challenge that I couldn't turn down.

How have your dreams changed? As I matured in my life and my career, I realized I wanted to be in a place where I could do meaningful work and make a real difference in the lives of human beings. Things became less about money, social status or a shiny title—and more about how I could make a difference in the world around me. Personally, I didn't want to just be a mouthpiece for an organization who is after the almighty dollar—the world has enough of those. I know I'll probably never be a millionaire, but I'll have hopefully made an impact on things that are truly important.

How have you changed? I've certainly changed my perceptions and definitions of success. Success for me is no longer defined by speedy career advancement, financial thresholds or other sociocultural expectations—no matter how others might have me believe. Success for me now lies in the ability to be solvent, happy and fulfilled in my work, and to make an impact in the lives of others. It's also helped to drive my involvement with social causes like LGBT+ activism, HIV/AIDS education, care and research and community mental health support.

What did you wish you had known? The most important piece of advice I wish I could have given myself is don't pigeon-hole yourself into one career path or one goal. Just like in a poker game, don't get tunnel vision when you see three-of-a-kind. You might miss the full house playing out right under your nose. (And you'd be a pretty terrible poker player.) Life is a series of opportunities and dreams can change. It's not just a straight line between you and one goal.

What has surprised you most about yourself or your career? I'm nowhere near where I thought I would end up, and that's okay! As a matter of fact, it's great. I have gone from coordinating VIPs and guest media on the maiden voyage of a $1.8 billion cruise ship to leading state-level government relations on organ donation, to delivering keynotes to hundreds of the nation's leading transplant surgeons. Each career opportunity has equipped me with invaluable tools that I have carried from one role to the next, and it's made me a better, more experienced and more marketable professional.

What advice would you give to someone in college now? A degree doesn't automatically mean you're ready for the workforce, nor are you entitled to a job making $75,000 a year. Be patient with yourself and be humble with others. Take advantage of internships. Learn soft skills. Don't underestimate the power of networking—and not just quick meet and greets, emails and "Congrats on your work anniversary!" messages on LinkedIn. If you want their attention, find ways to get involved with them and their work. Volunteer with their organization if possible, shadow, stay in contact. Show how passionate and valuable you are so that when an opening becomes available, there can be no question as to who their choice is. And when that happens, don't rest on your laurels. Never stop learning. Take advantage of career development opportunities, certifications and anything that continues to make you more valuable and competitive.

What do you wish young professionals working at your agency knew? Every person and every task has something to teach you if you're perceptive enough. Observational learning has taught me many things in my career: Traits and skills that I want to embody as an effective leader and communicator ... and maybe some things that aren't as effective. Take those learnings and shape yourself into the professional you want to be. Throughout it all, remain objective. Ask the hard questions, don't take things personally, and don't be afraid to advocate for yourself. Finally, I'll share one of the best pieces of advice I've ever received: Remember that compliments and criticism are like bubble gum. Unwrap it, chew on it for a while, but don't swallow it. It's just not good to digest.

More information about Corey Bryant can be found here: https://www.linkedin.com/in/joseph-corey-bryant/.

Social Responsibility

Social responsibility is an ethical framework that stipulates that organizations and individuals have an obligation to act for the good of the profession and society—to balance shareholder profits with benefits for society in general. Today, stakeholders expect organizations large and small to be socially aware and strive to make the world better for all people. Social responsibility is also an important aspect of an organization's reputation, as discussed at the end of Chapter 4. As professionals, we must conduct business in a socially responsible way that will meet the expectations of our employers, the industry and the public at large.

Corporate social responsibility (CSR) is a management orientation whereby companies integrate social and environmental concerns with their business operations and their interactions with stakeholders.[5] Ten years ago, very few Fortune 500 companies gave any thought to CSR, but with changing values in society and emergence of the millennial generation, who appear to be more concerned about social good than previous generations, more and more companies are discovering the benefits of a comprehensive plan that not only helps the world, but also makes good business sense.

CSR can take many forms, including providing dollars to match donations made by employees to non-profits, allowing employees to take time off to help local charities, or donating a portion of corporate profits to a good cause. TOMS Shoes may be one of the most famous examples of CSR being part of their essential business. TOMS was founded with this simple CSR idea—*match every pair of shoes sold with a new pair for a child in need.* Another example is the fast-food restaurant chain Chipotle's that launched the "Inglorious Fruit and Vegetable" campaign to help fight food waste by partnering with a non-profit to sell "ugly" produce at reduced prices rather than throwing it away. A classic example of CSR is McDonald's Ronald McDonald House that has been providing a free place for parents of hospitalized children to stay for almost 50 years.

CSR is also important because a corporation's positive social impact adds strategic value to the business. While "doing good," corporations have been able to capitalize on favorable public sentiment, particularly when the good actions are posted on social media. At the same time, socially irresponsible business practices are no longer hidden, again thanks to social media and hyper-aware consumers, making positive news generated by CSR even more important.

There are many positives for a company to implementing a CSR strategy—here are a few:

1   **Enhanced public image:** Consumers and publics like shopping and advocating with organizations that help the community.
2   **Increased media coverage:** The media has a vested interest in reporting on things of importance to the community.
3   **Boost employee engagement:** If an employee is proud of their company, they are more productive.
4   **Attract and retain investors:** Investors are more likely to be attracted and continue to support a company that has demonstrated a commitment not only to their employees, but also to the world at large.
5   **Forging corporate sponsorships:** Oftentimes social responsibility programs require partnership with other corporations or state and community organizations. These partnerships can be the beginning of long-standing relationships.

CSR campaigns can have a positive impact on an organization with the most important outcome being that of developing and maintaining relationships with the local community and making the world a better place for everyone.

Industry Insight

CSR and the World's Largest Retailer

Walmart has a multifaceted, comprehensive Corporate Social Responsibility plan that covers a wide variety of social needs and focuses on several key areas of importance. "Sustainability" to Walmart includes the goal of maintaining zero waste, upgrading with 100% renewable energy, and selling products that sustain resources and environment. "Opportunity" indicates that Walmart is dedicated to giving women more opportunities in the workplace. "Community" section provides hunger and disaster relief along with community development. All of these directives are published on their website in a bid to be transparent about their commitment to social responsibility and their local communities. Thus, when Walmart sponsors recycling programs, beautification efforts, education scholarships for local students, or other local initiatives, they are signaling to the public that they are an ethical company that cares about the world around them. During the COVID-19 pandemic, when Walmart mandated masks be worn in all Walmart and Sam's Club stores by all employees and customers, they put the long-term public good ahead of any concern about short-term back-lash or political pushback. The mandate was consistent with Walmart's CSR strategic plan.

Societal Issues in Strategic Communication

Despite the role of strategic communication in helping organizations to operate in a socially responsible manner, the practice of strategic communication can also be criticized for its negative influences on society. Marketing and brand communications are often blamed for creating demand for products that people don't need and for making society more materialistic, which leads to many negative societal outcomes, including environmental degradation. Public relations practitioners are sometimes called propagandists, particularly when they work for political candidates and twist the truth or artfully re-frame issues to benefit their client's re-election. Some see the profession of strategic communication as inherently unethical because of its attempt to shape public attitudes and behavior.

Academic Angle

What Is Propaganda?

Strategic communication is sometimes considered propaganda. But what is propaganda? Do strategic communicators practice propaganda? Are they propagandists? These are important questions for students of strategic communication to consider.

The word "propaganda" is mostly associated with government speech, especially during wartime. It evokes negative images, such as Goebbels-style brainwashing in Nazi Germany, Soviet rhetoric during the Cold War or, more recently, President Trump's accusations of "fake news from the lamestream media" or catch-phrases like "China Plague" when describing the COVID-19 pandemic. Few Americans can define propaganda, but they think they know it when they see it and most believe it to be bad.

Defining propaganda is difficult. The term *propaganda* has been attached to a broad range of persuasive communication from advertising to education to political speech. It is only in the last few decades that propaganda has developed a negative connotation. According to Barry Fulton, director of Public Diplomacy Institute at George Washington University, only after the mid-1960s did propaganda take on "the tone of doing something underhanded."[6] Before World War I propaganda was a virtually unknown concept—the 1913 edition of the *Encyclopedia Britannica* did not contain an entry for *propaganda*, primarily because people did not use the word or understand what it meant.[7]

Propaganda can be categorized into two types—*black propaganda*, which is associated with deception, misinformation and outright lies and *white propaganda*, which involves selective use of the truth, or the promotion of positive and the suppression of negative information. The stereotypical idea of propaganda is generally black propaganda and includes coercive, aggressive and non-objective communication, which may be completely false, such as a government's dissemination of exaggerated stories of enemy atrocities during wartime. However, a government spokesman's explanation and defense of its country's foreign policy to an international audience might be considered white propaganda. The United States has engaged in both types in its history.

Contemporary communications scholars Garth Jowett and Victoria O'Donnell, define propaganda as "the deliberate and systematic attempt to shape perceptions, manipulate cognitions, and direct behavior to achieve a response that furthers the desired intent of the propagandist."[8] Some may argue that current "media spin" from politicians, pundits and commentators qualifies as propaganda under this definition. They contend that the message is planned by a sophisticated organization and may be interpreted as one-sided, if not blatantly deceptive, and definitely self-serving. Others may attempt to label advertising as propaganda because it is an organized effort to convince people to buy products they may not need. However, advertising—if labeled propaganda—would be white propaganda, accentuating the positive qualities while omitting the negative aspects of a product. Advertising, as it is legally practiced in the United States, is therefore more accurately defined as persuasive communication.

Strategic communication is definitely persuasive in nature, therefore understanding the art and science of persuasion is important for the effective and ethical practice of strategic communication. Being a propagandist is not an ethical role for strategic communication professionals.

Advertising most likely cannot make us buy things we don't need or believe everything that political campaigns claim about their candidates. For every criticism, there are opposing views that suggest that strategic communicators don't always have the power that the critics assign to them. Some say that advertising drives our economy, making us wealthier and producing a better quality of life. In terms of public relations, the public is generally intelligent and most of us know when we are being lied to. However, there are some specific societal issues that are of special concern for strategic communication practitioners, which need our special attention. These include the use of distasteful messages and images; portrayals of race and gender; and, persuasive communication aimed at children and other vulnerable audiences.

Distasteful and Offensive Messages

Some media messages can make you uncomfortable because they are disgusting or use inappropriate words or images. While advertisers and other strategic communication practitioners want to garner attention with eye-catching creative approaches, when messages are distasteful and offensive to most people, the strategic communicator has crossed an ethical line. For example, when the animal rights group PETA posted billboards in Florida in 2009 with the headline "Save the Whales" above a close-up image of a grossly obese woman, the public found it offensive and pressured PETA to remove the signs.[9] Both the clothing label Benetton and ice cream manufacturer Antonio Federici used nuns in sexually explicit poses with men to promote their products. The combination of religion and sex is universally considered inappropriate.

Advertising, such as the outdoor billboard for the Protection and Ethical Treatment of Animals (PETA) above, are considered offensive and distasteful.[10]

Photo Credit: CC Attribution Non-Commercial Share Alike.

Offensive and distasteful messaging can include sensitive product categories such as condoms or personal hygiene, sexually explicit imagery and language, nudity, vulgarity and violence. Certain messages may be offensive in certain contexts, but not in others. A fast-food commercial, such as Carl Jr's spot featuring a woman seductively consuming a giant burger with dripping sauce, that is run in after-school programming when children are watching, is inappropriate, but the same ad might be fine if broadcast after children have gone to bed.

Of course, applying a standard of good taste can be difficult because it varies by the individual, time, context and culture. Nonetheless, strategic communication practitioners should be aware of and constantly monitor the sensitivity of their stakeholders, including particular cultural customs and traditions and try not to offend them or their communities. Even though the controversial messages can gain attention, especially when they are spread virally on social media, it still doesn't make it an ethically right thing to do.

Portrayals of Gender and Race

Portrayals in the media can have significant effects on society. For example, in the 1970s, television programs and commercials mostly portrayed women as housekeepers and mothers, while men were shown exclusively in professional roles. Despite the large numbers of women in the workforce at that time, these inaccurate gender portrayals persisted and fostered discrimination against women in society.[11] More recently, Hollywood has been criticized for the dearth of black actors in major motion pictures. When people of color are cast, they are typically hoodlums or drug-dealers, leaving the impression that minorities in our society are up to no good.

Negative portrayals of gender and race are sensitive and important issues for strategic communicators to consider. **Stereotypes**—a widely held, oversimplified image or idea of a particular type of person or group of people—can be helpful short-cuts in communication, but more often, stereotypes rely on negative qualities that are exaggerated and hurtful. When negative stereotypes are portrayed in the media, unfair caricatures are reinforced that are harmful to segments of society.

The enslaved black mammy stereotype reflected in the Aunt Jemima brand of flour, pancake mixes and syrups has been criticized for perpetuating negative racial stereotypes.[12] So much so that Quaker Oats, the brand's parent company, decided to replace and rename the well-known, 130 year-old breakfast brand in an effort to achieve racial equality. Also in 2020 during a period of heightened awareness of race inequity, Land-o-Lakes removed the Indian girl logo from their butter packages and the NFL's Washington Redskins announced that they would drop their mascot's name and image. Both actions were taken because the logos were offensive to Native American people.

Image of Quaker Oats Aunt Jemima brand before its name change in 2020.
Photo Credit: Mike Mozart/CC BY.

The debate about whether the media shapes or mirrors society is an important one for strategic communicators to consider. If you believe that media have the power to shape opinions and attitudes, rather than merely reflecting society back on ourselves, then media portrayals of gender and race become very important societal concerns. Strategic communicators have the power to choose how they portray people in their messages and should use that power to create a better society.

Targeting Children

Messages aimed at children and other vulnerable audiences are among the most controversial issues in strategic communication, particularly to marketing communications. Children do not have the experience or maturity to discern marketing messages and make informed consumer decisions. Therefore, strategic communicators should take special care in developing campaigns aimed at young audiences. The marketing of soft drinks, fast-food and candy to children has come under particular scrutiny in the last decade from governmental and non-profit agencies seeking to protect children from harmful products. Promoting alcohol and tobacco products to teenagers, especially black youth, is another area of concern for strategic communicators, as it has the potential to negatively affect the most defenseless segments of our society.

Regulation of Strategic Communication

In the United States, freedom of speech and the media is guaranteed under the First Amendment of the Constitution. Most western democratic countries also enjoy free speech rights, but have no constitutional imperative to guarantee it. Speech in other countries might rather be governed by libel, defamation or privacy laws. In the United States the Freedom of Information Act (FOIA) guarantees the right of the public and the media alike to request information from government. Some states have passed their own laws, called Sunshine Laws, such as Florida and Oklahoma, which are known for their strict rules to guarantee open access to records and processes for open government meetings and records.[13]

The broad freedoms that are enjoyed by the news media under the First Amendment do not always extend to other types of communication in the public sphere. Commercial speech, such as advertising, does not enjoy complete First Amendment freedom. In the U.S., advertising is regulated by a variety of federal agencies. At the national level, the Federal Trade Commission (FTC), whose purpose is to ensure fair business practices, is chief among government efforts to protect consumers from deceptive advertising. The FTC can issue cease-and-desist orders to advertisers, levy fines, and even order corrective advertising to be undertaken by a company to address the effects of untruthful or misleading messages on consumers. The Food and Drug Administration (FDA) and Federal Communications Commission (FCC) are examples of other governmental agencies that have legal authority over aspects of strategic communication practice. Regardless, the advertising industry has been criticized for the lack of consumer protection through deceptive or false advertising claims. Some states have their own laws governing advertising.[14]

In addition to federal agency oversight, national advertisers can sue each other in federal court, though doing so could be a long and expensive process. While the FTC has no authority to regulate local advertising, there are very few instances where products and services are so local that their advertising is not affected in some way by interstate commerce.

In most other countries, advertising is highly regulated. For instance, in many countries comparative advertising is not allowed by law, while it is encouraged in the U.S.

In addition to federal regulation in the United States, the advertising industry largely polices itself through an elaborate self-regulatory system that is discussed in the Industry Insight below.

Industry Insight

Advertising Self-Regulation: Truth and Accuracy

U.S. consumers are exposed to thousands of advertising messages every day, but do not necessarily know who is responsible for their truthfulness and accuracy. In the U.S., there is a certain amount of legal and government agency regulation of advertising messages, but many of the forces that shape the ads consumers are exposed to arise from self-regulation—efforts by non-government organizations and businesses themselves.

When advertising professionals and non-government organizations, rather than government commissions and legislatures, work to ensure the truth and accuracy of advertising, it is known as self-regulation. It can be as simple as an advertising agency art director correcting a visual to more accurately represent a product, a specialized attorney advising a marketing agency about regulations for medical products, or a television network previewing commercials for objectionable content. In U.S. cities, local offices of privately supported Better Business Bureaus (BBB) work to uphold fair business practices, including truthful advertising and marketing.

When national advertisers have disputes about advertising claims, they may enlist the National Advertising Division (NAD) of the BBB National Programs, which reviews the case and issues a decision. The NAD represents the primary U.S. advertising self-regulatory system concerned with the truth and accuracy of advertising claims. Another BBB national unit, the Children's Advertising Review Unit, monitors advertising to children, who are considered especially vulnerable to persuasive marketing messages, and another oversees online data privacy.

Over the years, the National Advertising Division has heard disputes regarding vacuum cleaner manufacturers about how well they suck dirt from carpet, makers of infant formula about babies' calcium absorption of their products, cosmetics companies about eyelash volume claims for mascara, and weight-loss products for their fat-burning capabilities. Decisions of the NAD can be appealed to the National Advertising Review Board (NARB), where a panel of industry and public members adjudicate a contested case. The five-person NARB panel consists of three members from advertiser companies, one advertising agency executive and one public member. Summaries of NAD and NARB decisions are announced through press releases and covered in business publications and are also available on a subscription-based database.

Decisions such as those from NAD and NARB are not legally binding, but if an advertiser fails to comply with an NARB decision, for example, the case can be referred to a federal agency such as the FTC or the Food & Drug Administration

(FDA). To read more about BBB programs, including NAD and NARB decisions, go to https://www.bbbprograms.org/media-center/decisions.

Contributed by Dr. Alice Kendrick, who is a professor in the Temerlin Advertising Institute at Southern Methodist University in Dallas, Texas and serves as a public member of the NARB.

Summary

Ethics are important at the individual and societal level. Understanding right from wrong not only guides the way we live and how we conduct our relationships, having a strong moral compass guides our professional dealings as well. The practice of strategic communication can have a powerful influence on the general public and impact on society—both positive and negative. Therefore, it is important to understand the potential ethical dilemmas that may arise in the workplace and be able to apply your own and the industry's professional code of ethics to morally questionable situations. Recognizing the mandate that strategic communication be socially responsible, strategic communicators should work to mitigate its harmful effects. Finally, as strategic communication practitioners, you must be familiar with the laws, regulations and self-regulatory mechanisms that govern the practice in order to serve the public and profession.

Discussion Questions

1 Develop your own code of ethics. Start by writing down ten things you value and how you want to act in your everyday life. Then share your code with your classmates and discuss differences you have in your code.

2 Why do you think that the public views advertising executives and PR practitioners as unethical? What would you do to change strategic communication's image problem?

3 This chapter lists three broad areas of societal issues that are considered problematic for strategic communication, including offensive messages, stereotypical portrayals and advertising to children. Can you think of other ways that strategic communication potentially has negative effects on society? What can the industry do to change these harmful activities?

4 Develop a Corporate Social Responsibility campaign for a company that you work for or have worked for in the past. Explain how your CSR plan will benefit the reputation of the organization.

5 Review the ethical dilemmas in the chapter opener. How would you behave if you were put in those situations? Would you feel pressure to act unethically to make your agency more profitable or because it is the socially acceptable thing to do? Why or why not?

Check out the online support material, including chapter summaries, useful links and further reading, at www.routledge.com/9780367426316.

Notes

1   Fullerton, J., McKinnon, L., & Kendrick, A. (2014, Fall). A comparison of advertising and public relations students on ethics: Attitudes and predicted behavior. *Southwestern Mass Communications Journal*, *30*(2).

2   Reinhart, R. J. (2020, January 6). Nurses continue to rate highest in honesty, ethics. *Gallup.* Retrieved from https://news.gallup.com/poll/274673/nurses-continue-rate-highest-honesty-ethics.aspx.

3   Retrieved from Public Relations Society of America website at: https://www.prsa.org/about/ethics/prsa-code-of-ethics.

4   Retrieved from the American Advertising Federation's web site at http://www.aaf.org/_pdf/aaf%20website%20content/513_ethics/iae_principles_practices.pdf.

5   United Nations Industrial Development Organization. What is CSR? Retrieved from https://www.unido.org/our-focus/advancing-economic-competitiveness/competitive-trade-capacities-and-corporate-responsibility/corporate-social-responsibility-market-integration/what-csr.

6   Powers, W. (2001). Brand of the Free. *National Journal*, *33*, 46–47.

7   Severin, W. J., & Tankard, J. W. (2001) *Communication Theories, Origins, Methods and Uses in Mass Media* (5th ed.). New York: Longman.

8   Jowett, G., & O'Donnell, V. (1999). *Propaganda and Persuasion* (3rd ed.). Thousand Oaks, CA: Sage Publications.

9   Van Hoven, M. (2009, Aug. 24). Peta backs down to pressure, replaces "blubber" billboard. *Adweek.* Retreived from: https://www.adweek.com/agencyspy/peta-backs-down-to-pressure-replaces-blubber-billboard/5152/.

10 https://www.huffpost.com/entry/petas-new-save-the-whales_n_261134.

11 Dominick, J. R., & Rausch, G. E., (1972). The image of women in network TV commercials. *Journal of Broadcasting*, *16*, (Summer), 259–265.

12 Kesslen, B. (2020, June 17). Aunt Jemima brand to change name, remove image, that Quaker Oats says is "based on a racial stereotype." *NBC News.* Retrieved from https://www.nbcnews.com/news/us-news/aunt-jemima-brand-will-change-name-remove-image-quaker-says-n1231260.

13 https://ballotpedia.org/Florida_Sunshine_Law, last accessed on March 25, 2019.

14 Pember, D. R., & Calvert, C. (2008). *Mass Media Law*. Boston, MA: McGraw-Hill.

Chapter 6

Research

Learning Outcomes

After you have read the chapter, you should be able to do the following:

- Understand the importance of research to strategic communication.
- Explain the acronym ROPE and how to implement it.
- Describe the steps in the strategic communication research process.
- Understand the difference between primary and secondary research and the methods used for both.
- Become familiar with the basic ethical principles of research.

Chapter Opening Vignette

Focus Groups: A Versatile Tool for Strategic Communicators

One popular option in the strategic communicator's information-gathering toolbox is the focus group. The name reflects the involvement of multiple participants who together discuss specific topics, products, brands or ideas. Focus groups are an example of qualitative research.

A focus group consists of around eight to ten carefully selected members of the targeted stakeholder group and is led by a moderator, who works through a discussion guide that has been approved by the research sponsor or client. The focus group discussion usually lasts about two hours. During that time the moderator leads the group through a conversation about their lifestyles, motivations, habits, opinions or attitudes regarding a specific topic. Topics that strategic communicators' might be interested in hearing stakeholders talk about include new products and brands, advertising campaigns, public policies or fundraising ideas, among others. The moderator can also guide focus group members through several activities such as word-association, storytelling, role-playing and creation of brand or concept collages to explore the participants' opinions about the topic.

If budget permits, one of the best ways to plan focus groups is with the assistance of a company that specializes in recruiting participants and then hosting the groups at facilities that allow video and audio taping as well as a mirrored wall that allows for real-time, anonymous viewing by the research sponsors. These research companies can also recommend a moderator if the agency or client does not have one. Most focus group facilities have kitchens that can facilitate preparing and organizing food samples for taste tests, just another aspect of their versatility.

Focus groups can be helpful at several stages of the strategic communication process. They are particularly useful at the outset of a project to identify what consumers see as key issues with or perceptions of brands and companies, as well as what their product category experiences have been like. They also are helpful in learning the consumer language around a product or category, which often is not the same terminology used by marketers or advertisers (for instance, a consumer may consider a bank checking account a "service," while the bank refers to it as a "product"). Focus groups are not useful in estimating total size of market, size of audience, sales projections or other types of information that require sample surveys to arrive at quantitative findings.

Focus groups also act to obtain stakeholder feedback regarding message concepts, appeals, rough drafts of communication materials or even finished content. Imagine the time and money saved if a potential advertising headline is found to cause confusion among consumers. If the focus group participants represent the target group a company is trying to reach, their initial reactions to even rough ideas or strategic directions can be quite valuable. Ultimately, communication success does not depend on the intent of the communicator, but how the recipient of the message evaluates and reacts to it. Focus groups are one way to obtain stakeholder reaction.

Dr. Alice Kendrick is a Professor in the Temerlin Advertising Institute at Southern Methodist University in Dallas, TX.

The First Step in Strategic Communication

The first step in the strategic communication process is research. It is through research that strategic communicators—whether they are working in advertising agencies, PR firms, political campaigns or non-profits—gain information and knowledge to help them make good decisions, prevent them from wasting money and achieve better outcomes. Research is vital to communication planning, and every aspect of the plan should be grounded in good research.

Research should be conducted before, during and after a communications campaign. Research will not only help determine the strategies and tactics during the planning phase of the campaign, but will also be used to monitor how the campaign is working while the campaign is running. After a campaign has ended, evaluating the results against objectives is another important use of research and allows communicators to improve planning for the next campaign. This is discussed thoroughly in Chapter 13.

Why Do We Need Strategic Communication Research?

Organizations—whether for-profit, non-profit or governmental—must spend their resources wisely. Research helps avoid mistakes and unnecessary expenditures. Time and money are very valuable to organizations; therefore, organizational leaders strive to be efficient in the way they do business. Research can help improve efficiency by discovering which approaches and ideas are best for the organization.

Research is a very important competitive tool in modern business. Organizations that do not conduct research about their products, markets and stakeholders are bound to fail eventually. Because of new technology and big data, companies have more information at their fingertips than ever before; understanding and applying this information puts companies ahead of their competitors. Overall, research helps an organization build and grow their business, achieve their goals and be more productive.

Strategic communicators conduct research for many reasons:

- *Research helps organizations learn about what their stakeholders (such as their consumer) wants in terms of products and services.* Understanding the customer's wants and needs is critical to the success of most businesses. As technology has developed, our method of determining these wants and needs has changed. For example, when the NFL's television ratings declined in 2016, the NFL management decided rather than simply trying to guess why their fans were turned-off by America's favorite sport, they would conduct systematic research to determine why. They contacted MediaScience, a research firm that examines the biometric responses of individuals to various media. NFL fans were invited into specially designed living rooms and asked to watch a game. As they were watching, MediaScience tracked their eye motion, heart rate and other biometric responses to determine what people enjoyed the most. By analyzing these data, the NFL was able to determine which features of their programs' viewers preferred and what wasn't viewed favorably.[1]
- *Research is an important tool when an organization is stuck and cannot decide which tactics to execute.* Should we launch a new television ad campaign or partner with a local charity to improve our company's image? Is package A or package B more likely to result in higher sales of a new laundry detergent? By conducting research,

organizations can test alternatives and, in some cases, uncover pathways that might not have been previously considered.

A/B Testing, sometimes known as split testing, is a hallmark of research within the communications industry. A/B testing is a type of experiment where the researcher randomly exposes two groups of stakeholders to two different versions of a communication piece, such as a website, a video or a slogan, and measures which one performs better. In A/B testing, one group sees the "A" version and the other group sees the "B" version. Preference measurements, such as "on a scale of 1–10 with one being very unfavorable and 10 being very favorable, how favorable are you toward this message?" are then taken among members of each group and their responses are averaged to get a preference score. By comparing the scores, the researcher can tell which version is preferable. In A/B testing, it is important that the individual stakeholders are assigned at random to one of the two versions in order to avoid bias that may come from the nature of the group. For example, if only men see version A and only women see version B, the researcher will not know if any differences that are found are because of the communication piece or because of some other difference that is inherent between men and women.

One organization that emphasizes the importance of A/B testing is Facebook. Imagine you are a small business that sells an innovative charcoal facial mask to young women, and you don't have a big budget. By using A/B testing, you have the option to set up two nearly identical ads for the facial mask on Facebook, with one minor difference between them, such as the image or headline. It will be easy to determine the most effective way to communicate with your target audience by measuring which ad gets more click-throughs. Picture this: Ad A has a video clip of a woman peeling off the facial mask easily and without issue, revealing supple, beautiful skin. Ad B has a video clip of a woman peeling off the same mask, the same way, but hilariously screaming as she does it. This type of A/B split testing allows advertisers to compare the effectiveness of the two ad executions with a real audience in a live media setting. Digital media platforms, such as Google and Facebook, can provide precise data measuring the effectiveness of these ads by capturing more than 140 metrics such as online impressions, website traffic, and click-through rates, (for more information on these online media metrics, see Chapter 11 "Evolving Media"). Your company may discover that although the video of the mask being easily removed portrays the product better, the hilarious video leads to more clicks to your website and ultimately more sales.

Research can prevent mistakes and save the company money. Field-testing a new product in one market before it is launched across the country or the globe is an example of using research to save time and money. The old marketing adage is that "if it plays is Peoria, it will play anywhere." For years, marketers have been using test markets to determine if a product will be a success or failure. Cities like Peoria (IL), Albany (NY), Tulsa (OK), Nashville (TN), Birmingham (AL), Greensboro (NC) and Wichita (KS) have been used by marketers to test the newest and greatest product ideas. These cities are chosen as test markets because they have characteristics that are demographically representative of America's general population, are generally isolated from larger media markets, and are small enough to be relatively affordable. Do you remember Wow! Chips, Cheetos Lip Balm, Satisfries from Burger King or Life Savers Soda? Probably not. The reason? The companies behind these brilliant products didn't utilize test marketing effectively. By not understanding what the markets wanted, the companies that launched these products took major financial hits. If they had used test markets, focus groups, in-home usage tests (iHUTs), and field studies, they may have learned their product ideas were going to fail. It's better to lose $50,000 in Albany than suffer a $50,000,000 loss nationally.

Ways of Knowing

We conduct research so that we can know about things in our world. There are many ways of knowing. You can rely on your own experience or the experience of others.

The best way of knowing, however, is through science. The scientific method of knowing uses systematic observation. In the same way we use our senses to systematically collect data in the world around us, scientists systematically collect data to understand the world. Through this collection and analysis, we confirm or reject beliefs, develop theories to explain how things work and understand the world better. Through scientific research we can achieve many goals including prediction, explanation, understanding and control.

Hypotheses and Theories

A hypothesis is a specific prediction about what will happen in a scientific experiment. Hypotheses are often called educated guesses. They are a hunch, guess or prediction about what will happen based on some previous knowledge (that's why they are *educated* guesses) and are the starting point for scientific research.

This previous knowledge is often based on a **theory**, a complex system of ideas that is intended to explain something. Theories are very useful because they can make broad predictions about how things in the world will behave. Theories are not just random opinions. It takes lots of science, hypothesizing, experimenting, confirming and rejecting before an idea rises to the level of a scientific theory. By using theory, we can predict, explain and understand the world around us.

The basic theories of strategic communication help us understand the best ways to communicate with our intended stakeholders and convince them to believe and behave in certain ways. For example, the theory of persuasion and its many sub-theories are the result of social scientists making hypotheses, collecting data with human subjects and then analyzing the data so that they could confirm or reject the hypothesis.

Academic Angle

Agenda-Setting Theory of the Press: The First Academic Theory of the News Media

The agenda-setting theory of the press states that there is a close relationship between the way the news media present issues and the order of importance assigned to those issues by those exposed to the news.

Bernard Cohen wrote in 1963: "The press is significantly more than a purveyor of information and opinion. It may not be successful much of the time in telling people what to think, but it is stunningly successful in telling its readers what to think about." This was an interesting notion, but was there proof that his statement was correct? Did the media really influence what the public thinks about?

Inspired by Cohen's writing, two journalism professors at the University of North Carolina—Maxwell McCombs and Donald Shaw—decided to conduct research to see if and how much the newspaper affected the public's thinking about issues in the country. They first tested the relationship in an empirical study in Chapel Hill, NC during the 1968 presidential election. The study examined the correlation between news content and responses people made to the question, "What are the major problems in the country?" The relationship was high. There was almost a 97% overlap between what the people mentioned as major problems and the articles in the newspaper.

However, after the Chapel Hill study, the question remained, which direction was the effect? Was it a cause-effect relationship? Did the media set the public's agenda or did the public set the media's agenda? To answer these questions McCombs and Shaw conducted another, larger study—this time in Charlotte, NC. The Charlotte study focused on the 1972 presidential campaign. In Charlotte, a randomly selected group of voters was interviewed in June and November of 1972 about what they thought were the most important issues in the country. The researchers also examined the content of the newspaper during this same period. According to their findings, the newspaper's "agenda" in June correlated with the voters' "agenda" in October to a much higher degree than the voters' agenda in June correlated with the newspaper agenda in October. This showed a cause–effect relationship and confirmed the researchers' hypothesis that, indeed, the newspaper set the agenda for the public.

McCombs and Shaw wrote,

> In choosing and displaying news, editors, newsroom staff and broadcasters play an important part in shaping political reality. Readers learn not only about a given issue, but how much importance to attach to that issue from the amount of information in a news story and its position. In reflecting what candidates are saying during a campaign, the mass media may well determine the important issues—that is, the media may set the **agenda** of the campaign.[2]

According to agenda-setting theory, the press makes people aware and knowledgeable about a variety of issues. It may not change their attitudes and behavior, however. But it still has an effect. It tells the public what to think about.

Agenda-setting theory was the first research area that was done purely by communication scholars. Prior to this time, psychologists and sociologists dominated the field of communication and media research. But, by the 1970s, Schools of Journalism and Mass Communications had trained their own PhDs, most of whom were former journalists and they brought their experiences from the newsroom to their academic work. Agenda-setting theory deals with the stuff that journalists know about—the press, editorial decision-making, politics, voter issues and the power of the media.

Scientific research grounded in agenda-setting theory continues to inform everyday practice by helping strategic communication practitioners understand how to effectively work with the media and shape opinions among targeted stakeholders.

Quantitative and Qualitative Research

In the social sciences, such as strategic communication, the data collection can be categorized as quantitative or qualitative, depending on how it is gathered. **Quantitative research** involves collecting data using numbers, such as sales figures, likability scales or number of click-throughs on a website. **Qualitative research** involves collecting data that uses words, such as a conversation, a written text or an interview.

Quantitative research can be more precise in terms of measurement and prediction. Since it relies on numbers, data collected using a quantitative method can be generalized to large populations using statistics. What is found in a small sample of a population, if the sample is selected at random, can be assumed about the entire population based on the laws of statistics. The Chapel Hill and Charlotte, NC studies mentioned above are examples of quantitative research.

Qualitative research does not use numbers or statistics but relies on the researcher to interpret systematically what the words mean, such as with the focus group example in the beginning of this chapter. Qualitative research seeks to know about the motivations, opinions and underlying reasons of a problem or behavior. It is helpful to understand the motivations of consumers. Qualitative research is often used when a problem is new and exploratory research is needed before it can be precisely measured using quantitative data.

Role of Statistics

Statistics are mathematical methods to collect, organize, summarize and analyze data. Statistics provide valid and reliable results only when the data collection and research method follow established scientific procedures. In other words, if your research is not set up properly, using statistics to analyze the data that you collect will not reveal the truth about the phenomenon under study.

Assuming the data collection is done properly, statistics can be very helpful to summarize research findings. Statistics help us to reduce lots of data into a format that makes it easy to interpret. A stack of paper surveys is hard to interpret by simply looking at them one-by-one. It is not until the responses are entered into a spreadsheet, tabulated, and analyzed using statistical methods (like averages, percentages and frequencies) that we can understand the results of the survey. Sometimes graphs are used to illustrate the statistics from the data. Statistics help us turn raw data into helpful information. Otherwise, data are just a bunch of numbers that have been collected, with no rhyme or reason to them. Statistics reveal the story in the data.

Applied vs. Basic Research

Basic research is the research done by scientists at universities or other laboratories. Its purpose is to build on a great body of knowledge, test theories and move our collective understanding forward. It lays the foundation for applied research.

Applied research seeks to answer specific questions about specific problems in the real world. The type of research that is used in strategic communication practice, and the type of research we will discuss in this chapter, is applied research. Strategic communication managers are looking for specific questions to real problems they face in the workplace and use applied research to find the answers and guide their decision-making.

The Strategic Communication Research Process

Strategic communication research is a tool to help communicators achieve overall organizational objectives. It allows organizations to see the bigger picture, answer questions and achieve their objectives. Therefore, research is the first step in the communications campaign planning process. Strategic communication strategies and tactics must be grounded in good research or risk being ineffective and wasteful. Strategic communication research is not only conducted prior to launching a communications campaign, but also should be done during and after the campaign, so that strategies can be adjusted, and researchers can determine if the campaign's strategies and tactics achieved the goals of the campaign.

Strategic communication research attempts to gain knowledge and find answers to questions that arise in the practice of strategic communication. Who is the target consumer for this product? Which media are best for reaching my audience? What should Twitter messages about our candidate say in order to win more votes? Research is the key to answering all these questions.

ROPE Process

In the field of strategic communication, some practitioners often use the ROPE model as a framework to guide their communications campaign planning. ROPE is an acronym that stands for Research, Objectives, Programming and Evaluation.

Strategic communicators can follow these sequential four steps to help them organize and implement effective campaigns.

- Research—this important first step involves learning about the client, the problem or potential problem to be solved and identifying the stakeholder groups.
- Objectives—this step requires carefully writing the goals and desired outcomes of the campaign. It is crucial to consider what is learned in the research phase when setting objectives. Unless objectives are stated up front there is no way to know if the campaign worked or not.
- Programming—this step is the heart of the campaign where actual implementation of the communication takes place. The message themes, paid media placement, special events and other tools are executed in the phase. Effective programming should focus on the stated objectives and be informed by the initial research. The Programming phase is sometimes called the Communication phase, in which case the acronym becomes RACE.
- Evaluation—in this final step, additional research is conducted which measures the outcome of the programming against the objectives to determine the effectiveness of the campaign.

How to conduct research, setting objectives, developing programming and evaluating outcomes are covered in detail in other sections of this book. This chapter on research is important because research is conducted in the first *and last step* in the ROPE process.

Professional Profile

Jacob Perez, Strategist

Jacob Perez—Strategist at McGarryBowen Advertising Agency.

Jacob Perez currently works at a major advertising agency, McGarryBowen, and is leading their strategy and innovation function for the consumer business of the agency's client American Express. Before joining McGarryBowen, Jacob led strategy for Johnson & Johnson, Ancestry, and Raising Canes at J. Walter Thompson. Jacob was also a Strategy Director at other large advertising agencies including Havas, Young & Rubicam, Saatchi & Saatchi NY, and Translation, working on a wide range of brands including McDonald's, Sprite, Bud Light, Mastercard, Johnnie Walker, Kettle One, Heineken, Nissan, KY, Lysol, and General Mills. Jacob began his planning career at The Vidal Partnership, one of the most respected multi-cultural agencies working on everything from retail to spirits to fast food.

Jacob is the model modern strategist—a digital native, and provocative thinker, who approaches strategy as an equal blend of business solutions, anthropological understanding, and creativity

> **What did you want to do with your career?** I actually didn't have a plan. It's been a journey of trials and errors, and it continues to evolve.

Are you doing it? I continue to go with the flow. I like to think that I'm on V.3 of my career.

What are you doing now? I'm leading strategy and innovation for the consumer business of American Express.

How did you get there? It's been a constant game of zig and zag. I've always been torn between creativity and having a more traditional business mind. When I was younger, the two felt like different ends of the spectrum. The business world has a funny way of categorizing people, and I just didn't feel like any of the labels I was given applied. I started in marketing client-side, but quickly realized I was a small part of a big machine. I jumped to the agency side in account management. The environment was better, but the role still felt limited. And then I got lucky and met one of the greatest creative minds in the ad industry, Mike Tesch. He told me I was a natural strategist and so I got into the Miami Ad School. Strategy felt right, and it was my home for a while. But the world keeps changing, AI and programmatic are playing a significant role in how brands go to market, so I felt the need to once more evolve. This time moving more upstream. So, I studied Design Thinking at MIT and later AI with an eye into its business applications. That's where I find myself today, designing products, experiences and strategies for one of the most customer-centric brands in the world, Amex. I'm curious to see what career V.4 looks like.

How have your dreams changed? I never had a big dream like most people do. I've had many aspirations along the way, mostly related to whatever stage of my life I find myself in. In that sense, I suppose it's fair to say my dreams are ever changing. For instance, I wanted to lead strategy for a Top 20 brand, and that happened. I want to see one of my product ideas be successful in the market, and I'm getting close to marking that off the list. Eventually, I want to write a book.

What has surprised you most about yourself or your career? The most surprising thing for me was the value of having meaningful mentors. I used to hear it all the time, and it sounded like a bit of cliché. I had people advise me along the way, and while useful, it wasn't transformative. That is until I found a couple of people who truly cared and took the time to know me. Thinking through ideas, decisions, aspirations with someone who knows you, understands the industry you are in and has life experience is invaluable. As one of them says, "you don't know what you don't know."

What advice would you give to someone in college now? Maintain a generalist mindset. Learn about everything and anything because you never know where your career path is going to go. I've met doctors who turned into lawyers. Engineers who turned into artists. Writers who became strategists. What you think you are good at today, what you think you want to do with your life is more than likely going to change over time.

More information about Jacob Perez can be found here: www.linkedin.com/in/perezjacob.

Steps in the Strategic Communication Research Process

There are ten basic steps in the research process. These steps can apply to all types of research, but we are going to talk about each one in terms of strategic communication research.

1   Determine the objectives of the research.
2   Select a problem.
3   Review existing information.
4   Develop a hypothesis or research question.
5   Determine an appropriate method/research design.
6   Collect relevant data.
7   Analyze the data.
8   Interpret the results.
9   Present the results in an appropriate form.
10 Take action to solve the problem.

Now, let's break down each of these steps and expand on the processes needed for each one.

1. Determine the Objectives of the Research

Before an organization begins a research project, they need to determine the objectives of the research. What does the organization want the research to achieve? Research usually starts with a question from someone in the organization, such as "I wonder how our social media is working?" or "What do our stakeholders think about our brand?" or "Are the mayor's policies making him more popular with citizens?" Other times the objective may be that a problem needs to be solved, such as "how do we improve our company's image?" Once identified, then research can be developed to solve the problem or answer the question.

Some questions are easy to answer. Executives in an organization often have good intuition about what should be done for the easy questions. However, it is not uncommon to conduct research just to confirm what the organization already knows instinctively. Sometimes, the questions and problems are too complex and/or important to rely only on intuition and they require systematic research. Since research requires time and money to conduct, launching a research project should not be taken lightly or attempted for questions that are unimportant or not well defined.

Before a research project begins, planning must be done and decisions must be made, including who will conduct the research? When do we need the results? What is the budget? And how certain must we be about the findings?

With any research project there are constraints. These constraints usually involve time, money and ambiguity. When you begin a research project, you need to decide how much time is available to get the results and how much money can be spent on it. Finally, you need to determine how much ambiguity or uncertainty about the findings can be tolerated. These three variables—time, cost and ambiguity—are trade-offs. For example, if the research needs to be done quickly, then it will require more money to get the data gathered. It may mean that you will need to hire more researchers to complete the data collection more quickly. If the budget doesn't allow for hiring additional researchers or paying overtime, then they will not be able to collect as much data. Gathering more data always provides clearer and more reliable findings, so when there are less data, the findings may be ambiguous. On the other hand, if you have a large budget and adequate time, you can design a well-thought-out research study in order to gather ample data that result in less ambiguous findings and clearer answers to the research problem.

2. Select a Problem

To conduct a research study, you need to narrow down the overall objectives to a specific problem or problems. Take the example of what people think about a particular brand. Do you want to know what current customers think or what non-users think about the brand? Do want to know consumers' attitudes (like/dislike) toward the brand in general, or are you just curious to see if they perceive the brand as too expensive? Do you want to know what they think about the brand relative to competitors? If so, which competitors and on what factors?

Maybe the real problem is that consumers don't know about the brand at all. If this is the case, then the research problem might be, "what is the level of awareness among consumers for our brand?" Usually a single research project can only handle one or two specific research questions at a time. It is important to clarify with the organization exactly what they want to know. Exploring all the aspects of the question and selecting one or two problems to answer will produce better and more usable research results for the organization.

Here are some popular questions for strategic communication research:

- Who are the stakeholders for my communication?
- Which media are best for reaching this audience?
- How much money should be spent to reach this audience most efficiently?
- Which messages should be used most effectively?

3. Review Existing Information

Sometimes the answers to problems and questions are already available in existing information and there is no need to gather new data. **Secondary research**—the summary, collation and/or synthesis of existing data—is often faster and less expensive to obtain. Secondary research may provide larger and more reliable data sets than could be easily obtained with a primary research. However, secondary research does not always provide the specific information to answer your problem. In some cases, the secondary sources may contradict each other. The details about how the original research was conducted may not be available, which makes it difficult to know if the findings are reliable or not.

A good researcher should always start any research project by finding out more about the problem or issue from already existing sources. That's right … secondary research is done first! These sources may be internal or external to the organization. The company's proprietary information such as sales reports and/or findings from previously conducted studies are valuable examples of internal secondary research (see Figure 6.1). External sources such as articles in trade magazines or on government databases can also be helpful to answering research problems. Understanding how to thoroughly search electronic secondary sources is an important skill. The section "Tips for Searching Secondary Sources" provides tips on how to do this effectively.

TYPE OF RESEARCH	WHAT IS IT?	PROS	CONS	SOURCES
SYNDICATED RESEARCH	Large-scale studies conducted by outside, commercial research firms and sold to multiple clients who need information.	Large ongoing study.	Not specific to one client's needs. Expensive.	Nielsen Arbitron MRI Simmons Gallup
TRADE AND POPULAR PRESS	Report national studies that often contain information about the communication industry, including salary surveys, listings of agencies, and annual information on media spending.	Easily available based on large, national samples.	Not always specific to your client's needs. Very broad in scope.	Advertising Age Adweek PR Newswire Industry specific publications such as Nation's Restaurant News Wall Street Journal New York Times
ACADEMIC JOURNALS	Publish academic research about strategic communication topics.	Helpful for gathering broad, theoretical information.	Often difficult to understand and interpret. May not relate to the "real world" problems of the client.	Journal of Advertising PR Research Journal International Journal of Strategic Communications
ASSOCIATIONS	Release studies relevant to the industry sector they're associated with.	Provide highly relevant data to their members.	Narrow to one industry. Sometimes the research is influenced by the association's personal agenda.	American Advertising Federation Public Relations Society of America Television Advertising Bureau
GOVERNMENT	Excellent source of secondary data on demographics, etc.	Free and available from databases on the web.	Information is very general.	U.S. Census Department of Labor Federal Trade Commission

Figure 6.1 Types of Secondary Research

ONLINE METRICS	Provide information about web site visits, social media sentiment, and click rates.	Free/Flat Rate, depending on source.	Need some training to interpret data and understand how the variables are measured.	Google Metrics HootSuite
EXISTING CLIENT DATA	Most companies conduct their own research studies.	Can save time collecting new data. Data are highly relevant to their products, employees, and sales trends.	May be out-of-date, incomplete or poorly collected. Information about the method and procedure for collecting the data is not always available.	Sales Data Previously commissioned research studies Employee records

Figure 6.1 (Continued)

Tips for Searching Secondary Sources

- Search by keywords
  - Think of all keywords.
  - Write down keywords and search systematically.
  - Combine keywords to narrow results. Utilize Boolean search tools "AND" "OR" and "NOT" (use caplock) to refine your search.
- Consult keyword lists of relevant articles.
- Scan abstracts for important information.
- Print or save articles that appear relevant.
- Notice dates—old information most often isn't relevant.
- Learn to navigate databases and spreadsheets for raw data.
- Make notes of sources for proper citation.
- Compare studies and findings and look for inconsistencies.

Reading Syndicated Cross-tabbed Data

MRI-Simmons and other marketing research firms conduct on-going consumer research among national random samples of consumers and report their findings on a regular basis to their clients. Often the data are reported in cross-tabbed format like the one in Figure 6.2.

Fall 2009 Product Electronics

Cellular/Mobile Phones/Pdas - Handset Brands
Apple iPhone
Base: Adults

		1 Total '000	2 Proj '000	3 Pct Across	4 Pct Down	5 Index
Stub						
Total		225,887	7,118	3.2	100.0	100
Educ: graduated college plus		60,806	2,903	4.8	40.8	152
Educ: attended college		63,023	2,350	3.7	33.0	118
Educ: graduated high school		69,801	1,246	1.6	17.5	57
Educ: did not graduate HS	*	32,257	619	1.9	8.5	61
Educ: post graduate		20,290	879	4.3	12.3	137
Educ: no college		102,058	1,864	1.8	26.2	58
Age 18–24		28,537	1,509	5.3	21.2	168
Age 25–34		40,349	2,157	5.3	30.3	170
Age 35–44		42,375	1,810	4.3	25.4	136
Age 45–54		44,155	1,010	2.3	14.2	73
Age 55–64		33,466	470	1.4	6.6	45
Age 65+	*	37,006	162	0.4	2.3	14
Adults 18–34		68,885	3,666	5.3	51.5	169
Adults 18–49		134,084	5,941	4.4	83.5	141
Adults 25–54		126,879	4,977	3.9	69.9	124
Men 18–34		34,689	1,932	5.6	27.1	177
Men 18–49		66,843	3,314	5.0	46.6	157
Men 25–54		62,815	2,757	4.4	38.7	139
Women 18–34		34,196	1,734	5.1	24.4	161
Women 18–49		67,241	2,627	3.9	36.9	124
Women 25–54		64,064	2,220	3.5	31.2	110

Figure 6.2 **Example of a Cross-tabbed Data Report**

To help you understand how to read and interpret the data the following key is helpful.

Column 1—Total '000 (Base Count): At the time of the Fall 2009 survey there were 60,806,000 people in the U.S. with at least a college degree.

Column 2—Projected '000 (Projected Count): Projected out to the entire population of this group, 2,903,000 of those with at least a college degree have an iPhone.

Column 3—Percent Across: Of those who have graduated college or more, 4.8% have an iPhone. Alternatively, if you picked a random person out of everyone who has at least a college degree, there's a 4.8% chance they'll have an iPhone.

Column 4—Percent Down: Out of people who have an iPhone, 40.8% have at least a college degree. OR, if you picked a random person with an iPhone, there's a 40.8% chance they'll have at least a college degree.

Column 5—Index: How likely is the group on the left to have used the product/service/etc. compared to average? 100 is average, so looking at the second line, those who've graduated college are 52% more likely to have an iPhone.

Unfortunately, sometimes the exact information to answer your organization's specific question may not be available via a secondary source. If this is the case, you will need to conduct a primary research study.

4. Develop a Hypothesis or Research Question

In the first three steps of the research process, many questions may arise as offshoots of the initial research objective. Some questions might be answered with secondary research, but others are so specific to the organization and its environment that you will need to collect primary data. If multiple new questions arose during the first three steps of the research process, you will need to identify which question will be tackled first.

At this point, the researcher must develop a research question or hypothesis. This is sometimes the most difficult part of the research process because hypotheses (a statement about how two variables might interact) or a research question (a specific question about specific variables) are difficult to formulate, especially if you do not fully understand the topic under study.

The more specific the research question is, the more helpful the findings of your research study will be. Let's go back to the example of understanding how people feel about a brand (research objective). In order to achieve this objective, researchers identified a key question—what is the level of brand awareness? To study this problem, we must formulate a specific research question using specific variables that have specific definitions, such as "What is the level of awareness for Brand X among adult consumers (18 years and older)?" The research question could be even more specific because awareness can be measured several ways. Unaided awareness is usually measured by asking consumers to name brands in a category that they can think of without any prompting. If your brand is mentioned without prompting, that is an indication of high levels of brand awareness. Similarly, aided awareness involves prompting, such as asking research participants if they've ever heard of Brand X. A hypothesis for this problem might be: Unaided awareness for Brand X will be found among 50% of U.S. adults.

Ways to Measure Common Variables in Strategic Communication Research

Awareness

Unaided

Please list the restaurants you have heard about in the past month.

_____

_____

_____

Aided

Which of the following restaurants have you heard about in the past month?

❑ McDonald's

❑ Burger King

❑ Wendy's

❑ Other _____

Knowledge

Jennifer Garner is spokesperson for which brand of credit card?

❑ Chase Freedom Unlimited

❑ Discover

❑ Capital One

❑ Platinum Rewards Visa

Conviction

In the next 30 days, which of the following items do you plan to purchase at least once?

❑ Coffee

❑ Cola

❑ Fruit Juice

❑ Milk

Attitude/opinion

Please place a check in the space that describes how likely you are to recycle.

Very Likely ___ ___ ___ ___ ___ Not Likely

Brand image

Place a check in the appropriate space for each characteristic you believe each of the following brands of cranberry juice possess.

	HEALTHY	TASTY	GOOD VALUE
OCEAN SPRAY	_____	_____	_____
MINUTE MAID	_____	_____	_____
TROPICANA	_____	_____	_____

Figure 6.3 **Brand Image**

5. Determine an Appropriate Methodology/Research Design

A research plan involves selecting a design and a method for the study. The design describes the type of study, and the method refers to how the data will be collected. Some research studies are descriptive—their objective is to describe the state or condition of a phenomenon. Correlational studies attempt to determine the relationship between variables, while causal studies seek to identify the precise cause of certain effects. The research objectives should guide the type of research study selected. Additionally, there are several research designs to choose from depending on the objectives of the study:

- **One-shot** designs are used for simple descriptive studies to provide a snapshot of a particular situation at a particular point in time. Such as an analysis of social media posts about your brand the day after you launch a new promotional campaign.
- **Longitudinal designs** are made up of a series of individual one-shot studies done the same way over time to measure change or trends. Longitudinal studies can be predictive of the future.
- **Pre/post tests** measure effects before and after a particular action. Advertisers often measure product awareness before a campaign and compare it to awareness levels for the product after the campaign finishes to see if there is an impact from the messaging.
- **Laboratory experiments** measure cause and effect in a controlled laboratory setting. The ability to control variables not under study is an advantage of a laboratory experiment, while the artificial environment of the lab can be a negative because research subjects may not behave normally in the artificial environment. For example, a political research firm may bring a sample of voters to a laboratory setting to view a video message about various candidates. The researchers will measure the voters' attitudes toward the candidates before and after viewing the commercial to determine if and how the messaging influences the favorability of the candidates among voters.
- **Field experiments** are often used in marketing communications research because they measure cause and effect in real situations. You might use a field experiment, for example, to measure the effects of an outdoor billboard for a local McDonald's on store sales.

RESEARCH METHOD	WHAT IS IT?
FOCUS GROUPS	• A specialized type of interview. • Bringing together a group of people (6–10) to talk naturally about some topic or group of topics. • Usually about 2 hour in length. • Moderator leads the discussion using a moderator's guide. • Moderator's guide or outline is derived from research questions and developed by the research team. • Typically recorded by video or audio for later analysis. • Often held in a room with two-way mirror so researcher can observe participants and take notes.
IN-DEPTH INTERVIEW	• Personal interviews between one person and the researcher. • May be face-to-face, on the phone, or over the Internet. • Beliefs, values, opinions.
ETHNOGRAPHY	• Anthropologists and sociologists use ethnography to study cultures by immersing themselves in the culture and observing its behavior and ritual. • For advertising and PR research, ethnographies may be about a brand or consumer behavior. • Observing how consumers use a brand, shop, or talk about brands is a form of ethnography. • The researcher is an observer and should remain impartial and be careful not to influence the behavior under study.
OBSERVATION	• Researcher observes ongoing behavior. • Studies behavior that happens naturally in natural settings. • Can be descriptive or correlational, but does not allow for causal explanations.
SURVEY	• Usually involves a single, cross-sectional study that generates a snapshot in time. • Ideally, it involves a random sample of a relatively large population, usually at least 100. • Using a questionnaire, subjects are asked the same questions in the same order. • The data come from self-reports. • Uncovers attitudes and opinions of large populations that are too large to observe directly.
EXPERIMENTS	• Limited and well-defined concepts. • Hypothesis testing. • The only type of research that can test cause-and-effect relationships. • The most demanding and most productive type of research. • Allow for prediction.
CONTENT ANALYSIS	• Describe what the typical viewer/reader sees over time in the media. • Quantitative Method employs counting of images, actions, words, portrayals, etc. • Descriptive only. • Cannot establish cause/effect, attitudes or social impact.

Figure 6.4 Common Research Methods for Strategic Communication

The research method is the foundation of the study. There are many research methods available. Choosing the appropriate method depends on the objectives of the research—what are you trying to learn from the research. For example, if you are interested in how consumers behave when shopping, observational method would be useful. In-store cameras can record consumer behavior, and researchers can analyze the video to make determinations about shopping patterns. If you want to understand the opinions and attitudes of large populations, survey method is most appropriate. However, to gain insight as to why people hold certain opinions and how it affects them, you might need to conduct a focus group or in-depth interview.

To gather data from humans, you will need to determine who the research participants will be. In survey research, the participants are called **respondents**. In experimental research, the participants are called **subjects**. In order to select the proper participants, the researcher must identify the population under study. What group of people are you interested in knowing about? From that population, research participants can be chosen. This smaller group of the population is known as a **sample**. In the case of a content analysis, when the population under study is media content, a sample of content can be extracted from the entire population of content.

Research is usually designed to understand traits about large populations. Since it would be too difficult, time consuming and expensive to study everyone in the population, a smaller sample must be obtained that is representative of the larger population.

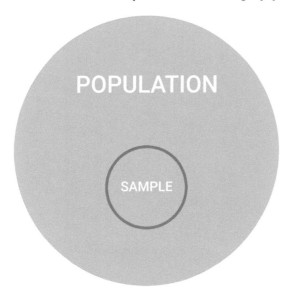

Figure 6.5 **Population: Sample**

For the sample to resemble the population-as-a-whole, random sampling is required. With random sampling (also called scientific sampling), a researcher can generalize the findings of the survey to the larger population. In a truly random sample, everyone in the population must have an equal chance of being chosen to participate in the research. Because it is difficult to obtain a complete list of the population from which to randomly draw a sample, truly random sampling is seldom achieved in strategic communication research. More often representative or volunteer samples are used.

For experiments, subjects do not need to be selected at random, as long as they are part of the population. However, it is important to randomly assign the subjects to the experimental groups.

Qualitative research methods do not require scientific samples but can use non-scientific samples such as convenient samples or volunteer samples. These types of samples allow the researcher to gather subjects who are readily available and willing to participate in the study.

6. Collect Relevant Data

Obviously, there are many details to be determined before the data collection begins. The actual collection of the data typically takes the most time and effort, and therefore usually involves an outside commercial research firm who selects the actual participants and collects the data using professional research protocols and ethical guidelines (see "Basic Ethical Research Principles" below).

If the collection of the data is outsourced, the researcher should oversee the process and make sure the research plan is being followed properly. Safeguarding the data is also important. Data stored on computers should be protected and backed-up to avoid losing the data or having anonymity of respondents violated because the data were not secured from unwanted intruders.

Collecting the data usually takes an extended period of time depending on the method, length of the questionnaire, availability of participants and other factors.

Basic Ethical Research Principles

- Do not involve people in research without their knowledge or consent.
- Do not coerce people to participate.
- Do not withhold from the participant the true nature of the research.
- Do not actively lie to the participant about the nature of the research.
- Do not violate the right to self-determination.
- Do not expose the participant to physical or mental stress.
- Do not invade the privacy of the participant.
- Do not withhold benefits from participants in control groups.
- Do not fail to treat research participants fairly and to show them consideration and respect.
- Subjects should volunteer and sign a form that says they agree to participate.
- Researchers should use language understandable to the participants.
- Researchers should tell participants they can withdraw from the research.
- Researchers should inform participants of the important things that might affect their decision.
- Prior consent must be obtained if participants will be filmed, taped or recorded in any form unless the research involves natural observation in public places.

7. Analyze the Data

Once the data are collected, they are in a raw form and of little use to the researcher and/ or the strategic communication manager. The data must be analyzed using statistical techniques or in the case of qualitative data, through coding and interpretation by the researcher. The use of computers for the collection and analysis of data has greatly enhanced the research process. Software such as Qualtrics and Survey Monkey can be used to gather data online. Statistical software such as SPSS allows researchers to conduct statistical analysis on large data sets in a matter of minutes. Microsoft Excel or other spreadsheet programs are often adequate for handling most studies in strategic communication.

8. Interpret the Results

Once the data have been analyzed and coded, and statistical procedures have been conducted, the raw research data can become useful information. It is at this point that the strategic communication researcher uses their skills and insights to understand what the data are saying and attempts to answer the research questions and/or hypotheses. While interpreting the results, it is very important to remain objective. The researcher should not "stretch" the data to apply beyond the situation under study. While the researcher may want to find positive news for their organization, it is important only to report what the data say and nothing more.

To help researchers be objective, they should go through each table and set of statistics in detail and write down their own conclusions. Then ask one or more uninterested colleagues to interpret the same data. If the other researcher comes up with different conclusions, then put both possible interpretations in the report. Look at the research questions and the objectives of the research and attempt to answer those questions as directly as possible from the data.

9. Present the Results in an Appropriate Form

The research study is not complete until the results are communicated to the decision-makers. The researcher must write their results, conclusion and recommendations based on their unbiased interpretation of the data. They should also include an introduction that explains the project, the objectives of the study, the findings of secondary research, the primary research questions and the method for gathering the data, including how the sample was drawn and what instruments were used. The final report should include the statistical analysis and possibly the raw data in a large binder or online in a .pdf electronic format.

The final written report is not the final step. Usually the researcher will communicate the findings in an oral report to upper management and other decision-makers. The report might include a power point presentation with charts and tables that visually communicate the data so that they are easy to understand. The findings of the research and conclusion of the researcher should be included in the presentation along with some recommendations for action.

10. Take Action to Solve the Problem

Research for its own sake is not valuable to the strategic communication practitioner. The purpose of research is to assist managers in making decisions and taking action that will benefit the organization and help achieve its objectives.

Too often, research reports are left sitting on shelves collecting dust or buried on someone's computer in rarely opened files, either because the findings weren't well received or the organization's goals have changed and the data became obsolete. Nonetheless, a good research study can be helpful even after its practical use has expired as a window into the organization's problems and history.

Summary

Research is vital to the professional practice of strategic communication. Understanding stakeholders, identifying client needs, measuring media impact are just a few important aspects of effective strategic communication that research can reveal. Although conducting research properly is sometimes tedious, time consuming and costly, the cost of not doing good research is much greater and often results in losses for the client. Therefore, understanding how collect, interpret and apply data to communication problems is a skill that every strategic communication professional should attempt to master.

Discussion Questions

1   What are some research questions that might be important to strategic communicators?
2   What is the difference between primary and secondary data? When should you use one versus the other?
3   Think of a popular consumer brand that you like, what type of research would you do before developing a campaign for that brand? How would you conduct it? What type of questions would you want to answer?
4   Explain the ROPE process. Why is it helpful to strategic communication?

 Check out the online support material, including chapter summaries, useful links and further reading, at www.routledge.com/9780367426316.

Notes

1   NFL Puts Fans in Labs to See What works as football seeks answers. (2017, July 17). *Advertising Age*. Retrieved online at: http://adage.com/article/media/nfl-puts-fans-lab-works-football-seeks-answers/309775/.
2   Mccombs, M. E., & Shaw, D. I. (1972). The agenda-setting function of mass media, *Public Opinion Quarterly*, *36*(2) (Summer), 176–187, https://doi.org/10.1086/267990.

Chapter 7

Strategic Communication Planning

Learning Outcomes

At the end of this chapter, you should be able to do the following:

- Be aware of the steps in strategic planning.
- Understand the elements of a situation analysis and create one on your own.
- Know how a SWOT analysis can impact the strategy and operations of an organization.
- Write an objective.
- Know the toolbox that strategic communicators use to execute strategies and tactics.

Chapter Opening Vignette

Request for Proposal at Saxum Public Relations Agency

"There's plenty of time, no need to rush." If you think this is what every strategic communicator thinks when they receive a Request for Proposal (RFP) from a new client, then you'd be wrong. What they are probably thinking is more along the lines of, "It's game time." They put on their game faces, figure out how to best solve their potential client's needs, roll up their sleeves and prepare to come up with a plan of attack.

Planning is important. Strategic communicators must plan every aspect of their campaign, from figuring out what the client's main issue is to developing tactics—timing is key. According to Ashley Wilemon, Senior Vice President of Client Strategy and Service at Saxum Public Relations in Oklahoma City,

> There are so many balls that you have to juggle in an agency. To really get the client, you have to know everything about them, what they want and what they actually need, then you have to be brave enough to execute it all, oftentimes on a really tight deadline. When you're writing the RFP, you have to account for strategies, target audiences, client needs, budgets, timelines, and more. Without strategic planning, we'd be lost.

Making a Plan

Planning is an essential part of our lives. Whether it is to plan our weekend or to plan our future, we are always making plans. What are we going to do this weekend? With whom? At what time? Where?

After we graduate from high school, we make our college plans. Our goal? Graduating in four years with a college degree. In order to do this, we develop strategies that help us succeed. These strategies include deciding on a major, the type of institution that we'll attend and so on. Finally, we get down to the details or tactics—which classes will I take this semester? Will I live at home or in the dorms? Each level of planning builds upon the next, all with aim of achieving an ultimate goal—earning that degree.

Think back to the definition of strategic communication in Chapter 1: Strategic communication is *deliberate* and *purposive*. Basically, it is *planned* communication. It is not random or spontaneous—it requires forethought, carefully crafted messages and thoughtful organized responses. Therefore, planning is a key element to practicing effective strategic communication.

Now reflect on Chapter 3, where strategy was discussed. This chapter is a continuation of the ideas articulated in Chapter 3, but this chapter will look at strategy and strategic planning on a more practical level, focusing mainly on the application stage. The implementation stage will be discussed in subsequent chapters concentrating on each area and finally brought together in Chapter 13—"Strategic Communication Campaigns."

Strategic Planning

At its basic level, *strategic planning* is the process by which organizations determine what actions they will take to achieve specific goals. Strategic planning requires people to think ahead about how the organization will achieve positive outcomes. Sometimes, this forethought is done collectively when organizational leaders come together for a strategic planning session. The main purpose of a strategic planning session is to develop top-line goals—a mission, vision and values—for the organization. After establishing these foundational goals, strategic planners determine objectives that can be applied to each activity area of the organization. Finally, strategies and tactics are developed to achieve each objective—all with the aim of meeting the foundational organizational goals.

Case Study

Domino's Pizza Strategic Planning

Strategic planning can be a great way to manage crisis, shift company culture and create a new direction for the future. Take Domino's Pizza for example. When a video prank by two Domino's employees went viral and damaged the company's reputation—costing them millions—the organization had to take a hard look at itself. By examining what went wrong and why, getting customer feedback and examining corporate policies, Domino's found the root of the problem and addressed it. Executives realized that the company had a bigger issue than a negative viral video—Domino's had lost its focus. People thought the food was bland, cheap and unappetizing. So, to turn around the organization and gain back public trust, executives embraced criticism head on, created a new strategic plan and set goals to make change. Their strategic planning allowed the organization a turnaround that expanded online ordering options and improved the taste of the food. This, in turn, then increased sales, market share and stock prices. Domino's CEO, Patrick Doyle, stated "You can either use negative comments to get you down, or you can use them to excite you and energize the process of making a better pizza. We did the latter."[1]

In complex organizations, there may be multiple goals that require lower-level objectives to achieve them. Corporations set long- and short-term goals every year, usually revolving around departmental needs or financial achievements, such as profits, sales and market share. Each department in the corporation writes a plan that focuses on activities that advance the overall goals of the corporation. Specifically, the marketing department would create a communication plan, which might include communication objectives, strategies and tactics.

For example, if a toy company sets an annual goal of increasing sales of dolls by 20% over the next year, each department at the company would draw up a plan to achieve this goal. The development department might set an objective of designing a new, more life-like doll. The manufacturing group might retool their machinery to accommodate more efficient doll production. The marketing department would write a plan that includes objectives to help make sales goals. These objectives would include communication strategies aimed at creating desire among young girls for the new baby doll through some sort of communication activity—like advertising on children's television programs. Often called a campaign plan or communication program plan, developing plans like this can be one of the most important things that strategic communicators do.

One of the leading scholars of strategic communication, Kirk Hallahan, wrote that effective strategic communication begins with analyzing the situations that confront organizations through research and then using that research to develop goals and objectives that specifically provide a foundation for planning a communication campaign or program, including strategy and message development.[2]

According to Hallahan's definition, strategic communication's planning has four discrete steps:

1. Analyzing the situation, also called the situation analysis
2. Research
3. Developing goals and objectives
4. Planning strategies and tactics, such as message development.

Thus, before the marketing department schedules hundreds of commercials for the doll, there are certain steps it must take first, including the situation analysis, primary research, and a SWOT (strengths, weaknesses, opportunities and threats) analysis. These initial steps set the stage for creating an effective strategic communication plan.

Situation Analysis

The primary purpose of a **situation analysis** is to explain the recent history and current situation and to create a framework for future recommendations. The situation analysis sets the stage for planning by collecting all the important information in one place. It helps reveal the areas where more information is needed and gives background information about the organization's history, sales, products, customers and competitors.

Typically, the communication manager will compile the information about the organization, product, brand, the customer and the competition into a single document. Much of the information needed to create a situation analysis is found through internal company records, annual reports, sales data, previously conducted research reports and through external industry research reports, trade articles and consumer trend data, which are discussed in more detail in Chapter 6.

A situation analysis for a corporation might follow this outline:

- Product/brand overview
  - Description of product/brand including benefits and features
  - History of brand
  - History of company
  - Current sales/market share (by week or month, if available)
  - Distribution (where is the product sold?)
  - Pricing (how much does the product cost?)
  - Current market positioning
  - Current communication strategies
- Stakeholder analysis
  - Demographic
  - Psychographic
  - Geographic
  - Behavioral (usage habits and loyalty)
  - Purchase cycle (how often do they buy?)
- Competitive analysis
  - Identify strongest competitors
  - Market share for each competitor
  - Positioning for each competitor
  - Promotional history for each competitor.

Problems and Opportunities

The next step in the planning process is research. The research process—both internal and external—is extremely important to writing a good strategic communication plan. Research at this stage is primarily focused on gathering information (both primary and secondary) about the organization, product or brand, the market, the various stakeholders and the overall environment that was not revealed in the situation analysis. To understand more specifically how and why to conduct research, see Chapter 6 of this text.

After the situation analysis is written, the research is collected, analyzed and presented, there is one more step before developing the objectives and strategies for a plan. This step links the situation analysis (what was done in the past) with the research (the current reality in the marketplace) to the plan (what we should do in the future). It is called the problems and opportunities phase.

The problems and opportunities phase is the process of strategically converting research findings into organizational goals and objectives. It is probably the most difficult and most important step of the entire process, because it requires careful, thoughtful strategic thinking. It takes talent and practice for strategic planners to look at the situation analysis along with newly uncovered research to discover strategic opportunities for the organization. The planner must take the research—which provides information about the external environment, competitors, stakeholder characteristics and societal trends—and simultaneously think about the organization's internal capabilities and shortcomings. Then, the planner must analytically and objectively blend this knowledge to create overarching goals that are beneficial and achievable. This is the key to the entire strategic plan.

In the example of the toy company above, research may have revealed a societal trend toward mothering. By recognizing this research finding as an opportunity in the external environment and combining it with the toy company's internal strength in producing and selling baby dolls, an overarching goal of increasing the sales of baby dolls by 20% was set. The organization realized that the most beneficial product to focus on this year is baby dolls. They will leverage their doll manufacturing and marketing expertise to take advantage of current market trends.

SWOT Analysis

Because the problems and opportunities step is so difficult, there are several tools that an organization uses to help determine the best path. One of these tools is called SWOT—an acronym developed by a group of management consultants in the 1960s that stands for strengths, weaknesses, opportunities and threats. (SWOT was discussed in Chapter 3, but we will also present it here because of its importance to planning.)

A SWOT Analysis for the doll manufacturing company, ToyCo, might look like this:

1   **Strengths** (internal positive qualities of the organization)
- ToyCo is the largest and most well-known toy manufacturer.
- ToyCo's baby doll division possesses the largest share of the doll market.
2   **Weaknesses** (internal negative qualities of the organization)
- ToyCo has not added new baby dolls to its product line-up in more than a decade.
- ToyCo dolls are typically higher priced that competitors' dolls.
3   **Opportunities** (external/positive to the organization)
- A societal trend toward "mothering" is creating demand baby dolls among little girls in the U.S.
- A mini baby boom in the middle of the last decade has increased the size of the children's market.

Figure 7.1 SWOT Analysis

4   **Threats** (external/negative to the organization)
  - New, smaller toy companies are entering the market with innovative toy designs.
  - An economic downturn resulting from the COVID-19 pandemic threatens disposable income of families in the U.S.

Case Study

The National Student Advertising Competition

In 2017, the American Advertising Federation's National Student Advertising Competition (NSAC) challenged students across the United States to create an integrated strategic communication campaign to make Tai Pei frozen Asian entrees, a brand of Ajinomoto Foods North America, more relevant to younger millennial consumers ages 15–25.[3]

One student group created an analysis of problems and opportunities for Tai Pei, shown below:

Tai Pei Problems and Opportunities

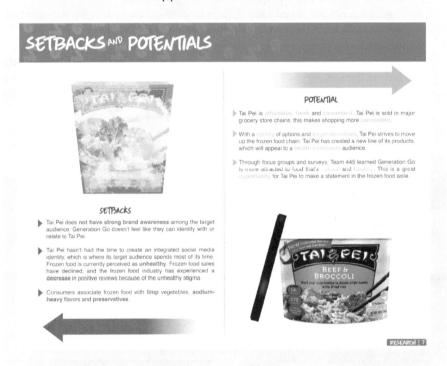

Prior to creating the analysis, students conducted primary and secondary research about the Tai Pei brand, the frozen food industry, Asian cuisine in general, Tai Pei's competitors and young millennials' food and media habits. From their research, they were able to identify the positive aspects of the brand as well as its shortfalls. The research also allowed them to identify trends in the external environment that might affect millennials' interest in Tai Pei. By organizing the findings in such a way, the company could evaluate strategic paths and develop the right tactics.

Outside-In Planning

As discussed in Chapter 1, the outside-in approach is a foundational element in strategic communication. The outside-in approach puts the focus of the plan on the stakeholder, not the organization. Ultimately, the stakeholder—customer, voter, public or constituent—determines the strategy for the organization. The most effective communication plans are those that look at the stakeholders first and then shape strategies to meet stakeholders' realities. The SWOT analysis should be developed from the perspective of the stakeholder. It is important for strategic communication planners to think like the stakeholder when they are developing their plans. Therefore, it is important to understand how the stakeholder is interacting with the external environment. What are they buying? What sites do they visit on the web? What sort of pricing and promotional incentives seem to be interesting to them? Account planning is a function in many communications agencies that assist in answer these questions.

Industry Insight

Account Planning

The professional discipline known as *account planning* or *communications planning* plays a special role in many strategic communication campaigns by providing stakeholder input at every step of the way. Account planners, who often hold such titles as communications planner, strategist, brand planner or connections planner, use a variety of research techniques to identify and understand various stakeholder groups.

Some argue that account planners have the coolest jobs in the agency or corporation, because they constantly keep up with trends in music, entertainment, government, business and other areas so that they can incorporate marketplace developments in their work. The result of their research, analysis and synthesis for a specific client is a strategic brief (in advertising called a creative brief)—a condensed one-page guide for those who create campaigns, events and other efforts designed to keep everyone on strategy.

Briefs, and briefings—highly detailed and often creative sessions during which planners present their work and the resulting strategies—vary in content, but almost all contain the following elements:

- Why are we communicating?
- With whom do we wish to communicate?
- Where do they live, work, shop and play?

- How can we best reach them?
- What do they currently think?
- What would we like them to think?
- What is the single most compelling thing we could say to them?
- What is our support for that communication? Why can we say that?
- Are there client mandatories or requirements for these messages (such as including a picture of the product or person, specific wording, legal requirements, etc.)?

And I like to add:

- Is our strategy and messaging sensitive to matters of race, ethnicity, sexual orientation, gender, religion, disability or other issues?

Account planning had its origins in the 1960s in London advertising agencies, where senior management felt the creative work fell short of its potential because of a lack of deep understanding of the consumer. Planning made its way to U.S. ad agencies in the 1980s, and by the 1990s almost all major agencies employed account planners on their business. Account planners represent a sort of hybrid position—part researcher, part creative, part media planner and part strategic leader—and because of that today's planners come from a variety of backgrounds, whether psychology, anthropology, business, advertising or other fields.

If you are the type of person who is constantly curious about what you don't know, likes to investigate a wide variety of topics, understands quantitative research but also has interviewing and observational skills that help in understanding people's motivation and mindset, and loves finding and communicating creative solutions to a team, account planning might be for you. The foundation of effective communication is understanding your stakeholders, by whatever name you might call them. The account planner's job is to serve up that understanding and leverage it for the benefit of the communications team.

Contributed By Dr. Alice Kendrick, professor in the Temerlin Advertising Institute at Southern Methodist University in Dallas, Texas.

Objectives, Strategies and Tactics

The next step in strategic communication planning is to articulate the objectives, strategies and tactics.

- **Objectives**—where you want to go?
- **Strategies**—how you are going to get there?
- **Tactics**—executional details.

One easy way to understand objectives, strategies and tactics is to think about going on a trip from Chicago to Los Angeles.

First you determine where you are currently (the situation analysis). You are in Chicago, Illinois. Then you try to understand what resources you have available (from the research). You have a car. There are highways available and you have $300 to spend on gas. Now to write your objective: Travel from Chicago to Los Angeles in four days with a $300 budget. The strategy is more specific. How will you get to Los Angeles in four days? Strategy: Drive my car approximately eight hours per day following Route 66. Tactics (the details): Leave at 9 a.m. from Chicago on Route 66 headed southwest. Drive to Springfield, Missouri, the first day; to Amarillo, Texas the second day; and to Flagstaff, Arizona, the third day. On the fourth day, arrive Los Angeles.

That is the plan. Very simple, right? You can use the same approach when you create objectives, strategies and tactics for a strategic communication plan. Start with the overall goal, then think of ways to achieve that goal and write that in the form of a strategy. For each strategy, detail the tactics that will be used to achieve the strategy.

Cascading Objectives/Strategies/Tactics

Most organizations use a cascading approach to planning. In the cascading approach, there is a hierarchy so that each succeeding step flows from the step before. It starts from the organization's mission and flows down to each department's plan, which cascades to each unit's plan. From there a communication plan is developed which informs the functional communication elements—advertising, promotions, social media, public relations, etc.

In a cascading marketing plan for a for-profit company, a strategy of the higher organizational level becomes an objective for the next level. Chesapeake Energy uses this kind of model to communicate initiatives with employees. Leadership crafts their objectives, passes these objectives on to management, which then cascades smaller objectives to departments and the individual contributors. These contributors are given "Blue Chips" goals so they know, specifically, what they need to accomplish. This way, all the productivity and activities in the organization are aligned, and every contributors' actions are a small step in accomplishing corporate objectives.

For example, think about a political campaign and cascading objectives and strategies. With any candidate, there is one goal: Get elected. But, the candidate can't do this alone. There are teams of people working behind the scenes on different aspects of the campaign. Most campaigns have three divisions—the field team, who are generally responsible for knocking on doors and getting the public excited about the candidate; the communications team, who are in charge of crafting the message strategy for the candidate and producing the materials to communicate that message; and the fundraising team, who get the money from donors to keep the campaign running. Each division is trying every trick in the book (i.e. strategies) to get their candidate elected. They all have different objectives, which all go back to overarching goal: Win the election!

What is important to remember, though, is that these strategies are going to be different for each division. For example, the communications team's objective may be to perfect the words and messaging that voters will see and hear about the candidate. To do this, they give individuals specific tasks (or tactics) to execute such as, building a website, utilizing social media and designing promotional materials. This furthers the overall goal and assists the other divisions at the same time. Without a website, how would people donate? Without donations, how would we pay to produce the promotional materials? Without a field team, how would the promotional materials get to the target audience? Without working together, how can they meet the candidate's goal? In short, they can't. Without the objectives and strategies cascading from above (i.e. the candidate), each team would flounder, and the campaign would fail. This is illustrated in Figure 7.2.

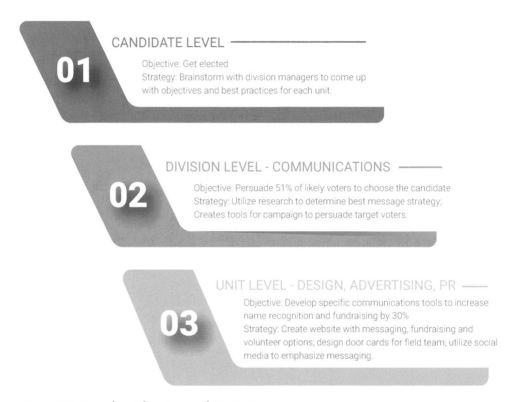

01 CANDIDATE LEVEL
Objective: Get elected
Strategy: Brainstorm with division managers to come up with objectives and best practices for each unit.

02 DIVISION LEVEL - COMMUNICATIONS
Objective: Persuade 51% of likely voters to choose the candidate
Strategy: Utilize research to determine best message strategy; Creates tools for campaign to persuade target voters.

03 UNIT LEVEL - DESIGN, ADVERTISING, PR
Objective: Develop specific communications tools to increase name recognition and fundraising by 30%
Strategy: Create website with messaging, fundraising and volunteer options; design door cards for field team; utilize social media to emphasize messaging.

Figure 7.2 **Cascading Objectives and Strategies**

Developing Objectives

Before developing the objectives for a strategic communication plan, it is important to realize what strategic communication can and cannot achieve. One mistake strategic communication managers often make is to set objectives in the communication plan that they cannot achieve through communication alone. For example, strategic communication activities (such as promotions, advertising, and publicity) cannot increase profits without support from other parts of the organization, such as finance, manufacturing and sales. Strategic communication objectives should be focused on outcomes that can be achieved with communication activities.

Generally speaking, communication objectives should be:

- Informational (mere awareness, recognition, recall, comprehension, knowledge, understanding)
- Attitudinal (favorability, beliefs, emotional responses)
- Behavioral (coupons returned, attendance at events, web site visits, donating, volunteering)
- Post-action behavior (repurchase, loyalty, positive remarks on social media).

Writing Good Objectives

Good objectives are simple statements with a single concept that usually start with an infinitive. In other words, "*to* [verb]". To create. To drive. To target.

An objective should:

- Be concrete and measurable
- Define the stakeholder
- Benchmark the degree of change sought
- Specify Time Period.

Objectives should state exactly what is to be achieved. They should not be vague, and it is very important that objectives are measurable. Otherwise, the planner will not know if the objective has been achieved. It is also important to define the stakeholder that is to be affected by the objective. All objectives should have set time periods for which they must be completed. At the end of a campaign, the outcomes of the campaign are evaluated based on the objectives. Only well-written objectives that are concrete, measurable and define both the stakeholder and time period can be properly measured to determine success or failure of the communications program.

The objective statement always starts with "to" followed by an active (or power) verb. Figure 7.2 provides a list of power verbs to consider when you write an objective statement.

VERBS APPROPRIATE FOR OBJECTIVE STATEMENTS

Address	Administer	Analyze	Approve	Arrange	Assign
Attain	Authorize	Build	Calculate	Catalog	Communicate
Complete	Conceive	Conduct	Confine	Contract	Control
Convince	Coordinate	Correct	Create	Decide	Decrease
Delegate	Demonstrate	Design	Develop	Diminish	Direct
Disapprove	Distribute	Document	Draft	Educate	Employ
Enhance	Enlarge	Enlist	Establish	Evaluate	Examine
Expand	Finish	Gain	Generate	Govern	Group
Guide	Hire	Identify	Implement	Improve	Increase
Index	Inform	Initiate	Institute	Interview	Investigate
Justify	Keep	Locate	Maintain	Make	Motivate
Negotiate	Notify	Obtain	Organize	Outline	Overcome
Persuade	Plan	Position	Prepare	Present	Preside
Protect	Provide	Publish	Raise	Reassure	Recommend
Record	Recruit	Rectify	Reduce	Regain	Release
Remove	Request	Require	Research	Reshape	Retain
Revise	Schedule	Secure	Select	Sort	Start
Stimulate	Strengthen	Supply	Teach	Tell	Trace
Track	Train	Verify	Write		

Figure 7.3 **Verbs Appropriate for Objective Statements**

SMART Objectives

One tip for writing good objectives is to ask yourself, "Is this SMART?" Using the acronym SMART will help create strong objectives that will guide the planning process.

- **S—Specific:** Are you identifying something concrete or is it too vague? Would someone from another division in your organization be able to understand what you are talking about? Being specific helps you create concrete proof of your work, which can often keep people motivated and build relationships between divisions.
- **M—Measurable:** If you don't set levels of measurement, how do you know if your objective was met? Connecting a measurable goal to your work will allow you to show the value of what you've done. Besides, if you make your objective measurable, you have something to work toward, and generally, employees that work toward a goal are more successful.
- **A—Attainable:** It's great to aim high, but be careful not to overpromise. Are you setting objectives that can actually be accomplished? Without the right skillset, tools or budget, it can be difficult to achieve lofty goals. If your objective seems unattainable, go for something smaller and build toward the end goal. Just make sure you have the budget and resources to get to the moon … or whatever objective you set, because with every project, those resources are finite. So, be realistic.
- **R—Relevant:** Is your objective relevant to the larger goals of the organization? Is it cascading from the objectives set from leaders above? You need to determine if the objective is relevant to the people on your team as well as organizational goals. People want to know how objectives impact them, and how they are contributing to organizational goals. You wouldn't ask a communications specialist to do the job of a rocket scientist and build a rocket to Mars. It just isn't relevant … or safe.
- **T—Time-bound:** Time management and project management are actually something in which students naturally understand. Whenever you get an assignment, the first thing you ask is "When is this due?" You need to know how much time you have, so that you can manage your other tasks and can finish your work on time. It's no different when writing and accomplishing objectives. You need to know how much time you have to achieve your objective, so you can make a plan and execute it.

Think again about the toy company. A strategic communication objective for the toy manufacture might be:

To increase desire by 10% for dolls among young girls in the U.S. by the end of the 8-week campaign period.

The objective concretely identifies one variable that communication can affect—Desire. It specifies the stakeholder—young girls in the United States. The degree of change sought is a 10% increase. The time period is the 8-week campaign period.

Rationale Statement

A component of an objective statement that comes in very handy is the rationale statement. A rationale statement is a brief summary provided after the objective statement of why you decided on this objective, reminding the reader about the research findings that support the objective. Rationales make sure your objectives solve the problem hindering your mission.

Look again at the analysis for the toy company. It directly provides the rationale for the objective stated above:

- Research showed there is a societal trend toward mothering.
- The company's internal strength is producing and selling baby dolls.
- This will leverage the baby doll manufacturing and marketing expertise to take advantage of current market trends.

Once objectives are set and readers have been reminded of the reasons why this objective has been set, the organization develops strategies to reach those objectives.

Strategies and Tactics

Communication strategies are the functional part of the strategic communication plan. Depending on the objectives of the campaign, the strategic communicator can choose from a toolbox of strategies and tactics. One way to think about strategies and tactics is by types of media used. In Chapters 10 and 11, you will learn more about media strategies and in Chapter 9, we will discuss message tactics. Media and messages essentially make up the communication plan. You will see how they are all brought together to achieve communication objectives in Chapter 13, where the campaign process is discussed.

The Strategy Toolbox

Strategies are action plans that are used to achieve objectives. There are a variety of actions that can be chosen, depending on what is to be achieved. One way to think of strategies is to visualize a toolbox. What tool is best utilized to achieve the objective at hand? Do you need to hang a painting on the wall? Then, open the toolbox and choose a hammer. But, if you need to remove the back of your remote control to change the batteries, a screwdriver might be a better tool.

Below is a list of tools that might be in the strategic communicator's toolbox. There are certainly other tools, but this list will get you started thinking about strategies. When creating strategies, think about which tools might work best in the current situation to achieve your communication objectives.

Organizational—An organizational strategy is just as important to consider when developing a plan as other areas of communication. First, organizations must consistently communicate with its external public. Having an informative, easy-to-navigate website and professionally produced collateral materials are just two organizational strategies that may help. Second, organizations must also communicate with internal audiences. Utilizing strategies to engage employees, such as a company newsletter, employee events and incentive programs can create a more positive working environment that benefits the firm.

Traditional Media—When most people think of traditional media, they think of newspapers, television and magazines. As a strategic communicator, you can utilize this strategy by sending out press releases, creating media kits, making video news releases and any number of strategies to get coverage for your clients. Although media have changed, traditional media is still a very powerful strategy, which can reach many people. Traditional Media strategies are discussed in detail in Chapter 10.

Digital Media—Digital media refers to newer online forms of media, such as websites, blogs, online video and other formats. Traditional media that is digitized and distributed over the internet is also considered digital media. Social Media is a form of digital media. It is an important strategy for most organizations whether they are selling product or raising money for a charity. Having a presence on social media platforms such as Facebook, Twitter and Instagram allow stakeholders to interact with the organization in real time. Social Media conveys information about the organization and its activities, as well as participates in a larger dialogue about the organization in the public sphere. The personality of the brand can also be transmitted on social media. You can have a little sass and little fun with your stakeholders—as long as you don't cross a line. Wendy's Twitter account is a perfect example. They regularly roast their competitors and stakeholders, and people love it. Their sassy tweets get thousands of retweets and are regularly shared on other social media sites. By communicating their irreverent personality, Wendy's social media managers are making a greater impact than simply replying to questions that may be posed online. Digital Media is evolving and rapidly changing and therefore a powerful strategic tool for communicators. Digital Media is discussed in detail in Chapter 11.

Advertising—Advertising is paid communication that is carried on the media. Advertising is a strategy that has the advantage of reaching mass audiences and niche audiences depending on the goals of the campaign. It also can be controlled by the organization since the time and space are paid. Advertising can be expensive, and it is sometimes ignored because it lacks credibility. When done well, however, it can create an image and personality for the brand. Think of that talking duck from Aflac insurance company. Did you hear him quack the brand name? That's because the brand has incorporated him into the advertising. He's a consistent message that allows you to create top of mind awareness. You see him on TV, in magazines, billboards and even football games. Aflac creates a consistent brand message in all its advertising in the form of a duck.

Interpersonal—Utilizing interpersonal strategies allows for face-to-face interaction with both internal and external stakeholders. Although this type of strategy doesn't reach as many people as traditional media or advertising might; it does allow for a deeper connection with your stakeholder and when you partner it with other strategies—like traditional media—it can become a very powerful tool.

Let's think about Barack Obama's campaign for president as an example. As he went from town to town, he used interpersonal strategies to engage both internal and external publics to garner votes—he would visit campaign headquarters to thank volunteers and give them the energy to keep going; he would have a beer with locals; and his team would videotape the encounters to get him more coverage on the news. On an interpersonal level, these one-on-one moments made a powerful connection with the individual. Can you imagine how people might have felt when Obama stopped to talk to them? When you have a stronger connection like this, the ability to persuade can be much more powerful.

Publicity—Publicity is basically unpaid exposure in the media about an organization or brand. When the media present stories about a brand—such as an article in an online newspaper—it reaches large stakeholder audiences. Publicity is free, but its content is also out of the control of the organization. If the publicity is positive, then this can be very beneficial for the organization. But if the publicity is negative this can hurt the organization's reputation. Strategic communicators in their role as publicity agents work with journalists to gain positive coverage for their brand, organization or event.

Let's think about Wendy's again. Because they manage their social media account and roast people without damaging their reputations, they regularly get free publicity from various websites, such as Buzzfeed or Bored Panda. People see and hear about Wendy's without much effort. However, there have been companies that haven't been as savvy and nearly ruined their reputations with bad the publicity that came from it—just ask United Airlines. When the airline broke the guitar of Dave Carroll and refused to reimburse him for the loss, the musician made a song about it ... and it went viral. In just six weeks, more than four million people viewed the "United Breaks Guitars" YouTube video. Public response was swift. Some reports indicated the company lost nearly 10% of its stock value—an estimated $180 million.

Experiential—Experiential marketing, also called event marketing or engagement, is a strategy to allow stakeholders to participate with the brand directly, often through some type of experience. Experiential strategies directly engage stakeholders and invite them to develop a relationship with the brand through production and co-creation of marketing programs or brand extensions.

One example of an immersive, experiential marketing strategy is that of the lifestyle website for women, Refinery29. Each year, they curate an exhibit called 29Rooms, "an interactive funhouse of style, culture and technology" that is sponsored by brand partners. Musicians, artists, car companies and consumer products all vie to create the most immersive, vivid, hands-on experiences for visitors. Every room is designed to inspire the creative juices and social media posts. For example, Dunkin' Donuts created a Lichtenstein-inspired kitchen, where visitors felt like they were in one of the iconic paintings. This experiential strategy provided brands stylish and savvy ambassadors who willingly created top of mind awareness to a larger, highly sought-after audience—millennials with expendable incomes. This is such a popular event that tickets sell out in minutes. Those who purchase a ticket find an Alice-in-Wonderland-style world of 29 highly curated and interactive rooms that take experiential marketing to the next level.

Sales Promotions—Sales promotions are all those activities that create an incentive to try a brand. Coupons, gifts with purchase, contests and sampling are all considered sales promotions. Short-term promotions might include a free dessert when you order a pizza. Long-term promotions include frequency programs like American Airline's AAdvantage program that rewards American customers with free trips after they fly 20,000 miles on American. Think of your favorite holiday. No matter which one it is, you'll probably find someone giving you a discount or great deal. By offering a short-term promotion—such as 30% off for a limited time—it can increase traffic and sales for the company.

ORGANIZATIONAL	TRADITIONAL MEDIA	DIGITAL MEDIA	ADVERTISING
Employee newsletters, e-blasts, research reports, annual reports, user kits, corporate branding, website, employee engagement, incentives, company outings	Newspapers, magazines, radio, television, news fact sheets, interview notes, news releases, feature releases, ANR, B-roll, VNR, media kit, photograph	Social media releases, apps, Twitter, Facebook, YouTube, LinkedIn, Snapchat, influencer marketing, Reddit, podcasts, blogging, vlogging, live-streaming, e-magazines	Newspaper ads, magazine ads, billboards, yard signage, transit, promoted posts, digital targeting, celebrity endorsements, product placement
INTERPERSONAL	PUBLICITY	EXPERIENTIAL	SALES PROMOTION
Volunteering, donation drive, organizational involvement, speech, rally, demonstration, product exhibition, convention booth, meet and greets, public forums, door knocking	Media advisory, story pitch, position statement, letter to editor, guest editorial, interview, news conference, studio, satellite media tour, editorial conference, partnerships	Guerilla marketing, civic events, sporting events, contests, holiday events, historic commemorations, social events, happy hours, fundraising	Coupons, in-store sampling, promotional items, branded clothing, branded office/home accessories, direct-mail items, postcards, catalogs

Figure 7.4 **The Communication Toolbox**

There are multiple strategies that can be employed in a strategic communication plan and with each strategy, the planner must think through each specific tactical step in order to implement the strategy. The more details provided in a communications plan, the more likely the organization will meet their goals and achieve success. Planning, therefore, is an important element in strategic communication.

Packaging Communication Tactics

For each tactic that you plan out, you need to think about the details. The timeframe—when the project is due, the budget, who is responsible for it, any special considerations and evaluation techniques—should be laid out with the description of the strategy and tactic. Doing so helps you understand the details of your idea and see the bigger picture of your plan. Here's an example for a ballet company that is trying to get more young professionals to support them:

> **Strategy:** To partner with the other young professional groups to increase membership and interest in ballet events.
> **Tactic:** Host a joint membership happy hour with the philharmonic young professional group. This will serve as a membership recruitment event and fundraiser.
> **Due Date:** October 1
> **Budget:** $200 for food and drink tickets, $40 for social media promoted posts
> **Owner:** Marketing Director, Amy
> **Special requirements:** We will need to coordinate plans with the partnering organization to split costs for the event. Need to get approvals for the social media posts through supervisors at both organizations. Also need to plan copy for email blast to promote the event with current members of each group.
> **Evaluation:** Assess the interest in the event by the number of members from each organization who attend the event. Interest and success can also be evaluated through Facebook measurements and email click-throughs.

This isn't the only way to write out the details of the tactic, but when you're learning how to package it all together, it's a great method to help you remember all the details. (We'll get into budget, timelines and evaluation in Chapter 13.) Tactics can be organized in your plan by tactical category (like above), by public, by objective, by strategy or by department. How you organize really depends on what your client needs. For example, let's say your client is a non-profit which has two totally different groups with whom they need to communicate—both donors and those in need. Since there may not be a large overlap in strategies, organizing the plan by target audience would be smart. Or, maybe your client is a political candidate; since her team is divided into three units (field, communication and fundraising), it would be smarter to organize the plan by department. Whoever the client is, you need to figure out the best way to organize the plan based on what works best for them.

The Planning Matrix

At this point you are well-equipped with understanding the steps, terminology and process for putting a specific strategic communication plan together. To help you even more, the planning matrix on the following page can assist a great deal to put all your tactics and strategies together in a systematic way. You can make the matrix bigger or smaller to fit your

OBJECTIVE	To promote and create awareness for the new festival, which profits go to charities in the region. This will be a multi-phase launch that will focus on a variety of announcements leading up to the festival, which is planned for the first weekend in October.
STRATEGIES	We will focus on local and regional story lines, emphasizing the cultural significance and economic impact of the festival. We will incorporate messaging that features partnerships with non-profits throughout the state as well as the artists performing.
TARGET AUDIENCES	• Men and women age 18–39 living within 100 miles of the festival venue • Music lovers who regularly attend festivals • Active adults who are engaged in the community and care about nonprofits
TARGETED MEDIA	• Local and regional papers, newsletters and magazines • Regional television and media outlets • National Industry/Special Interest publications • Local chambers; convention and visitors bureaus
MESSAGE	The new music festival will bring incredible music into the region, have a positive impact on the local economy and bring much-needed aide to local non-profits.
TACTICS/ MEDIA MATERIALS	• Fact sheet—One-sheeter with at-a-glance information about the sponsors, artists and non-profits that will benefit. Will refer to website for consistency. • Quotes—Quotes about the event from festival organizers, headliners, and spokesperson from non-profits • VNR—Video news release of planning of festival, interviews with non-profits and b-roll of performers to provide to stations not at event(s). • Social Media—Posts will be made regularly interacting with locals, hyping artists, making announcements and generating buzz about the festival. • Press releases—Release and media advisories to announce the new festival. In addition to initial release, updates about new artists and other key festival information.
PERSON RESPONSIBLE	Account executive will be the lead for this account. More will be added to tasks as needed as events approach.
TIMELINE	Below is a tentative timeline of press-worthy events and/or announcements. All timeline items are contingent on the timing of the project, in addition to the approval of releasing information to the public/media. • Jan 10—Launch of website & social media pages • Jan 15—Interviews and b-roll production • Feb 1—Announcement of the festival • Feb 15—Festival Tickets On-Sale • Feb - Oct—New digital media content on a daily basis. Monitoring and responding daily. See appendix for content calendar. • Sept 15–30—Countdown to the festival. Schedule a variety of local and regional press events and interviews leading up to opening day. • October 3–5—Festival. All hand on deck. Account team will handle interviews with artists, answer media questions, monitor mentions on social, respond to any crisis, and coordinate with festival production crew to create a positive framework for the festival. • October 7–10—Post-festival media opportunities (i.e. concert throwbacks on social, feature of checks to non-profits, showing positive economic impact to region, etc.)

Figure 7.5 **The Planning Matrix**

SPECIAL CONSIDERATIONS	• Launch of Website and Social Media Pages—Be sure to have this up and operational before any announcements to the local media. Begin having content produced and ready to go before this goes live. Have information about sponsorships, tickets, maps, FAQs, artists and the non-profits that the festival will be helping. Have consistency between all platforms. • Interviews and b-roll production—Release to media interviews with artists and non-profits as the festival nears. Incorporate how the artists are glad to be helping the community and how worthwhile it is. Show video of who, exactly, the proceeds will be helping with an emotional angle. Releasing this information prior to the festival can keep an on-going mention of it in the news. • Announcement of the festival—Once confirmed, announce artists, sponsorships and non-profits that are connected to the festival. Send information to local and regional media. • Festival Tickets On-Sale—Create announcement and social information about how to purchase tickets. Ensure the website is fully operational and ticket account with ticketmaster is correctly set up. • New digital media content on a daily basis—Create a detailed content calendar for social media posts, emails, video content, snapchat, and other digital tools to keep generating buzz about the event. • Countdown to the Festival—We will provide media with a series of stories previewing the festival. These media opportunities are intended to increase awareness of the festival, gain media coverage and disseminate new information about the event. • Festival—Little to no new media promotion. This will be mainly maintaining schedules, posting events on social, monitoring media trends, and creating a positive framework for the festival. • Post-Festival—As the festival unfolds, record events, schedule meet & greets between artists and non-profits and find post-festival stories. Material will be used in post-festival media. (i.e. concert throwbacks on social, feature of checks to non-profits, showing positive economic impact to region, etc.)
BUDGET	Social Media Monitoring and Content Production $5,300 Website production $2,700 TicketMaster Hosting $2,500 VNR & b-roll Production $4,500 Estimated Subtotal $15,000 Contingency $1,500 **Total Estimated Production Costs $16,500**
EVALUATION TECHNIQUE	Success will be measured through outputs of ticket sales, website click, the number and quality of stories by local press, and calculating the AVE of the stories. In addition, we will gauge measure outcomes of the event such as post-festival attitudes toward the festival.

needs by adding or subtracting as many stakeholder groups as are required, add more or fewer strategies to reach stakeholders, and tweak the message strategies where necessary. However, the most consistent component of your plan should be the message. No matter what your strategy is, the stakeholder group should receive the same message across all tactics used. (For more details on message strategy see Chapter 9.)

After you have completed the matrix, you can at a single glance see what resources you will need in terms of budget and people skills. Check out the example for how a plan might look if you were planning a new music festival.

Summary

Once you win the business of your client, the client will have high expectations for you. Without a solid plan in place, your agency may flounder. Fortunately, you've learned that utilizing strengths and finding the potential opportunities can really help your client grow. By taking a deeper look at who your client is and what weaknesses they have, you can address any threats they may not be able to see. Essentially, your SWOT analysis helps guide your plan for the client. Without it and the situation analysis, your strategic plan might just go off track. By understanding the SWOT and utilizing the strategic communication toolbox, your strategic plan can be executed quickly and effectively—you just have to keep all those balls that Ashley Wilemon mentioned at the beginning of this chapter in the air.

Discussion Questions

1   How can strategic planning influence the daily operations of an agency or business?
2   What are the steps in communication planning?
3   What does SWOT stand for? Which SWOT elements consider factors internal to the organization and which elements look at external factors?
4   How does a SWOT analysis guide a communication strategy?
5   Why should objectives, strategies and tactics be cascading?
6   What are the elements of an objective?
7   Why should you include a rationale statement?
8   Can you explain some of the differences in the types of resources that are available in the strategic communicator's toolbox (such as advertising vs. publicity)?
9   Complete the planning matrix for the doll company described in this chapter.

Check out the online support material, including chapter summaries, useful links and further reading, at www.routledge.com/9780367426316.

Notes

1   Maze, J. (2018). How Patrick Doyle changed Domino's and the restaurant industry. *Restaurant Business Online* (June 25, 2018). Retrieved online at https://www.restaurant-businessonline.com/leadership/how-patrick-doyle-changed-dominos-restaurant-industry; source: https://www.youtube.com/watch?v=AH5R56jILag.
2   Hallahan, K. (2015). Organizational Goals and Communication Objectives in Strategic Communication. In D. Holtzhausen, and A. Zerfass (Eds.), *The Routledge Handbook of Strategic Communication (pp. 244–266). New York: Routledge.*
3   Ajinomoto Windsor, Inc. to sponsor 2017 national student advertising competition (2016, August 22). Press release from the American Advertising Federation. Retrieved at https://www.aaf.org/AAFMemberR/Press_Room/2016/NSAC_2017_Client.aspx.

Chapter 8

Stakeholders

Learning Outcomes

- Define and identify different types of stakeholder groups.
- Explain the situational theory of publics and how it helps inform strategic communication practice.
- Know the basis of segmentation and be able to give examples of each.
- Understand the stages of the consumer decision-making process.
- Identify factors that influence consumer decision-making.
- Learn about the diverse nature of stakeholders and how to communicate with people that are different from you.

Chapter Opening Vignette

In Search of Stakeholders

Imagine that the cosmetic company you work for discovers a brand-new, revolutionary way to combat the effects of aging. This product is extremely effective, easy to use, made from natural and organic compounds, but is expensive.

Now, imagine you've been hired to represent a political candidate in an election. Your candidate is a moderate who believes in more liberal social policies but is fiscally conservative.

Finally, imagine you own a record label and have signed a new recording artist, who mixes traditional country music with a Latin influence. How do you make it possible for each one of these clients to break into an already crowded market and become a success?

If your first response was to post on social media, run radio spots or have a launch party to generate excitement about your client, the next question should be "*Who* are we trying reach with these messages?" When you ask your clients this question, their first reaction might be "Everyone!" But, in reality, it can't be 'everyone' because reaching everyone is practically impossible, and if you could actually do so, you would need an enormous budget and lots of time. But most importantly, there really isn't a product, brand, idea or concept that appeals to everyone anyway. For example, a 16-year-old boy won't run out to buy that anti-aging cream and he isn't old enough to vote in an election. He may not even like country music.

Every brand, product, idea or concept appeals to a different segment of the population. Figuring out who needs to hear your client's message is a key part of strategic communication. You must find the people who have the biggest stake in what you're advocating. You must reach the stakeholders.

Stakeholders

In strategic communication, **stakeholders** are the people to whom the communicative entity aims to send messages. There are many different types of stakeholders and they serve many different purposes for the CE. In marketing situations, the stakeholders might be **consumers**, customers or target markets. In advertising, they are usually called **target audiences**. In public relations practice, these people are typically referred to as **publics**. All these terms have slightly different meanings, but they can all be described as stakeholders. Stakeholders can also be voters, citizens, employees or elected officials. Anyone who has a stake in the CE's message is a stakeholder.

This chapter will look closely at the concept of stakeholders and the integral role they play in strategic communication. We'll examine the difference between active and passive stakeholders. We will break down who the stakeholders are, where to find them, how to attract them and how to keep them. The chapter will also discuss consumer stakeholders, their behavior in the purchasing process and how they can shape the brand. Finally, the chapter will examine the role diversity plays in strategic communication and provide tips to help you identify and target the most appropriate stakeholder group.

Who Are Stakeholders?

The concept of stakeholders, defined as individuals and groups that can affect or be affected by the messages, actions, goals and policies of the CE, began in the 1980s and relates to the idea that people have a stake in what happens with organizations in the public sphere. These groups of people are intrinsically invested and care—on varying levels—about the CE's actions.

Identifying stakeholders at all levels, both present and potential, is an essential job for the strategic communicator. Understanding who these people are, and how your organization relates to them, are among the first steps in strategic communication planning, even before writing your strategies and tactics. After all, you can't develop a communication plan without first knowing with whom you are trying to communicate and you can't make a list of media that you prefer to use when you don't yet know which media your stakeholders are using.

Stakeholders can be divided into internal and external groups. Internal groups are within the organization and include employees, managers and owners. External stakeholders are outside of the organization. External stakeholders include customers, investors, supplier/partners, society, government and even creditors.

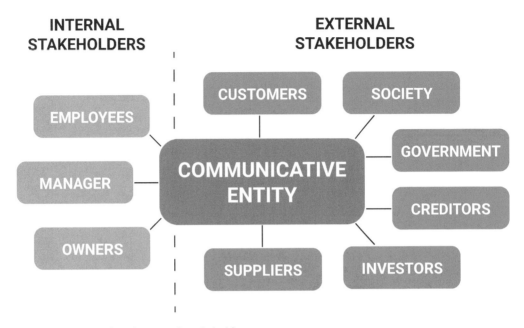

Figure 8.1 Internal and External Stakeholders

Stakeholders also can be categorized according to the amount of involvement they have. Primary stakeholders are impacted directly—positively or negatively—by the actions of the organization, while secondary stakeholders are affected indirectly. Key stakeholders may not be affected at all, but still have a significant ability to influence the organization, such as a regulatory body or government agency. Identifying the primary, secondary and key stakeholders is necessary to a successful strategic communication campaign.

Stakeholder Groups

Another way to identify stakeholders is to analyze how they are linked to your organization. Communication scholars Grunig and Hunt[1] established that four main linkages exist—*enabling, functional, diffused* and *normative*. To understand this concept, it might help to think about your university. A university is a complex system that affects thousands of people. These people can be placed in different stakeholder groups by the way they are linked to a specific university. For example, Congress, State Legislators and the Board of Regents are all linked to the university in the same way—they enable it to operate through funding, regulations and guidance. These groups have some level of control over the organization. If the organization's relationship with these groups runs into problems, resources might become scarce. These stakeholder groups are *enabling* the organization to exist.

Faculty, staff and other employees are another stakeholder group that help the university function on a daily basis. By giving their input (i.e. time, energy and knowledge), they create the products and services (such as your education) that the university offers. This stakeholder group is typically highly invested in the success of the organization—what happens within the organization will affect them directly. Students, such as yourself, are another functional stakeholder group in your university. You consume the university's output—in this case your education—which directly affects you.

Other groups, like fans of the university's athletics teams, the media, alumni and even the citizens of the town where the university is located are also considered stakeholders. However, these relationships are more *diffused* than the previously mentioned groups—the actions of the organization may affect them, but less so. This group of people becomes more involved as actions of the organization affect them. For example, fans and alumni will tailgate during football season, but not during final exam week—finals don't affect them.

You may not realize it, but an organization's competitors, peers, academic and professional societies and associations are all considered stakeholders as well. Since they all have a common goal with the organization—the education of students—they are known as *normative* stakeholders.

Shifting Responsibilities

As discussed throughout this text, the rapid evolution of technology has dramatically changed the media environment. In the past, the advertising and PR industries would send finely crafted messages *to* stakeholders to consume. Today, however, traditional marketing, public relations and advertising methods have evolved into new techniques that are designed to communicate *with* the stakeholders. This is another attribute of the outside-in approach. So, the question you may be asking is: Why? Why would communicators deliberately change their message strategy? The answer is simple: It's because stakeholders *demand* it. Societal and technological changes resulted in stakeholders realizing they too have power and are prepared to exert it to get what they want and need.

No one has been more affected by the changing communication technology than stakeholders. They no longer just watch TV, go to the movies and read magazines filled with messages from organizations. They tweet, Skype, post on Facebook and Instagram, they stream entertainment when they want it and cruise the internet to consume and actively create content for others to consume. Stakeholders are sending messages to organizations and expect a response. Most of today's stakeholders demand instantaneous information that is up-to-date, accurate and most importantly tailored to their own individual needs.

If it sounds like a lot of work to corral these unpredictable, ever-changing populations, it can be. Fortunately, technology provides communicators with the tools to help make your stakeholders happy. Whether it's sending an email to a board member or responding to a tweet, two-way communication is key. And because of this, communication professionals should remember that stakeholders are actually the co-creators of your brand. From the chairman of the board, to the random twitter account, how you react and respond to stakeholders will determine the success of your organization, your client and your brand.

Here's an example. Your company is developing a new soft drink. After spending two years in research, developing a marketing campaign and spending millions of dollars to come up with a drink you think will really spark the interest of the public, you release it and it flops. Stakeholders are going to have different reactions. The enabling stakeholders, like the board of directors or investors, are livid that you wasted so much money. The functional stakeholders, such as the research team and consumers, are upset. The research team is confused as to why the input they put into the product failed, and consumers don't like the output of the research team. The media, a diffused stakeholder, won't stop reporting about the failure, and your competitor, a normative stakeholder, is cackling with glee because they will have more sales after your blunder. How you communicate with your stakeholders about the failure will depend on their level of interest, the power that the group has and the urgency of the situation. No matter how much money or how confident you were with the new product, your stakeholders are the ones who decide the success or failure of your endeavors. They are that important.

Case Study

Harry Potter and Fandom

Fandom is a phenomenon that has changed a great deal in the 21st century. It was created in the early 20th century to describe people who were fascinated by and enthusiastic for a phenomenon, such as a movie star or a sports team, and continued to expand throughout the 20th century. At the beginning of the 21st century, it became associated with major brands, particularly in the entertainment industry. Examples are movies, such as *Star Trek*, and other science fiction genres such as novels, video games and comic books.[2] At this time, it is particularly associated with music superstars such as Beyoncé's *BeyHive*, Justin Bieber's *Beliebers* and Taylor Swift's *Swifties*.[3] There are literally hundreds of these groups that can be best described as subcultures. They can be overenthusiastic and are often not very tolerant of the opinions of others when it comes to the object of their fandom. On the opposite side there are the haters, who are virulently opposed to the brand. The way CEs deal with their fandoms shows how brands now use the outside-in approach, so typical of modern strategic communication.

An outstanding example of how influential fandom groups have become, is the case of the Harry Potter books. Members of Harry Potter's fandom are called *Potterheads*.[4] The author of the series, J. K. Rowling, embraces Pottterheads, who create websites, podcasts, expand on the books' characters and even write their own fiction extrapolating on the characters and events in the books. They follow the actors from the movies, create online series based on the characters' lives after the story ended and host conventions. Rather than fighting the Potterheads, Rowling uses them to further interest in her fiction.

Even some of the most famous names in the entertainment industry must bend the knee to fandoms. In the past, members of fan-based groups often got into copyright trouble for using the characters or visual materials. Now, brands have realized that they must allow their stakeholders to do with the brand as they please. If not, the fans will revolt against the brand, call for boycotts and use the internet to shame or harm the brand. In the case of Harry Potter fans, Warner Bros., which owns all rights to Harry Potter and anything associated with the brand, wanted to shut down the websites and fan activities for copyright violations. The company was unsuccessful in doing that and eventually embraced the fans, understanding that working with them is much more beneficial than being confrontational. They now involve corporate webmasters of powerful Harry Potter-related sites in their strategic communication programs. The webmasters became *enabling stakeholders*.

Even organizations that would prefer to not follow the outside-in approach now realize that fans are more powerful than brands and brands are often at the mercy of the stakeholders. Smart brands allow this to happen without interference—and might even encourage it—because they realize that the engagement is beneficial to the brand. Warner Bros. executives finally realized that while many fans are disappointed that certain elements of the books are left out of the movies and theme park, they do not try to avoid criticism but realize, "bringing the fan sites into the process is what we feel is really important."[5]

Active vs. Passive Processing

Another way to approach stakeholders is to analyze how they engage with the media and your messages. Almost everyone consumes media content. Understanding how people consume media is important in understanding how to engage stakeholders. Some stakeholders are actively involved with mediated messages (they are deeply interested in specific issues and events), while others are more passive. For example, you're having a fundraiser for an important and popular charity. You sent out 500 invitations via regular mail. What are people going to do with that invitation? Is everyone going to reply? No. No matter how great an organization it is, it's nearly impossible to get a 100% to respond. Even though everyone may be interested in the cause, some will just ignore the invitation (passive) while others will jump at the chance and RSVP right away (active). Stakeholders will have either a passive or active reaction to your messaging and they will shift between the two depending on their interest level.

Active stakeholders respond with action. They are motivated by their beliefs and desires and are easily persuaded by the goals of an organization or the ideas of their peers. They can also be strongly motivated to oppose an organization. They are actively seeking out information about an organization and/or its messages. They then use this information to either make a decision, personally invest more time and energy for a particular cause and answer a call to action, or in some cases, they may decide to revert back to a more passive mode.

If it sounds like active stakeholders are selfish, in a way, they are. They seek out only what interests them and leave other information behind. Active stakeholders are more prone to achieve gratification from media content for their own psychological and social needs. This is far from being a bad trait, because these stakeholders are more prone to be your best advocates. They are the people most inclined to go to work for your cause. They are also the people who will be active members of your organization and help in spreading the message. They may be your most loyal customers and actively tell others how great your products are. In turn, they will be more demanding of the organization. They will be more critical and require your attention, since they care so deeply about the cause. Just ask Becky with the good hair. In 2016, after super-star Beyoncé dropped the *Lemonade* album, her fans—known as the Beyhive—were determined to find out who this rumored side-chick was. Numerous women were accused and harassed online by this extremely active group of stakeholders.[6]

It would be wonderful if all stakeholders were active, but that is not the case. Most, in fact, are **passive stakeholders** who passively respond to media messages rather than emotionally or intellectually engage in the content. They are not necessarily disinterested, they are just not invested enough to actively engage. You might think of these people as the "mass" in mass media or the "main" in mainstream media.

To contrast the two types of stakeholders, think of the fans of your school's athletic program. Some fans, especially alumni, actively engage in athletics, seeking out information about recruiting, coaches and team statistics. They are often ardent social media users and they belong to online discussion groups. They attend games and booster club meetings, and some financially support the program with sizable financial contributions. Conversely, other fans are more passive in their support. Although they may care about the outcome of games, they may not necessarily pay as much attention to media coverage and they may be less inclined to buy tickets or contribute money. The strategic communication practitioner should try to influence both types of stakeholders because both are integral to the success of the organization. It is important to remember that the passive stakeholder can become active if properly motivated, in this example, as a fan of an athletic team that has a winning season and goes to a championship game. Passive stakeholders do have a vested interest in a given organization, its cause and its messages. They just have a lower, less active interest level.

Situational Theory of Publics

As mentioned earlier, although the term "stakeholder" is often used interchangeably with the terms "publics" or "audiences," there are some important differences. Although there are some overlapping areas between the two, stakeholders are identified by their relationship to the organization; whereas, publics are grouped by the messages that they receive. A public, is a group of people who face a similar problem, recognize the problem and organize themselves to do something about it. To explain this process, J. E. Grunig developed the **situational theory of publics**, which posits that stakeholders shift into different groups and will communicate in an active manner, passive manner or not at all, based on the situation at hand.[7]

As situations with an organization or issue arise, stakeholders shift into groups of publics that will adopt an active or passive approach. Stakeholders who are not affected by the CE and do not interact with it become **non-publics**. Those who see a situation but don't see it as a problem or are not affected by it are known as **latent publics**, because they have the potential to become active. Those who are aware the organization or issue is affecting them but are waiting for an event to trigger them into action are known as **aware publics**. Finally, groups that are aware of an event and are actively seeking information about the situation are **active publics**.

Let's think about your university again. How your university communicates with different publics will vary. For example, let's say your school's football team is going to the national championship. Congrats! It's going to be an amazing experience. Think of all the hype, new gear and one heck of a tailgate. Your school is going to want to communicate all that with the groups of people that care about it the most.

A group that your university's communications department won't bother with creating messages for is the non-public—people who are not fans of the school or have no interest in football. Another group that might not have messages geared toward them is a latent public. These would be people who are aware of that there's a national championship but are not fans of the school's sports teams. It would be a waste of the communication team's energy. Latent publics are much too passive for the university to take the time to create a message strategy aimed at them.

As we progress, we begin to see more active groups for which your school will want to communicate. For example, an aware public for your university to communicate with may be a bandwagon fan. As soon as they are triggered by the positive press about your school going to the national championship, they'll start seeking out messages from your university simply because it caught their interest. The messages that your school will send to this group may be different from the messages they send to true fans of the school. This final group, the active publics, are the people that your university will prioritize in their message strategy.

Key Influencers

Each group that your CE becomes involved with may have different reactions to the message strategy—either active/inactive and supportive/non-supportive. As you determine how people are reacting to your messages, you can shift to target your publics. You may want to prioritize certain groups with your messaging. The groups that you want to communicate with first is known as your **key public**—they may have the greatest influential power, urgency or most involvement, either negative or positive.

Even within public groups, there are individuals that hold a lot of sway over the rest of the group. These people, known as **influencers**, have thoughts and opinions that hold a lot of weight within the group. So, before you start sending out messages, you should make sure you know the influencers within these groups who can help communicate your message. They can often make or break your campaign.

For example, think about Chrissy Teigen. The model and social media maven is a powerful influencer online. When she makes a comment or statement about a topic, millions of her followers might just follow suit. In 2018, when Donald Trump had his 72nd birthday, Teigen donated $72,000 to the American Civil Liberties Union (ACLU) to help them fight injustice against immigrants. She then encouraged others to do the same—whether it was $7.20 or $72. In 24 hours, Teigen's efforts raised over a million dollars in donations—that is influence! It also is an example of an issue driven in opposition to the CE.

Because of the influence of publics on CEs, it is one of the most important functions of the communication strategists. They must scan the environment and always be aware which issues are developing that might affect the CE. Here the segmentation of the environment (remember the macro level) in different sectors, as discussed in Chapter 4, is a valuable tool to identify these emerging issues.

Segmentation

Let's think about "everyone" as discussed in the chapter's opening vignette. Everyone in the world is a lot of people—almost eight billion, in fact. These billions of people are spread all over the globe and can be very different from one another. In fact, they are totally unique individuals, but they do share some common characteristics. The key to strategic communication is to understand *who* among these eight billion people will be receiving, engaging and responding to your messages. What language do they speak? Where do they live? What customs do they have? How old are they and what do they like and dislike about your brand, idea, concept or organization? In order to effectively communicate to these people, you must know something about who they are. The more you know, the better and more effective the communication will be.

It is also important to be efficient with your communication. To be efficient means sending one message that appeals to many people. One-on-one, individual communication is costly and takes lots of time. To be a good strategic communicator you need to aim your messages at *groups* of people. Therefore, it is important to break the billions of people in the world into smaller, more manageable, groups with similar characteristics. Breaking the total population into smaller homogeneous groups is called **segmentation.** By using segmentation, you can send one message that will appeal to many people, which is a very efficient and necessary way to communicate in the public sphere.

Characteristics of Segments

Creating segments from large heterogeneous masses is a bit tricky. Not all groups make good segments. It is important that you have meaningful, identifiable groups made up of like-minded people in order to be effective and efficient with your messaging. Therefore, when forming segments, it is important that they are distinguishable, homogenous, important, large enough to matter and reachable.

Distinguishable

You must figure out the characteristics of the people the CE wants to communicate with. For example, if you were to create messaging for an haute couture fashion line, you'd probably want to set some parameters, such as those who make more than $250,000 a year, those who shop at high-end lines or those who have shopped with the fashion line before. You must distinguish who you are targeting so you can be efficient with your messaging. After all, not everyone can afford haute couture.

Homogenous

According to the dictionary, to be homogenous is to be the same or alike. So, when you are determining which stakeholder groups to communicate with, you should find some characteristics that unite them. Perhaps it is a political party or a professional association. Perhaps the feature that unites the group is that they are all fans of the same sports team. Perhaps it's the generation in which they were born. Whatever it is, you can use the fact that they are homogenous to your communication advantage—many of your message strategies can be uniformly tailored toward them.

Important

Non-profits care deeply about donors; without them they would cease to operate. Publicly traded business care about their stockholders. Organizations care about groups that affect their bottom line. Sometimes, the voice of one person can impact an organization in a significant way. The segment needs to be important to justify the time and energy spent to reach it.

Large Enough to Matter

Fringe groups that complain about a product but don't generate press or impact don't really matter to an organization. They may be aware of them, but they are not likely to change their communication strategy to respond to them. However, thousands of voices united can matter. Think about "March for Our Lives" and the National Rifle Association (NRA). Small groups fighting for gun reform may not make an impact on how the NRA creates their messaging on a day-to-day basis. However, when those thousands of people organized to fight for gun reform, the NRA paid attention and shifted its communication strategy. Whether you agree or disagree with gun reform, when a small group became large enough to be important, the organization they were targeting sat up and paid attention.

Reachable

Think about your client's dream customer. How difficult will it be to communicate with them? How expensive will it be? What methods should you use? Without the ability to reach stakeholders, do you really need to try to target them? That's the idea here. If you are trying to reach soccer moms, you must figure out the best methods to actually reach them. Whether it's streaming music, commercials on their kids' favorite television shows or magazines filled with celebrity news, it's up to you to determine if you can get their attention and how much it might cost you to do it.

Basis of Segmentation

Typically, the main basis of segmentation can be broken into four categories of characteristics—geographic, demographic, psychographic and behavioral. Simply stated, your demographic represents "who you are"; geographics represent "where you are"; psychographics represent "why you are"; and behavioral represents "how you are." By utilizing the information about your stakeholder, you can determine who and where your customers are. Companies pay big money for insights into customers. We briefly touched on these segments in Chapter 4 when we discussed CEs' external environments, so let's use this next section to explore in more depth what these classifications mean.

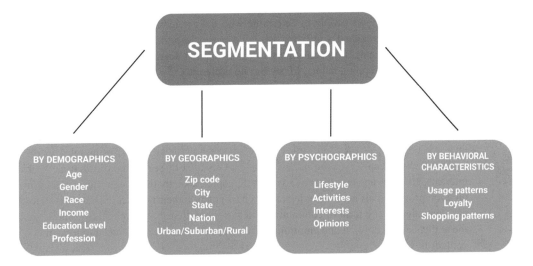

Figure 8.2 **Basis of Segmentation**

Demographics

Demographics ("who you are") is the statistical study of populations, especially human beings. As a very general science, it can analyze any kind of dynamic living population. It is a "just the facts" approach that allows you to segment people by simple characteristics that everyone could fall into, such as age, gender, race, profession, socio-economic group or other physical characteristics. For example, if a company wants to sell a line of clothes that is young and trendy, they could target women between the ages of 16–26, because those are the people most likely to be interested in young and trendy fashion.

Geographics

Geographics ("where you are"), or the location that your stakeholder is in, can tell you a lot about them. Something as simple as a zip code can give you a plethora of information about whom you should target. You can know what region your stakeholder is from, if they are urban or rural, and even the type of neighborhood they are in.

By breaking your entire customer base into small, manageable groups, you can create targeted messages that help you spend your budget more efficiently. For example, imagine you are the marketing manager of a new Mexican restaurant in your town that makes the best queso around. You know it, but you just don't have enough customers that know it. The owner of the restaurant says you can run a small, $2,000 campaign to bring in customers. So, how do you determine whom to target? The best way, especially for a retailer, is geographics. You could easily blanket the entire city with mailers. But it would be very expensive, and most would be delivered to homes that are not near your restaurant, so they would likely end up in the trashcan. Instead of blanketing the entire city, you only send the mailers to houses within three miles of your restaurant. Because you were efficient with your campaign, you have brought in customers that live nearby and may become regulars, without wasting money on people across town and who have other restaurants near them that are much more conveniently located.

There are some great resources to help you with both demographic and geographic segmentation. One resource is a program called Nielsen PRIZM—a customer segmentation system that allows people to determine who their potential customers are by simply looking up their zip code. By utilizing available census information, The Nielsen Company has been able to categorize consumers in to 66 distinct segments, which allow them to understand their shopping habits, lifestyles and preferences.[8]

Psychographics

Although demographics and geographics are valuable and can be used as a starting point, they don't shed light on the lifestyles and interests of an audience. Psychographics ("why you are") dive deeply into the human psyche. This area of segmentation focuses on the interests, affinities and emotions of a group of people—exactly the things strategic communication professionals need to understand to best position their product or message. Before any campaign or any form of communication to your audience, it is critical to connect with the audience on a cultural and emotional level to ensure that the look, feel and tone of your content fits.

A person consumes goods for reasons beyond age and income. By exploring other aspects of their life, you can use psychographic segmentation information to better understand the decisions of a consumer. It could be their personality; it could be their attitude; or it could be their lifestyle. When thinking of "lifestyle" think AIO—activities, interests and opinions.

Activities could include what kind of work, hobbies or shopping style a consumer might have. If you have an indication of someone's daily routine, you can begin to see what purchase habits they have. A person that bikes to work, exercises and only buys organic foods, will undoubtedly have different product preferences than someone who is a couch potato. Strategic communication professionals can use this information to their advantage to create targeted, efficient messaging.

Interests pertain to what they invest their time and energy into—whether it is in food, fashion or recreation. How people spend their time will reveal a lot about their habits. Opinions may be a dime a dozen, but if communication professionals know what those opinions are and where their allegiances lie, they may be able to create targeted messages and utilize brand loyalty. For example, if a person thinks plastic is causing harm to the ocean, an eco-friendly company might see this information as an opportunity to change its message strategy.

Behavioral

Behavioral segmentation information will provide information about the rate of use, what benefits the consumer is seeking from the product, how loyal they are to the CE and how ready they are to purchase. In other words, how a stakeholder is using the product and what they are doing with it. Are they making impulse buys at the register? Do they use coupons? Do they prefer to order things online rather than go to the store? These behaviors matter to strategic communicator because they provide insight into how to create message strategy. With information like behavioral segmentation information, you begin to see the whole person and really gain insight to your stakeholder groups.

There are many ways to segment audiences, beyond demographics, geographics, psychographics and behavior. Depending on the situation and strategy, the strategic communicator may want to segment according to sexual orientation, life stage or product benefits. From politics to religion, the characteristics of your stakeholders matter and can have a significant impact on why they make the decisions they do. Perhaps a man only buys groceries on sale because he is worried about making ends meet. Perhaps you can influence voters to support your candidate because they share the same faith. No one *really* knows the impact these elements have, but they do provide insights and patterns.

Aggregation

With the availability of **big data**—large computerized data sets that reveal trends and patterns in human characteristics and behavior—strategic communicators can access information about people on an individual level. Unlike in previous decades before supercomputing, information about groups of people were gathered through surveys and generalized to larger populations. Instead, today big data gives us a granular perspective. However, individual-level data are not especially helpful to marketers, advertisers or PR practitioners in their work, because it is not "large enough to matter." It must be aggregated into larger groups with distinguishable, homogenous characteristics. Whereas segmentation starts with a big heterogeneous mass and breaks it into smaller homogenous groups, **aggregation** takes individual data and groups it into larger meaningful segments. Aggregation and segmentation are opposite actions to achieve the same result—to produce identifiable, like-minded groups of people that can be efficiently and effectively targeted with messages by the strategic communicator.

While Big Data can be used to segment people into large groups, it also allows for the individuals making up those segments to be known and targeted individually. For instance, when you do a search on your computer or access social media platforms, your online behavior is tracked. Later you will find ads for certain products appear on your screen. This is due to the ability of companies who use big data to identify and communicate with you individually according to your geographics, demographics, psychographics and your internet search behavior.

Segmentation should be a consideration at the beginning of any communication campaign you implement. It is an essential part of the research phase and requires all the good primary and secondary research skills that you have mastered. Remember to connect with the stakeholder—from their age to their income to their hobbies to their shopping habits.

Consumer Behavior

As discussed earlier in this chapter, there are many types of stakeholders. One important stakeholder type—especially for marketing and advertising practitioners—are consumers. **Consumers** are individuals, or groups of individuals, such as companies, governments or organizations, who purchase products and services for personal use. **Consumer behavior** is the study of how these individuals or groups select, purchase, use, or dispose of products, and the needs and wants that motivate behaviors.

Stages in the Consumer Decision-Making Process

When consumers purchase a product, they go through various stages in their decision-making. Academics who study consumer behavior generally point to five stages in consumer decision-making—need recognition/problem awareness, information search, evaluation of alternatives, purchase act and post-purchase evaluation.[9] The exact path that consumers take depends on the type of product and the buying situation. From the consumer's perspective, buying a car is not the same as buying a hamburger. Sometimes, consumers' decisions are made with very little thought about the product, especially purchases that have low perceived monetary or social risk or for products for which consumers are brand loyal. Consumers' buying habits differ by individuals, products, categories and situations. Therefore, strategic communicators need to know how the decision process works for their specific product category and what triggers consumers to choose certain brands.

Figure 8.3 **Stages in the Consumer Decision-Making Process**

Need Recognition and Problem Awareness

The consumer decision-making process typically begins when the consumer realizes that they need something that they do not have currently available. Maybe they simply ran out of toothpaste or dog food or frozen pizza. Sometimes they are dissatisfied with their current brand, for example, the McDonald's hamburger that they just ate was not very satisfying and so they decide that next time they are going elsewhere for lunch. Sometimes consumers realize that they have new wants or needs (especially if they get a raise and have more money) or they may be made aware of new products that they want to try. Buying one product—like a new smart phone—may lead to recognition that they need related products—like a new phone case. There are lots of reasons that people realize that they have a problem that product consumption can solve.

Information Search

Once the consumer recognizes that they need a product or service, they begin searching and gathering information related to attaining it. They may conduct an internal search by reflecting on what they know about the product category. Additionally, they may engage in an external search, which could include searching the Web or visiting a store. It is during the search stage that the consumer creates an **evoked set**, which is a short-list of products/brands that they are favorably considering.

Evaluation of Alternatives

Once the short-list of possible choices is determined, consumers begin evaluating each option. They use **evaluative criteria** or features that they consider important in making their choices among all the alternatives in the evoked set. The evaluative criteria could include factors such as price, style, color, flavor or convenience. The criteria will vary according to the product under consideration. For example, when buying a car, you might focus on the miles-per-gallon rating, cargo space and/or driver technology. You will compare and contrast each criterion for each make and model during this phase of the consumer decision-making process.

Purchase Decision

Eventually a purchase decision will be made. Often the decision is made rather quickly in a physical store or while shopping online. Other times, purchase comes only after considerable thought and consultation with friends and family. If the consumer has a high degree of brand loyalty in the category, then the purchase decision may be quick, but if they are unfamiliar with the product, it may take time to carefully search and evaluate different brands. Depending on the price, the purchase decision may go quick, or take many months if the item is costly.

Post-Purchase Behavior

The process does not end when the purchase is made. When the consumer takes the product home they will decide if it was a good choice or not. This experience after buying will impact the next purchase decision, so it is important for strategic communicators to follow-up with consumers on their purchase choices, either through personal contact or with other communications such as advertising. Seeing an advertisement about the product helps positively reinforce the brand as a good choice in the consumer's mind and makes the next purchase that much easier. Sometimes, however, consumers are not happy with their purchases and they may feel buyer's remorse. This psychological uneasiness about a purchase is known as **cognitive dissonance**. Companies do not want customers of their products to feel uncomfortable about their purchases, so they do what they can to alleviate this feeling, such as offering money-back guarantees and/or 30-day refund policies. Happy customers become loyal customers and represent future sales for the company.

Variations in Consumer Decision-Making

Depending on the type of product that consumers buy, the decision-making process may be long and complex or short and simple. Think about what you consumed for lunch today. If you ate food from a restaurant, you spent some time thinking about which restaurant you preferred. You probably considered things like the price, convenience and the type of food available. Maybe you grabbed your "usual" from the sandwich shop on campus, or because it was your birthday and you were eating with friends, you spent several weeks contemplating and planning for the perfect restaurant meal. There is variation in the consumer decision-making process according to the amount of time and type of purchase.

Routine Response Behavior happens for low-priced, frequently purchased products that consumers buy out of habit. Products like toothpaste or gasoline might be bought using routine response behavior, that is, consumers will buy the same brand from the same place routinely as their supply is depleted. It is difficult to get consumers to change their habits and switch brands if they are purchasing in this mode.

Limited Problem Solving may be used if the consumer has a limited amount of experience with the product. In these buying experiences, consumers may take some additional time to explore other options before buying, but if the product is relatively inexpensive and has little risk, the purchase may occur rather quickly after some shopping. Clothes are a good example of a product that is purchased with limited problem solving. Consumers will do a short search online or in stores to select styles and colors that they like. They will often look for good prices and try clothes on before they buy.

Extended Problem Solving usually happens for big-ticket items, such as a car, house or computer. If the consumer lacks knowledge regarding the product, then it will take time to establish criteria for evaluating the alternative brands. In extended-problem-solving situations, strategic communication practitioners needs to provide consumers with detailed information about the product and in some cases, may require one-on-one personal selling.

It is important for strategic communicators to understand which variation of consumer response behavior is being used for their products, because each type of decision-making requires a different communication strategy. For routine behavior, keeping the brand top-of-mind with the consumer is important, and requires frequent messaging. For limited and extended problem solving, consumers are actively seeking information about the product. The brand that can provide the most relevant information will likely be chosen for purchase.

External and Internal Influences on Consumer Behavior

Consumers, like all types of stakeholders, are influenced by the people around them. External factors that influence consumer behavior relate to the external environment, such as culture, social class, reference groups, brand communities and family. These factors are exerted by other people and can affect a person's consumer behavior. When strategic communicators are analyzing the macro-environment, as discussed in Chapter 4, they must consider how culture affects stakeholders in certain situations. For example, the Mexican-American culture is very family oriented and Mexican-Americans tend to live together in large, multi-generational family units, therefore they often consume products that are sold in large quantity packaging and are promoted as "family-friendly." **Reference groups** are groups of people with whom an individual identifies and therefore assumes some of their values—reference groups may be families, church groups or professional organizations. For college students, fraternities and sororities are common reference groups that can influence the consumer decisions that chapter members make.

Stakeholders are also influenced by internal factors. These factors happen inside the person's mind, such as psychological influences, needs/wants, personality, attitudes and motivations. **Motives** are internal forces that move a person toward a goal. In consumer behavior, motivations can be powerful. For example, if someone is hungry, they are motivated to get food. At mealtime this motivation grows, so sending messages about restaurants just before dinner is very effective. **Attitudes** are a person's overall favorable or unfavorable feelings toward some object. Stakeholders can hold attitudes toward almost everything—a brand, product, social movement or political candidate. Attitudes are usually very stable, which means that knowing how to change them is an important skill for strategic communicators. Personality is made up of all traits, experiences and behaviors of a person. Strategic communication sometimes appeal to personality characteristics such as individualism, competitiveness or ambition.

Academic Angle

Maslow's Hierarchy of Needs

In 1943, American psychologist Abraham Maslow developed a theory of human motivation. Maslow's theory is presented as a pyramid that starts with human's basic needs at the bottom and moves through five less critical needs toward the top of the pyramid. The theory states that the needs on the bottom must be satisfied before a person is motivated to fulfill the higher-level needs.

At the base of the pyramid are physical needs, such as food, water, warmth and rest—basic things that humans must have to survive. If you find yourself without food or water for an extended period you will become completely focused and driven to get nourishment or you might die. Clothing is also a basic, physical need to keep humans warm.

The next level on the pyramid is also very basic—the need for security, such as shelter. However, in the modern, industrialized world, we usually have plenty of food and water, and most of us have a place to live and feel safe when we sleep at night. Therefore, we seldom think about the basic needs and, as a consumer, spend most of our time trying to achieve higher-level desires.

Once the basic needs are met, according to Maslow, humans are motivated to satisfy psychological needs. The first level of psychological needs is social. Social needs are centered on being loved, having intimate relationships, friends and family. The next level of psychological needs is for esteem or a feeling of accomplishment and prestige. Being popular and famous is a need that only some may achieve, but for which we are all driven to some extent.

Finally, the top of Maslow's hierarchy is self-actualization—the need to achieve one's full potential, including things like creative production, focusing on others, giving back to society and educating one's self. According to Maslow, most people never transcend to self-actualization and spend their life trying to survive, make friends and be loved. Therefore, the tip of the pyramid is quite small. Very few rise to that level but many might strive for that.

Applying Maslow's hierarchy of needs to consumer behavior helps identify consumer segments for products. Depending where a consumer is situated on Maslow's pyramid determines their interest in consuming certain products. If a consumer is trying to satisfy esteem needs, they are likely to desire products that make them look good and cause them to be admired by others, such as fancy cars, a nice house, a country club membership and probably credit cards. For the small percentage of the population that has satisfied all the lower-level needs and has advanced to self-actualization, marketers can leverage their desire for travel, higher education and contributing to charitable organizations.

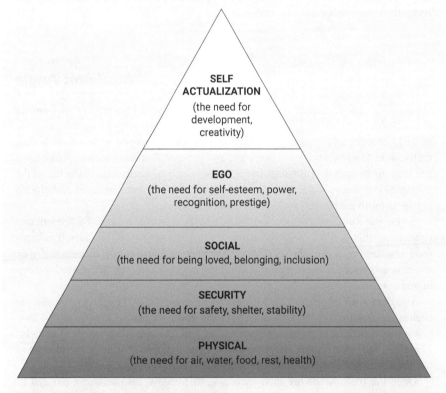

Figure 8.4 Maslow's Hierarchy of Needs

Stakeholders and Their Diverse Nature

We have been discussing the importance of segmenting stakeholders into homogenous groups; however, it is important to remember that there is much diversity in the world. Understanding and embracing that diversity makes the world interesting and is an important skill of strategic communication. Though stakeholders for any organization may be united by a single goal or commonality, they are very often made up of people from differing cultural and ethnic backgrounds. They may be both national and international in their thinking and represent diverse viewpoints on attitudes toward gender, religion, health and relationships.

It's very difficult to work with a culture that is not your own. For example, how would you facilitate a campaign targeted to people of a different race or ethnicity than yours? Things that define us in terms of our race or ethnicity are often deeper than just our skin color or country of origin. We have many other factors—such a customs, language, family and religious backgrounds—that also become part of racial or ethnic identity.

A strategic communicator's job is to serve as the bridge between organizations and their audiences. Sometimes, organizations fail to understand the complexities of their own stakeholder groups, making diversity education an important part of the training for people entering this profession. The training is often intense, requiring interpersonal and diversity education, for which you must leave personal prejudice behind.

As a strategic communication professional, it is up to you to find, understand, cultivate and keep your organization's stakeholders as happy as possible. It's a tough job. Oftentimes, you must deal with multiple groups, each radically different from each other. It doesn't make it easier knowing that your success is entirely dependent upon your mastery of understanding each stakeholder's unique needs. Once you understand them, however, you will be in a better position to help them, and your organization will be better for it.

Cross-Cultural Communication

Cross-cultural communication refers to how people from different cultures speak and perceive the world around them. Within an organization, cross-cultural communication may involve understanding different business customs, beliefs and communication strategies. Having a mastery of cross-cultural communication allows companies to build and maintain relationships across diverse stakeholders and is critical to communication in a globalized world.

Understanding how cultural values differ among people from various national backgrounds is important in effective strategic communication. There are several frameworks and theories that apply to cross-cultural communication. For example, you may want to revisit Chapter 4, where we briefly discuss Geert Hofstede's research on cultural dimensions.

Another prevalent theory uses low context versus high context to explain differences in communication style across nations and cultures. Anthropologist Edward T. Hall developed a framework to explain how people from different cultures communicate according to the importance they place on the context of the message rather than the actual words that are spoken.[10] According to Hall's work people from low-context cultures, like the United States, place low importance on context, but instead view the explicit words as the most important part of the message. By contrast, people in high-context cultures focus mostly on what is *not* said and rather on the context of the communication—the situation, tone of voice, body language and other non-verbal elements. It is difficult to understand the message in a high context without a great deal of background, whereas information is clearly and directly communicated in low-context cultures. Asian, African, Arab, central European and Latin American cultures are generally considered to be high-context cultures while the United States and Australia are generally considered low-context cultures.

Hall's framework can be very helpful to strategic communicators who are operating in a global environment. High-context cultures prefer face-to-face communication, while individuals in low-context cultures are more comfortable communicating electronically and in writing where explicit details can be articulated. People from high-context cultures are more interested in the relationship between the speakers and not the specific words that are spoken. When conducting business globally, US executives sometimes lose a deal because they fail to value the relationship with the other party and are too focused on the explicit conditions of the agreement.

Watching television advertising around the world is a great way to understand the differences between high- and low-context cultures. In the United States, ads are often loud and direct—"come to our store and get the best deal in town!" Advertising in other cultures, such as Europe, is much more subtle and nuanced, so much so that an American may not even know what is being advertised. Europeans are often put off by loud "ugly Americans," while people from the United States accuse Europeans of being aloof and pretentious. These misguided attitudes often arise from not understanding how people from different cultures communicate.

Creating a campaign targeted at international audiences can be a difficult task. A well-done campaign can build brand loyalty, while a poorly executed campaign can cause irreparable damage and mistrust and can destroy an organization's credibility. Communication scholars Cameron, Wilcox and Reber suggest five basic cross-cultural rules to consider when designing strategic communication campaigns for diverse audiences.[11]

1   Organize team members who have knowledge of the customs and values of the stakeholder group. If you are Caucasian and your team is composed of all white people, would you see a problem with conducting a campaign targeting African Americans? If you are in an all-male team, would you feel confident in designing a campaign aimed at a female audience? If you have never been to the Middle East, do you feel competent to design a campaign aimed at promoting an American company to audiences in that region? Probably not. After all, the nuances of cultures that are not our own are difficult to understand. However, with some cultural sensitivity, you can surround yourself with people from targeted background for every campaign—or at least research other cultures with an open mind—and create campaigns that effectively accomplish a client's communication goals.

2   There is no such thing as "one size fits all" standardized messages. Messages must be customized for specific audiences. Understand that stakeholders in different cultures respond better to messages that have been customized for them.

3   Most audience members tend to be loyal to communications that match their lifestyle and cultural customs and backgrounds. A carefully tailored message can create a bond between the stakeholder and the organization you represent. This loyalty can be enduring, but that allegiance can quickly evaporate if the strategic communication firm does not remain dedicated to serving the needs of the specified audience.

4   Use the primary language of the cultural group you are trying to reach. This may sound like an easy task, but it is actually quite difficult because people too often forget that not everyone speaks English or understands the intricacies of the English

language. Learning another language also means learning about the culture that uses that language.

5   Use a spokesperson that represents the targeted culture. Research has shown that we respond better to people who look and act like we do. Therefore, it makes sense to use someone already trusted by the culture to deliver the message or sell the product.

Industry Insight

Making Work That Travels

As companies continue to expand into new markets, one of the challenges they face is finding the most interesting and relevant way to tell their story to different people in different countries. And crucially, they need to figure out how to tell the story efficiently, both in terms of their time and budget.

When I moved from a mainly North American role in New York to a truly global role in Amsterdam, I thought one of the big challenges would be learning about the nuances between markets in order to make work that resonates with consumers in different countries.

But one thing you learn very quickly in a global role is people around the world are more similar than different. Global strategic communication starts with a strong insight based in a universal human truth (the same type of truth you might see played out in a Disney or Pixar film). You're not exempt from doing research, but you can conduct research while you are developing the creative brief in the few countries you think will be most different to find what they have in common.

Second, make sure your truth plays against a cultural tension. An insight without tension will lead to flat, uninteresting communications. Instinctively, global communications tend to shy away from tension, for fear of making a misstep and facing consumer backlash. But there's no empirical evidence to show bad communications have ever had a long-term negative impact on sales. Companies shouldn't fear consumer outrage, they should fear consumer indifference.

The next thing you need is a good Big Idea. This should be rooted in your human truth and tied to your brand, and I capitalize the "b" in "big" because your idea should be big enough that each local market team can make the idea locally relevant. That's where the local insight and nuance should sit—with the local team. They'll always know their market better than you do.

I've found stress-testing an idea to determine whether it's big enough isn't exactly scientific. You'll know you've found the right one when the room is excited, when proof-of-concept tactics are generated quickly and it's easy to explain why it's right for the consumer, right for the brand and right for the strategy brief.

You need to carry that excitement with you as you sell in to clients and help them move it through their organization Or, if you're a client, as you sell it through your organization. Good ideas need a core group of advocates from inception to execution, especially at the global level where the communications face a larger group of stakeholders than at the local level.

A common misconception about global communication is that the central piece—whether it's a film, a partnership or an event—needs to be the most locally relevant. This often is voiced as consumers not being able to "see" themselves in the communications. An idea built on a human truth will resonate anywhere. Great communications are magnets, drawing people in, not mirrors trying to reflect an image of who the brand thinks the consumer is.

The reality is that local relevance can and should come to life in the other executions not developed by the global team. Whether that's through local sponsorships, partnerships, content or any of the other tactics available for strategic communication, as long as it comes from the same idea and makes use of the campaign's tone and visual elements, it will feel coherent to the global campaign and bring the local relevance needed for success.

A good idea will always travel. The final piece to successful global communications is to participate in or help organizations share back local adaptations of global campaigns with the global team, and with other markets. This is beneficial in several ways: It gives global some oversight to understand how campaigns are being implemented (and where improvements might need to be made in the future) and it allows best practices to be shared within the organization. A tactic from one market might be relevant for another, or two markets might have tried the same tactic with varying success, and can help improve the tactic for other markets. We call this "borrowing and building."

Creating a successful global strategic communications campaign isn't an easy task, but with some strategic rigor, a strong Big Idea and the team and tools to rally an organization behind that idea, the task is far less daunting than it might seem.

Wes Young—Communications Planning Director, Wieden+Kennedy Amsterdam.

Stereotypes

Communicating with diverse stakeholder groups can be a difficult task, but as discussed earlier in this chapter, understanding other cultures and the differences between you and others, can make interacting cross-culturally very rewarding and fun. However, there are two traps that humans can fall into when attempting to deal with people who are different from themselves—stereotyping and ethnocentrism. As mentioned in Chapter 5, **stereotyping** is a form of categorization that mentally organizes experiences and guides your behavior toward a particular group of people. Though some stereotypes may be positive in nature and provide helpful mental shortcuts, most of them are hurtful to the particular stakeholder group, for example, "Americans are loud" or "Germans drink all the time." Everyone tends to use stereotypes to some degree, but for a strategic communication practitioner this should be avoided, if possible.

Stereotypes can hinder communication with diverse audiences for the following reasons:[12]

- Stereotypes *act as a filter*, keeping out information that people don't already subscribed to. They promote cognitive dissonance, meaning messages are more difficult to understand, attend to, or be acted upon when the information presented is not the same or compatible with the receiver's own thoughts or ideas.
- Stereotypes assume that all members of a group have exactly the same traits. We know this not to be the case. There are no monolithic societies in the world where population is exactly the same. Individual difference must be recognized and respected.
- Stereotypes keep you from successfully communicating because they oversimplify, exaggerate and overgeneralized. They distort because they are based on half-truths and offer untrue premises and assumptions. They fill communication channels with noise oftentimes blunting the true message of the sender.
- Stereotypes, once started, are hard to break. Because they are often repeated stereotypes only strengthen over time and become more difficult to combat. Some say that stereotypes can create self-fulfilling prophecies. Individuals tend to see behavior to confirm their expectations even when that behavior is absent.

It should be mentioned that demographics and stereotypes are not the same thing. In the next section, we will analyze some of the most recognizable demographic groups. Demographics are based on facts and rooted in scientific research methods. They're not based on fear, innuendo or insecurity, as stereotypes can be.

Ethnocentrism

Ethnocentrism is the view that one's own group is the center of everything, and others are scaled and rated with reference to it. It is the practice of evaluating other cultures by the standards and customs of your own culture. National ethnocentrism is a strong devotion that places one's nation above all others. It goes beyond national pride and patriotism and possesses the more negative impacts of national superiority.

Ethnocentrism is universal. Everybody has varying degrees of it. Think of your country, your college or university, and your car. Chances are you're very proud of where you live, where you study and what you drive. It is a normal human reaction. But think how you feel when someone, for example, a rival university starts throwing shade about your school. Automatically, you try to rationalize how this person can be so misguided and you start to think of all the ways your school is better. This is a low stakes example, but just imagine if stakes were higher—like in government-to-government diplomatic exchanges. It is important for strategic communication professionals to not show ethnocentric bias to their stakeholders.

Ethnocentrism can work in a two-fold manner within the profession. First, practitioners should be conscious of how they promote their client's messages and products, so as not to further ethnocentrism. Professionals should think their products and the organizations they advocate for are the very best, but this can turn negative when a practitioner views their system as the only system, or worse, tries to force others to use the same system. If that were to happen, then the strategic communication professional would be working to further ethnocentrism. The easiest way for professionals to combat ethnocentrism is simply to be open to new viewpoints. Learn to step into the other person's shoes and ask yourself, without bias, why do people think the way they do. The answers may lead you to a potential new stakeholder who supports your organization, message and/or product without reservation.

Important Stakeholder Groups

The most difficult skill for a strategic communicator when dealing with stakeholders is to understand and be able to effectively communicate with people who are in different demographic groups than their own. Think about how hard it is to explain something to your mother or grandmother. These are people that you know and love, but because they are older and have different life experiences, it can be hard to talk to them. As a strategic communication professional, it is critical to put yourself "in other people's shoes." You must understand individuals well enough to communicate your message clearly and persuasively, even though they may not be like you. One place to start is through gathering a basic knowledge about some key demographic groups. This type of information changes quickly, so it is important to keep up with the most current research on large demographic groups in society. Here's a basic framework to get you started.

Age Groups

Age is a popular and easy way to segment the U.S. populations. Depending on when a person is born, attitudes, lifestyles and attitudes vary. People identify with people their same age. They tend to hold similar opinions and have similar buying habits because they share similar life experiences. Three important age groups in the U.S. currently are labeled Baby Boomers, Gen Xers and Millennials.

"Baby Boomers" (born 1940–1964) account for the ever-growing population of senior adults and have the equivalent of about four trillion dollars in consumption in our economy. Here are some of the major points that distinguish this group:

- They are more skeptical than most age groups and they demand value for their money because they live on set incomes.
- They are less influenced by fads.

- They take time to volunteer in community organizations as a way of filling their spare time.
- They tend to be reliable voters.
- Issues that affect their well-being, such as health care, are especially important to them.
- They still read newspapers and increasingly watch more television, making them a target audience for advertising on legacy media outlets. Although their use of social media is increasing, they tend to find more credibility in newspaper, magazine, radio and television content.
- They are discriminating shoppers. They are not fanatically loyal to brands; rather, they will always look for the best value.
- Baby boomers are becoming more non-conformist as they age. They are "free spirits" and often rebel at social norms.

Generation X consists of those born between 1965 and 1980 and are a dominant segment of the workforce. They tend to be extremely independent, highly valuing their self-sufficiency and innovation. They have been referred to as "America's middle child," bridging the gap between seniors and Millennials. Gen Xers are:

- Suspicious of large corporations and more discriminating about attempts to brand those companies. They are cynical, and yet, more easily swayed on some issues.
- More diverse and unique in terms of ethnicity.
- They appreciate a large variety of media formats, from social media to legacy platforms, as they grew up on traditional media at the time it began to change.
- They are the primary users of Facebook.

Millennials (or Generation Y) were born 1981 to 1996 or so, a period of great change in American society, especially in terms of technology. These stakeholders have a strong sense of community, both global and domestic, but can be also be narcissistic and reliant on their appearance. This generation is known for:

- Being socially conscious, and more attracted to public-service-related professions. They tend to align their careers with their passions.
- They tend to be more competitive than Generation X.
- They are highly networked, reliant on technology for social interaction and even dating, but lacking in their interpersonal communication skills.

Most of the readers of this book are part of the newest generation, which is currently being labeled as **Generation Z**. Demographers don't know much about you yet because you are still in high school and college and are just now developing your own unique traits that will define you as a generational group. Being the first truly digitally native generation, Generation Z mostly gets their news on social media and visits YouTube daily. Apple and Google are among their favorite brands. Politically, Generation Z is more liberal, more comfortable with big government and less U.S. centric than the generations before them.[13] There is no doubt that current events, such as the COVID-19 pandemic will impact this generation, leading some to call this group "Zoomers" because of their time spent in virtual school via the online video platform Zoom.

Professional Profile

Ayanna Jackson—Vice President, American Advertising Federation

Ayanna Jackson—Vice President, American Advertising Federation (AAF).

Ayanna graduated from the University of Louisiana, Lafayette with a bachelor's degree in Communications and a minor in English. She has spent most of her career working in advertising sales for the world's most notable media companies, but transitioned to the not-for-profit sector, still with a focus on advertising.

> **What did you want to do with your career?** I wanted to be the next Oprah Winfrey.
>
> **Are you doing it?** Not quite.
>
> **What are you doing now?** I am responsible for promoting diversity within advertising and media industries, as well as educating the future "Mad Men (and Women)" in our industry. I manage and create programs that promote Diversity, Equity and Inclusion (DEI) not only in the advertising industry, but in media, as well. Creating awareness around the lack of fair and equitable treatment for diverse communities, addressing the "why" it even exists and what we can do to course-correct these issues is what I do. It's hard, because it requires me to change mindsets and behaviors. It can be exhausting, but when you hear someone tell you that you've affected the trajectory of their lives, it makes it all worth it.
>
> **How did you get there?** Prayer. I literally prayed for a job that would allow me to be of service to others. I never thought it would be in the advertising industry. My career had been spent helping major brands market themselves to make a ton of money. I didn't know there was a place that would allow me to have such an integral impact on young people's lives in the industry. I also didn't

know the AAF existed. By coincidence (or divine intervention) a former colleague from many, many, many years ago told me about the organization and suggested I reach out to his ex-wife who was the chief operating officer. I'd just moved back to DC and I wasn't looking for a job, I just wanted to learn more about the advertising landscape in DC. I connected with the COO and she was very open to talk to me. We stayed in contact and when I was ready for a new professional opportunity, I reached out because I knew she was well connected. Little did I know that the opportunity would be to work for her at the AAF. I'd never worked in the DEI space. But, I did know that many times in my former job, I was the only face that looked like me at certain events and that needed to change. My current position has afforded me the opportunity to understand the glaring disparities between diverse communities and others within the industry.

How have your dreams changed? In wanting to be the next Oprah, I wanted to effect change. Now, I just do it in a different way, so I guess they haven't changed all that much. My current job is aligned with my personal goals—to be of service to others.

What has surprised you most about yourself or your career? In my current position, I'm still fighting to secure equity for all. The fact that we're still having the discussion about diversity in 2021 and that the lack of representation of certain demographics, especially within the Black community, is at times disheartening. But, I'm also optimistic that I can move the needle, whatever that may look like.

What advice would you give to someone in college now? Take advantage of every opportunity you have to network and of the resources at your disposal. Be aggressive and make your own opportunities. Be unapologetically you and know your value.

More information about Ayanna can be found here: https://www.linkedin.com/in/ayanna-jackson-6a24408/.

Racial Groups

Though it sometimes isn't easy to talk about, race is a very important factor in distinguishing stakeholders because minority racial populations are growing in the United States. Indeed, America continues to racially diversify. By 2050 it is estimated that non-white populations will outnumber Caucasians. Therefore, today's companies need to lay the groundwork for the inevitable changes in communication strategies that will accompany this shift in the population. But while racial composition is important, it cannot be the sole way of targeting minorities due to regional, cultural, religious factors and other differences that can occur within a given racial subculture.

The three largest minority populations in the U.S. are Hispanics, African Americans and Asian Americans. Hispanics are currently the fastest growing sociocultural group in America, and they represent a very large sector of the economy, spending roughly $1.5 trillion annually in 2018, which is expected to grow 50% in the next five years. This is a young group, as it makes up about a quarter of the U.S. millennial population. The culture is, of course, bilingual, meaning that strategic communication messages must be available in both English and Spanish. Other factors about Hispanics includes that this group tends to be loyal to organizations, products and brands and are very family oriented.

African Americans represent about 13% of the U.S. populations and their buying power is approximately $1.3 trillion in 2018. As a group, African Americans tend to be early adopters of products, especially new technology. Blacks watch more TV than other demographic groups. Asian Americans are a smaller population group, only about 6% of the U.S. population, but represent about $1 trillion in spending power.[14]

Other Important Stakeholder Groups

LGBTQ+ members, the disabled and religious groups are examples of other important segments of the U.S. society. Because these groups contain a large population, they deserve the attention of strategic communicators. Understanding the unique characteristics of these groups, including shifting trends is essential to the practice of strategic communication. For example, the LGBTQ+ population represents tremendous spending power and are heavy users of all types of media.

All the demographic differences represented here are just a few of the audience considerations that a strategic communicator must consider when targeting stakeholders on behalf of clients. It is important to thoroughly research stakeholders to avoid cultural insensitivity that will decrease the impact of messages, cause distrust toward the client and/or offend the targeted stakeholders.

Summary

Stakeholders are the people who the communicative entity is trying to reach with their messages. Stakeholders are anyone who has a stake—either positive or negative—in the organization, including customers, employees, investors and advocacy groups, among others. The term stakeholder is very broad. Depending on the situation, they may also be called consumers, publics or target audiences. Consumers are an important stakeholder group for marketers, who must understand how they shop, purchase and use products.

There are many diverse stakeholder groups that require special strategies and consideration in order to effectively reach them. Strategic communication professionals need to have skills in inter-cultural communication and avoid stereotypes and ethnocentrism when working with diverse stakeholders. Understanding stakeholders may be the most important task for the strategic communication professional and doing a good job will go a long way to assure success.

Discussion Questions

1   Define the concept of stakeholders. What is the difference between internal and external stakeholders? Publics, consumers and audiences are all stakeholders. How are they different from each other?
2   Big corporations, like Apple, have a variety of stakeholders. Can you identify their active stakeholders and passive stakeholders? Who are their key influencers?

3 Pretend you are working for a company that manufactures jeans and other denim clothing for teenage girls. The owner wants to expand the company's business by marketing to other segments beyond young women. What segment do you think the company should appeal to? Describe the segment demographically, geographically, psychographically and behaviorally.

4 Explain in detail the consumer decision-making stages that you might go through when you are buying a new personal computer. Which brands would be in your evoked set? What kind of information search would you conduct? What criteria would you use to evaluate the alternatives? How would you deal with buyer's remorse?

5 Why is it important for strategic communication professionals to understand diverse stakeholder segments? Give an example of a brand that segments according to race.

Check out the online support material, including chapter summaries, useful links and further reading, at www.routledge.com/9780367426316

Notes

1 Grunig, J. E., & Hunt, T. (1984). *Managing public relations*. New York: Holt, Rinehart and Winston.
2 https://en.wikipedia.org/wiki/Fandom.
3 https://en.wikipedia.org/wiki/List_of_fandom_names.
4 https://toxicfandomsandhatedoms.miraheze.org/wiki/Harry_Potter_Fandom_and_Hatedom.
5 Italie, H. (11 April 2007). "P\lku8 tter sites wild about Harry". *Toronto Star*.
6 Menta, A. (2016, Aug 3). We finally know who "Becky with the good hair" is in Beyoncé's song. *Elite Daily*. Retrieved from https://www.elitedaily.com/entertainment/beyonce-becky-with-good-hair-means/1571962.
7 Grunig, J. E. (1997). A situational theory of publics: Conceptual history, recent challenges and new research. In D. Moss, T. MacManus, & D. Vercic (Eds.), *Public Relations Research: An International Perspective* (pp. 3–48). London: International Thomson Business Press.
8 www.nielsen.com.
9 Kotler, P. (2000). *Marketing Management: Millenium Edition*. Upper Saddle River, NJ: Prentice Hall.
10 Hall, E. T. (1959). *The Silent Language*. Garden City, NY: Doubleday.
11 Wilcox, D. L., Cameron, G. T., & Reber, B. H. (2015). *Public Relations: Strategies and Tactics* (11th ed.). New York: Pearson.
12 Samovar, L. A., & Porter, R. E. (2001). *Communication between Cultures*. Belmont, CA: Wadsworth/Thomson Learning.
13 Morning Consult (2020). Understanding Gen Z. https://morningconsult.com/wp-content/uploads/2019/06/Morning-Consult-Understanding-Gen-Z.pdf.
14 Simon S. Selig Jr. Center for Economic Growth at the University of Georgia University of Georgia (2018). The multi-cultural economy. https://www.newswise.com/articles/minority-markets-have-3-9-trillion-buying-power.

Chapter 9

Message Tactics

Learning Outcomes

After you have read the chapter, you should be able to do the following:

- Understand the importance and role of message strategy.
- Learn how to communicate messages across all aspects of the organization and to all its stakeholders.
- Describe the 5C's of good storytelling.
- Demonstrate the effective development of creative briefs.
- Describe the process for writing different types of message tactics, including a print ad, news release and social media content.

Chapter Opening Vignette

The Apple Experience

When Steve Jobs returned to Apple in 1997 as interim CEO—he had been fired by Apple's board of directors in 1985—one of the first things he did was to launch the "Think Different" campaign. In doing so, he explained, "we believe that people with passion can change the world for the better." Jobs maintained that this core value is what drives Apple to create the best products.

Staying true to that passion for innovation is the reason that Apple products have been so consistent, and it is the reason that you can walk into any Apple store across the world and get the same experience. From sales associates to top executives, Apple is united by a common culture with a straightforward message.

It is that culture that ensures that Apple customers enjoy the experience that they have come to expect when they interact with Apple. The company works to ensure all the domains of practice are working together. Apple is often recognized for its ability to build pre-launch product buzz and let media outlets help tell their story. When you visit an Apple store, it looks and feels very similar to the experience you have when you visit Apple.com. When you purchase an Apple product, whether it be a computer, wireless ear buds or a new charger, you will notice that the packaging also reinforces the light, airy and high quality look and feel of the product, the store, the website and the advertising. Even the user manual that is included with its products has the unique Apple look and feel.

Every aspect of the Apple experience reinforces its brand identity and message strategy. What do you think of when you think of Apple? Products? Advertising? In-store experience? The message strategy and the products tell the story of making people's lives better through innovation.

Apple Store in Palo Alto, California.
Photo Credit: By FASTILY—Own work, CC BY-SA 4.0.

Messaging

In strategic communication, messaging involves how an organization portrays itself, shares information about itself and the value it provides. The story of Apple demonstrates the importance of the message strategy. Message strategy is about engaging stakeholders, fostering relationships, and working together to tell the story and, in the process create the best message for the brand or communicative entity (CE). Effective strategic communication messaging must work in harmony across all aspects of a communicative entity, like a symphony orchestra that mixes instruments together in unity to set the tempo and shape the sound of the ensemble.

This chapter will help you learn the steps and strategies that are required to develop an effective message strategy for a CE. It will focus on communicating that message within the company, where relevant, and then using media to communicate the message to the public.

Developing a Message Strategy

Effective messaging is always simple and consistent. In today's marketplace, people expect and demand individual and personalized communication from CEs. Stakeholders rarely support a CE, or buy just a product or service; rather, they evaluate its value or utility and buy into the vision of the CE, its essence and its people. This is true for organizations and individuals, such as musicians and sports stars. Consistency is also very important to an effective message strategy. A simple and consistent message drives relevance, awareness and action. For instance, if a consumer believes in a beauty product because the manufacturer's core value of no animal testing in product development aligns with her own, she will not only buy the organization's products, she will become a fan and spread the word to others. This section will focus on how to develop the message that will resonate with all of your stakeholders.

Core Values and Messaging

In Chapter 3 an entity's value system was discussed as part of the foundational stage of strategic planning. It was not only included as a step in a plan. It has real value and everything the CE says and does should reflect those values. This is very much the case with message development. An organization must always keep its core values in mind when developing its message. Messaging is not simply created by an agency or marketing department. A good message strategy emerges from the founder's vision, from product research and development, and from listening to employees and other stakeholders. If the organization does not stay true to its own core values in its messaging, why would its customers or fans stay true to the organization?

At the same time, message strategies must be nimble and adaptable based on what's going on in the world, in the marketplace, and in the lives of an organization's stakeholders. This does not mean that values are situational. While consistency in values is vital in messaging, strategic communicators must also be flexible and adaptable. An effective message strategy requires listening, improving and adjusting the plan. The message strategy must always stay true to the organization's mission and values, but it also must be creative, innovative and fresh. There are many examples of how brand messaging changed because the value system was no longer reflected in the message. Numerous brands have recently changed their brand names and logos because they no longer reflect their core values of equality and respect for all stakeholders. Examples include the Washington Redskins, which at this time has chosen a placeholder name of the Washington Football Team, and Aunt Jemima will now be known as the Pearl Milling Company.

Messages should also be communicated effectively and consistently. In evaluating message strategy, an organization should be able to ask its stakeholders, including employees and customers, the following questions and find their answers to be consistent:

- Who are we?
- What problem are we solving?

- How are we different from our competitors?
- Why should people buy our product or service?

If the answers are not consistent across all stakeholders, then the organization is missing the mark on effective communication. Ineffective communication, particularly in the long term, almost certainly affects an organization's bottom line, which leads to organizational failure.

Channels of Communicating the Message

As social media technology continues to drive consumer activism, organizations are realizing that it is essential to effectively communicate how their company, brand or organization bring its core values to life in order to retain its relevance and vitality among stakeholders. Good strategic communication starts from the C-suite—the chief-level executives—chief executive officer (CEO), chief financial officer (CFO), chief operating officer (COO), and chief information officer (CIO). This communication then permeates throughout the organization and all stakeholder groups.

Strategic communication messages are delivered through multiple channels or methods. A person, such as a sales representative, repair department employee, security guard or customer service representative can deliver and receive messages. Customers or fans also deliver messages. These are typically called word-of-mouth (WOM) messaging. Messages are also delivered to larger audiences through media channels such as TV, radio and social media. However, the challenge for strategic communicators is that the impersonal nature of the media can make it difficult to craft the message that resonates with stakeholders on a personal or meaningful level.

Let's take the user manual for an automobile, for example. Is it a brand message that communicates the essence of what an organization is? The answer is typically no, because many organizations fail to take the opportunity to craft a user manual or other technical writing to support the brand identity and company values. But, it is a missed opportunity to enhance relationships with stakeholders. When strategic communication is working at an optimal level, an organization uses all its channels and methods to consistently tell the same story and celebrate its core values. As mentioned in the chapter opening vignette, Apple carefully crafts its user guides to reflect its brand image and voice, because the organization understands every aspect of the brand from the store to the packaging, including the user guide, can influence how customers and stakeholders think of the brand.

We have established that an effective message strategy is in sync with the company's core values. But how is a message strategy communicated? The channels in which communicative entities must tell their stories increase almost daily. Let's look at just some of the channels or activities available to communicate messages.

Advertising

Advertising is a form of persuasive communication that is run in the media and paid for by an identified sponsor. There are multiple venues where a company's advertising is disseminated. These include newspapers, magazines, television, radio, outdoor advertising such as transit vehicles or billboards, direct mail and online advertising including paid search, social media, streaming video advertising and digital display advertising. We will explain paid media in more detail in Chapters 10 and 11.

Sales Promotions

Sales promotions are designed to increase sales or encourage the use or trial of a product or service. Sales promotions activities can help customers in the decision-making process by providing incentives for action. They can be a big part of a messaging strategy. There are many different types of sales promotions, and they are common in both consumer and business-to-business markets. Sampling, loyalty programs, sweepstakes and contests are all examples of sales promotions. Sales promotions are often used in conjunction with advertising and other communication efforts. As part of the strategic communicator's toolbox, sales promotions are also discussed in Chapter 7.

Free giveaways, also known as premiums, are another sales promotion technique, which can be utilized in many ways. A common messaging strategy and sales promotion for cologne and cosmetic brands, for example, is a gift with purchase. You've heard of SWAG, right? While it can mean different things, in the context of strategic communication, it stands for branded stuff we get for free or Stuff We All Get. When you receive a free tote bag, with a company's brand logo on it, when you go to an expo or an event, it is a sales promotion technique to get you to notice and build a relationship with that brand.

You are surely aware of **coupons**, which are another sales promotion technique that can be utilized in different ways. Coupons can be associated with paid advertising, such as including a coupon in newspaper or magazine ads or in a direct-mail campaign. The most steadily growing use of coupons is through coupon codes shared online. Coupons also can be offered on packaging and through **point-of-purchase (POP)** displays. POP displays are product displays in supermarkets and retails stores that are separate from standard shelving. The goal of POP displays is to draw attention to the brand and products with 3-D elements and fun, eye-catching visuals, so shoppers will be drawn to buy those products over the countless other choices.

Free trials or sampling are yet another sales technique that has exploded in the digital market. Have you visited the app store lately? One of the most common techniques to sell subscription-based apps is to offer a try-before-you-buy approach. These are just a few examples of sales promotion options.

Here is a more comprehensive list of sales promotions:

1   Coupons
2   Sampling
3   Premiums
4   Loyalty Programs
5   Sweepstakes
6   Contests
7   Brand Demonstrations
8   Cash Back
9   Free Trial
10 Bonus Packs
11 Shared Programs
12 Logo Merchandise
13 Experiences.

As we have discussed, communication strategy works best when you employ multiple channels, strategies and tactics together to support each other. Sales promotions are just another example of that. For example, McDonald's did not roll out its latest Monopoly Sweepstakes game promotion in the UK without employing communication channels such as paid advertising. These included TV, radio, print, traditional and digital billboards, as well as social activity on Facebook, Twitter, Instagram and Snapchat, not to mention a custom website and online game board.[1] McDonald's also informed its sales staff of the sweepstakes and prompted them to encourage customers to "get peeling for that winning feeling" with game pieces featured on promotional food packaging. The goal is to use as many communication channels as needed to get the promotional message out to all potential stakeholders.

Public Relations (PR)

Every major organization or company has a public relations person or unit through which they trumpet the core message. The most common tactic for disseminating a message through PR is the **news release**, but there are several other forms of PR messaging. News releases are written with the look and feel of a news story and sent to media outlets to generate interest in an organization or communicative entity. News releases can be used to make an announcement, such as an increase in quarterly profits, as a follow-up after an event such as when a local brewery wins a state-wide competition, or in response to a trend, current event or unfolding crisis. News or press releases are written for and shared with print media or "the press." PR professionals also create broadcast news releases, such as a **video news release (VNR)** or an **audio news release (ANR)**. A video news release is simply a news release in the form of broadcast news story, complete with video, voice-over and additional video footage, still photographs and animation known as b-roll footage, which can be used to enrich the story and give the media outlet flexibility in editing. The broadcast stations can use the video provided with voice-over and graphics created by the PR professionals as is, or they can use the **b-roll footage**, or video images without voice-over and graphics to enhance their own stories. An ANR is the same concept, but designed to be played on the radio.

Media kits are another tool used to generate media coverage for an organization or communicative entity. Media kits consist of a **fact sheet** about the organization or event, biographic sketch of the major people involved, a straight news story, news-column material, a news feature, a brochure, photographs, and audio and video segments. The materials are designed and packaged professionally in line with the organization's branding and sent to media outlets. Magazine publishers create media kits to help attract advertisers by explaining their pricing and ad sizes and specs, describing their audiences and quality of their content.

News conferences are utilized to garner media attention for an announcement, a breaking event, follow-up to an investigation or other items that would be of interest to news organizations and their audiences. The communicative entity or representative usually makes an announcement then allows time for reporters to ask questions. To prepare for a news conference, strategic communicators must write an opening statement, a briefing paper for the person answering the reporter's questions and social media content that can be shared during or after the news conference. Like writing news releases, strategic communicators must understand what makes news and prepare their news conference information to meet those standards.

Events are utilized by strategic communicators to develop and enhance brand relationships, and they continue to grow in popularity each year. In fact, many media outlets utilize events to help sell their own media and add value for their advertisers. From the trade shows to tasting tables in the grocery store, events help brands come alive to consumers and stakeholders. Events are not only planned to give the attendees an authentic, engaging and motivating experience, but also they are designed to be news worthy and attract media coverage.

Strategic communicators also must be prepared to provide **responses to media inquiries** even if they have not sent out a press release, held a press conference or hosted an event. Often, in the event of a crisis or another news event, an organization or communicative entity may have a connection to the story and receive requests from the media for comment. Strategic communicators must be available to help gather information, develop and deliver a timely response to help build or maintain a positive relationship with the media on behalf their client—the CE. Cooperating with and keeping the media informed is also important to maintaining a positive image with customers and stakeholders.

Whether it is writing a press release, holding a news conference, hosting an event or responding to media inquiries, it's just like writing and creating good advertising. It comes down to telling a good, compelling story. Remember, a good story can be a true story, and good strategic communication is about authenticity.

The Five C's of Storytelling

Creating a good story means presenting important or interesting information that will engage the audience and keep them wanting to learn more. To engage an audience with a good story, you want to fully understand them. Think about how you talk with your friends versus how you talk with your grandparents. Would you tell your grandparents a story the exact same way, using the same language that you would if you were telling the story to your friends? No, you would likely change it up. You would craft the message for the audience. Your grandparents think differently than your friends. They've had different experiences. They value different things. A good story is meaningful to the listener. You must have a good understanding of the listener in order to connect with them on a real level.

We sort of just know that instinctively when interacting with people. We don't necessarily strategize in our everyday interactions. Or do we? What about when we are trying to persuade people into doing what we want them to do? Let's say you want to go on a study abroad trip to Europe over spring break. You have a chance to talk to your mom about it first, then you will see your dad in a couple of days and ask him about it then. Will you use the same tactics to persuade your mom, as you would use to persuade your dad? What will your mom want to know? Will they value the same things?

Academic Angle

Theories of Persuasion[2]

Strategic communication often functions to persuade audiences in favor of a sender's message. Therefore, in order to extend our understanding of strategic communication, it is important to study the large body of scientific research dealing with persuasion and attitude change.

Persuasion is defined as *attitude change resulting in exposure to information from others*.[3] The discipline of persuasion goes back to the days of Plato and Aristotle. For the Greeks and Romans, persuasion could take the form of an argument, debate, discussion or public speech effectively arguing a point of view. Techniques required for effective persuasion were honed, practiced and applauded in the public arena. Much of America's government and legal system is derived from these ancient societies who had great respect for public discourse and informed discussion—the tools of persuasion.

When applied to advertising, persuasion is used to *change consumer's attitudes* toward a particular product, brand, person or idea, which ideally leads to *buying* the product, voting for a political candidate or accepting an idea, such as "only you can prevent forest fires."[4]

Carl Hovland (1912–1961), a Yale psychology professor attempted to uncover the "magic keys of persuasion."[5] After World War II, Hovland sought the perfect set of conditions and combinations of variables that would allow persuasion to take place without fail. Naturally, Hovland was unable to discover the perfect persuasion formula, primarily because human beings are very fickle subjects whose behavior is very unpredictable. He did however make some important discoveries that continue to serve as the basis of understanding of how persuasion works. A few of those discoveries are reviewed here, including source credibility, sleeper effect, one-sided versus two-sided messages and audience personality factors.

Source credibility research has established that more credible sources are more effective in persuading an audience. That is why advertisers often use doctors to sell medicine or celebrities to tout fashion. However, this is not always the case. Hovland's research revealed that over time the receiver tends to forget the source but remember the message. Therefore, source credibility ultimately may not be a critical persuasion variable.

Research supporting one-sided versus two-sided messages is interesting. One-sided messages, those that only present arguments in favor of the desired change and ignore counter arguments, are most effective in persuading people who are already in favor of the message and those who are less educated. For an audience opposed to the message and/or a well-educated audience, a two-sided approach—one that presents both sides of the argument—is more effective. Presenting the arguments for and against the favored position allows the receivers to acknowledge their point of view before accepting the other side. Two-sided messages also serve to *inoculate* the audience against future efforts at persuasion.

Hovland and other post-WWII researchers established the concept of *individual differences* and maintained that receivers have different backgrounds, personalities, values and environments. Individuals will interpret and react differently to the same message. Mass communication messages are not *magic bullets* that strike everyone in the same manner and result in an immediate, uniform, direct effect, as early propaganda scholars believed. Often effects are much more moderate, and vary according to the characteristics of the individual receiver.

Hovland also found that less educated people and those with lower self-esteem are easier to persuade than more educated and confident receivers. Further, attitude change may not happen quickly. Receivers who show no attitude change immediately following exposure to a persuasive message may be persuaded later—as long as six weeks after exposure. This phenomenon is called the *sleeper effect*.

By exploring the academic literature on persuasion, many strategies can be learned and used to not only make us better communicators, but also to help us resist persuasive attempts that we may encounter as citizens and consumers.

Strategic communication messages not only present interesting information that is valuable to the audience, but also the messages are designed to change attitudes and/or behavior. The messages need to be memorable and lead to short-term or long-term action or both. In order to change attitudes and behavior, the audience or stakeholders must be emotionally moved by the message. The key to effective message strategy is storytelling. Our brains are designed to remember stories. Humans are much more likely to remember a story than facts and figures. A great story takes the reader/listener/audience on a journey with characters, locations, ups and downs, conflict and resolution. Strategic communication falls short when communicative entities fail to tell a complete story effectively. To ensure a story is complete, you can use 5C's of storytelling as a good checklist of what is essential to telling a complete story.

Context

A good storyteller breathes life into the story from the start by introducing the environment and providing rich details to understand place, time, social order and who the characters are. Context helps the readers/listeners/viewers develop enough stake in the story where they can, feel the extreme temperature, smell the intoxicating aroma, hear the pounding sound of the rain, see themselves in the situation and care about it.

Characters

Good stories have interesting characters with whom the readers/viewers can relate. Compelling stories feature a heroic figure, who overcomes obstacles and conflict for the betterment of others. What do you think of when you think of Progressive insurance? What about Budweiser beer? If you said, Flo and Clydesdales, then you answered the question of how characters help tell a brand's story.

Conflict

A story would be boring without conflict. The hero cannot make it to hero status without facing conflict or battling the villain. The conflict drives the story and helps the hero achieve his/her goal. One of the most iconic ads that uses conflict, specifically individual vs. the society machine conflict is Apple's "1984" ad that launched the original Macintosh computer. The full 60-second spot ran only once on national television during the third quarter of Super Bowl XVIII on January 22, 1984. The ad features a woman throwing a sledgehammer through a screen violently disrupting a brutally conformist system and set the tone for its "Think Different" campaign. The Apple brand was the hero of breaking free of a world of PC conformity.

Climax

A compelling story has exciting conflict, but that conflict must lead up to something. The conflict must come to an end, and it should be exciting. David must slay Goliath. Superman saves Lois. The astronauts make it back into the earth's atmosphere. The climax is the turning point in the story, and no good story is complete without it.

Conclusion/Change

One of the worst things an author can do is to leave the audience hanging at the climax. Your conflict doesn't have to have a positive solution—tragedies are stories that ended badly after all. But a good story has a resolution and that means a change takes place within the central character. Think of a caterpillar entering a cocoon. Once he does so, one of two things will happen: (1) He will either transform into a butterfly, or (2) he will die. But no matter what else happens, he will never climb out of the cocoon as a caterpillar.

Your story should be consistent. Once your central character faces the conflict, s/he should either be transformed into someone smarter or more beautiful, or s/he will succumb to death or despair. Of course, in strategic communication storytelling, it is best to write positive resolution stories for your clients' and their brands/products/services.

In strategic communication, communicative entities need to tell stories with rich detail in which their customers or stakeholders are the heroes of their stories and the product or service should help the heroes to overcome its enemies, but not without an epic battle that reaches a pinnacle. It's important to consider what theme you want your audiences to walk away with and what action you want them to take as a result. In order to persuade your parents into sending you on that study abroad trip, tell them a story about how the experience will bring you value, which aligns with what they value, such as you getting a good job after you graduate. See the FIFA Case Study for an industry example of storytelling.

Case Study

FIFA World Cup Messaging

The FIFA World Cup finals is the most widely viewed sporting event in the world. The FIFA World Cup, often simply called the World Cup, is an international football (known as soccer in the U.S.) tournament held once every four years. It is contested by the men's national teams of the member associations *Fédération Internationale de Football Association* (FIFA), the sport's global governing body.

The current format of the World Cup involves 32 teams competing for the title, at venues within the host nation (or nations) over a period of about a month. The 2018 FIFA World Cup was held in Russia. The sporting event is televised across the world, including the U.S. where all of the the matches have been televised live since 1998. The United States has participated in every World Cup since 1990 until they failed to qualify for the 2018 competition after a loss to Trinidad and Tobago in 2017. Even though the U.S. did not have a team competing in the 2018 World Cup, American viewers still tuned in. Germany's stoppage-time win over Sweden on June 23 pulled in 5.4 million viewers on Fox, making it the most-watched non-U.S. men's group stage game on English-language TV in 28 years.

Showing a commercial during the World Cup is a huge opportunity for advertisers to get eyeballs on their brands.[6] Volkswagen (VW) recognized the fact that sports fans like to have a team to get behind and cheer onto victory. So, what's the average American soccer fan to do when their country is not competing? "Jump on the Wagen." The campaign by New York-based ad agency Deutsch aired on Fox and Fox Sports and provided American viewers with some help on which team to cheer for. The company developed a light-hearted series of ads around the tournament, in which representatives of different countries pitch for their teams using customs of their country. The ads, with the tagline "Jump on the Wagen," are all set in VW cars putting the brand/product at the center of the story. In one of the spots, a carload of Swiss people promote their country as the home of Swiss army knives and tweezers. A couple of Argentinians demonstrate their "passionate" nature by arguing over what's playing on the car stereo. A Brazilian woman shows off a trunk-full of soccer trophies.

This campaign is an example of crafting the message around what's going on in the stakeholder's lives and helping them feel valued. The campaign also featured digital extensions through social media channels encouraging fans to adopt a team, as well as Snapchat filters for countries still playing in the last two weeks of the tournament. Jim Zabel, Senior Vice President of Marketing for Volkswagen of America, said, "Overall, it was meant to appeal to the Volkswagen fan's affinity for soccer, delivered with our brand's signature wink and smile."[7]

The Creative Brief

Effective strategic communication begins with research and strategy, as we discussed in the earlier chapters of this book. Before communicative entities can become creative storytellers, they must get into the mind of the consumer or stakeholder in order to craft an interesting and effective message for that audience, which is often identified as insight. The communicative entity must listen closely to what their stakeholders are talking about and how they express themselves, which is best accomplished through qualitative research, such as focus groups or personal interviews, and listening through social media. Listening and understanding stakeholders lead to insights that drive the strategy and spark the creative message.

In order to connect insights and strategies into messages, most advertising agencies and communications firms develop the **big idea**. In order for a campaign to pierce through the noise of competing messages and generate the desired attention from the target audience, the CE must develop a clear, impactful and differentiated concept or the "big idea."

Another tool called a **creative brief** is a written document that the CE uses to show their agency that they understand the problem and have a strategy for solving it. The creative brief outlines the client's vision and ensures everyone involved with the campaign is on the same page. The creative brief accurately and concisely summarizes the consumer/target audience, the product or services, market research of the brand and its competition, and key insights. It's a 1–2-page document that helps to paint a picture of the brand's position and value in the marketplace. The creative brief is a collection of facts, but the purpose of the brief is to inspire the creative team to create the most effective communications to solve a particular problem.

Fifteen Questions for a Creative Brief

The brief, as its name suggests, should be clear, concise and actionable. There is no one-size-fits-all method of developing a creative brief. The format and style of creative briefs vary greatly. However, the creative brief should include the answers to these 15 questions, not necessarily in this order or format.

1   **What's the problem?** Describe the problem. You cannot merely take the client's word for this question. The client might not fully understand the depth of the problem. Dig at the problem until you find the root cause. You have to ask a lot of questions and examine the problem from multiple perspectives to understand the core issue. Until you know the complete answer to this question, the rest of the brief likely will not matter.

2   **Who has the problem?** Determining the target audience is essential to all strategic communication. It's impossible to craft an effective message without knowing to whom you are speaking. The more you know about the target audience, the better you can tailor the message that is meaningful and memorable to them. How is the target audience currently solving this problem? What options do they have that they are not using?

3   **What is the product/service/brand solution that we are offering as the solution?** You need to know as much as possible about product/service/brand. You want to be able to offer the solution in terms that are clear and easy to understand.

4   **What is the product's/service's/brand's existing core values?** You want to be able to align the core values with what the audience values. You must stay true to who the organization or brand is, so it's important to include it in the brief.

5   **What is the rationale and emotional reasons to make people believe us?** You need to provide rational truth to why the product/service/brand is the best solution. But you cannot rely solely on facts, you must provide an emotional angle with which the audience can identify.

6   **What is the big idea?** The development of the big idea enables the CE to create a campaign with a clear, creative focus that can be executed through multiple channels and connects with the target audience in new and innovative ways. The big idea emerges when you have a thorough understanding of the target audience and blend it with a comprehensive knowledge of the product or service.

7   **What will we say?** What are the key words or messages that we must convey? What words, images and sounds will help the target audience understand the emotional reasons to believe our product is the best solution?

8   **How will we communicate our messages?** What communication channels will we use and how will we use them? How will they work together to strengthen our messages?

9   **What action do we want people to take once they receive our messages?** On the surface this seems easy: You want people to become the organization's customer or

fan. But it's not that simple. Each of the communication channels must have its own call to action. Ideally, you want to leverage the communication channel to meet the buyer where she goes for information throughout the buying journey and move the buyer forward.

10 **How do we want people to feel?** Almost all decisions are emotional. They can also be rationalized after the decision has been made. You need to understand how you want people to feel during the engagement/buying process and after they've bought what you have sold. If a customer regrets her decision soon after the purchase, what is the likelihood that she will be back to buy from your organization again? Slim. Repeat customers are easier to retain than it is to attract new ones. A good message strategy should seek to retain, as well as attract customers.

11 **What are the goals of the project?** Setting goals establishes that the direction and result. Goals should be established using the **SMART goals framework** (which is described in detail in Chapter 7): **S—Specific:** Set specific numbers and percentages to achieve. **M—Measurable:** Progress can be supported with data. **A—Attainable:** Set goals that can actually be accomplished. **R—Relevant:** Goals should align with long-term objectives of the organization. **T—Time-bound:** Goals should be achieved by a specific deadline.

12 **How will we measure success?** What is the campaign trying to do? Raise awareness? Drive web traffic? Increase donations? Increase market share? Your goals will drive how the campaign will be measured.

13 **What brand guidelines should we be aware of?** What must be included in the final project? Examples of this include a tagline, logo, images, signature sound, timeline, budget, approval process, key stakeholders who need to approve, and so forth. You might also consider including what cannot be included, such as a specific color (the color of the client's competitor) or words or phrases to be avoided.

14 **Who is the competition?** The client's competitors have a big impact on any campaign. Describe the key competitors, their market share and their communication and media strategy.

15 **What is the context that may affect the campaign?** Describe the context of the campaign. What is happening in terms of current events or ideas that you can leverage to achieve your goals? Identify how your product/service/brand is seen in the marketplace and how you can improve it.

Let's look at an example of a creative brief. This one is for Fossil smartwatches.

In summary, the creative brief is like the playbook that has been developed by the coach, with input from the team, and describes the rules, the goals and objectives, the competition and the common values of the team. The brief helps to maximize the talents of all the players involved and avoid unnecessary confrontations about the direction or focus of the game. The creative brief is also used to review draft work. When evaluating creative strategies and messages, the team should always ask if the work aligns with the big idea and the direction of the brief. It should be the guide for all the communication that the organization is involved in from the message found on the homepage of the campaign website to the message found on the "About" section of the press release. The paid advertising such as TV spots and billboards, sales decks and social media content strategy should be in line with the framework of the creative brief.

Message Strategy

WHAT ARE WE COMMUNICATING AND WHY?

Fossil has taken fifth place in the smartwatch market worldwide, but awareness is still extremely low. The goal is to establish Fossil as a smartwatch competitor and raise overall awareness and sales of the Hybrid Q and Gen 3 smartwatches.

WHO ARE WE COMMUNICATING TO?

Women 18-35 who prefer style over or in addition to technology; secondary target audience is men 25-35 who work and/or travel frequently.

WHAT DO THEY CURRENTLY THINK?

There is room to make a first impression because most people have not yet heard of Fossil smartwatches. People like Fossil as a brand, but they view smartwatches as unnecessary.

WHAT DO WE WANT THEM TO THINK?

Fossil looks better on their wrists than competitors' watches and elevates their statuses without overwhelming them with features.

WHAT IS THE MOST IMPORTANT THING TO CONVEY?

Women like things designed specifically for them. Apple's and Samsung's watches are gender-neutral, as are a few of Fossil's watches, but many more of them are fitted and styled for one or the other.

Men who travel and have full-time jobs are constantly in meetings and traveling. Features like the automatic time zone updates will convince them a hybrid watch will make life easier for them.

Style Women will like the style of the Fossil watches much more than the style of other watches.

Status The Fossil watch is more professional for a meeting/interview setting where status matters.

WHY SHOULD THEY BELIEVE US?

Fossil's hybrid and smart watches offer customers a stylish, professional-looking watch that they can wear to the gym or to the office. We will speak their language on platforms they are familiar with to convey Fossil's timeless image to the modern smartwatch world.

ARE THERE MANDATORIES OR CONSTRAINTS?

The Fossil watches will ease the tech-apprehensive millennials into the "smart" world. They prioritize style more than competitors' watches and look better while having the same desirable features. There are no mandatories or constraints in the campaign, but each advertising piece should have the Fossil logo to create a brand image along with the awareness campaign.

WHAT IS THE TONE?

Understanding/relatable while giving the impression of elitism, trendy, young.

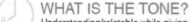

A sample of a creative brief produced by a group of students at Oklahoma State University.

Executing the Message Strategy

The channels and activities available for communicative entities to execute its messaging are virtually endless in the 21st-century media and marketplace. No single medium or class of media is enough for an effective message strategy. The message must be delivered, received, recycled and shared through a well-crafted blend of media channels and organizational activities. Let's explore an example of messaging from each of the four categories of media channels: paid, owned, earned and shared.

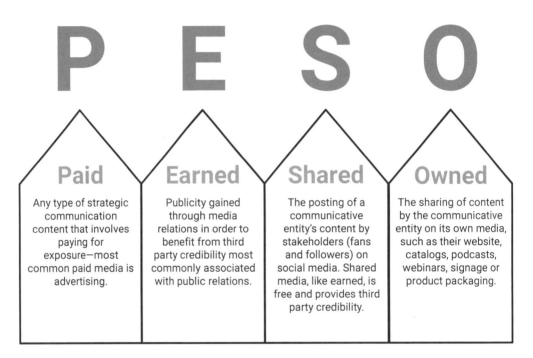

Figure 9.1 The PESO model

Paid Media

Paid media is what you commonly think of as traditional advertising including magazine ads, newspaper display ads, television and radio spots, billboards and online advertising such as digital display ads and paid search. Paid advertising also includes hiring an influencer to participate in a campaign or promote a product and paying bloggers or offering the products for free in exchange for reviews. Creating and writing the messaging for each of these media tactics are all quite different as you can imagine. Developing the script for a radio spot requires a different thought process and mechanics than writing a headline and body copy for a magazine ad. We don't have time in this chapter to discuss how to write for each of these channels, so let's take a glimpse of creating paid media messages by exploring how to write effective print ads.

First and foremost, the inspiration must start from and align with the creative brief. The composition of a print ad include the following components: (1) *a headline*, (2) *a sub-head* (optional), (3) *body copy*, (4) *imagery*, (5) *white space*, (6) *call to action* and (7) *contact information*. Start with the **headline**. A good headline is essential to an effective print ad. It is your first and maybe only opportunity to grab the reader's attention. The headline should hook the reader and compel them to learn more about the product or service.

Industry Insight

Headline Quiz

The following is a list of what are considered to be great headlines followed by a list of brands/products. Read over them and try to guess what product the headline is advertising.

Headlines:	Brand Products:
They don't write songs about Volvos.	Jack Daniel's
Life. Liberty. Getting Crap Done.	Chevrolet Corvette
The song isn't born to be status quo.	WD-40
It's unusual to drive the vehicle you were conceived in.	Nike
Think training is hard. Try losing.	Volkswagen Van
Freedom is a right. Independence is a choice.	Harley-Davidson

What do you think? Was it difficult? These headlines help tell the story of their brand. Volvos might be safe and practical, but driving a Corvette is so amazing that artists like Prince, the Beach Boys, and many more have written popular songs about the sports car.

Here are the answers to headlines quiz:

"They don't write songs about Volvos." Chevrolet Corvette.
"It's unusual to drive the vehicle you were conceived in." Volkswagen Van.
"Think training is hard. Try losing." Nike.
"Freedom is a right. Independence is a choice." Jack Daniel's.
"Life. Liberty. Getting Crap Done." WD-40.

Take a moment to think about what story each of the headlines listed above are telling. Does the story or message fit with what you think about the brands/products?

Writing a good headline is essential to a good print ad. Some print ads do not require a headline because the image is so powerful that the message can be conveyed without a headline, but that is very rare.

The next thing to consider is a **sub-head**. You won't find a sub-head in all ads, but a sub-head can be used to draw the reader in even further. If the headline asks a question, the sub-head can answer it. If the headline makes a cryptic statement, the sub-head can reveal more. Examples of effective use of subheads:

Headline: Our graduates often get called names. Sub-head: Like Sir. (Sheffield Business School.)

Headline: To all those who use our competitor's products: Sub-head: Happy Father's Day. (Durex Condoms.)

Headline: Want a job here? Sub-head: Keep an eye on the obituaries. (Shiner Beers.)

Aren't those fun how they work together to tell a story with just a headline and sub-head?

Next is **body copy**, which also helps tell the story. The body copy elaborates on the message that is introduced by the headline. However, you have very limited space in a print ad, so your body copy must be concise. Make every word count. Write in a conversational tone. Explain why the product/service is the best solution for the problem. It's worth repeating: The body copy should be concise, using as few words as possible while still telling a complete story. The ad should tell the story of how the brand/product/service solves the problem that the reader/stakeholder is facing, as in the following Harley-Davidson ad.

The problem is being stuck in the mundane of following the rules, lack of adventure and owning a boring car. Harley-Davidson is the answer.

Headline: The song isn't born to be status quo.

Body copy: We never did one like this before. Check out that rear fender and the stretched fuel tank. Note the immaculate front end, the chrome oil lines, the bullet turn signals. It's classic Harley. Yet it's unlike anything the road has ever seen. The Softail "Deuce" lives to push the limits. Maybe you should follow suit. 1-800-433-2153 or www.harleydavidson.com. The Legend Lives On.

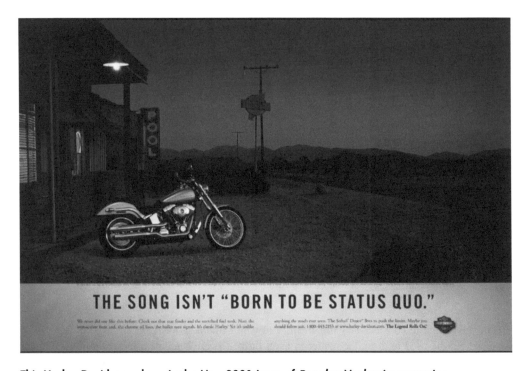

This Harley-Davidson ad ran in the May 2001 issue of *Popular Mechanics* magazine.

The Minneapolis ad agency, Carmichael Lynch created the ad, and it ran in Popular Mechanics in May 2001. They tell a great story of excitement and rebellion against the mundane. It sure makes me want to get on a bike and "push the limits."

Imagery—Occasionally, you will see print ads without any images. It's rare, but sometimes the headline/copy is all you need. It's rare because visuals and imagery are attention-getting and memorable. Images help to tell a story as much or sometimes more so than the text. Images evoke emotion and tell you what you need to know in a faster and more powerful way than text alone can do. People remember pictures better than words, especially over longer periods of time. This phenomenon as we know it today, is called the Picture Superiority Effect.[8]

> Based on research into the Picture Superiority Effect, when we read text alone, we are likely to remember only 10 percent of the information three days later. If that information is presented to us as text combined with a relevant image, we are likely to remember 65 percent of the information 3 days later.[9]

There is another very important aspect of the Picture Superiority Effect that must be understood: It's not just any image. It needs to be an image relevant to the content or body copy, which reinforces the message.

White space is just as important to your print ads as the copy you write. White space helps your visuals and copy to breathe and stand out more, which allows the reader to be pulled in. If you don't grab the reader's attention and pull them in, your message will not be received.

Call to action—You caught the reader's attention through powerful imagery, a compelling headline and interesting body copy? What should the reader do now? If you don't tell them, they'll just put your ad down and move on to something else. Tell them to shop now and provide a link to your website. Tell them to call now to receive a 50% discount. Tell them to come into your store by a certain date to get a free trial or sample. You want to make your reader feel a sense of urgency, so they will be more compelled to act on your message.

Contact information—Make it easy for prospects to contact you and get the exact information they want. If you only provide a phone number or a generic URL, you're going to lose valuable prospects—not everyone will be ready to pick up the phone, and it can be tough to find specific answers from your home page. You can create a landing page with a specific URL that provides specific information related to the campaign. Provide a phone number for a specific sales group that can provide help and details related to the campaign.[10]

Professional Profile

Kaleb Mulugeta—Associate Copywriter

Did you have any internships in college? I did! I landed my first internship the summer after junior year. I flew up from Dallas to Chicago, to be a copywriter intern at an advertising agency called TracyLocke. Alongside the other interns, I presented campaigns to the agency every Friday. We gained real-world experience sitting in on

Kaleb Mulugeta—Associate Copywriter.

client meetings, pitching to C-level executives, creating and selling ideas to global brands. My second internship was for my college, writing social media and email newsletter copy. My third was my biggest: A post-graduate internship at a juggernaut advertising agency in New York City. However, the summer of 2020 was interrupted by the COVID-19 pandemic, so that internship didn't happen.

How important do you think those internships were? Vital. You need that experience. No matter how much you learn in the classroom, it just can't capture the essence of working at an agency: meeting deadlines, rapid turnarounds, collaborating and communicating across disciplines. The best way to learn is by doing, that's what internships are for. Lastly, internships expand your network. The advertising industry is a small world; the people at your first internship are likely to know some of the people at your next one. Make a good impression.

What did you want to do with your career? I wanted to be a writer and comedian. I aimed to get my start working in advertising, building an extensive portfolio of successful work, before venturing off into the entertainment industry to pursue comedy full-time. Right now, my goal is to produce work that entertains and empowers.

Are you doing it? So far, so good.

What are you doing now? I am currently an Associate Copywriter at TBWA\ Chiat\Day New York. My role consists of creating and pitching ideas for brand campaigns, writing copy for social media content, scripting TV commercials (now known as Online Videos), and more. I usually collaborate with an art director, while being guided by our creative directors. So far, I've worked on brands like Hilton Hotels, Bubly, and Mountain Dew, to name a few.

How did you get there? Hard work, networking and luck. At Southern Methodist University, I built a portfolio of speculative work (fake commercials) I produced under the direction of my professors. That portfolio, along with recommendation letters, and countless hours spent applying to internship programs, got me into a prestigious program called MAIP—The Multicultural Advertising Intern Program. Created by the American Association of Advertising Agencies (4A's), it partnered the best agencies in the country with the best diverse talent. I interviewed, got selected and benefitted from hands-on training while connecting with hundreds of talented students of color entering the industry. As a historic, well-respected program, my involvement with MAIP afforded me access to some of the best creatives in the business. I was very active on LinkedIn, and a comment of mine caught the eye of the right recruiter. This led to an interview, which led to another interview, resulting in a full-time job offer.

What did you wish you had known? The world is a small town. That agency you dream about working for? Your professor knows someone who knows the head recruiter. Learn how to network. Be friendly, but persistent. Also, the two most important words in the dictionary are as such: Add value. Everyone wants a job, everyone wants to take, everyone wants to win. You see where I'm going with this, right? Focus on adding value to every room you enter and watch things start to work out for you.

Don't know how to add value? Ask.

What advice would you give to someone in college now? Find what makes you different and stick to your guns. You're in a sea of thousands of talented students competing for the same roles. The one thing they don't have is your story, personality and perspective. Use those to forge your path, because they are yours, no one else's. Oh, one last thing: Ask for help. Resources and opportunities won't come rushing to you, you have to seek them out. Okay, the last thing for real: Being a genuine, eager, hard-working person will open more doors than name drops and a fancy resume. Be a great person before being a great candidate.

Owned Media

Owned media is anything under organizations' direct control such as websites, newsletters, catalogs, social media sites and blogs. The CE fully controls the content and its distribution. The foundations of an owned media strategy are your content channels—the vehicles through which you deliver content to audiences directly, unmediated by a third party. The most common channels are your website, catalogs and newsletters. You should also consider your stores and mobile apps as communication tools. The key to a successful content channel is that you have engaging content that is relevant and valuable, and that you are using all available data to personalize the experience for the user.

Earned Media

Unlike paid and owned media, which are guaranteed, earned media is, well, earned and therefore requires a third party to communicate your organization's message to its stakeholders. Your brand must do something that earns press coverage, positive reviews and recommendations. Being in control is often very important to organizations, but earned media is far more trusted than paid and owned media. So, giving up that control and building relationships with journalists and your customers/fans and trusting them to communicate your message makes your message more likely to be heard and trusted.

Earned media refers to publicity or media exposure you've earned through media relations and word-of-mouth. Earned media is the result of distributing fantastic content, the influence of your **search engine optimization (SEO)** efforts, delivering a fantastic customer experience, or a combination of all three. It's getting your company, product, service, expert opinion or ideas included in a news story—online, print, radio, TV, podcast, and so forth. Earned media involves a media outlet, such as a newspaper, magazine or even a blog, featuring information about your brand, product or service. It's appearing on a local or national TV morning show or the evening news. Earned media placement on trusted outlets can validate your owned content and give your brand third-party credibility and endorsement. Credibility increases with each additional mention by the media. It's what most people think of when they think of PR or publicity. Earned media can also include mentions on corporate social media, reviews and blog posts referencing you.

You can facilitate earned media by helping journalists write articles, or contributing your own thought leadership content to industry publications.[11] There has been much debate about the value and efficacy of the press release since the UK's executive director for government communications, Alex Aiken, declared that "the press release is dead." A few years later in an interview with PRWeek, Aiken changed his tune a bit regarding the press release and admitted that the press release still has a role to play in modern communications.[12] He explained that because the way that people consume their news and information, and the way they communicate with one another is changing and evolving, so strategic communication must reflect and adapt to those changes. Earning publicity is not easy because too many PR practitioners are pitching to too few journalists. PR professionals outnumber journalists five-to-one in 2018.[13]

Here are some guidelines for writing a press release

FOR IMMEDIATE RELEASE: (DATE)
Contact Name
Organization (Agency or Company)
Phone Number
Email

Headline

This is a title, which should grab the reader's attention while explaining what the release is about. The reader should be able to read the headline and understand that the release is for a product launch, a ground-breaking invention or an inaugural festival.

Location: Identify the city and state where you are and where the news is taking place.

Lead (introductory paragraph): Explain your newsworthy content in one strong sentence that clarifies what you are announcing and why it is important. A good lead is critical to the success of a release. Try to tap into an emotional connection with the audience. Answer the 5 W's: Who, What, When, Where and Why.

Quote (second paragraph): The second paragraph is the best spot for quotes. Shape your message with quotes from partners or industry leaders who will benefit from the news you are releasing.

Body (third and fourth paragraphs): The body of the release should offer clear, poignant and relevant information that is easy to skim and understand. Include the most important information at the top and get into less vital details later. Journalist call this approach to writing the inverted pyramid. Avoid adding fluff that doesn't need to be there. Journalists love to get exclusive information and data that supports it. Be direct and comprehensive. The body can include additional quotes to support the story.

Boilerplate: This a placeholder for few words (3–4 sentences) to describe your company, including what your company stands for, to the audience and a link to your website. You can also include your logo here.

Press contact: Provide the name and contact information of the media coordinator or communications specialist that the reporter can contact to get more information.

After writing the press release, it is a good idea to circulate it to key organizational stakeholders for comments and questions. Make sure that you schedule the time of the release appropriately. If you have a blog, it is important to write and post a blog post that coincides with launch of your press release. Likewise, you want to make sure you schedule social media posts that complement the release. You want to make sure your employees are in the loop, so if they are asked questions, they can provide knowledgeable and supportive responses. It is also a good idea to communicate with customers about the news. You can launch an email to customers that explains how they will benefit from the big announcement. They will appreciate hearing the news directly from the source, and they will be more likely to share the news through their own social media. Finally, create a list of message points for anyone on your team that would serve as a spokesperson.

Shared Media

Shared interaction and engagement with branded content on social media platforms like Facebook, Twitter and YouTube is "shared media." Paid and owned media often inspire shared media. When shared media starts to gain a lot of attention, it can lead to earned media. For example, do you remember the Barbie "You Can Be Anything" campaign in 2015? It started with the television spot "Image the Possibilities" showing five girls playing out what they want to be when they grow up, including a veterinarian, a professor, a businesswoman, a museum guide and a soccer coach. The young actresses in the spot not only got to choose their careers, but also pretend to be those professionals in real-life settings, unscripted in front of unsuspecting adults while being filmed for the spot with hidden cameras. At the end of the spot, the girl playing the professor is shown in her room holding her Barbie, who is standing in front of "an auditorium" of other Barbies, giving a lecture. It started with paid and owned media. It was a commercial spot that aired on television (paid media), and the video was available through the Barbie YouTube channel (owned media). The ad touched people and the video went viral with people sharing it through social media (shared media). Because the video was gaining so much attention, it started gaining attention in the news, talk shows and trade magazines talked about and released stories about the endearing video (earned media). The content of the ad was inspired by the philosophy of the creator of Barbie, Ruth Handler, who said Barbie represented the fact that women have choices and that a girl can be anything she wanted to be through the doll.[14] One of the goals of the campaign was to shake the negative image and criticism Barbie has received for its lack of diversity and unrealistic physique that has been attributed to poor body image issues among young girls.[15] It is an excellent example of a message strategy that utilized all four buckets of the PESO media model.

Like in the Barbie example, in order for shared media to be successful, it needs to start with interesting, compelling and authentic content that speaks to people and makes them say, "hey, look at this" and share it with friends. When used effectively, social media and its users can help CEs to reach not only their audience but also the friends and followers of their core audience—and convert them all into fans and followers. Like with any media platform or message strategy, there's not a one-size-fits-all guide to creating content that is guaranteed to be shared. It is important to craft a message that creates emotional bonds with your audience. Like paid, owned and earned content strategy, shared content will be louder and more effective when it reinforces the organization's identity and core values. That's what Barbie did by going back to the philosophy of its creator, "girls can be anything they want to be through Barbie," which is the brand's core value.

Shared media messages should be not only tailored for the audience but also for the best platform to reach that audience. First you must determine who you want to communicate with and what platforms they use. Once you have a good idea of who your audience is and where your social strategy is taking place, you need to know what kind of content you'll create. As we mentioned above, your aim should be to design content that's relevant to your business or brand and its values. A CE should never simply post content for the sake of it. Instead, messages should be carefully crafted to connect with the audience. You can create online communities through social media if you develop and curate useful content, as well as listen to and engage with audiences. Social media can help CEs strengthen bonds with their audiences and develop loyalty. One of the main keys to strengthening those bonds is listening. Social listening, that is listening to audiences on social media, can help CEs discover consumer and cultural insights.

Listening is just one of the keys. Like any good conversation, you must listen and respond. You need to engage in conversations with your customers. Think about brands that you are loyal to and enjoy. Do you follow them on social media in any way? If so, why? Do they share information that is valuable to you? Do they offer discounts that you use? After CEs identifies its audience and where they spend their time, the next step should be finding out more about what they want to see from the brand. Questionnaires and polls are fun and effective ways to start engaging your audience. Asking customers to share feedback can help a CE listen and strengthen connections with its customer community. Customers love it when they are retweeted or get a response to their tweet or post by their favorite brands. For example, Leigh Ann Cleaver, a Kansas City Chiefs fan and a passenger on Southwest Airlines had a positive experience on a flight to SuperBowl LIV. She really enjoyed the flight attendants' customers service, so she gave a shout out to @SouthwestAir on Twitter, and Southwest Airlines responded and showed Leigh Ann that they care about what she cares about.

Chiefs Airlines aka @SouhwestAir has arrived! #ChiefsKingdom #SuperbowlLIV.

The tweet included a video of a plane full of excited Chiefs fans. Courtney from Southwest Airlines responded:

> Looks like ya'll are ready for some football! Let's hope Mahomes can bring it home for ya. Enjoy your travels!—Courtney.

The conversation did not stop there. Leigh Ann responded with a photo of a flight attendant holding a giant cardboard Patrick Mahomes:

> Crew was fantastic too! They embraced our Mahomie 🖤🏈 #ChiefsKingdom #SuperBowlLIV.

@SouthwestAir replied:

> This is awesome. 😃 Enjoy the game on Sunday!—Courtney.

Southwest is known for being more flexible than other airlines, and for recruiting and retaining motivated employees.[16] People who work for Southwest appear to love their jobs, and as a result provide a positive customer experience. This series of tweets that was initiated by a customer communicates those values. By listening and engaging with customers on Twitter, Southwest helps to reinforce those core values and make the customer feel even better about her experience.

Instead of looking at a well-executed message strategy for shared media specifically, let's conclude this chapter by exploring an effective message strategy that employs multiple channels to engage, inspire and persuade its stakeholders and employs them to help communicate its message. The Domino's "Paving for Pizza" Campaign, launched in June 2018, is an excellent example.

Case Study

Domino's Social Responsibility Campaign

Domino's and its ad agency Crispin Porter + Bogusky (CP+B) utilized paid, owned, earned and shared media to generate excitement, engagement and action from stakeholders. They addressed the problem: Pothole-ridden roads damage your take-home pizza. The Domino's brand offers the solution to fix the potholes and save the precious pizza. This campaign is in line with the organization's core values: "Domino's is a brand that is relentless in its pursuit of making everything about the pizza experience better, from how it's made to how it's ordered and delivered," Kelly McCormick, creative director at CP+B, said.

To help ensure that their product gets to the homes of its customers in perfect condition, Domino's decided that they needed to help fix potholes in roads across the country. CP+B approached the cities of Athens, GA; Bartonville, TX; and Milford, DE, offering them each grants of $5,000 to help them repair potholes in their towns. After accepting the grants, the cities were asked to repair the roads, take photos or videos of the repairs, and stencil on a Domino's logo and the tagline "Oh yes we did."

CP+B exchanged hundreds of emails with the municipalities. The towns were pleasantly surprised by the offer and grateful for the cash; as Milford city manager Eric Norenberg explained in a Washington Post op-ed, the grant really made a difference for his town, which has an annual budget of only $30,000 for road repairs. Milford was able to patch 40 potholes with its $5,000—and treated its staff to a pizza party with the $200 in Domino's gift cards. Athens fixed 150 potholes and Bartonville did eight.[17]

The campaign was a quick success earning 100,000 site visits, 31,000 zip code registrations from all 50 states, 700 media stories, 100,000 Twitter mentions in two days after the campaign launched. It also landed in the number-one spot on Reddit. The launch ad has been viewed on YouTube more than 300,000 times. Domino's was celebrated on social media as a hero, but others (including Bernie Sanders) criticized the fact that a pizza chain had to help make basic street repairs.[18]

When the campaign originally launched, the project budget of $100,000 was enough to fix potholes in 20 cities. Soon after the campaign launch, the response was far greater than expected, so Domino's and CP+B have decided to increase the budget and repair potholes in at least one city in all 50 states.

The campaign tells a story that is timely, addresses a problem that relates to a wide audience and features the brand as the hero of the story. Some of the tactics utilized to communicate this message strategy include paid advertising such as national TV spots, media relations, civic marketing, sales promotion and social media such as YouTube. They created a website for the campaign: Pavingforpizza.com. The site opened an opportunity for customers to nominate their own city for a pothole makeover.

They also developed an interactive Pothole Impact Meter so you can see first-hand just how ravaged the pizzas are by potholes. By engaging its audience, Domino's is creating an opportunity to draw people in and get them talking. The site shows where they have fixed roads and what cities they are planning to visit next, keeping the content fresh, so people will come back to the site for updates.

By utilizing civic marketing, they created a story that journalists and media outlets found to be newsworthy and shared on both the local and national level. When people saw that roads were being fixed in their communities, they began telling the Paving for Pizza story on their own social media platforms. Advertising and public relations trade publications, such as AdWeek and Advertising Age shared the story to discuss the merits of the campaign. It is an example of an organization properly executing a message strategy across all its channels and using methods to consistently tell the same story. The campaign celebrates its core values, engaging stakeholders, fostering relationships and looking to stakeholders to share the message. The campaign shares a simple and consistent message that drives relevance, awareness and action. Domino's and CP+B has stayed consistent in its message, but they have also listened, improved and adjusted the plan by extending the budget to fix roads in more cities and get more people invested in the brand.

Summary

Messages are the building blocks of strategic communication practice. Creating effective and relevant messages that break through the media clutter and reach targeted stakeholders is critical to success as a strategic communicator. Understanding to whom you are directing your messages allows strategic communicators to be most effective in reaching their goals and objectives for the brands and/or their clients' brands. A creative brief is a document that serves to define the strategy for the campaign and informs the messaging throughout. Different types of media require different message strategies and tactics. Advertising calls for interesting headlines, concise body copy and compelling images. News releases allow the strategic communicators to provide news content to journalist, while shared media functions to spread news about the brand and recruit fans and followers.

Discussion Questions

1   How does a company's core values play a role in its messaging strategy?
2   Can you name five types of channels of communication?
3   What does PR stand for? What category of media is PR typically associated with?
4   What is the difference between a news release and a media kit?
5   What are the 5 C's of storytelling and why are they important to developing messaging?
6   What is the purpose of a creative brief?
7   What are the components of a print ad?
8   Can you explain how a news release works?
9   How did Domino's capitalize on cities having poorly maintained roads as part of their message strategy?

Check out the online support material, including chapter summaries, useful links and further reading, at www.routledge.com/9780367426316

Notes

1   Glenday, J. (2018, March 21). McDonald's goes hands on by bringing back "peelable" Monopoly campaign. *The Drum.* https://www.thedrum.com/news/2018/03/21/mcdonald-s-goes-hands-with-peelable-monopoly-campaign.
2   Excerpted from Fullerton, J., & Kendrick, A. (2006). *Advertising's War on Terrorism: The Story of the U.S. State Department's Shared Values Initiative.* Marquette Books.
3   Olson, J. M. & Zanna, M. P. (1993). Attitudes and attitude change. *Annual Review of Psychology, 44*, 117–154.
4   The "Smokey the bear/Only you can prevent forest fires" campaign began in 1944 and remains the longest running public service announcement ever produced by the American Ad Council. To learn more, go to: https://smokeybear.com/en/smokeys-history/about-the-campaign.
5   For a full discussion of Hovland's persuasion research see Lowery, S., & DeFleur, M. (1995) *Milestones in Mass Communication Research: Media Effects* (3rd ed.). White Plains, NY: Longman, 165–188.
6   https://www.impactplus.com/blog/2018-world-cup-marketing-campaigns.

7   https://www.venturavw.com/blog/volkwagen-reveals-new-jump-on-the-wagen-campaign-for-the-2018-world-cup/.
8   Nelson, D. S., Reed, V. S., & Walling, J. R. (1976). Pictorial superiority effect. *Journal of Experimental Psychology Human Learning and Memory*, *2*(5), 523–528. https://www.researchgate.net/publication/22152101_Pictorial_superiority_effect.
9   Medina, J. (2008). *Brain Rules*. Seattle, WA: Pear Press.
10 http://www.marketingmo.com/campaigns-execution/how-to-get-the-most-from-a-print-ad/.
11 https://www.axiapr.com/blog/whats-the-difference-between-earned-media-shared-media-and-owned-media.
12 https://www.prweek.com/article/1215044/reports-death-press-release-greatly-exaggerated.
13 https://muckrack.com/blog/2018/09/06/there-are-now-more-than-6-pr-pros-for-every-journalist.
14 https://www.thedrum.com/news/2016/06/30/marketing-moment-91-barbie-s-imagine-possibilities-video-goes-viral.
15 https://www.refinery29.com/en-us/2015/10/95826/barbie-ad-girls-can-do-anything-mattel.
16 https://www.investopedia.com/articles/investing/061015/how-southwest-different-other-airlines.asp.
17 https://www.washingtonpost.com/news/posteverything/wp/2018/06/13/why-i-let-dominos-fill-my-citys-potholes/.
18 https://www.adweek.com/creativity/as-dominos-expands-its-pothole-paving-to-all-50-states-heres-how-to-bring-it-to-your-town/2/.

Chapter 10

Traditional Media

Learning Outcomes

By the end of this chapter, you should be able to do the following:

- Be able to distinguish among the different types and meanings of "media."
- Understand the PESO model and give examples of paid, owned, earned and shared media.
- Identify the traditional paid media classifications and understand how advertising is purchased by each type.

Chapter Opening Vignette

A Media Diary

It's 6:00 a.m., you wake up to the voices of Lady Gaga singing "Rain on Me." Before Ariana Grande begins singing "living in a world ...," you tell Alexa to turn the volume down as you reach for your iPhone to check your Instagram. You ask Alexa to turn on the lights as you hop up and get in the shower. As you are getting dressed, you turn on the TV to ESPN to watch the highlights of last night's playoff games. You get in the car and ask Google to show you the route to work with the least traffic. As you drive to work, you laugh and agree with the sports talk radio announcers discussing the bad calls that consistently benefitted the Golden State Warriors while glancing out at the billboard boasting that $1 Nacho Fries are Taco Bell's biggest product launch ever. You take the elevator up to your office and check your Twitter and the *New York Times* app. You stop at the reception desk to peruse the headlines above the fold of the local paper before heading down the hall to your office.

You've been up about two hours and in that time, you have been immersed in media, yet this description barely scratched the surface. It is common knowledge that U.S. consumers fill most of their waking hours using the media, but did you know that adults in the U.S. now spend more than half the 24-hour day—12 hours and 7 minutes on average—with major media?

What Is Media?

The word media is a complex term that comes with multiple meanings depending on the context; hence, it can mean different things to different people. Media is the plural of medium, and as we will explore in this chapter, it is a term used to refer to communication channels through which news, entertainment and promotional messages are disseminated. These channels include television, radio, magazines, newspapers, billboards, direct mail, the internet and social media. According Merriam-Webster, "the singular media seem to have originated in the field of advertising over 70 years ago." The word media is also used in the worlds of art, science, the paranormal and data. In art, medium can refer to both the type of art, such as a painting or a sculpture, as well as the materials an artwork is made from, such as watercolor pencil, marble or clay. In science, medium usually means an intervening substance through which something is transmitted. Medium can also refer to a person who communicates with the dead. Finally, tools used to store and deliver information or data are also referred to as media. DNA and RNA, handwriting, phonographic recording, magnetic tape, optical discs, USB thumb drives, and online storage or "the cloud" are all examples of storage media.

In the United States, in particular, the term media is often used synonymously with news media to collectively refer to journalists or crews working for news outlets. The news media are a big part of the collective term, media, but it is more than that. Media not only include communication channels used to disseminate news, but also media include entertainment channels, such as film and gaming and promotional channels, such as direct mail and outdoor advertising. Communication channels used at locations and events are also part of the world of media. For example, the Jumbotron at a sports arena, digital signage at airports and interactive screens at supermarkets are all considered media.

Media—the term and the concept—continues to evolve and takes on new significance with the advent of new technologies and changing audiences. In strategic communication, the role of the media is to help create, sustain and strengthen relationships with stakeholders. Today's audiences are flooded with undifferentiated information, and they are pro-active consumers who decide what they want, when they want it and how they want it. As discussed in Chapter 1, we now live in a society that exists within the media—not with the media, as it did for earlier generations. As media technologies have emerged and evolved, people have evolved with it. With print media, we were readers. With radio, we also became listeners. Television shaped us into viewers, which includes reading and listening. The personal computer, coupled with word and design software, allowed us to become publishers. The internet has allowed us to become media producers and broadcasters.

The selection and use of media are critical to the practice of deliberate and purposive communication by an organization or communicative entity, and it is increasingly requiring more creativity and imagination than ever before. The plural noun, **media**, is a blanket term for all types of print, broadcast, out-of-home and interactive communication. The singular noun **medium** refers to a specific type of media. TV is a medium. Radio is a medium. Newspapers are a medium. Social media are a medium. A specific publication, TV channel, radio station or social media platform are media vehicles. Examples of media vehicles are CBS, NPR, USA Today and Facebook. When a communicative entity "buys media"—a industry phrase that means purchasing advertising space/time—it is really buying access to the audiences of specific media vehicles.

In the world of strategic communication, media are categorized into four types: paid, earned, shared and owned, which is referred to as the PESO model. You will remember we discussed PESO in Chapter 9. This model emerged from the field of public relations and has be around since 2010 when *AdWeek* published an article, "How to define shared media on Facebook,"[1] which explains "shared media is the documented engagement between a brand and a user where that engagement is reflected in both of their networks and not fully owned by either entity." Digital marketing expert Gini Dietrich is often credited for creating the PESO model when she published her book *Spin Sucks* in 2014.[2] While the model has been both widely adopted and highly criticized, it is an excellent way to organize your thoughts and explain all aspects of media options available to communicative entities.

Case Study

Fake News

On February 17, 2017, U.S. President Donald J. Trump tweeted: "The FAKE NEWS media (failing @nytimes, @NBCNews, @ABC, @CBS, @CNN) is not my enemy, it is the enemy of the American People!" With this tweet (and others like it), news media took on a whole new meaning for many people. Like the broader term media, *fake news media and fake news* have come to mean different things to different people. At its core, fake news is defined as news stories that are false and included fabricated information without verifiable facts or sources. Fake news goes far beyond false news stories. Claire Wardle, of FirstDraftNews.org, developed a chart to explain the complex notion of fake news in what she describes seven distinct types of problematic content sit within our misinformation ecosystem. Some people, especially politicians, call news coverage that is unflattering or critical of them or their positions, "Fake News," when it is accurate, verifiable reporting and does not fall into any of the categories below.[3]

Figure 10.1 Types of Fake News

Different Types of Media

As discussed in Chapter 9, PESO stands for "*P*aid, *E*arned, *S*hared, *O*wned," and serves as a way to organize communication channels into discrete groups, which allows us to recognize the strengths and weaknesses of the different channels and develop the best strategy for integrating multiple channels. As we have discussed earlier in this book, advertising, public relations and marketing all originated as very separate academic disciplines and professional practices. Communications professionals often focus and rely on media with which they are most comfortable. Advertising folks lean toward paid media, while PR professionals will steer toward earned media seeking the validation of an unbiased journalist communicating the message, and content marketers are most often drawn toward owned media. Good strategic communication plans combine all the four outlined channels. Integrating the four media types leads to a more comprehensive strategy that includes influencer engagement, partnerships and incentive programs that maximize communication efforts. Let's look at how each of the four media is defined.

Paid Media

Prior to the digital revolution, advertising and public relations were two very separate disciplines that utilized paid media efforts and earned media efforts respectively. Advertising focuses on developing and disseminating creative, persuasive paid media messages that contain an identified sponsor. Paid media is what you know of as advertising, which is essentially paying media owners for distribution of marketing messages. Paid media includes purchasing ad space in magazines, newspapers, on a television or radio program, on billboards, on a website, via Google Ads, on a bus or in a subway station, among other options. The communicative entity, usually via its agency, is paying for their messages to be seen and/or heard.

It is important to understand that advertising has been critical to the affordable distribution of news and entertainment for more than 150 years in the U.S. In most of the world's countries, the media are supported and controlled by government. However, the media in the U.S. and other democratic societies, are kept free from government control. This is made possible because of advertising support of the media. For example, you could not get in your car and turn on the radio and access hundreds of stations for free without advertising. You would not be able to access major television networks, such as CBS, NBC and ABC, with just an HD antenna without advertising. While these "free" media sources are becoming less and less popular because of the rising popularity of streaming services, such as Netflix, Hulu and SiriusXM, it is still important to understand advertising's role in the development of the free press in the U.S. The first amendment is a constitutional guarantee that the government cannot encroach on a free press, but without advertising paying most of the costs and creating a revenue stream, news and entertainment media that Americans have grown up with would not be widely available and accessible. Even social media has been able to survive and thrive while remaining free to users because of advertising.

Examples of Paid Media

Paid media can be any type of strategic communication that involves paying for exposure. Paying a blogger to write a blog about a product, paying a celebrity to wear a product at a highly publicized event, or paying a movie producer to feature a product in a film, all fall under the category of paid media. Super Bowl commercials are the most recognized and celebrated form of advertising or paid media. In fact, many people tune in to the Super Bowl to watch the commercials instead of the game.[4] The NFL championship game remains the best way to reach as many people as possible at once. An advertiser can reach more than 100 million viewers with a single Super Bowl commercial, which is dramatically more people than any alternative program or medium. Of course, reaching that large of an audience does not come cheap. For example, NBC Sports charged more than $5 million for a 30-second spot during the Super Bowl LII.[5]

Paid advertising can also take the form of **influencer marketing**, which is essentially when a company pays individuals who have a fan following or audience to promote their brand, usually online. Paid advertising can also take the form of **influencer marketing**, which is essentially when a company pays individuals who have a fan following or audience to promote their brand, usually online. The power of the influencer economy was said to be discovered by a campaign for Coach purses over a decade ago. The campaign involved a collection of purses designed by fashion bloggers. The purses sold out in a single day, which demonstrated to the vice president of communications at Coach, Raina Penchansky, that influencers were going to change strategic communication. Penchansky went on to co-found an agency that matches bloggers and social media influencers—people on social media with a large following—with sponsors. The influencer market has grown to more than $1 billion on Instagram alone.[6]

How to Measure Paid Media

Paid media, particularly if it is distributed online, is one of the easiest forms of strategic communication for which to measure effectiveness, as online advertising platforms usually come with their own analytics software to track how many and who sees the ads. If you advertise on Google for example, Google provides analytics that allows you to filter data three ways—organic, referral and paid traffic. **Organic traffic** is search results that are populated from natural popularity, not because an organization paid to have their site listed higher on the Google results page. **Referral traffic** occurs when users find a website through another website, other than a major search engine. **Paid traffic** refers to search engine results from paid search advertising, such as Google Ads.

Collecting audience data are an important part the advertising business because having good data about the audience allows advertisers to spend their money more efficiently and effectively. Advertisers collect these data in several ways. There are many companies that collect and sell data and information to advertisers so that they can track performance across any number of advertising platforms, such as Google Analytics, Funnel and Adobe Advertising Cloud. The sophistication of targeting audiences is more enhanced than ever because of advancements in viewing technology, increased complexity of media habits and the precision of data and analytics technologies. CEs can target people who are more likely to be interested in their products and services, which translates to less ad waste and more people acting on the advertising. Ad waste means advertising to people who don't care and will not care about your brand, products and services.

Earned Media

Instead of paying for exposure, public relations professionals work to secure strong relationships with journalists in order to achieve **earned media**, which is also known as publicity.

Earned media is messaging about a brand or communicative entity that is not paid for, but run free-of-charge as part of their editorial content. Earned media is gained through relationships that the strategic communicator develops with the media and other influencers in order to benefit from third-party credibility. Media relations involves convincing reporters/editors to present news coverage about an organization, person or event by saying or doing something that the news media will choose to report on as part of their usual task of informing the public. **Third-party credibility** means that individuals give information presented as part of a news story more credibility than if the same information was presented in an advertisement. The system was set up long before the internet to make sure that paid media did not impact earned media. In fact, publishers would make sure that there were actual walls within their organizations to prevent advertising dollars (paid media) from influencing editorial content (earned media). This divide between paid advertising and editorial content is often referred to as "the separation of church and state."

Just when you think you have a handle on the difference between paid and earned, then you learn about native advertising or sponsored content. **Native advertising** differs from traditional advertising in that it isn't visually separated from editorial on the printed or digital page. In fact, it is designed to look like editorial content. So much so, that sometimes, the audience can't tell the difference between the two.

But, native advertising isn't earned media or traditional editorial content either because it's paid for by a sponsoring CE. Native advertising is **sponsored content** that looks and reads like original media content, instead of paid advertising. However, somewhere on the page, or at the beginning of a video segment, there is a notification that signifies that it is paid content. The average consumer often overlooks the notification or is not aware of its meaning. Different media vehicles use different terms to specify paid content, including advertising, sponsored content, brand voice and presented by. Native advertising can be very successful because it provides an opportunity to provide a custom, detailed message that readers/viewers may find more interesting than traditional advertising. However, native advertising is often criticized for its ambiguity, approaching the line of mistrust and deception. Sponsored content or native advertising, despite being decades old as a concept, remains confusing to readers.

Academic Angle

Native Advertising and the Persuasion Knowledge Model

In 2015, The Stanford History Education Group (SHEG), based at Stanford University, conducted a nationwide study called "Evaluating Information: The Cornerstone of Civic Online Reasoning" to assess young people's online civic reasoning skills or "the ability to judge the credibility of information that floods young people's smartphones, tablets and computers."[7]

Part of the study included a section in which middle school students were presented with a paper copy of the home page of *Slate* magazine's website (pictured). The students were asked to identify highlighted items on the page as advertising—yes or no—and explain their answer in a space provided. The study found that more than 75% of the middle school students answered correctly when identifying traditional advertising and traditional news stories (item #1). But, when it came to identifying native advertising (Item #3), 82% of the students failed to identify an advertisement marked "sponsored content" as an ad.[8]

When the same test was given to college advertising majors in another study,[9] they scored better than the middle schoolers, but not as well as you might expect for college-age students who were studying advertising. Almost three-fourths (74.2%) of the college students properly identified the item labeled "sponsored content" as an advertisement. About 20% of the students who marked the item wrong, expressed the sentiment that "Sponsored content isn't always an ad." Clearly many students did not consider native advertising as "advertising." A few students explained that it isn't advertising, but it is "PR" or "promotion." Clearly the students are confused—paid media is by definition advertising.

Research such as the two studies described above raise concerns about the ethical nature of native advertising because academic research shows that consumers who recognize advertising messages treat those messages with more skepticism than messages that they consider to be something other than advertising and therefore more objective or neutral. According to the Persuasion Knowledge Model,[10] consumers interpret persuasive messages such as advertising and "cope" with each persuasive episode. The coping may not necessarily include resisting the persuasion, but implies

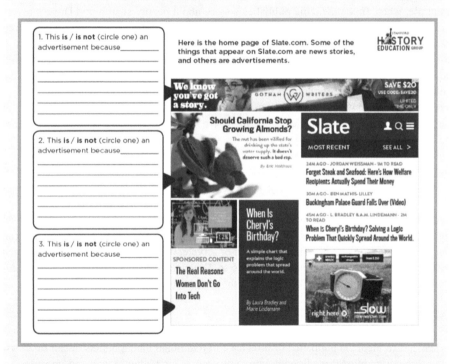

Instrument used to measure young people's ability to discern between advertising and editorial in online media.

that resourceful consumers maintain control of the outcomes to meet their own goals. The Persuasion Knowledge Model underscores the importance that consumers who are targeted with persuasive attempts know that they are engaged in a persuasive episode in order to cope. When consumers think that they are in an objective or neutral interaction, such as when they are reading editorial content, they may not engage in the same cognitive and physical defenses that they would in a persuasive episode. Native advertising and sponsored content may be an attempt on the part of marketers and publishers to mask persuasive intent and therefore prevent the triggering of consumers' coping ability.

Examples of Earned Media

Earned media is what most people refer to as traditional public relations (PR); it is also described as media relations or publicity. Historically, a communicative entity (a brand, a celebrity, an organization) would hire a PR firm because of the firm's relationships with journalists. The firm shares newsworthy information about the communicative entity with journalists from various news outlets, so they will utilize the information in their news articles. As mentioned earlier, stories told from a third-party perspective are looked at as credible and trustworthy, which is known as third-party credibility. For example, when *Time* magazine publishes a story about beauty soap brand Dove's use of primary research about women's self-esteem and body image, it would be considered earned media.

If earned media is free and more trusted by consumers, then why do CE's buy paid advertising? Well, it's not that simple. Media relations is expensive for the communicative entity, because it takes a great deal of time and effort for strategic communication professionals to get the right information to the right journalists and to get media outlets to cover the story. And even with all that work involved, there are no guarantees. Paid media is guaranteed to be published and controlled by the advertiser. Earned media may or not be published and the CE loses control of the message—the media might change the message to suit their editorial focus.

Earned media can go beyond relying on news media to share the story, as the customer becomes the channel. Customers post and share reviews and ratings on e-commerce and consumer websites, and positive reviews are considered earned media. This type of earned media also can be negative, so there is some risk in this strategy. Industry influencers can lead the conversation about a brand, product or service, which is another example of earned media, if those influencers are not paid to do so. When the CE pays the influencers as mentioned in the example about Coach purses above, it is considered paid media.

How to Measure Earned Media

When earned media is published or broadcast in traditional media outlets, it can be measured through traditional media measurements such as circulation, reach and impressions. We will define and discuss these terms more later in the chapter. Because earned media often exists outside of an organization's own marketing channels and is independent of its own content, earned media also can be tracked using brand monitoring tools. These are tools that scan the internet and social media platforms for mentions of a brand's name. By excluding mentions resulting directly from the brand's own efforts, it can effectively measure brand influence and exposure. Another way of measuring earned media could be to look at things like backlinks to the brand's web content. **Backlinks** are links to a website from another website, and by their nature are easier to track and will also act as a boost to search engine optimization. **Search engine optimization (SEO)** is the practice of increasing both the quantity and the quality of traffic to your website through organic search engine results. In other words, with improved SEO, you have a better chance of people finding your website through a search on Google or another search engine. We will explore backlinks and SEO further in Chapter 11.

Shared Media

Paid and earned media are the most traditional forms of garnering exposure for a communicative entity, but as social media platforms became widely adopted, another form of distribution emerged—shared media. In the days of only traditional or legacy media, the CE and its agency were responsible for the creation, production *and* distribution of advertising. Audiences were only receivers of the message. In today's world, digital communication allows for a level of interaction and dialogue between CEs and consumers or stakeholders. Prospects, customers and stakeholders are able to establish their own media brands through social media platforms and blogs. They are able to share and publish content on their own platforms for a brand, product or service. Stakeholders no longer are limited to receiving messages, they can distribute the message to others, thus have a say in what is being communicated. Shared media is like earned media because its purpose is to get someone else to advocate for your organization or brand and thus provide third-party credibility. Most people trust recommendations from friends and family over any other type of advertising. When people share a CE's content to their social networks, that's shared media. Paid and earned media can inspire shared media. To maximize shared media, strategic communicators strive to create content that is valuable, entertaining and encourages sharing. For this to happen, the organization/brand must have fans and followers who feel passionately about the brand and want to engage and share information with their friends and followers. This can happen organically—that is people have a natural desire to share their affinity for a product or service. Often shared media is a result of a strategic communication campaign where the CE provides tools, to its own loyal audience to create and share branded content with their peers, as a form of guided **word-of-mouth (WOM)** marketing.

Many CEs take advantage of customers and stakeholders ability to create and distribute marketing messages, by creating campaigns that solicit and encourage **user-generated content (UGC).** Instead of creating the ad for the Super Bowl in 2007, Doritos asked its fans to create their own originals videos for a chance to win the Super Bowl spot. This approach to having customers develop the advertising for the brand generated a great deal of buzz and engagements as fans of the brand submitted thousands of videos and pulled together to comment, vote, and share their favorites. Doritos continued this approach for a decade. UGC thrives in the market of experiential entertainment, and no brand capitalizes on this trend better than GoPro. Drawing on its massive follower base of almost

20 million, GoPro launched a photo-of-the-day competition where GoPro posts the best user-submitted GoPro image each day.

Examples of Shared Media

Earned media and shared media are very closely connected and often overlap. When a fashion blogger posts a blog about a hot, up-and-coming brand of clothing without being asked to do so by the brand, it would be considered earned media. When the followers of the blog share the blog with their friends via word-of-mouth or social media, it would be considered shared media. While it can take on many forms, shared media is essentially when a brand or communicative entity has fans and followers who feel passionately about the brand/entity and want to engage and share information about it with others. These folks are sometimes described as **brand advocates** or ambassadors. For shared media to work effectively, the brand either has to be giving away something of significant value, consistently providing interesting and useful content, or providing the stakeholders with amusement. Snapchat, for example, with its branded filters that enable users to create and share branded selfies or videos with their Snapchat friends, has proven that, given the right tools, consumers will market on behalf of the brands they love or that provide them with fun, amusing tools. Taco Bell got a lot of publicity when it created the taco-head filter for Cinco de Mayo. The filter performed extremely well. For an average of 24 seconds, over 48 million Snapchatters transformed into tacos thanks to Taco Bell's Cinco De Mayo lens. It was viewed 224 million times. They paid an estimated $750,000 for 24 hours of that filter. That works out to be one-third of a penny per view! People thoroughly enjoyed playing with the filter, which generated considerable engagement with the Taco Bell brand and helped increase Taco Bell's sales.[11]

How to Measure Shared Media

Shared media is generally about creating a positive image of a brand through its content and social media interactions. In this sense it is measured in much the same way as earned media is, with more emphasis on the general mood and positivity toward a brand. In the world of shared media, opinions can form very quickly, so reputation management, as discussed in Chapter 3, is crucial in heading off negative commentary.

Owned Media

Communicative entities have the means to produce and publish their own content through newsletters, catalogs, brochures, informational white papers, websites, webinars, podcasts, blogs and social media platforms. These materials became more prolific and effective in the digital age. **Owned media** involves aggregating an audience that seeks out the content that an organization or communicative entity disseminates to add value to its stakeholders. Gone are the days when organizations and brands simply push out information about its business, products and services and brag about being number one. Today, organizations have to create and share content that is valuable, interesting and informational for its stakeholders.

In order to utilize owned media effectively, a communicative entity must develop a quality content strategy that directly reflects the brand image. Owned media needs to be creative and entertaining, much like paid advertising needs to be creative and entertaining to be effective. When an organization or brand develops and shares effective content through its owned media, it leads to shared media as stakeholders share the content within their own networks.

In fact, effective strategic communication campaigns combine all four types of media in a deliberate and purposive way that generates synergy. In other words, good strategic communication develops and executes a content strategy that integrates paid, earned, shared and owned media in which the combined effects are greater than the sum of their separate effects.

Examples of Owned Media

Owned media refers to all the assets that the communicative entity owns and controls. It includes websites, catalogs, newsletters, pamphlets, packaging, social media and user guides and manuals. Signage, packaging, and point-of-purchase material (displays in retail stores) are also forms of owned media. These are all examples of communication channels that the CE owns and controls and through which it communicates with its stakeholders.

When we think about effective owned media, we're not just talking about content on a website that promotes about how great the brand or company is—although that is also considered owned media. We're talking about content that is valuable, interesting and informational for the brand's audiences. Effective owned media includes informative material that the brand or communicative entity produces like videos, how-to webinars, informational whitepapers, podcasts, blogs and eBooks, that create value by giving away great ideas that benefit the audience. Owned media is perhaps more important than it ever has been as the digital world has shifted consumer habits. More and more people will independently seek out high-quality content before making purchases or utilizing services. This means that a website and other online assets cannot be all about the brand and how great it is. A brand's website, YouTube channel, Facebook page, must give people information and entertainment that they actually want, more so than simply trying to sell products and services.

In this way, owned media can be seen as directly affecting shared media by providing content people want to share. Marriott International, Inc., a leading global lodging company with more than 7,000 properties across 127 countries and territories, is an example of a brand that creates useful owned media to engage audiences. Marriott has multiple blogs relevant to the lodging industry, such as Marriott Traveler and Vacations by Marriott.[12] They consistently provide useful information about traveling, such as information on culture and style of vacation destinations or tips and trends to make travel more enjoyable. Marriott provides information that their target audience seeks. As a result, the audience pays attention and engages with the Marriott brand.

How to Measure Owned Media

Like paid digital media, owned media can be easily tracked with tools like Google Analytics and Facebook Analytics or by any other number of third-party options. The trick isn't so much tracking data, it's knowing what data to track and how to interpret it in the right way. Owned media is the backbone of marketing communication. Much of a company's marketing activity will be about driving as much traffic to their owned media (offline and on) as possible.

Professional Profile

Brandon Havens—Digital Media Specialist

Brandon Havens—Digital Media Specialist at Oklahoma's Credit Union.

Did you have any internships in college? I did. I realized early on in journalism school that I would need internship experience. Side note to current students—professors don't drone on about the importance of internships for no reason—they're so valuable. I had a semester-long internship my junior year at a local news station in Oklahoma City. I was so excited about it because my dream was to be in broadcast journalism, and I knew this would help me get a foot in the door. I was able to shadow reporters, anchors, camera crew and senior staff members throughout the semester. The internship was even more interesting as it was during the 2016 presidential election year.

My second internship was non-traditional, but just as valuable. I participated in the National Student Advertising Competition (NSAC) my senior year. Although this wasn't an internship, it taught me more about advertising, marketing and communications than most of my classes did. We created a hypothetical nationwide advertising campaign for Tai Pei Frozen Asian Foods, and I was able to be part of the creative team and was a presenter at competition.

How important do you think those internships were? I can't stress how impactful my internships were for my career. Sometimes, internships will reveal to you that your chosen career path is perfect for you. Often, internships can have the opposite effect. I walked into my first internship at the news station confident I was going to be a field reporter after college who eventually landed at the anchor desk. I walked out of the internship with a degree path change and the realization I would never be a journalist. I enjoyed the internship, but I quickly realized that career wasn't the right fit for me. I ended up adding a second degree (strategic communications) to my initial journalism degree. I'm so thankful I had the internship because otherwise, I might have realized I didn't want to be a broadcast journalist after graduation.

My experience with NSAC was the opposite. NSAC was my first experience with advertising, and I fell in love with it. Being part of the Oklahoma State University NSAC team showed me where my career was meant to be.

Internships not only teach you life lessons the classroom can't, but they can also reaffirm or challenge your life plans. College is about learning about yourself as much as it is learning in the classroom, and internships are no different.

What are you doing now? I'm the digital media specialist for Oklahoma's Credit Union (OKCU) located in Oklahoma City. OKCU is a mid-sized credit union with about 45,000 members across Oklahoma and the country. In my position, I manage communication through our digital channels. I write content for and manage our website and social media channels. Additionally, I create all digital advertising creatives and placements and manage our digital advertising budget. I report directly to the chief marketing officer and often report to our executive suite and the board of directors regarding our digital communications.

How did you get there? After undergrad at Oklahoma State University, I was encouraged to stay in the program to earn a master's degree. It was a fantastic decision. I worked full time for a marketing department on campus and was able to graduate from graduate school in a year and a half. After graduating with my master's, I moved to Oklahoma City and joined the team at a digital marketing agency. It was a small team and we had a lot of clients. The work was fun, but after a year, I wanted a change. In the midst of COVID-19, I quit my job and searched for something different. I landed at Oklahoma's Credit Union because of my prior experience in digital marketing and advertising.

How have your dreams changed? In college, my dreams were to be at an anchor desk, then they were to work for an advertising agency where I could work on national accounts. After being in the field for a few years, my dreams have changed drastically. Now, I dream about doing impactful work that helps people. At OKCU, we help people do more with their money through community outreach, supporting local businesses and providing financial literacy. Every day I see the work I do help people in need, and it feels great. I've learned that I can achieve my dreams by taking small steps toward a bigger picture. Just a few years ago, I measured my success as an all or nothing measurement. Now, I understand my dreams are fluid and they change a lot, and if the work I do daily makes me happy and fulfilled, I'm quickly on my way to achieving my dreams.

What did you wish you had known? Being well-rounded in your industry (and outside your industry) is extremely valuable to employers. Take that photography class. Get experience in motion graphics. Enroll in a public speaking seminar. Simply doing what your coursework requires gets you a degree, but it doesn't set you apart. When an employer looks at two potential employees who are equally qualified, think about what you can do to make you special.

Also, don't take yourself too seriously. We can make plans all day long, but at the end of the day, they change due to a myriad of reasons. Stay on the path you're on, work hard and enjoy the journey. It sounds cliché but it's true.

What advice would you give someone in college now? Take any opportunity you can to get real-world experience. This isn't limited to internships. Apply for extra-curricular programs like the National Student Advertising Campaign. And if you're thinking about getting a degree beyond a Bachelor's, do it while you can. It's easy to graduate and think "I'll come back to it," but you probably never will. You're already in a learning-mindset. Keep it going and get that next degree.

Integrating Media

As mentioned earlier, Super Bowl commercials are the most expensive and most well-received form of paid media. However, even the most expensive and celebrated form of paid media does not work independently. Advertising on the Super Bowl also garners earned and shared media. Super Bowl commercials have long been the topic of morning news shows segments, newspaper and trade magazine articles, blogs, late-night talk shows both before and after the Super Bowl each year. So, Super Bowl spots have been benefitting from earned media for decades. But in more recent years, brands are being more deliberate to create owned, earned and shared media in conjunction with the Super Bowl ad (paid) to get more bang for their buck. In fact, Volkswagen's successful Passat commercial aired in 2011 is credited for revolutionizing the way advertisers approach the Super Bowl. The ad, titled "The Force," portrays a young boy dressed as Darth Vader trying to apply "the force" on different subjects around his house and he finally succeeds with a little help from his father and the Volkswagen Passat, in the end. Volkswagen first released the spot on YouTube (owned) four days before the Super Bowl and generated 12.4 million views before it aired the 30-second version (paid) during the big game. The video was shared more than 5 million times on social media (shared). Because of the eloquent storytelling, the minute-long YouTube version was an instant hit, and the exposure did not stop with social. Media outlets such as CNN and *Time* magazine were talking about the ad (earned) and its enchanting star, Max Page, who plays the mini Darth Vader. The cute, young commercial actor suffered from a heart condition, which made the "The Force" all the more compelling. Volkswagen also ran a 15-second teaser spot that aired on "Saturday Night Live" the night before the game, to create momentum that continued through the Super Bowl. The early release of the ad—which has since become a widespread practice—created unprecedented pre-kickoff buzz around the commercial, helping it earn the titles of most-shared Super Bowl ad of all-time and second most-shared TV commercial ever.[13] This campaign is an excellent example of leveraging PESO to gain maximum strategic communication benefit.

Case Study

Challenging the Way People See Beauty to Better a Brand's Bottom Line

Dove's Real Beauty Campaign, which has evolved into the Dove Self-Esteem Project, is an excellent example of strategic communication designed to utilize synergy by developing a campaign that incorporates paid, earned, shared and owned media. In the early 2000s, Dove executives began looking for a way to revive a brand that was being overshadowed by other companies. They were moving beyond the bar of soap and launching products such as shampoo and body wash. Their PR agency, Edelman, conducted a study of more than 3,000 women in ten countries in order to learn about women's priorities and interests. They released a report from the study that showed that only 2% of the women interviewed considered themselves beautiful. In light of these findings, Dove executives believed that instead of talking about their products, they should start a conversation about beauty.[14]

In 2004, Dove launched an interactive campaign that featured images of "real women" on billboards with two tick-box options next to them such as "fat?" or "fit?" and "ugly spots?" or "beauty spots?" Passersby could text their vote to a number on the board, and the percentages appeared next to the image on the billboard. The Campaign for Real Beauty website quickly received 1.5 million unique visitors to the site. The company wanted to go beyond advertising and actively engage its audience. It was evident that the campaign tapped into a topic that women wanted to explore and discuss. They knew the campaign would be considered mere lip service, if they did not go beyond marketing. Dove partnered with organizations like the Girl Scouts, Boys & Girls Clubs of America and Girls Inc. to create a fund and raise awareness about online bullying, and share photography depicting the beauty girls see in the world around them.[15] A series of short films were also used to raise awareness about the fund and the larger campaign. "Evolution," was the title of one of the series, which demonstrated how makeup and digital alterations can make an average woman look like a supermodel. The series became very popular on YouTube, very quickly. After "Evolution" was released, the Campaign for Real Beauty had people taking notice, talking about it and sharing it with others. Young women discovered that they had been faced with narrow definitions of beauty all their lives. The campaign and the video series started a conversation that drove women to examine how the beauty and fashion industry had manipulated their understanding of what beauty means and how they see themselves.[16] The video series originally posted on YouTube in October 2016, has more than 20 million views in 2020.

In attempt to better understand its stakeholders and target audience, Dove launched two studies to examine self-esteem, body image and body confidence among women and girls. After interviewing 10,500 females across 13 countries, the *Dove Global Beauty and Confidence Report* found that women's confidence in their bodies is on a steady decline, with low body esteem becoming a unifying challenge shared by women and girls around the world—regardless of age or geography. Dove's research was groundbreaking and newsworthy, garnering significant media coverage. To coincide with the launch of the *Dove Global Beauty and Confidence Report*, the brand announced a goal of doubling is social impact by 2020—committing to positively impacting an additional 20 million young lives over the next four years.[17]

Although Dove has been met with considerable criticism throughout its journey to engage women in a discussion about beauty, challenge stereotypes and address self-esteem issues among women through strategic communication, it is an excellent example of creating interactive communication designed to leverage research, data and all four types of media (PESO) in order to stay relevant in the minds of consumers by providing interesting content, while striving to stay true to the brand's essence.

A billboard from Dove's Real Beauty Campaign.
Photography ©Rankin.

Traditional Media Classifications

In addition to understanding the four media types (paid, earned, shared and owned) it is also important to understand four traditional classifications of media (print, broadcast, out-of-home and interactive) and how advertising is paid and earned within these classifications. As mentioned earlier, because of the internet and social media, these media classifications are outdated and limiting media because now stakeholders can access and engage with a media vehicle's content from many different platforms. However, it is important to understand the origins of these media classifications and how to leverage them strategically. Leveraging paid media is the art and science of **media planning** and **media buying** that involves strategy, negotiation and placement of ads. We will discuss the different media classifications, how they are measured, priced and purchased.

Print

Print media include newspapers, magazines, brochures, catalogs, direct mail, packaging, fliers and all other forms of message dissemination that involves printing text and/or images on paper or other materials such as T-shirts, pens and hats. Newspapers and magazines are the most prominent form of print media, and most print media vehicles are no longer merely print vehicles because they have interactive capabilities through the internet, mobile apps and social media. Print media sell advertising space as well as accept news releases, which can be effective in generating publicity (earned media).

Newspapers

Newspapers take many shapes and sizes, and they are published periodically, most often daily or weekly. Newspapers provide information about current events. Most newspapers are businesses, and they pay their expenses with a mixture of subscription revenue, news-stand sales and advertising revenue. Newspapers have traditionally been published in print (usually on cheap, low-grade paper called newsprint). However, today most newspapers are also published on websites as online newspapers, and some have even abandoned their print versions entirely.

The *New York Times*, nicknamed the Gray Lady, is the most prominent newspaper in the U.S., but it is more than just a newspaper. The *New York Times* includes a newspaper, a weekly magazine, a website, a mobile app, as well as offering a wide variety of signature live events available for sponsorship. A communicative entity can buy advertising space on all these versions of the *New York Times*. The print newspaper advertising includes display advertising, which is sold by the column inch. The *New York Times* consists of six columns in width and 21 inches in length. Advertisers can purchase a full-page ad, which is 6×21 or 126 column inches or all the way down to a 1-column inch ad, which is described as a 1×1 and every size in between. The advertising rates are based on the number of readers the vehicle reaches, which is called **circulation**. The weekend edition of the *NY Times* has a circulation of 4.8 or almost 5 million people. The media kit for the digital version of the Gray Lady boasts that *NYT Digital*, the online version of the paper, is a global powerhouse with 119 million unique readers worldwide at the time this was written. By having multiple forms, newspapers such as the *New York Times* can bundle their advertising offerings to gain exposure through reach (number of people) and frequency (number of times people are exposed to the message).

Print newspapers have two types of advertising, display ads and classified ads. Display advertising includes ads throughout the editorial content and various sections of the paper. With the *New York Times*, and many other newspapers, the different sections of the newspaper have different advertising rates. For example, the nationwide weekday, ad rate for the Fine Arts/Antiques section of the *New York Times* is $727. This rate must be multiplied by size of the ad to determine the cost of the ad. Ad size is determined by column inches. To calculate column inches, you simply count the number of columns the ad is wide by the number of inches it is tall. A small ad that is two columns wide by two inches tall is four column inches. A small 2×2, 4-column-inch ad in the Fine Arts/Antiques section of the *New York Times* on a Monday would cost $2,908. Four column inches multiplied by the weekday rate of $727 equals $2,908.

The weekday rate is less expensive than the weekend rate because the circulation is higher on the weekend. An advertiser would pay $954 per column inch for the same ad in the same place on Sunday, when the circulation is higher. The business section rate is higher than the Fine Arts/Antiques section, because that section has a higher readership. An advertiser would have to pay $1,762 per column inch to reach the nationwide audience in the business section on Sunday and $1,541 on a weekday. How much is the total cost of a full-page ad in these sections? A full-page ad is six columns wide by 21 inches long, which equals 126 column inches. You multiply the size of the ad in column inches by the ad rate.

	Weekday	Sunday
Fine Arts/Antiques Section	$126 \times \$727 = \$91,602$	$126 \times \$954 = \$120,204$
Business Section	$126 \times \$1,541 = \$194,166$	$126 \times \$1,762 = \$222,012$

It costs an advertiser almost double to purchase a full-page ad in the business section than it would to advertise in the Fine Arts/Antiques section of the *New York Times*. These are rates for the printed newspaper, but an advertiser can purchase ad space in the printed newspaper, *New York Times* magazine, nytimes.com and NYTLive, which is events. The *New York Times* media kit offers 30 different digital ad types from a leaderboard to virtual reality. This one media vehicle is an excellent example of how complicated campaign and media planning has become in the digital age.[18]

Magazines

Magazines are also periodical publications that are printed and/or electronically published. Magazines are generally published on a regular schedule, weekly, monthly, quarterly or annually (that's why they are called periodicals). Magazines and other periodicals are generally financed by advertising, by single copy purchase price, by prepaid subscriptions, or a combination of the three. The key advantage to magazine advertising is the potential for high-impact messages. Magazines provide brands/companies with the ability to show-case their products or services in a high-quality, glossy format that is rich with color and attention-getting, visual imagery. Magazines allow "bleed" images, meaning that the image extends all the way to the page edges, without a border. Magazine print advertising is most often sold as full-page ads, covers, half-page or quarter-page ads. The most expensive ad space in a magazine is the back cover because it gets the most exposure. The inside front cover and the inside back cover are also sold at a premium price above other full-page ads.

There are a few general interest magazines, such as *Time*, but most often magazines are considered to be niche media because they focus on a specific topic reaching a specific audience. Magazine readers typically have strong interest in the theme or topic of a given magazine. There are hundreds of magazines often targeting niche interests. By leveraging readership demographics, you instantly ensure that your message is being seen by the right people—the ones most likely to buy your product. Finding this close link between readers and the brand/product being advertised is critical to the effectiveness of the advertising message.

Contributing to the effectiveness of magazine ads is the potential for ongoing, repeated exposure. Homeowners and businesses commonly have magazine racks or other spaces where they keep magazines for other readers or repeat use. This gives advertisers the potential to reach many people with one copy and the same reader multiple times. Plus, since magazines are a static medium, readers can look at the ad for as long as they want, unlike broadcast media, which is fleeting—here one instant and gone the next.

Like newspapers, magazine ad rates are based on readership for print and unique visitors and page views for online. Ads in national magazines commonly cost several thousand dollars per issue. You can opt for smaller, quarter-page or half-page ads to save money, but those often get lost in the clutter of a large magazine with lots of advertisements.

Publications sometimes offer discounts for early submissions and for ads arranged through an advertising agency. Advertisers can also save money by advertising in the same magazine numerous times in one year. The more ads a company places within the publication, the less expensive each ad will be. *Car & Driver* is an example of a niche magazine that reaches car enthusiasts. The published rate for a 4-color, full-page ad in *Car & Driver* in 2018 is $258,500. The reach of the magazine in 2018 was approximately 19.6 million readers. Car & Driver offers digital advertising for both the mobile and online versions of the magazine.[19]

While advertising in print media is on a steady decline, there are still advantages of purchasing paid advertising and earning publicity in print media for communicative entities. For example, audiences are less receptive and attentive when they are watching TV or scrolling the internet. Print readers typically don't multitask when they read a magazine or newspaper, and they are more likely to pay attention to ads in print media.

Broadcast

Radio and television are considered broadcast media because the audio and/or video content is distributed to a dispersed audience via any electronic mass communications medium in a one-to-many model. Radio and television broadcasting, which includes the production and transmission of educational, entertaining and news-related programming, is a practical application of audio and visual technologies. Like print media, radio and television sell advertising space (or time) as well as accept news releases and video releases, which can be effective in generating publicity. Local stations often cover special events, such as a grand opening of a store or a sports event by doing on-site broadcasts. Broadcast media can be helpful in supporting event marketing efforts.

Examples of broadcast media vehicles include broadcast networks such as ABC, NBC, CBS and Fox, cable networks such as CNN, USA, Bravo and Discovery, and radio networks such as iHeart Radio, Inc. and Entercom.

Television

First let's talk about television. Both broadcast and cable channels appear on your local cable or satellite system, but you must buy airtime separately. You can purchase local airtime on the broadcast stations from that station's local representative in a certain market or area, you can buy cable channel airtime from the local cable system's representative, or you can buy national airtime across all markets. Smaller businesses often purchase cable airtime because cable channels will sell airtime for the entire market or individual cable systems, just one area of the market. Television rates are set up with pricing for a 15-second, 30-second or 60-second commercial in a particular television program. You can also purchase "rotators," which are commercials that will fall somewhere within a specified time period, such as prime time—7 p.m. to 10 p.m. on a particular day.

Television Markets

In order to understand how to buy television advertising or airtime, it is important to understand the term, market. The term is also known as a media market, broadcast market, market region or DMA (designated market area) and is defined as a region in the United

States in which the population receives the same television and radio station offerings. Designated Market Areas, as the name suggests, do not overlap for the purpose of media planning, buying and evaluating. Determined by the Nielsen Company, there are 210 DMAs in the U.S. and are usually defined based on metropolitan areas, with suburbs combined within. Advertising rates are more expensive in the top or largest markets because more viewers have an opportunity to see the advertising in those markets. The metro areas with the highest populations are the called the "top DMAs."

The top ten DMAs for 2019–2020

1   New York
2   Los Angeles
3   Chicago
4   Philadelphia
5   Dallas-Fort Worth
6   San Francisco-Oakland-San Jose
7   Washington, DC
8   Houston
9   Boston
10 Atlanta.[20]

As we mentioned, television advertising can be purchased nationally across all 210 markets, or by individual markets. When evaluating where and when to advertise, it is important to weigh the opportunities and costs of advertising nationally or within a few key DMAs that best reach the audience most effectively and efficiently. For small businesses with a small budget, it is especially important to make sure they are advertising at the right time, the right place and the right price. Advertising in the top DMA: New York will reach the most people. It will also cost more than advertising in any other DMA. Is it worth it? Is it the most effective and efficient television market? It depends. If the communicative entity's product or service is most heavily used in New York, then advertising in that market will be effective and efficient. However, if the communicative entity's product or service is mainly purchased in the southern U.S., then advertising in the top DMA doesn't make sense. It's about getting as many eyeballs on the ad as possible each time it airs, but it also needs to be the right eyeballs. Brand and media companies work to match the demographics of the viewers of each show to the target market of the product or service being sold. The popularity of the program and number of times the advertiser agrees to air the ad all affect the total cost of running the ad.

Rates and Ratings

Television rates are generally based on the size of the audience for the program, but there are other factors that can influence the rate. TV rates fluctuate greatly with supply and demand. If a station has limited inventory or commercial airtime available, the price usually increases because it is in high demand. If the station has a lot of inventory left, the price is usually lower because the demand is low. However, low is a relative term, television advertising is not cheap. The average cost of a national 30-second TV commercial is approximately is $115,000. Television advertising airtime is considered "perishable" because like vegetables at the grocery store, it has a limited shelf life. Once the program airs, the inventory is gone and cannot be sold.

Ratings are important to selling advertising and determining cost. The Nielsen Company does most of the U.S. television ratings and broadcasting research. Nielsen estimates that there are approximately 120 million households in the U.S. To determine the size of a program's audience, Nielsen conducts a survey of approximately 41,000 households, which means the study sample is a little over .03% of the actual households with televisions. Like most valid research, the study sample (41,000 households) is intended to represent the total population (120 million households). The rating is based on their estimates of the audience from their survey. A "1" rating equals 1% of the population in the demographic segment you are wanting to reach. For example, if you want to know how many adults between the ages of 25 and 54 are watching a certain show, a one rating indicates that 1% of the total population of adults 25 to 54 watch that show. It is important to clarify, it is 1% of the total population of adults 25 to 54 in the country, not 1% of the people watching television.

The percentage of people watching television is called share, which is another important measurement, but it is not used much in pricing airtime. Pricing for TV inventory is determined by a variety of factors including how many viewers a program gets, the demographic segment the advertiser wants to reach and the type of programming, and a metric called **gross rating points (GRPs)**.

What is a GRP? It is essentially a math equation used to determine how many people an intended audience might have exposed to an ad or ads. This equation was developed in the 1950s, and it is still used today to get an estimate and measure the total exposure of an ad among a target audience or how many people within a specific group are reached by advertising in a TV program. Rating points are key performance indicators (KPIs) specific to **media planning** and **media buying**. GRPs are used as a cumulative measure of the **impressions** an ad campaign can achieve. Impressions are the total number of exposures to an ad. Calculating GRPs is a simple formula that takes the universe impressions and divides it by the universe population. The **universe** is the population of the group being measured and needs to be identified prior to evaluating all metrics. For example, adults over 18 is a universe, while millennials (adults 22–38) is a target demographic segment within that universe.

$$GRP = \frac{\text{Total Universe Impressions}}{\text{Selected Universe Population}} \times 100$$

Reach and Frequency

To understand how to calculate GRP's, we first have to define and understand reach and frequency. While the concept of reach and frequency are most closely tied to television advertising, it applies to any promotional activity you undertake: direct mail, direct selling, media coverage and even networking. *Reach* is the *number* of people you touch with your message or the number of people that are exposed to your message. Frequency is the average number of *times* a person is exposed to your message. In a world of unlimited resources, you would maximize both reach and frequency. However, all budgets have their limits, so communicative entities have to make decisions to sacrifice reach for frequency or vice versa. For example, is it more effective to expose 100 potential customers to your message once or expose 25 potential customers to your message four times? On the surface, it may appear simple, reaching more people is better, right? Not exactly. Strategic communication is process of building relationships with customers and stakeholders. Like friendships, relationships built through strategic communication grow as a result of encounters and touchpoints that happen over time. You might have an instant connection with someone upon first meeting or interaction, but a friendship or relationship will not grow without nurturing or spending more time together. That's frequency. A common mistake among communicative entities is sacrificing frequency for reach. There is a great deal of noise or other messages competing for your target audience's attention, so doesn't it make sense that telling them something once or even twice might not even stand out enough for them to remember hearing it, let alone act on it? So back to the question of exposing 100 people once or 25 people four times—the answer should now be clear that your message will be far more effective if you choose to expose fewer people more often. Frequency not only allows a communicative entity an opportunity to build a better relationship through more exposure, but also it increases the likelihood that the message will cut through the clutter of competing messages through repetition.

Now that we have a general understanding of reach and frequency, we can calculate GRPs. Reach is the percentage of the audience reached and frequency is the average number of times the audience is exposed to the message, and GRPs measures the gross showing of an ad campaign over time. GRPs are a way to quantify the number of exposures (which are impressions) as a gross percentage of the population. It's important to note that GRPs do not determine the influence your messages have over people, but it merely relates how many people were tuned in to the station at the time your ads were airing and how many times on average they were exposed to the messages.

$$\text{Reach} \times \text{Frequency} = \text{GRPs}$$

Let's apply the formula. First, add up your total reach. Each percentage is equal to one rating point. For example, if you reach half (50%) of the viewers, you have a reach of 50. If your commercial was aired five times, you have a frequency of 5.

$$50 \times 5 = 250$$

It is possible to get a number larger than 100 because GRPs includes duplication. You can use the formula for each show in which your air ads. Ad A airs three times on a program that reaches 15% of viewers. Ad B airs five times on a program that reaches 10% of viewers. To calculate the total GRPs for the combined advertising on the two programs, you solve each individually then add the totals.

Ad A:	$25 \times 3 = 75$
Ad B:	$20 \times 5 = \underline{100}$
Total GRPs:	**175**

Calculating GRPs is a simple formula that takes the universe impressions and divides it by the universe population. GRPs tell you how much of the audience you're reaching, but in order to determine the reach of your specific target audience, you will need to calculate target rating points (TRPs). GRPs and TRPs are slightly different but the terms are often used interchangeably. TRPs quantify the gross rated points achieved by an ad or campaign among targeted individuals within a larger population.

In addition to reach, frequency and rating points, broadcast media planning involves how, when and which content your audience consumes, so that you can determine the networks and programs that fit your audience, the television markets or areas of the country to advertise in, what time of year and what time of day to advertise, and the length of the commercial spots. The size and composition of the viewing audience is very important to understanding TV advertising. The audience size and composition determine the amount the network or station can charge for commercial time. When a television show is cancelled, it almost certainly means that it has failed to attract enough viewers to make advertising during the program attractive to communicative entities.

Future of TV Advertising

Traditional television advertising is on the decline because viewers are "cutting the cord" and choosing streaming services like Netflix and Hulu, instead of paying for cable or satellite TV services. As online video streaming platforms are experiencing massive growth in viewership, advertising is following the eyeballs and shifting toward video streaming or over-the-top advertising. The term *over-the-top (OTT)* refers to the service used to stream digital content to TV, the devices include streaming boxes like Apple TV, Amazon Fire TV, HDMI sticks like Roku, Chromecast and Smart TV apps like Netflix and HBO Go. OTT or streaming advertising is on the path to overcome traditional advertising for several reasons. TV advertising is limited to television, but OTT advertising allows brands to get their message in front of viewers via television, smartphones, tablets, laptops and desktops. Advertising on video streaming platforms is also easier to track, measure and optimize advertising while being cheaper than TV advertising. Communicative entities can make changes to their OTT advertising campaigns much easier than traditional advertising because they can track when viewers click through to their sites and purchase products. Traditional TV advertising is more expensive for a few reasons, but most importantly it's because OTT advertising is able to better select who will be exposed to the advertising and only pay for that personalized audience. Traditional TV advertising relies on targeting audiences by general demographics such as age, gender and geographic region. Streaming advertising makes it possible to collect and mine personal data on viewers on an individual level. As with all advertising, by making sure you are only paying to advertise to a smaller, more tailored audience, it is much cheaper than paying to advertise to a larger, broader audience.

Radio

Like television, radio audiences and advertising has been negatively affected by streaming options, such as Pandora and Spotify. In March 2020, when countries started locking down due to the COVID-19 pandemic, fewer people were commuting to work every day. Businesses were struggling to stay afloat and they were spending less on advertising, if any at all. These conditions strained the radio advertising market. According to eMarketer, radio is predicted to bounce back and spending for advertising is expected to level off at $30 billion for a few years.[21] Despite its recent advertising decline, traditional radio continues to play a role in the lives of billions of people worldwide. Radio even overlaps with streaming options, as traditional radio stations have downloadable apps and ability for listeners to livestream their stations from virtually anywhere with internet access. According to Nielsen, radio reached more than 90% of U.S. adults on a weekly basis in the first quarter of 2020.[22] Because of the nature of radio, it has several unique qualities that continue to make it a viable advertising medium.

First and foremost, radio is a local medium that helps listeners find out what is happening now in their communities, such as news, weather, traffic, sports and entertainment. Radio is mobile, and that portability allows it to be a constant companion for listeners with them wherever they go. The accessibility of radio allows advertisers to meet consumers in places other media can't. For example, radio audiences can be reached while at work, driving, gardening, at the beach, going for a run and so much more. Radio audiences tune in throughout the day, which gives advertising messages more opportunity to reach its target audience. Those audiences can be targeted by specific demographic segments and communities, around events and genres. For example, radio stations in the same town can attract very different and specific audiences.

> **Audience 1:** Adult men ages 18–34 who love anthem rock, Longhorn football and live in the 75217 zip code.
> **Audience 2:** Adult women ages 35–54 who listen to country music, love NASCAR, shopping at Target, and live in the 75217 zip code.

Radio is an intimate medium. People often listen alone, and they form strong relationships with their favorite stations. That intimacy, loyalty and ability to reach a very specific audience who is on-the-go makes advertising on the radio highly effective when the message is crafted properly. The emotional connection to radio makes listeners more receptive to advertising when the message is designed and placed for the right audience.

The key feature of a radio station is its format, which is the type of programming that it features. Some of the most common radio formats include:

- Top 40
- News/Talk
- Classic Rock
- Country
- Adult Contemporary
- All Sports
- Urban Contemporary.

One of the main strengths of radio advertising is its low cost, which gives the communicative entity the opportunity to build higher reach and frequency with less money than other media. Radio is more cost-efficient than local television, print advertising and direct mail. Radio is not only cost-efficient, but also time efficient. Radio commercials can be produced very quickly, and they have a very short lead-time, which means ads can be produced and scheduled on very short notice. Advertisers can craft their messages and change it almost up to the time it goes air. Radio stations offer promotional activities that support and add value to a radio advertising buy, such as live broadcasts from a client's event or place of business, on-air personalities giving away tickets to an event or promotional items with the client's logo.

Purchasing radio time is very similar to purchasing television, as advertisers can buy network, spot or local. The cost of a radio commercial will depend on the length of the commercial, the time of day that the ad runs and the frequency of the ad broadcast. Morning and evening drive times are usually the most expensive because the radio audience tends to peak during commuting hours. Most radio advertising is purchased locally from individual stations by local companies, such as car dealerships, retailers, restaurants, bars and financial institutions. Some local stations are affiliated with national broadcast networks, such as CBS. There are both national and regional radio networks. Advertisers can utilize networks to minimize the amount of negotiation and legwork needed to gain national or regional coverage at a lower cost than paying individual stations. National advertisers can also use spot radio to purchase advertising on individual stations in various markets, with greater flexibility than purchasing through a network. Purchasing spot radio also allows an advertiser to adjust the message for local market conditions.

In summary, radio offers advertisers the ability to appeal to narrow segments of the market and the opportunity to build high reach and frequency at a very efficient cost.

Out of Home Advertising

Out-of-home (OOH) or outdoor advertising, most commonly identified with billboards, is considered the genesis of all advertising. Commercial advertising can be traced back to ancient walls or rock paintings throughout Asia, Africa and South America. Billboard advertising has been used in the United States since the 1800s. Out-of-home advertising opportunities available in many markets can be numerous, almost to the point of overwhelming, including billboards, bus shelters, transit ads, benches and more. Out-of-home gives advertisers the opportunity to take advantage of place and meet audiences where they are. Outdoor advertising is buying location and length of time. Because outdoor advertising has a longer life span than most other media, it offers consistency and stability, which is very beneficial for improving brand awareness and brand recognition. The prevalence and ubiquity of out-of-home advertising is a testament to its ability to attract attention and compel consumers to make purchasing decisions over time. Next time you visit a major city, take the bus or subway, attend a sporting event in a large stadium or arena, take a few moments to discover how many different forms of advertising that you are exposed to and ask yourself what the experience would be without the advertising.

Billboards

Let's explore the different types of out-of-home advertising. **Billboards** are essentially the king of OOH. Billboards are large-format poster displays found in areas of high consumer traffic, such as busy highways and city centers. Advertisers can purchase static or digital billboards. Static billboards are the traditional style billboard with, you guessed it, a static image and message. Static billboards are the only medium that offers constant exposure that cannot be turned off or thrown away, and they are very hard to ignore. Billboards come in a lot of different sizes, including bulletins, posters and junior posters. Bulletins are the largest and most standard-size billboard with a vinyl face. Bulletins offer maximum exposure, visibility and impact. Poster billboards are smaller than bulletins and used to gain exposure and utilized to reach customers where they live, work and play. Posters are often used to flood the market at one time by displaying the same message in multiple locations throughout the city/community. Junior posters are the smallest in the billboard family. They are often used to promote special events, new products and seasonal offerings. Static billboards are not necessarily confined to the standard size and horizontal rectangle shape. Advertisers can use creativity and design eye-catching 3-D forms and extensions to help communicate their messages.

Digital billboards are computer-controlled electronic displays that gives advertisers greater flexibility, allowing the message to be changed or updated easily. Digital billboards can be set to have a customized schedule to reach viewers at specific times of the day and days of the week. For example, a fast-food chain can advertise the breakfast burrito in the morning, the limited-time-only spicy chicken sandwich around lunch and the combo meal in the evening. The changing message alone grabs viewers' attention and because of production costs, digital can cost less than static billboards. When it comes to choosing between static versus digital billboards, the campaign goals should guide the decision, and the answer might just include both. While static billboards are exclusive with a constant message, advertisers who choose digital billboards will be sharing screen time with as many as five other brands. Digital billboards give advertisers the opportunity to not only gain attention for their brands, but also give customers the opportunity to interact with the brand. For example, Netflix utilized a digital billboard display in Toronto to promote the film, *Daredevil*, in 2016. The display included four boards, and viewers were asked to tweet in support of one of the characters featured on one of the boards: #daredevil, #elektra and #punisher. The winner of the hashtag fight was revealed as the character with the most mentions would then damage the other character's posters, which appeared as bullet holes, bruises and cuts.[23]

Several other forms of out-of-home advertising are available. We will discuss a few of these options, but for a more comprehensive list see Figure 10.2.

Type of OOH Advertising

Billboards	Street Furniture	Transit	Place-Based
Static	Bus Shelters	Airports	Cinema
Digital	Bus Benches	Buses	Arena and Stadiums
Bulletins	Newsracks / Stands	Rail / Subway	Wall Murals
Posters	Phone Kiosks	Digital Transit	Digital Place-Based
Junior Posters	Urban Panels	Taxis	Shopping Malls
Wallscapes	Digital Street Furniture	Mobile Billboards	In-Window Street Ads

Figure 10.2 Type of Out-of-Home Advertising

Transit Advertising

Transit advertising has been around for a long time, and it takes advantage of the fact that millions of people utilize commercial transportation. Advertisers can reach a "captive audience" while they ride the bus, train or taxi and while they wait at the station, platform or airport. Public transit offers numerous placement possibilities including bus wraps, platform displays, posters inside the bus. Advertisers can even opt for station domination, which means purchasing every media space in the station to create a full brand experience. Advertisers can adorn walls, add floor graphics, wrap entry/exit turnstiles, and virtually any surface of the Station's interior or exterior. Transit advertising includes three separate media forms: inside cards, outside posters, and station, platform or terminal posters. **Inside cards** are the ads placed in a wall rack above the windows inside the bus or subway car. The ads are typically 28 inches wide by 11 inches tall. **Outside posters** are ads that appear on the backs, sides and/or roofs of buses, taxis, trains, subway and trolley cars, and even rickshaws. Station, platform and terminal posters are what you would expect, posters in these locations. However, advertising in stations and terminals can take many forms including floor displays, kiosks, island showcases, electronic signs, and dioramas. Advertisers can add interactive digital elements with face-recognition technology and 3-D prop installations, such as a life-size Chick-Fil-A Cow, to keep commuters engaged.

Street Furniture is yet another great way to reach audiences on the move. There are numerous street furniture formats, but the most common types are bus stops, transit shelters and bench ads. Street furniture ads can be static or digital, but most importantly when it is used creatively, it can transform a space and give audiences a unique experience. For example, when Caribou Coffee launched its hot and fresh Daybreaker breakfast sandwich, its advertising agency Colle McVoy, utilized transit advertising. They transformed bus shelters into ovens complete with real heaters and working clocks to showcase Caribou's new "Hot 'n Wholesome" menu items and keep Minnesotans warm while waiting on the bus in frigid temperatures.[24]

Caribou Coffee turned bus shelters into ovens, with real heat, to promote their new hot breakfast sandwiches.

Place-based advertising is available in various places including malls, cinemas, health clubs, restrooms and more. But nothing really compares to arena and stadium advertising because of the electrifying atmosphere of passion, competition and the glory of victory. Attendees are emotionally connected to the game, and as a result they are more receptive to advertising messages than they are in many other settings. Stadium ads allow advertisers to reach a captive audience with guaranteed exposure, and your brand could also be shown on TV and reach viewers outside the venue as a bonus. Stadium and arena advertising can be very effective; however, advertisers better be ready to pay to play. Stadium advertising can be purchased for a season, but often multiple-year contracts are required.

Out-of-home advertising is a broad medium with many options and opportunities for reach, frequency, creativity and wow factor to increase brand awareness and product purchase decisions. Out-of-home advertising can be purchased in different ways, including contract periods for multiple boards or faces, purchased individually or by rating point level. Contract periods vary; bulletins are typically purchased for 12 weeks or longer, while smaller billboards and other OOH can be purchased in a single 4-week period.

Summary

This chapter introduced you to the vast world of media, its impact on strategic communication and the countless opportunities it provides communicative entities to reach their stakeholders. The media are classified into four categories, paid, earned, shared and owned. These categories provide a framework understanding how to best employ different channels and the best strategy for integrating multiple media channels for a successful campaign. Paid media is what we would typically think of advertising, such as TV commercials and full-page ads in magazines. Earned media involves gaining publicity through media relations in order to benefit from a third-party sharing news about a product, service or brand. Shared media involves getting people outside the organization to advocate for your organization or brand. It requires valuable, entertaining content that leads to followers of your brand sharing their positive experiences and affection for your products or services. Owned media is content that is created and shared through communication channels that the organization owns, including newsletters, websites, podcasts and social media. We also explored strengths and weaknesses of PESO media, how to purchase and garner media exposure and how to measure the results. We discussed the importance of integrating media from all four categories of media to gain exposure and engagement that leads to behavior change and brand loyalty.

We explored the different types of traditional media classifications: print, broadcast and out-of-home. The media are pervasive, and we have barely scratched the surface here. The following chapter will explore evolving media formats beyond the traditional or legacy media discussed in this chapter.

Discussion Questions

1   Make an hourly calendar of your daily media usage. Start when you wake up and log the media that you use throughout the day. If a CE wanted to reach you, which media would be most effective for them?
2   Think of a popular brand that uses the PESO model in an integrated way. Give examples of its paid, earned, shared and owned messaging.
3   What is third-party credibility? Why is it important to CEs? How is it achieved?
4   What brand messages have you shared on your social media recently? Why did you share? What about that brand or those messages made you share?

5   How much would it cost to run a 4×10 display ad in your local newspaper? Find out the column inch rate for the paper and calculate the cost of the ad.

6   If McDonald's purchased 1,200 GRPs for a month-long television campaign and it reached 80% of the audience, what is the average frequency for the campaign?

7   What are the advantages and disadvantages of out-of-home advertising?

Check out the online support material, including chapter summaries, useful links and further reading, at www.routledge.com/9780367426316.

Notes

1   Cohen, J. (2010, August 18). How to define shared media on Facebook. *AdWeek.* https://www.adweek.com/digital/shared-media-facebook/.

2   Dietrich, G. (2014). *Spin Sucks: Communication and Reputation Management in the Digital Age*. Pearson Education.

3   https://firstdraftnews.org/latest/fake-news-complicated/.

4   https://www.huffpost.com/entry/yougov-super-bowl-commercials-game_n_56b105d3e4b0a1b96203f436.

5   Carroll, C (2018, January 11). How much does an ad for this year's Super Bowl cost? *Sports Illustrated.* https://www.si.com/nfl/2018/01/11/super-bowl-lii-ad-cost.

6   https://www.businessoffashion.com/articles/news-analysis/the-evolution-of-the-influencer-economy.

7   Stanford History Education Group (2016), *Evaluating Information: The Cornerstone of Civic Reasoning.* Retrieved from: https://sheg.stanford.edu/upload/V3LessonPlans/Executive%20Summary%2011.21.16.pdf.

8   McGrew, S., Ortega, T., Breakstone, J. & Wineburg, S. (2017). The challenge that's bigger than fake news: Teaching students to engage in civic online reasoning. *American Educator*, *41*(3), 4–11.

9   Kendrick, A., & Fullerton, J. (2019). Can US advertising students recognize an ad in editorial's clothing (native advertising)? A partial replication of the Stanford "Evaluating information" test. *Journal of Marketing Communications.* DOI: 10.1080/13527266.2019.1655086.

10 Friestad, M., & Wright, P. (1994). The persuasion knowledge model: How people cope with persuasion attempts. *Journal of Consumer Research*, *21*(1), 1–31.

11 https://www.adweek.com/digital/taco-bells-cinco-de-mayo-snapchat-lens-was-viewed-224-million-times-171390/.

12 https://www.marriott.com/marriott/aboutmarriott.mi.

13 https://time.com/3685708/super-bowl-ads-vw-the-force/.

14 https://www.huffpost.com/entry/dove-real-beauty-campaign-turns-10_n_4575940.

15 https://www.dove.com/us/en/home.html.

16 https://www.dove.com/us/en/home.html.

17 https://www.prnewswire.com/in/news-releases/new-dove-research-finds-beauty-pressures-up-and-women-and-girls-calling-for-change-583743771.html.

18 https://nytmediakit.com/.

19 http://www.caranddrivermediakit.com/r5/home.asp.

20 https://mediatracks.com/resources/nielsen-dma-rankings-2020/.

21 https://www.emarketer.com/content/radio-ad-spending-will-decline-by-25-0-this-year.

22 https://www.nielsen.com/us/en/solutions/capabilities/audio/.

23 https://www.thedrum.com/news/2016/03/31/netflix-uses-billboards-ignite-social-media-battle-daredevil-season-two-launches.

24 https://www.adsoftheworld.com/media/outdoor/caribou_coffee_ovens_out_of_transit_shelters.

Chapter 11

Evolving Media

Learning Outcomes

After reading the chapter, you should be able to do the following:

- Explain how the media have evolved with advances in technology.
- Detail how the modifiers that we use to describe media limit progress in media and campaign strategies.
- Apply PESO model to better understand the complexity of media.
- Discuss how the digital giants—Facebook, Google and Amazon—have had an impact on media consumption and advertising revenue models.
- Describe and distinguish different marketing communication strategies including social media marketing, affiliate marketing, influencer marketing, mobile marketing and content marketing.
- Articulate how strategic communication and how people interact with media have changed with artificial intelligence, augmented reality and the Internet of Things.

Chapter Opening Vignette

Chickasaw.TV

The Chickasaw Nation wanted to connect its people and share the story of its rich history with the world. Instead of building a traditional website or posting videos on a YouTube channel, the tribe decided to utilize **brand journalism**. Chickasaw.tv was launched in January 2011. It is a high-definition, video-rich internet network documenting the culture, legacy and continuing contributions of the Chickasaw people.

The Chickasaw Nation was created after the Chickasaws were forced to relocate from their ancestral homelands by the U.S. government to Indian Territory after the passage of the Indian Removal Act of 1830. The Chickasaw Nation has a jurisdictional territory that includes 7,648 square miles of south-central Oklahoma and encompasses all or parts of 13 counties. Bill Anoatubby, governor of the Chickasaw Nation since 1987, says the online network does for the 47,000 Chickasaws worldwide and the public as a whole what black-and-white television did for him as a 10-year-old: It opens doors to information they didn't have—or didn't have as readily—before. Anoatubby said:

> It's an outlet to show our people the many ways in which our culture is still thriving. Actually, we're creating new chapters in our history and our story and that story is being written every day. We bring these two things together—what has happened today and our rich history—and really one is very connected to the other.

To tell their story of both past and present, the tribe went to Branded News Worldwide, a division of Oklahoma City ad agency Ackerman McQueen, to oversee the design and development of the network and its content. When the network launched, it offered nine channels and more than 1,200 videos and featured CNTV news, with current events and public affairs coverage.

The options for information are plentiful whether it's "Hearing Elders Speak Chickasaw" on the History and Cultural Channel or "Tours to Our Homelands: A Spiritual Connection" on the Destinations Channel or "Bedré Chocolate" on the Commerce Channel.

Ackerman McQueen is one of the leaders in brand journalism. Since 1999, years ahead of the creation of YouTube, Ackerman McQueen adopted a strategy of opening dedicated media channels for its clients. According to Ackerman McQueen, initially, brand-focused media channels were met with skepticism. Brands were supposed to be advertisers, not news outlets. Journalism schools laughed at the philosophy, local stations thought it was cute, and the media refused to see these brands as peers. The brands who decided to become "their own media company," explains the agency, "recognized that there was white space in a narrative that they could control with years-long dedication to owned storytelling."[1]

Introduction

In Chapter 10, we discussed the role of media in society, through the lens of the PESO model, and how to utilize and measure media in strategic communication. Technology is moving so fast and there is so much going on that we need to take a deeper dive into the media, how it is evolving and how it can be leveraged for effective strategic communication. We will explore the terms legacy, traditional and digital media and try to answer the question, isn't it all media digital today? We will examine how the largest and most powerful companies have changed the way people access news and information, as well as drastically impact the way the news organizations and broadcast networks generate revenue. Finally, we will identify various marketing communication strategies that are thriving and emerging as a result of the evolution of media.

Traditional Media and Technology

In order to better understand strategic communication, it is important to understand the media industry, which is critical to disseminating messages and engaging stakeholders. It is also critical to understand how quickly the media are changing due to the rapid advances in technology. The media industry has always evolved with technology—even before the internet. Let's look at newspapers, for example. The newspaper industry began to take shape in the mid to late 19th century with the advent of the printing press. Paid advertising fueled the newspaper industry, which created a single printed product for about 200 years. Advancements in printing occurred over the 20th century and the press was eventually replaced by computers. Paperboys, newsstands and supermarkets were only some of the many distribution channels that newspaper companies employed to get their paper product out to as many people as fast as possible. Those physical distribution outlets are now largely replaced by digital delivery online. The proliferation of the world wide web and the development of tablets and smartphones prompted newspapers to evolve from a single print product to a multi-media company. Newspapers are still producing printed copies on paper, but for the last decade they have also been producing video, web shows, podcasts, social media, live weather reports, events, and more.

Legacy Media

Traditional media, like newspapers, is also called mainstream or **legacy media**. The term legacy media generally refers to media that existed before the internet, such as radio, TV, newspapers and magazines. Legacy media is also associated with the elite 'Old Guard' and is typically owned by big corporations.

The internet radically changed legacy media to the point of evolution or even death of some media outlets. The few media companies that have survived did so by changing and expanding. Many started offering content and engagement through digital platforms and experiences. Legacy media vehicles such as **The New York Times**, **CBS News**, and **Forbes**, are still very relevant and remain leaders in the media landscape because they added "digital media" platforms. **The New York Times** is not just a newspaper. **CBS News** is not just a national television news network, and **Forbes** is not just a magazine. These media vehicles have become major media companies that produce content and engage audiences across multiple media platforms. CBS News, for example, introduced CBSN, the 24/7 internet streaming service launched in 2014. In January 2019, CBS announced the launch of a new streaming service targeting local audiences. CBS News also uses its social media platforms to provide real-time information to its audiences.

The Digital Revolution

As mentioned above, legacy media have evolved into "digital media," producing and disseminating news and advertising through numerous channels or platforms. **Digital media** in this context means content disseminated via the internet, including desktop, mobile, social and gaming.

The digital revolution also empowered brands to become their own news networks and advertising vehicles. Like Chickasaw.tv mentioned in the chapter opener, communicative entities and brands are becoming their own media outlets and creating networks to tell their stories because they no longer need traditional media. Another example of this is highlighted in this chapter's Industry Insight.

The media landscape is complex and ever-changing. Strategic communicators must constantly study the trends and stakeholder perceptions of media channels in order to adapt strategies and tactics to be successful.

Case Study

NRATV

Oklahoma City-based advertising agency Ackerman McQueen created a media channel for its client the National Rifle Association (NRA) in 2004 called NRA News. By creating its own "news" content, the advocacy group was given unlimited opportunities to communicate that gun control was a question of freedom more than safety. NRA News, which was expanded and rebranded as NRATV in 2016, is an example of brand journalism. NRATV ceased production in 2019 amid controversy between the agency and its longstanding client of more than 30 years.

The NRA News channel was billed as "the most comprehensive video coverage of Second Amendment issues, events and culture." As Ackerman McQueen explained on its website in detailing its job for the NRA, political free speech is restricted to the news media, so it makes sense to go into the news business yourself. It also helped the NRA evade legal restrictions on political advertising by creating and producing its own content.

Creating a news business for the NRA and serving as their agency of record for nearly four decades proved very fruitful for the Oklahoma ad agency and "shaped the NRA's public identity, helping to build it from a niche activist organization into a ubiquitous presence in American popular culture."[2] In addition to NRATV, Ackerman produced the NRA magazine **America's 1st Freedom** and created many memorable and successful ad campaigns. The firm and its affiliates reportedly earned $40 million from the NRA in annual earnings in 2017.

The NRA, a non-profit, has also directed $18 million since 2010 to a private company jointly owned by executives of Ackerman and the NRA, as reported by **The New York Times**.[3]

The NRA and Ackerman had a rather unique relationship becoming so interconnected that it's difficult to determine where one ended and the other began. For example, retired Lt. Co. Oliver L. North, who served as the NRA president in 2018–2019, had a contract with Ackerman in which he was paid approximately $1 million a year. North, a former Fox News pundit, hosted media programming and special events as part of that contract.[4] Dana Loesch, a former Breitbart News editor, was also a show host for NRATV and paid by Ackerman. Loesch frequently drew criticism for her controversial remarks about the mainstream media, and social justice movements including the #MeToo movement and Black Lives Matter. Loesch provoked widespread outrage when she mocked the popular children's program

Thomas & Friends for their efforts to show ethnic diversity by portraying the show's talking trains in Ku Klux Klan hoods on NRATV.[5]

In addition to NRATV being available online, the channel was also available through digital streaming platforms including Amazon Fire TV, Apple TV and Roku. In the aftermath of the Parkland, Florida high school shooting in early 2018, the role of NRATV came into focus as the organization's below-the-media-radar voice, according to **Deadline**. A group of Hollywood activists called on Amazon to drop the NRA's online video channel from its streaming service utilizing social media and the hashtag #StopNRAmazon.[6]

The criticisms of NRATV started to take its toll. A little over a year after #StopNRAmazon was trending on Twitter, a rare airing of an internal debate at the NRA, two prominent board members expressed concerns about NRATV to **The New York Times**. Their statements were released through the NRA itself, amid what was described as an internal review of NRATV and its future.[7]

In June 2019, the NRA was in an organizational and financial crisis and shut down the live production and news site, NRATV, and severed its longstanding relationship with its ad firm Ackerman McQueen. In addition, the NRA's second-in-command, Christopher W. Cox, resigned. NRA News that evolved into NRATV is one of the most successful and controversial examples of brand journalism that eventually ends as a tale of caution.[8]

Digital Media Giants and Their Impact on Legacy Media

As presented in Chapter 1, the field of strategic communication emerged because of the dramatic changes in media technology, which resulted in a paradigm shift—a new way of thinking—about how CEs communicate with their stakeholders. The digital revolution has changed the way society views and uses the media. Media flipped from being scarce to abundant in a blink of an eye.

The Meaningless Media Divide

Strategic communication still utilizes traditional or legacy media for the purposes of advertising within the context of how they originated—television ads on broadcast networks and display ads in newspapers, and so forth. However, many media buys include purchasing ad time and space on the media outlet's digital platforms, including its website or streaming services. In fact, digital and online media advertising, shared across multiple digital media platforms, is now the dominant U.S. advertising medium. Despite the COVID-19 pandemic in 2020, digital and online media contributed to a 4% increase in advertising for the year, while cable television lost ground, with a 15% drop in advertising.[9] This shows how dominant these media became in the advertising sphere. It is important to remember that advertising is driven by eyeballs, that is, advertisers are attracted to online and digital media because their stakeholders are viewing the content, and not because they like it better.

While we have used terms like traditional media, legacy media, new media and digital media in this book, those modifiers are no longer enough to describe how types of media interact in strategic communication planning. Tom Goodwin, CEO and founder of the Tomorrow Group, explained in a blog in 2014 the obsession between non-digital and digital is not only meaningless but also limits progress and innovation among marketers and strategic communicators:

> There is not a more meaningless divide and obsession than the notion of digital media. Media channels were once clearly distinguished and named from the physical devices that we used to consume them. Radio ads played on radios and were audio, TV ads played on TV's and were moving images, newspaper ads were images in the paper while outdoor ads were the images around us. In 2014 the naming legacy is both misleading and of no value. I listen to the radio on my phone, read the newspapers on a laptop, watch YouTube on my TV and read magazines on my iPad. Our old media channels mean nothing yet their names survive and mislead us into artificially limited thinking.[10]

Goodwin argued that we should stop distinguishing between different types of media channels, yet old habits die hard. The silos are still alive and well, primarily because of the way we buy, sell and measure media. Let's look back at the PESO media model discussed in Chapter 10. Where do legacy media and digital media fit within PESO? The answer is both legacy and digital media fit into all four categories of paid, earned, shared and owned. However, if you stay within the context of the old categories, one could argue that legacy media are paid and earned media, while shared and owned are digital media. But that is more of a historical perspective.

Paid, Earned, Shared and Owned Media Redefined

With the birth of the internet, communicative entities were given the options of owning their own digital platforms (owned), such as company websites, e-newsletters and blogs, and social media platforms to disseminate their messages. Stakeholders and consumers were also empowered to have their own media channels, such as blogs, vlogs and social media, which was the catalyst for the growth of shared media. Earned and shared media provide third-party credibility to the message because someone other than the communicative entity is telling or sharing the story, which makes it more trustworthy. For instance, a news report about a product or brand generated by a journalist is more believable than an ad message paid for by the brand itself. A Facebook post or Tweet shared or redistributed, are perceived as more trustworthy than a self-produced Tweet or Facebook post, particularly if it is shared thousands or millions of times.

Strategic communicators must recognize that legacy media have a presence in all four types of media: paid, earned, shared and owned. Media presence has always been paid and earned. In the digital age strategic communicators were among the first to embrace and leverage their own websites and social media (owned), and of course have others share their stories (shared). However, other entities sharing legacy media content, via Facebook for example, has created opportunities and challenges for legacy media. The opportunities include increased access and consumption. Access to news and information is literally at people's fingertips with digital technologies. With the explosion of media options, society's consumption of media has also exploded. Advertising and branding messages being delivered has also grown exponentially.

On the surface increased viewership of content seems like a great thing. However, it has caused considerable problems with monetization of the media, which is essentially how they make money. The growth of digital media has increased the challenges of generating revenue among media companies. Historically, legacy media produced news and entertainment content that created audiences and generated revenue through advertising. This is because for decades legacy media was the only way to reach the masses. It was critical for communicative entities to reach prospects, customers and stakeholders. For instance, Seinfeld, the most popular sitcom from 1994 to 1998, had more than 20-million viewers per episode. Its final episode generated 38-million viewers—half of the entire television watching audience.[11] Not long after Seinfeld signed off, the internet and digital technologies started changing the way audiences receive information, news and entertainment. As a result, companies and advertisers no longer have to pay legacy media to reach people, so the revenue streams of media outlets are being drastically affected. Audiences of 20 million people are no longer tuning into prime-time sitcoms all at one time as they did in the 1990s and 2000s. In fact, only one sitcom, Young Sheldon, was in the top 25 in the 2019–2020 TV ratings. The proliferation of online and digital media is chipping away at television audiences. People are turning to on-demand and streaming platforms and watching when they want, instead of being forced to watch during broadcast media time slots. As a result, media outlets are losing their ability to sell ads as effectively as they were. Their content is reaching fewer eyeballs, so they are selling less advertising.

Digital Natives

In 2017, Facebook and Google accounted for 99% of all the growth in digital advertising, according to one estimate based on Interactive Advertising Bureau data.[12] For legacy media to become viable in today's media landscape, they have become dependent on the digital media giants Google, Facebook and Amazon. Legacy media are still producing news and entertainment, but audiences are accessing the content from other channels, such as social media and search engines, which have drastically affected the way legacy media generate revenue. These **digital-native media companies** are not only claiming almost 70% of digital ad revenue, but people also see them as media companies. Facebook's news feed has become for young adults what the front page of the newspaper was for older generations of people. More than two-thirds of American adults say they at least occasionally get news on social media. Consumers turn to Twitter for breaking news, and they search Google for news updates.[13]

Legacy media organizations are reliant on Facebook and Google, often referred as the duopoly, to get their articles in front of people, fighting for attention alongside fake news, cat videos and websites that share the content of legacy media without permission. People are still consuming news from legacy media, but instead of going directly to the news sources such as nytimes.com or usatoday.com, people are reading those Times or USA Today stories on Facebook or accessing the stories via Google.

As a result, CEs are paying Facebook and Google to reach their stakeholders more often than they are paying legacy media companies. Google and Facebook do not create news and entertainment content, yet they dominate the digital advertising market, draining revenue that once paid for the quality journalism that Google and Facebook now share for free. Even as audiences consume more news content, the publishers that undergo the expensive process of producing it are not reaping the monetary rewards.

Google passed the entire U.S. newspaper industry in advertising revenue in 2010. In 2019 Google's ad revenue was more than $134 billion, while the newspaper industry's ad revenue is under $20 billion.[14] This comparison is somewhat misleading because Google's ad revenues are global, while the U.S. newspaper industries are not. However, the numbers do help tell the story of how the duopoly have affected legacy media. Media outlets at the local and national levels have had massive layoffs spanning the country in the last five years. Thinking ahead, who will provide the important role of in-depth journalism and investigative reporting if the legacy newsrooms no longer have advertising revenue to fund their work? This is an important challenge for democracy and the future of free, independent press.

Industry Insight

News Media vs. Facebook/Google

The newspaper industry trade organization, News Media Alliance, is leading a charge to collectively bargain with the two media platform giants—Facebook and Google—asking Congress for a special exemption that would allow newspaper companies safe harbor from antitrust law as a way to seek collective bargaining. News Media Alliance president David Chavern explained in a *Wall Street Journal* op-ed in 2017, that the problem "is that today's internet distribution systems distort the flow of economic value derived from good reporting."[15] Chavern also maintains that one of the worst things Facebook and Google do is to make all media look the same, with uniform layouts and design specs. This, says Chavern, is deadly for news brands in a world of unlimited choices. In January 2019, House Antitrust Chairman David Cicilline (D-RI) re-introduced the "Journalism Competition and Preservation Act," which would provide a limited safe harbor for news publishers to collectively negotiate with Facebook, Google and other platforms for better business arrangements.[16]

After much criticism of the duopoly and the efforts of the News Media Alliance, Facebook and Google have both launched initiatives to support journalism. First Google announced efforts to support the media industry through the Google News Initiative and pledged to invest $300 million over three years beginning March 2018. Facebook followed suit almost a year later announcing a $300 million investment over three years to support journalism, with an emphasis on promoting hard-hit local new organizations. These efforts have been both celebrated and dismissed by the media and media scholars. Matthew Ingram of the Columbia Journalism Review maintains that these efforts are more about convincing newsrooms and journalists to use the company's products more. Ingram explains that nothing is going to make that much difference unless Facebook and Google pay for the content they are displaying.[17]

Media are complex. Legacy media—newspapers, magazines, radio, television and outdoor—are still available to reach audiences not only through print and broadcast, but also through their digital channels. Digital-native companies Facebook, Google and Amazon have emerged as the leading means to reach audiences, claiming more than 70% of digital ad revenue. It is important to understand that we need to move beyond distinguishing among legacy, traditional, new and digital media because the modifiers are antiquated and limiting. Strategic communicators need to develop tactics to engage stakeholders with messages and experiences that transcend media platforms.

How to Leverage Evolving Media in Strategic Communication

What does this all mean for strategic communication? First, communicative entities must understand how to leverage all types of media channels. Second, the digital giants are impossible to ignore. Strategic communicators must seek to understand how and why people are consuming media and what the likelihood is that exposure to the CE's message will lead to desire and action among stakeholders. Strategic communicators must understand how to purchase advertising space on the evolving media platforms.

Facebook Advertising

You now know that Facebook is one of the digital media giants and therefore a great way to reach your stakeholders. Facebook ads can be purchased for desktop or mobile. More than 20% of the world's population is made up of active Facebook users, including almost 70% of adults in the United States.

Facebook is extremely popular, but is advertising on Facebook a good **return on investment (ROI)** for communicative entities? ROI is a way to measure the efficiency of an investment such as paid advertising and is explained more fully in Chapter 13. There are certainly data out there to support that Facebook can be a very effective strategy in the strategic communicator's toolbox. Studies have shown that more than 70% of consumers are influenced by social media referrals. Facebook's hyper-targeted Custom Audiences feature lets advertisers target so specifically that they have seen their new customer acquisition costs decline dramatically.[18] Several important factors can determine the success of your Facebook campaign.

Facebook Pixels

So, if you are convinced that Facebook can generate a positive ROI, what's next in planning and executing a campaign utilizing Facebook? The most critical place to start is with your **Facebook pixel**. The Facebook pixel is a code that you place on your website. It collects data that helps you track conversions from Facebook ads, optimize ads, build targeted audiences for future ads and remarket to people who have already taken some kind of action on your website. If you want to target someone who has been on your pricing page, gallery or even filled out a contact form on your website with Facebook ads, you can do that, as long as you install the snippet of code on your website. Facebook advertising, like all strategic communication, must cut through a lot of clutter.

Targeting

Second, like with any campaign, you must know and understand your target audience. It is perhaps even more imperative with Facebook because it allows you to target consumers with remarkable precision including narrowing down who will be exposed to your message by creating an audience defined by metrics including, but not limited to age, gender, location, interests, occupation, income and much more. The communicative entity can also target based on behaviors. Boutique hotels can target people traveling to their area, who have used travel apps within the last 30 days. E-commerce businesses can absolutely target based on historical shopping behaviors, tapping into consumers who are likely buyers of skin care products based on their actual past purchasing behavior. No matter what you are promoting or selling, with Facebook Custom Audience, you can deliver your ads directly to the people you need to see those ads, so you do not pay for promoting to people who don't need to see them.

Audiences and stakeholders are constantly being bombarded with messages, and people rarely use social media to be solicited or sold to. Instead, they are using Facebook to connect with old friends, brag about their children's t-ball prowess or share their frustration with the NFL ref's ugly pass interference no-call. In order to stand out from the personal posts and be noticed on social media, communicative entities must deliver great content that directly appeals to the target audience.

Retargeting

Facebook can also target people who've already engaged with a business or communicative entity with retargeting ads. Facebook retargeting involves finding people who have visited a CE's website and then using that data to find their Facebook profiles. CEs can run ad campaigns to target those people on Facebook and persuade them to return to CEs website. The **click-through rates (CTR)** of retargeted ads are ten times higher than the CTR of regular display ads.[19] Click-through rates measure the number of clicks advertisers receive on their ads per number of impressions. Remember, impressions are the number of times content is displayed, no matter if it was read or clicked on or not. If you think about it, retargeting makes a lot of sense when you think about how people use the internet for e-commerce and social media. People have multiple tabs open at once and jump around from one app to another. A customer might visit your site and fill up the cart, then get distracted before checking out and fail to return. By offering a little nudge to return to your site via Facebook retargeting, CE's can get customers to finish those purchases that otherwise may have never been thought of again.

Visual Relevance

Facebook ads need to be visual. Visual content is not only treated more favorably in the Facebook algorithm, but it's also more likely to be shared and remembered than written content. Relevance is critical for success when using Facebook advertising. Ads must be closely connected to, and appropriate for, the target audience. Facebook offers ad relevance diagnostics which helps CEs determine whether the ads ran on Facebook were relevant to the audience reached. The more relevant your ad image, ad copy and destination page is to your audience, the higher your score is—and the more favorably Facebook will treat your ads.

A Value Proposition

Facebook ads should include an enticing value proposition. A **value proposition** tells the reader why they should click on your ad to learn more about your product. Your value proposition should be believable. For example, saying you have the greatest sandwiches in the world will not make people come to your business' page. But claiming you have the best Philly Cheesesteaks in Philadelphia and your Yelp results support it, people will believe it.

Call-to-Action

Finally, it should have a clear call-to-action. A beautiful and relevant ad is great, but without a **call-to-action (CTA)**, your viewer might not know what to do next. As we discussed in Chapter 9, CTA is a phrase usually at the end of an ad that tells the audience what action to take and how to take it. Your CTA should encourage people to click on your ad now or buy now, subscribe now or whatever you want them to do and when. Now is often used because it creates a sense of urgency.

Instagram

Instagram may be younger and smaller (have fewer users) than its parent company, Facebook, but Instagram is the hot new member of the family that everyone is talking about and looking to for action. Instagram has had a steady incline in users since its launch in 2013, which reached more than 800 million users in 2020. Like many other social advertising platforms, Instagram gives you the granular control to target specific genders, age ranges, locations, interests, behaviors, and more. You can even target a direct list of leads or those who have a similar makeup.

Instagram Uses the Facebook Interface

Instagram does not have its own ad manager; Instagram ads are managed through the Facebook Ads user interface. Like Facebook, Instagram ad campaigns will help communicative entities increase brand awareness, reach, increase traffic or clicks to a website, page in the app store, app installs, engagement and conversions. Even more so than Facebook, Instagram is a visual platform that requires an image, set of images or video to communicate a message, all of which can be accompanied by text.

Organic Posts

When people are on Instagram and see a post about your brand without your paying to have it placed in front of them, they are seeing it organically. Organic Instagram marketing is viable because users frequently engage with businesses' content on Instagram, more so than on other social platforms. In fact, 90% of users follow at least one brand on Instagram. Organic Instagram marketing involves posting regularly on the business' or CE's Instagram while curating the posts specifically for the intended audience and strategically using Instagram tools, such as Stories and IGTV. **Instagram Stories** are short videos, approximately 15-seconds long on average, and they are only visible 24 hours after they're posted. Stories will disappear after 24 hours, but users can save them to their highlights, where they will stay until the user deletes them. Stories generate 2–3 times more engagement than regular Instagram posts, which are called Feed posts. Companies that use organic Stories can add questions and polls to engage users, and add a "swipe up" CTA that takes users to the CEs website or profile page.

One of the issues with marketing on Instagram has been getting your fans on Instagram back to your website. Clickable links cannot be added to organic feed posts, brands must direct Instagram followers to the link in their Instagram bio instead—and continuously update that link as they post new products. An Instagram bio is the section under the Instagram username where the Instagram user (including business accounts) publishes information about themselves and/or the brand. Paid Instagram posts can include links to websites. Ads can include the "Shop Now" button, which takes readers directly to a product page. Instagram ad formats, specifications and sizes change and new features emerge often.

Ad Types

Like other social media ad platforms, Instagram advertising changes and evolves rapidly. Currently, Instagram offers image ads, video ads, story ads, carousel ads and shoppable posts. Rather than directing customers to your website, shopping on Instagram provides a seamless customer checkout experience for anyone who discovers your products in their Instagram feed. E-commerce brands can tag products in Instagram posts and turn engagement into purchases with the shopping on Instagram sales channel. More than 130 million users click on a shopping post at least once a month.[20]

In addition to purchasing ads on Instagram, which hasn't always been available, communicative entities can utilize sponsored posts. This requires negotiating privately with Instagram influencers and asking them to promote your brand on their account. We will discuss paid influencers more later in this chapter.

Google

Like with any type of strategic communication and ad campaign, to get good results from Google Ads you need to start with your strategy: Who are your customers and how are you going to reach them. Google Ads currently offers four types of campaigns: search, shopping, display and video.

Google Ads is split into two networks, the Search Network and the Display Network. When advertising on the Search Network, businesses place text ads in the search engine results. On the Display Network, businesses instead place display ads on a huge network of sites across the internet. Each of the campaign types can be successful if you approach them the right way. Campaigns reach buyers at different stages of consumer decision-making process, which is discussed in Chapter 8. It's important to understand that Google is very progressive and changes its offerings and updates it processes often. Google Ads are more complicated than one might think at first glance because of the many options within options.

Auction

Auction is a key term in understanding the process of Google Ads. The auction determines whether an ad actually shows and whether the ad will show up first, second, and so on. All ads go through the auction. When someone does a search for electric blankets, for example, the Google Ads system finds all ads whose keywords match that search. The system ignores any ads that aren't eligible, such as ads for a different country or ads that violates Google policies. All eligible ads are ranked based on bid, ad quality, the context of the search and the expected impact of extensions and other ad formats. This ranking is called Ad Rank thresholds, which are determined at the time of each auction. Ads with higher thresholds appear higher in the search results than ads lower on the page, which is called ad position. Innovative advertisers are using search trends and their account data to inform their marketing. Ads for electric blankets in hot climates would rank low.

Search Ads

Search (or text) ads are what most people think of when discussing advertising on Google; after all, it is a search engine. Simple, right? Not really. There are different types of campaigns with search ads. Advertisers can use search trends and their account data from their search campaigns. For example, Kleenex developed a search campaign by combining the keywords "fever and runny nose" and correlated it with government data that revealed regional cold- and flu-related activity. This allowed Kleenex to target its ads in areas where higher numbers of people were suffering from the cold and flu and seeking relief.[21]

Examples of search ad campaigns:

▪ **Branded search campaigns:** A search campaign that targets your brand name. When someone searches a company's branded terms, such as "Nike" and "Just Do It," paid advertisements will show up above the organic listings. These are usually the cheapest and most profitable campaigns.

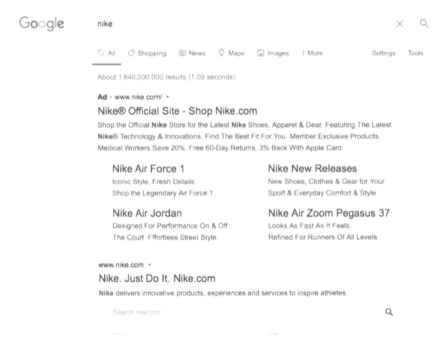

▪ **Competitor brand campaigns:** A search campaign targeting your competitor's brand. When someone searches for your competitors branded terms, paid advertisements for your brand show up above the organic listings. For example, instead of Reebok running a search campaign with Reebok as the search term, they use Nike to try to attract consumers looking for Nike products and convert them. This is a riskier approach, and it is sure to annoy your competitors. Google's focus is to make sure searchers find what they're looking for, so they provide a quality score to determine what paid ads show up first. The quality score for competitive campaigns will be lower than branded search, which means it's unlikely competitive campaign ads will show up in the first position.

▪ **Product brand search campaigns:** If you are a shoe store selling specific brands of shoes, you can borrow some of the brand power of the shoe brands, such as Nike and New Balance. You can run campaigns targeting searches for their brand/product/SKUs. This can be expensive without a high ROI because of all the competitors who also sell these brands. But if you are the only store in a regional area that sells these brands and you limit the search to that area, it will likely have a high CTR and ROI.

Shopping Ads

Shopping ads are now at the top of search results on Google, and search ads are getting pushed further down the page. If you want to make sure your products are visible when potential customers search for them, you can no longer ignore Google Shopping Ads. The product photo, title and price allow a potential customer to see at a glance if a retailer has the product they are looking for. More and more retailers are moving their ad budgets from text to Shopping Ads.

Display Campaigns

Display campaigns have a couple of different options on how to find the perfect audience. With campaigns on the Display Network, you'll show banners with attractive offers to people on Google's Network of 3rd party websites. Communicative entities can target people that have similar characteristics with remarketing audiences that they have already reached. Or you can target groups by uploading email lists. Since these are people familiar with your brand or store, the response rates on these campaigns can be effective. However, display ads are losing their luster, and tend to have poor click-through rates overall.

Examples of display ads.

Video Campaigns

Video campaigns are also available in Google Ads. While video ad content must be hosted on YouTube, video ads can appear on YouTube and on video partner sites and apps across the Google Display Network, including on tablets and mobile devices (depending on your format and settings). Communicative entities can create video campaigns with a range of video ad formats to engage customers in different ways on YouTube and across video partner sites.

Let's discuss a few of the video formats available. **Skippable in-stream ads**, which play before, during or after other videos, and the viewers has the option to skip the ad after five seconds. **Non-skippable in-stream ads** also play before, during or after other videos, but viewers don't have the option to skip your ad giving advertisers a better opportunity to reach viewers with a full 10- to 15-second message. Designed to increase video reach at an efficient cost, **outstream ads** begin playing with the sound off, and only appear on websites and apps running on Google video partners. Viewers have the option to tap and unmute the video, and advertisers are charged when viewers see the video play for two seconds or more. Depending on the video ad format, advertisers will be charged by impressions (CPM) or by views (CPV). With CPM (cost-per-thousand impressions) bidding you pay based on impressions. Bumper ads use CPM bidding, so you pay each time your ad is shown 1,000 times. Cost-per-view (CPV) bidding allows advertisers to set the amount you'll pay for TrueView video ads in Google Ads. With CPV bidding, you'll pay for video views or interactions. A view is counted when someone watches at least 30 seconds of the video or the duration of the video, if it is less than 30 seconds. An interaction would be clicking on a companion banner ad that takes the viewer to the advertiser's website, for example.[22]

Search Engine Optimization (SEO)

A key aspect of owned media is search engine optimization (SEO), which is the practice of increasing the traffic to your website through organic search engine results. It is important that you not only increase the quantity of traffic but also the quality of traffic because you want to attract people who are genuinely interested in your products or services. Advertising makes up a significant part of search engine results pages (SERPs).[23] Organic traffic is search results that emerge from popularity and don't require paid advertising. Search engines are the primary way people access information today. For example, when you type a question into the Google app or ask a question via the Google assistant and a long list of links to webpages that could potentially answer your question appears.

But how do the search engines determine the list of links and how to rank them? Search engines go out and gather information about all the content they can find on the internet and build an index of the information. That index is then fed through an algorithm that tries to match all that data with a search query. For CEs and companies to get their websites and brands discovered through search—the primary way people access information—they must have an SEO-friendly site that has content the search engines will be able to understand. Quality owned media means writing content that both search engines and people searching will value. Search engines aim to match the highest quality, most relevant information with the search queries of their users—but if you're not creating content sharing this information, your information has no chance of getting found or being ranked. Title tags, meta descriptions, backlinks, keywords and fresh content are a few ways to optimize a website or develop SEO.

Title Tag

Title tag is an HTML (hypertext markup language) element that specifies the title of a web page and provides an accurate and concise description of a page's content. They are displayed as clickable headlines on SERPs.

Meta Descriptions

Meta descriptions are HTML attributes that provide a brief summary of a web page, which are displayed on search results often influencing click-through rates.

Code sample

```
<head>  <meta name="description"
content="This is an example of a meta description.
This will often show up in search results."></head>
```

Meta description HTML code sample.

Meta descriptions are restricted to 160 characters, so CEs must be creative and succinct in writing a great description that conveys what the brand represents, values and offers. In the example pictured for Febreze, they start with a question to draw the reader in. It explains what the company stands for, odor elimination, and makes it personal offering tips to breathe happy.

www.febreze.com › en-us ▾

Febreze: Air Fresheners & Odor-Eliminating Products

Searching for freshness? Welcome to **Febreze**.com, home of true odor elimination. Find your favorite **Febreze** products and get tips to breathe happy.

As its name suggests, an internal link is meta description that points to another page on the same website.

Keyword Research

Keyword research is essential for successful content marketing. Keywords are the terms that people type into search engines. They can be one word, or they can be phrases of several words. Regardless of their length, targeting keywords in your content, including your title tags and meta descriptions, is one of the fundamental elements of SEO and it is an easy way of tracking the progress of your SEO efforts.

Backlinks

The other major factor in SEO is backlinks, also known as inbound links, or incoming links. Backlinks are the foundation of Google's original algorithm, and remains a key factor in ranking today. When other websites link to your site, Google views it as a vote for your site. As you get more votes, Google starts to view you as a respected authority and bumps up your site in the rankings. What's the easiest way to get backlinks? You guessed it. Produce great content that educates and entertains, and that people want to link to and share. Optimization can take many forms. It involves everything from making sure the title tags and meta descriptions are both informative and the right length, to pointing internal links at pages you are proud of.

Keep It Fresh

Lastly, search engines value websites and resources that are updated consistently. So, when a company publishes content regularly, its website will likely rank significantly higher. On the other hand, when a website stops producing content, search engines will assume the website is out-of-date and stale, so it'll drop the site's rank to avoid sending people to mediocre content.

Brand Journalism and Content Marketing

It is cliché, but it is true: Content is king when it comes to optimization. Two effective strategies for achieving high SEO are brand journalism and content marketing. Strategic communication and marketing have been described as professional publishing, which is essentially the rise of owned media. Rather than paying to advertise around other people's content or relying on a news organization to cover a story of their company, savvy CEs are creating their own narratives and platforms.

Born from the boom of branded magazines aimed at consumers, **brand journalism** has emerged as an effective tool in strategic communication. Companies that want to build awareness and cultivate brand affinity, craft content that their audience want, rather than sell, sell, sell. When consumers feel like a brand cares about them and provides them valuable news and information that helps them achieve their goals or serve their needs, they are more likely to become brand loyal.

Brand journalism tell stories that convey the brand's personality. For example, Red Bull owns its own Media House, which publishes a magazine, produces documentaries and movies. Like the examples of the Chickasaw Nation and the National Rifle Association, brand journalism is communication often presented in the style of a news organization, but with its own online platform.

Content marketing is another useful tool in strategic communication that is different, but complementary to brand journalism. Joe Pullizzi, founder of the Content Marketing Institute, defines content marketing as a "marketing and business process for creating and distributing valuable and compelling content to attract, acquire and engage a clearly defined and understood target audience—with the objective of driving profitable customer action."[24]

Content marketing has been around for decades, but the discipline has gained incredible popularity in the last decade, according to Google Trends. Blogs are commonplace in content marketing. When a CE freely shares content, it builds trust with readers. Providing readers with industry tips and information, for free, will keep visitors returning to the blog, which often leads to transforming them into buyers.

Blogs are just the tip of the iceberg. CEs can utilize e-books, books, videos, webinars, emails, games and more to share information and convert customers. Content marketing may sound like brand journalism, but the buying process and lead generation are two common reasons cited why you should not use the two terms interchangeably. Brand journalism is meant to connect with stakeholders on a personal level to create a relationship and a favorable brand impression. It is a reputation building tool. Content marketing is meant to move prospects along the consumer decision-making process by providing useful information to capture and nurture interest while building brand credibility. It is a sales tool. Ultimately, the two approaches share the goal of creating valuable, compelling content that is useful for prospects and customers.

Affiliate Marketing

In addition to the duopoly, legacy media have increasingly become reliant on Amazon, the go-to site for online shoppers and merchants alike. Amazon does not share news and information like Facebook and Google, but it does lead the world in e-commerce, logistics, payments, hardware and data storage. With its estimated 100 million subscribers in the U.S. and a billion active users worldwide, Amazon provides access to audiences through e-commerce.

To diversify and create additional revenue streams, media companies like Condé Naste tried their hands at e-commerce through sites like style.com which was sold to farfetch.com in 2017. Condé Nast is a media company that originated as a publishing company and its portfolio includes some of the most iconic titles in media: *Vogue*, *Vanity Fair*, *Glamour*, *GQ* and *The New Yorker*. While the merging of publishing and e-commerce did not allow Condé Nast or other legacy media that tried to do it on their own, to thrive, media companies are still making money via e-commerce through Amazon and other online retailers with what are called affiliate links or affiliate marketing.

Affiliate marketing is the process by which an affiliate earns a commission for marketing another person's or company's products. Magazine and newspaper companies along with bloggers provide links in stories to external sites where readers can buy products. Affiliate links generate revenue for the media companies when readers purchase products on sites like Amazon, Wal-Mart and Nordstrom after getting to those sites from the links in the stories. The sales are tracked via affiliate links from one website to another.

Many e-commerce sites use the affiliate link model to drive traffic to their site, but Amazon is the most dependable. It is the e-commerce giant, which means affiliate links to Amazon are more likely to lead to revenue for media outlets and communicative entities.

After accessing Amazon from an affiliate link, the publisher gets a percentage of any purchase for the following 24 hours. Like Facebook and Google dominate the digital content traffic including news, Amazon is the online shopping powerhouse, so partnering with Amazon via affiliate links is virtually unavoidable.

Condé Nast, an international magazine publishing giant, has not given up on leveraging e-commerce in order to stay competitive in today's rapidly changing digital media climate. In February 2019, *Vogue* debuted *VogueWorld*, a distinct digital sub-brand combining the title's celebrity and street style content with e-commerce. VogueWorld will live on Vogue.com, and *Vogue*'s online app will rebrand as *VogueWorld*. Though Condé Nast was unsuccessful when it tried to meld its fashion coverage into e-commerce via the revamped Style.com in 2016, the new *VogueWorld* will rely on an affiliate link model through Skimlinks, Amazon and select direct retailers, like Moda Operandi, to increase streams of revenue for the title.

Professional Profile

Cailin Bula—Media Strategy Supervisor

Cailin Bula—Media Strategy Supervisor.

Did you have any internships in college? Yes, two. My first internship was a semester at a shopper marketing agency and the second was a summer spent in the marketing department of a consulting firm.

How important do you think those internships were? They were valuable for certain reasons but not the core experiences to what I'd credit the start of my career. I spent all four years of college playing a varsity sport. As rewarding as that that was, it also left little time for internships. The two that I did manage to take on armed me with confidence to be around people who came from all over, with significantly more experience, doing work I knew little about. This gave me a peek into "the real word" workforce environment that I would not have had otherwise. However, most of the skills that I exercise in my daily work come from my time playing sports—teamwork, determination, work ethic, strategy and resilience. Everyone comes from different backgrounds with different levels of experience. What matter's the most is that you've taken the time to push yourself, learn something new, accept challenges, and have something to show for it at the end of the day. Whether it's internship experience with an award-winning agency, a self-made project started in your basement, or in my case a life dedicated to sport, do something that shows there is more to you than just "work experience" and know how to speak to it.

What are you doing now? I do Media Strategy and Planning for one of the largest automotive brands in the world.

How did you get there? After spending two weeks in New York City for a May term summer class taught by one of my favorite professors, I became infatuated with not only the city but the field of media. The trip gave us access to all kinds of professionals across various advertising disciplines in the mecca of the industry. This experience in my opinion was better than any internship I could have had. Our professor had set up a visit to one of the largest multi-national media companies and it was then that I realized there was a discipline in advertising that could blend creativity with the business side of things. That day I put a target on the back of the company, kept up with the professionals I had networked with, and a year later got hired to be one of their Digital Investment Planners. I shortly after moved accounts and began working on Auto and have been there ever since.

What has surprised you most about yourself or your career? Sometimes the work you're most comfortable with ends up being the least fulfilling, while other times you'll be pleasantly surprised by the opportunities and innovation that can come with something unfamiliar and new. One of the most rewarding parts of my career thus far has been planning multicultural initiatives. I've planned everything from major award show integrations to award-winning ad experiences that allow consumers to choose their language preference while viewing. It's required me to immerse myself in other cultures and work harder to find unique ways to take an insight and turn it into something meaningful that resonates with people. Advertising is becoming more and more grounded in audiences. People want to be seen for who they are and where they come from. This makes it that much more important that we as advertisers can communicate in equally unique and representative ways. My ability to find ways to do just this has absolutely surprised myself and even a few others.

What advice would you give to someone in college now? You don't need to have it all figured out and if you think you do there's a 98% chance it's going to change anyway. Your first move out of school does not mean it's going to be your last. If there is one thing about this industry that never ceases to amaze me it's the incredible variety in backgrounds of the people I've worked with. No one path is the same so trust your gut and enjoy where it leads you. Take risks, challenge yourself, try new things and don't be afraid to fail especially while you're young.

What do you wish young professionals working at your agency knew? Every single job no matter what discipline or level it may be, has a learning curve. You're required to understand new materials, business problems/goals, unfamiliar person-nel, processes, etc. You'll never come into a job knowing exactly what you'll be doing and how you'll be doing it. That is out of your control. What you can control is your attitude and how hard you work to learn. I'd never expect anyone new to come in knowing everything. In fact, I almost expect them to know nothing. However, if they have a positive attitude, are determined to provide value and can prove to be resilient to failure, they're going to be just fine.

Influencer Marketing

Communicative entities can purchase advertising on social media such as Facebook, Instagram and YouTube, as discussed above. But it is also important to understand **influencer marketing**, which allows a communicative entity to target an audience of like-minded people who follow an influencer they trust.

A **social media influencer** is a user on social media who has established credibility in a specific industry, has access to a large audience and can persuade others by virtue of their reach and authenticity. Built on the foundation of word-of-mouth recommendations, influencer marketing is not a new phenomenon. Social media has simply revitalized the power of this marketing technique. Influencers can be celebrities, but one of the most exciting aspects of influencer marketing on social media is the incredible mixture of regular people who cover all kinds of niches, from all over the world. Personal trainers, fashion bloggers, interior designers, chefs and more share their knowledge and experience on social media and develop a following.

While some of these influencers have follower counts exceeding those of traditional celebrities, they are viewed quite differently. An influencer's life will often feel more relatable. If they decide to collaborate with a brand, most of the time their opinion is not only genuine, but also it will be taken more seriously by their followers. An influencer's audience isn't limited to their actual followers; they can connect with the followers of their followers who share their content. As a result, they engage in many sponsored posts, allowing them to be paid for what they share on Instagram, YouTube or other social media.

Huda Kattan is described as the world's most influential beauty expert, with a wide-ranging social media outreach. She started as a blogger and has transformed her Instagram page, @hudabeauty, to gain 29 million followers for the makeup tutorials she puts out. Instagram is the ideal outlet to promote makeup and beauty products. After all, beauty is largely about appearance and Instagram is all about visuals. Her keys to success have been showing off successful makeup applications, establishing makeup trends, sharing reviews and creating how-to's. Huda now has her own makeup line, and her page is filled with vid-eos showcasing people applying their makeup, product plugs, occasional fashion advice, and more.

Instagram influencers can have a significant impact on brand outreach considering influ-encers garner more social engagement than the brand's advertising. Consumers are much more likely to like and comment on influencer's post, as well as be influenced to purchase a product by an influencer than they would from a brand's social media post or a paid ad. However, Instagram is certainly not the only game in town when it comes to influencer marketing. More than 80% of internet traffic is expected to be video by 2021. From cord cutters such as Netflix and Hulu, which are replacing cable and satellite TV with streaming services to Gen Z turning to Snapchat, Instagram stories and TikTok for entertainment. The internet itself could be called the world's largest television network.

While Snapchat, Instagram, Facebook and Twitter all feature some kind of video sharing and viewing features, YouTube is still the biggest mobile video platform around. Its very name is synonymous with mobile video; it accounts for more than half of all the video traffic gobbling up bandwidth on mobile phone networks. There's never really been a serious competitor to what YouTube is doing, and it's a hot spot for influencer marketing. YouTube and its dominance of the video streaming segment aren't going anywhere for the foreseeable future. In-Stream and Pre-Roll ads make the company tons of money, but influencer marketing is still the best way for brands to reach consumers. People seek out content from influencers, and they are far more likely to watch a video created by an influencer that they are to watch a traditional ad.

The growing popularity of mobile video in general, and the continued dominance of YouTube specifically, makes it even more important for marketers to find the right creators with whom to work. There are platforms, such as Upfluence, NeoReach and many more, available to help communicative entities find YouTube influencers. If a communicative entity wants to utilize influencer marketing, they can hire one of many traditional advertising agencies that have widened their offerings to include it, but influencer marketing has become so widespread there are also agencies that specialize in it. Florida-based influencer marketing agency, Americanoize, helps their clients to strategize, create and execute influencer marketing campaigns. They include big-name companies in their client roster, including AT&T, Hitachi, Ray-Ban, McDonald's, Samsung and Apple.

Mobile Marketing

As with legacy media vs. digital media, mobile vs. digital is somewhat misleading. Look at Facebook for example. Facebook is a digital app that can be accessed via desktop or mobile. So, when you purchase Facebook ads, are you buying digital advertising or mobile advertising? The answer is the communicative entity must decide. You can purchase Facebook ads for desktop or for mobile. You have to create a campaign for both, if you want your ad to show up no matter which platform the audience is using, but it can get expensive. This is true of most app-based marketing.

Most digital revenue is generated from desktop because there's more room for ads, but nearly three-quarters of audience engagement happens on mobile devices, according to Raju Narisetti, former CEO of Gizmodo Media Group and currently a professor at Columbia University's Graduate School of Journalism.[25] The gap, between where digital revenue comes from and where audiences are engaging, is growing. So, should you buy ads for desktop because there is more space, or because it's easier to measure? Mobile provides many more opportunities for communicative entities to grab people's attention, but adoption has been slow and there is not a standard way to measure consumption across multiple platforms.

Mobile marketing is the art of marketing products and services to appeal to mobile device users. With an estimated 5 billion mobile users on the planet, engagement with mobile devices is higher than ever and continuously growing. When done right, mobile marketing provides customers or potential customers using smartphones with personalized, time- and location-sensitive information so that they can get what they need exactly when they need it, even if they're on the go. More users are spending larger amounts of time engaged with mobile devices than ever before. We can expect this trend to continue. If forecasts are correct, it will soon be eclipsing desktop usage. Communicative entities have a variety of options when utilizing mobile marketing, including app-based marketing, in-game mobile marketing, QR codes, location-based marketing, mobile search ads and text messages:

- As its name suggests, **app-based marketing** is advertising involving mobile apps. Advertising in the Facebook app is different for desktop and mobile. Services like Google AdMob help advertisers create mobile ads that appear within third-party mobile apps.

- **In-game mobile marketing** refers to mobile ads that appear within mobile games including banner pop-ups, full-page image ads or even video ads that appear between loading screens.

- **QR codes** (abbreviated from Quick Response codes) are codes scanned by users using a smartphone, who are then taken to a specific webpage. QR codes are often aligned with mobile gamification and have an element of mystery to them. QR codes have been around for more than two decades and their popularity and usefulness has waxed and waned. During the COVID-19 pandemic, QR codes gained a surge in popularity as restaurants began using them as a safer alternative to physical menus, which can spread germs.

- **Gamification**, which is the process of using game mechanics and gaming attitudes in order to engage users, is a big trend. Gamification is essentially adding game play and rewards to nongame activities. For example, marketing rewards programs are relying on gamification to increase brand loyalty. The U.S. Army uses gamification on its web-site as a recruitment tool. Visitors to the site can play military training games as a way to increase interest in joining the armed forces. The COVID-19 pandemic was also a catalyst for increased use of gamification in strategic communication. For example, the Army turned to videogame tournaments to reach prospective soldiers, since the traditional methods of visiting high schools and setting up booths at state fairs and career fairs were unfeasible.[26]

- **Location-based marketing or geotargeting** is mobile advertising that reaches people in designated key areas from a geographic location, which can be done on the city or zip code level via IP address or device ID, or on a more granular level through GPS signals, cellular data and more using geofencing. CEs can set up a virtual boundary around a geographical location, which is known as a geofence. With latitude and lon-gitude coordinates, advertisers target from mobile apps and browsers when a user has the apps location services turned on. For example, a restaurant might target beachgoers within a three-mile radius to entice them to eat at their location. An excellent example of utilizing geotargeting, Purple, the mattress company, targeted social media users living in warm climates such as Phoenix, Arizona with its "Sleep Cool" campaign.

- **Geofencing** is a location-based service in which an app or other software uses GPS, RFID, Wi-Fi or cellular data to trigger a pre-programmed action when a mobile device or RFID tag enters or exits a virtual boundary set up around a geographical location, known as a geofence.

- **Mobile search ads** are basic Google search ads built for mobile, often featuring extra add-on extensions like click-to-call or maps. Mobile search has long surpassed desk-top, accounting for around 60% of traffic (U.S.) and click-through rates (CTR) are a percentage point higher for mobile vs. desktop. Mobile search has also seen the biggest growth in ad spend.

- **Mobile image ads or display ads** are image-based ads designed to appear on mobile devices. The smartphone has started to take over a lot of the tasks that used to be completed on desktop computers, and advertising is following the trend. For example, online retail has moved into the mobile space in a big way. Display ads on mobile are simply website banner ads that are shown on mobile devices, instead of desktop.

- **SMS marketing** involves capturing a user's phone number and sending them text offers. SMS stands for short message service marketing. When done correctly, texting is one of the most effective forms of communicating and engaging with customers. The likelihood of getting your message to the intended target is vastly higher than with email, pay per click, organic search or social media. However, audiences must opt-in to receive SMS marketing. It's neither ethical nor legal to send unsolicited messages with text-message marketing. Fortunately, customers have an easy way to opt themselves in—or out—straight from their mobile phones with most text-marketing services. SMS marketing delivers quick, simple messages that direct subscribers back to your site. The opportunities with SMS are endless. The message can be personalized, directing users to fun games where they can win coupons and tracking every step of the conversion process. If a communicative entity is trying to communicate in countries where WiFi is less common and data are expensive, SMS marketing may be the best tool for delivering marketing communication.

Case Study

The Role of QR Codes

Thanks to the invention of QR codes, more businesses and industries are turning to gamification as a means of creating higher levels of engagement, and that even applies to academia. Adding gamification to your mobile app will enhance your fan's engagement with the brand.

A Korean company used shadow QR codes to increase their lunchtime sales. If scanned during the right hours, (12 PM to 1 PM) the customers will be taken to a mobile website where they receive a coupon for up to $12 and discount offers. Customers shop and utilize the coupon or discount offers through the Emart App.

The items would then be dispatched directly to the customer's home. By mixing a simple game element, camera on the smartphone, an app and a shadow QR code, the company increased its lunchtime sales up to 25%.

Experiential Marketing

The migration from messages to experiences is not a new concept among marketers and strategic communicators. Ajaz Ahmed, AKQA agency founder and chairman, and Stefan Olander, Nike's vice president of digital sport, co-authored a book in 2012 titled *Velocity: The Seven New Laws for a World Gone Digital.* Ahmed said: "Our belief is that audiences want to have more engagement and more of an experience, rather than be bombarded with endless messages."[27]

Case Study

Red Bull Jumps to New Heights

Experiential marketing has been around for more than a decade, but it is expensive and difficult to scale. Remember the Red Bull: Stratos? If you were online October 14, 2012, you would have likely come across a live stream of the "Stratos" jump.

Red Bull has been at the forefront of extreme sports coverage for almost as long as the brand has existed. But in 2012, the company brought its content marketing to new heights—a world-record height, actually. Red Bull's super terrestrial marketing campaign, *Stratos*, featured Felix Baumgartner, a skydiver from Austria who partnered with Red Bull to set the world record for highest skydive. That record: 128,000 feet, about 24 miles above the Earth's surface.

To pull off this amazing stunt, Red Bull housed Felix in a small communication capsule and sent him up to the stratosphere using a large helium-filled balloon. What's truly remarkable is that his ascent and preparation to jump, alone, allowed him to break another record before landing safely back on Earth. Red Bull streamed the entire event online and saw the highest viewing traffic of any live stream ever broadcast on YouTube—at just over 8 million viewers. In case you missed this iconic example of experiential marketing, you can check out the recap video on YouTube.

As its name suggests, **experiential marketing** helps consumers and stakeholders experience a brand. Experiential marketing can help humanize a brand, and create experiences that leave lasting, positive brand impressions and ultimately foster customer loyalty and improve **customer lifetime value (CLV)**. CLV is the total worth of a customer to a business over the whole period of their relationship. It is an important metric as it costs less to keep existing customers than it does to acquire new ones. Increasing the value of existing customers is a great way to drive growth. The Stratos example is an extreme example. Most experiential marketing is cool with a wow factor. All too often however, it is also expensive and difficult to extend the lifecycle of the narrative to produce an effective return on investment.

Artificial Intelligence, Augmented Reality and the Internet of Things

New technologies are becoming available to make strategic communication much more enjoyable for stakeholders, and far more effective than traditional communications, and those technologies don't interrupt or distract but rather enhance daily lives and provide real value. Much like the internet and mobile have radically changed the media landscape, the rise of artificial intelligence, the Internet of Things and virtual and augmented reality are likely to have similar impact.

Artificial Intelligence (AI)

Artificial intelligence is a constellation of technologies—from machine learning to natural language processing—that allows machines to sense, comprehend, act and learn. Artificial intelligence will transform the relationship between people and technology, charging our creativity and skills. The future of AI promises a new era of disruption and productivity, where human ingenuity is enhanced by speed and precision. For example, the search industry is in a constant state of change. One notable area of development is the rising use of voice search and the growth of visual search technology. Search will soon rely more on AI with increased trust being placed in virtual assistants, such as Amazon's Alexa, and improving visual search technology. Communicative entities are exploring how to move paid search spend from text to voice ads, and from investing in clicks to answers and actions.

Artificial intelligence enables communicative entities to discover, gather and curate content and deliver it to stakeholders in a very personal way. Content curation should not be confused with content marketing. AI allows information to be gathered from different datasets and delivered to stakeholders in an organized manner. An example of AI content curation is a coaching system developed by UnderArmor, a sports apparel company, and IBM, an information technology company. Powered by IBM Watson, the goal of the system is to transform personal fitness. Using data from the UnderArmor record app, the brand offers relevant training advice and meal planning:

> A 32-year-old woman who is training for a 5K race could use the app to create a personalized training and meal plan based on her size, goals and lifestyle. The app could map routes near her home/office, taking into account the weather and time of day. It can watch what she eats and offer suggestions on how to improve her diet to improve performance.[28]

Virtual and Augmented Reality

The worldwide market size for augmented reality (AR) and virtual reality (VR) is projected to grow from $3.5 billion in 2017 to more than $198 billion in 2025. While many marketers focused their attention on the potential uses of virtual reality over the past few years, that attention has now shifted to augmented reality. **Virtual reality (VR)** creates a digital environment that replaces the user's real-world environment. The user's real-world environment is replaced with a fully rendered digital environment with body- and motion-tracking capabilities in a 360-degree experience, usually by way of a headset. Lowes' Holoroom How To is an example of using VR in strategic communication. Lowes created the Holoroom How To VR experience to assist do-it-yourself (DIY) home improvement consumers. The Holoroom How To guides users through a visual, educational experience on the how-to of home improvement using HTC Vive headsets. The Holoroom How To provides a virtual training clinic in various stores across the country offering education on everything from painting a fence to tiling a bathroom. Participants feel like they are actually there in the bathroom, grabbing tiles, dipping sponges in water. The VR training not only made the learning experience more fun than a video or a book, but also participants were much more likely to recall information, skills and apply them when they got home.[29]

Augmented reality (AR) overlays digital content into the consumer's real world featuring transparent optics and a viewable environment, real-time interaction and accurate 3D registration of real and virtual worlds. Augmented reality has already begun to show its true value through simplifying shoppers' journeys and adding value for consumers. For example, the rise of virtual try-on is transforming the beauty industry, and, in the automotive sector, users are now able to use augmented reality to immerse themselves in the experience of driving the car they are looking to purchase. AR has an astonishing wow factor. However, while this is a great way to draw people into an experience, it is easy to rely on the novelty and forget how to create true added value for the consumer. Leading brands and retailers, such as Sephora and Jaguar Land Rover, are offering new and better ways to engage with their brands. For example, customers can use an app that applies makeup to their faces so customers can virtually try Sephora before they buy. While Jaguar Land Rover put customers in the driver's seat of its new car to test drive from the comfort of their own homes. The web AR solution launched from Jaguar Land Rover's mobile ads with no need for a download. Consumers could virtually sit inside the car seeing their real world around them in full 360-degree views. Customers could use hotspots to change color, trim and wheels, as well as book an actual test drive. Running across the U.S. and Portugal, the campaign saw average dwell times of 121 seconds, and a click-through rate of 38%. These experiences have led augmented reality to yield results unprecedented in traditional marketing and advertising. The AR campaigns lead to better dwell times or time spent on a webpage or in an app, increased interaction rates and higher click-through rates to purchase. The numbers from the AR campaigns dwarf anything across print, online or television advertising.[30]

The founder and CEO of augmented reality company EchoAR told Hill.TV that 5G will dramatically improve the quality of interactive experiences. "'Pokemon Go' was a 4G experience. You were just seeing one small asset in the real world, but with 5G, you can stream a lot more data," he added. "You get much more meaningful experiences."[31]

Brands have seen higher engagement rates with their AR advertisements, so it's no wonder that many are shifting their focus toward AR. But the real impact of AR is yet to come and augmented shopping has a big role to play. The CEO of Levi's predicts that there will be no more sizing, and consumer will receive made-to-order finishing through body scanning. The industry is planning for a revolution and fundamental shift that will have deep effects on manufacturing, supply chain, merchandizing and so much more. Augmented shopping is expected to transform the way consumers buy clothing, furniture, beauty and makeup, automobiles and shoes.

This transformation will not happen overnight. Technological advances in 3D assets and WebAR are critical to providing a quality user experience across multiple platforms, such as Apple and Android. **3D assets** are three-dimensional models of physical products that users can interact with in AR/VR experiences. **WebAR** refers to AR experiences delivered via a web browser, which does not require downloading a third-party application.

The Internet of Things (IoT)

The Internet of Things involves multiple technologies and devices working together to create efficiencies and reduce waste for companies and consumers alike. These devices include smartphones, medical devices, door locks, fitness trackers, security systems, smoke detectors, and more. IoT is opening up a new era of economic growth and competitiveness. In the same way that Shazam app does with music, the IoT can make television commercials interactive to provide consumers with discounts, digital downloads, such as mp3s, or to let them play cool games. Augmented reality (AR) will be the IoT's user interface, adding a visual layer on top of advertising and creating media value for consumers. Audiences can receive a quid pro quo exchange from media for their time and attention.[32]

Amazon's Dash Buttons are one example of IoT in strategic communication. Dash buttons allow consumers to automatically order products when they're running low with just a click of the button. The buttons, about the size of a pack of gum, feature the product logo, connect to WiFi and link to the Amazon app. More than 300 different buttons are now available for specific branded products such as coffee, laundry detergent and tissues. Tide is one of the companies working with Amazon to help customers automatically order Tide detergent with one click of the button and it appears on the customer's doorstep in a couple of days.[33] However, Dash buttons have been banned in Germany, and not used in other countries because they violate consumer protection directives. CEs do not have to create a connected device to capitalize on the IoT for marketing. The volume of data that is generated from IoT devices is enormous. CEs can use that data to track and access consumers in the customer journey. The potential applications of IoT data are endless for communication entities that know how to harness it.

Summary

Strategic communicators and communicative entities have more options to engage audiences available to them than ever before and more options are popping up daily. High quantity and diversity of options can be beneficial in planning effective strategic communication, but unlimited options also make planning more and more complicated. It is critical for strategic communicators to remain current on today's ever-evolving media landscape. Effective strategic communication leverages ideas and creativity to use communication channels to their fullest extent. As technology continues to evolve the media landscape, communicative entities will seek to provide stakeholders with experiences and rely less on disseminating messages. Level of attention is a filter of quality to measure a medium's ability to provide a brand experience. The challenge will be to balance all the considerations and complexity of the media landscape with making choices within budget allocations. How to allocate vast sums of money to the best opportunities of achieving the communicative entity's objectives, is what makes communication strategy a subtle, strategic craft.

Discussion Questions

1 How has the rapid changes in technology had an impact on media and strategic communication?
2 What does PESO stand for? Why are the four categories useful?
3 What are media outlets associated with the term duopoly and why did they receive that identity?
4 What is retargeting? Explain its benefits.
5 What is SEO and how is it important to CEs?
6 How does content marketing complement brand journalism?
7 What is the difference between affiliate marketing and influencer marketing?

8 Based on the chapter and your own experience where do you see Artificial Intelligence, Augmented reality and the Internet of Things taking strategic communication in the near future?

Check out the online support material, including chapter summaries, useful links and further reading, at www.routledge.com/9780367426316

Notes

1   https://qz.com/1214801/nra-advertising-agency-ackerman-mcqueen-built-a-media-empire-to-push-guns/.

2   https://www.thetrace.org/features/nra-financial-misconduct-ackerman-mcqueen/.

3   https://www.nytimes.com/2019/03/11/us/nra-video-streaming-nratv.html.

4   https://www.newyorker.com/news/news-desk/secrecy-self-dealing-and-greed-at-the-nra.

5   https://www.nytimes.com/2019/03/11/us/nra-video-streaming-nratv.html.

6   https://deadline.com/2018/02/alyssa-milano-nra-tv-video-channel-amazon-boycott-hollywood-1202300178/.

7   https://www.mediamatters.org/nratv/mismanagement-cronyism-and-self-dealing-following-shuttering-nratv-turmoil-continues-nra.

8   https://time.com/5614707/nratv-shutdown-cox-resigns/.

9   https://www.mediapost.com/publications/article/355287/tvs-slow-recovery-projected-to-drop-10-for-2020.html.

10 https://www.theguardian.com/media-network/media-network-blog/2014/dec/18/future-advertising-digital-media-technology.

11 https://en.wikipedia.org/wiki/Seinfeld.

12 https://www.businessinsider.com/facebook-and-google-are-now-media-companies-2017-10.

13 https://www.journalism.org/2018/09/10/news-use-across-social-media-platforms-2018/.

14 https://www.statista.com/statistics/266249/advertising-revenue-of-google/#:~:text=In%20 2019%2C%20Google's%20ad%20revenue,almost%20134.81%20billion%20US%20 dollars.

15 https://www.wsj.com/articles/how-antitrust-undermines-press-freedom-1499638532.

16 https://www.postandcourier.com/opinion/commentary/commentary-newspaper-execs-push-for-safe-harbor-to-negotiate-with-google-and-facebook/article_89251336-d64b-11e9-98af-571d727cafcb.html.

17 https://www.cjr.org/the_media_today/google-pays-publishers.php.

18 https://totallyinfused.com/blog/easy-facebook-posting-ad-strategy/.

19 https://www.singlegrain.com/digital-marketing/set-up-facebook-retargeting-campaign/.

20 https://blog.hootsuite.com/insta-shopping-tips/.

21 https://www.thinkwithgoogle.com/marketing-strategies/search/how-advertisers-are-using-search-for-brand-building/.

22 https://support.google.com/google-ads/answer/2375464?hl=en.

23 https://moz.com/learn/seo/what-is-seo.

24 https://www.delawareinc.com/blog/qa-joe-pulizzi-ceo-of-the-content-marketing-institute/.

25 https://www.adweek.com/digital/media-companies-need-to-partner-with-brands-if-they-want-to-survive-in-the-digital-age/.

26 https://www.wsj.com/articles/army-deploys-videogames-to-reach-recruits-amid-pandemic-1589734800.

27   https://www.businesstoday.in/magazine/book/book-review-velocity-the-seven-new-laws-for-a-world-gone-digital/story/184790.html.
28   https://medium.com/@14ideas/artificial-intelligence-and-business-4dfdcd87dde0.
29   https://blog.hubspot.com/marketing/vr-marketing-examples.
30   https://www.thedrum.com/opinion/2018/03/29/three-things-marketers-should-know-about-adopting-augmented-reality.
31   https://thehill.com/hilltv/boundless/424340-tech-ceo-says-5g-will-drastically-improve-augmented-reality.
32   https://www.adweek.com/digital/looking-to-the-future-means-implementing-an-internet-of-things-based-strategy/.
33   https://blog.hubspot.com/marketing/internet-of-things-examples.

Chapter 12

Branding

Learning Outcomes

After you have read the chapter, you should be able to do the following:

- Describe the elements of a brand and explain why brands are important.
- Explain how to create a brand image through tangible and intangible attributes.
- Understand how brand relationships work to create brand loyalty.
- Detail how companies build and manage brand equity.

Opening Chapter Vignette

Can a Nation Be a Brand?

According to the concept of place branding it can. **Place branding** is a strategic communication concept that applies similar techniques used in branding products and services to cities, regions and countries.

Tourism and tourism promotion are one area of place branding. Tourism promotion may be the most powerful way to create an image of a nation in the minds of global citizens. For example, many people around the world, who may have never actually visited Australia, have an image of the country that was largely formed by the iconic, 1980s advertising campaign featuring actor Paul Hogan, who invited world travelers to "put an extra shrimp on the barbie."[1] Paul Hogan later appeared as the adventurous Crocodile Dundee in a 1986 film of the same name, as discussed in beginning of Chapter 1.

Unlike most industrialized nations, the United States did not have a national tourism board to promote tourism internationally until May 2011 when the Tourism Promotion Act created the non-profit Corporation for Travel Promotion, now known as Brand USA. Brand USA is a public/private partnership between the U.S. government and the tourism industry mandated to increase international visitors to the United States and to enhance the U.S.'s image worldwide through an international strategic communication campaign.[2]

The Brand USA advertising campaign included both traditional and nontraditional communication elements—television commercials, outdoor billboards, bus shelters, subway advertising and 4-color print ads. Digital elements included an online portal for travel planning and internet banner ads that linked to the site. The social media campaign featured country-specific Facebook and Twitter pages along with Pinterest and a customized YouTube site loaded with multiple versions of the commercials.

The target stakeholder for the Brand USA campaign was "Americaphiles," a term for those who were favorably disposed toward the United States. According to advertising agency, J. Walter Thompson, Americaphiles "embrace the American spirit, feel a strong kinship with America and Americans, identify with American culture and personal freedom, are fans of the idea of American travel and actively encourage others to go."

Research on the campaign suggested that the campaign accomplished its primary goal of increasing tourism to the United States, bringing 5.4 million incremental visitors to the United States between 2012 and 2017.

Beyond the economic benefits of international tourism, are there other advantages that a country might gain from creating a positive brand in the minds of global citizens?[3]

Introduction

Branding is an important element of strategic communication. Originally, a brand was just the name of the product that was being marketed to a consumer. Later, branding became the action of identifying and differentiating the product from other similar products in the marketplace. In the 21st century, the concept of the brand has evolved beyond products and services to include people, causes, concepts and ideas. Essentially, the brand is everything your mind connects to a company. Companies, stores, celebrities and universities are all brands. Philosophies, political parties and nations can also be brands.

There are many definitions for the word **brand**, however, generally it is a name, term, symbol or design—or a combination of these elements that is intended to clearly identify and differentiate a seller's products from a competitor's products. In other words, a brand is the bundle of attributes—the features, functions, benefits and uses—that set a product apart from its competition.

Think about your favorite soft drink. Is it Coke or Pepsi? Or is it a completely different brand? When you think about that soft drink, what about it stands out? Is it the taste, the design on the can, the memories and feelings you have associated with drinking it? All that is part of the brand. These attributes create an emotional shortcut linking the product and the consumer. A company can utilize these emotional shortcuts to inspire, motivate, connect with and inform consumers.

Branding is an important aspect in strategic communication. This chapter will overview the concept of branding, in general including the various brand elements, such as logos and how to name a brand. It will also discuss how strategic communicators create brand image through communication campaigns. Finally, the chapter will focus on maintaining and managing the brand.

Brand Elements

The brand is the emotional shortcut a company uses to connect with consumers. The brand not only encompasses the name, symbol and logo but also includes the image the product possesses in the minds of consumers. A brand can be thought of as the product's reputation. According to ad man-turned-government-adviser Simon Anholt, a brand "is nothing more and nothing less than the *good name* of something that's on offer to the public."[4] The role of branding in strategic communication is building and maintaining a positive reputation.

Industry Insight

Why Build a Brand?

By Mallorie Rodak

A brand is the blueprint for a company's future. Of all the things a company can own, nothing is more important than its brand. Nothing's as valuable. Nothing's as enduring. Industries and competition evolve. Technology becomes obsolete. Patents expire, and copyrights and proprietary procedures go into the public domain. But there's only one thing that never expires: a brand. A brand enables a company to attract and retain the best employees and affiliates, leverage competitive opportunities, become an industry leader and increase economic value.

As a Brand Planning Group Head at The Richards Group, I act on this belief that clients' brands are among their most valuable assets. And that's why our role as an advertising agency isn't just that of an ad-maker, but rather, a brand-building partner.

But how do you package up the sum of a brand? Is a brand simply a logo, a tagline, an ad campaign? Are the Chick-fil-A cows a summation of the Chick-fil-A brand? No, these are elements, touchpoints and even spokescows, but they are not the brand itself.

We believe a brand is a promise. Everything you say, everything you do, is a promise you make to people. And there is something inherently special and meaningful about a promise. If I make a promise to someone, it means we have a mutual understanding of what to expect. If I break that promise, I've likely done more harm than good.

That's why the strongest brands uphold their promises over time with three vital characteristics: conviction, consistency and connection. First, everyone within the organization has an unwavering certainty about what the brand is, why it exists, whom it reaches and what benefits it offers. Next, they portray the brand consistently across time and at every touchpoint, so regardless of how people interact with the brand—whether at a brick-and-mortar location, on the web or on social media—they come away with the same impression. And lastly, connection. The endurance of an idea is simply its ability to connect with people. The strongest brands have a sensitive and insightful understanding of their customers at a deep level.

When our clients approach us with a business challenge, we never address it as a one-dimensional exercise sprinkled with random consumer insights. Rather, we use our proprietary process called Spherical® branding, where we gather the information and research deemed necessary to understand the brand's current opportunities and challenges (discovery) and conduct a collaborative brand development workshop with key brand decision-makers that concludes with a one-page brand promise.

A brand promise consists of four parts. First, the brand vision. Brand vision is the reason why the organization exists; the deep-seated human needs and desires a brand fulfills. Disney's vision is "keeping the magic of childhood alive."

Second, the brand positioning strategy defines the way you want the consumer to think about a product, store or service. It includes three interrelated components: the target audience, the brand's competitive set and the most compelling benefit the brand offers. For instance, The Home Depot's most compelling benefit is providing "know-how to make any project a success." The Home Depot doesn't just sell hammers and nails, they give you know-how and, ultimately, instill confidence.

Next, the brand personality captures the human characteristics that help build or enhance a relationship between your brand and consumers. Suspend disbelief for a moment, and imagine a scenario where the Motel 6 brand and a handful of other motels walk into a room as human beings. How could you tell them apart? With Motel 6's commonsensical and good-humored personality, you can see (or rather, hear) how a brand personality can become an iconic part of a brand promise that can separate a brand from its competitors, like the voice of Tom Bodett has for Motel 6 for more than 30 years.

Lastly, people don't just buy brands, they decide to join them. Brand affilation is a description of the users of the brand that paints your customer in an attractive light. It is an indisputable fact that birds of a feather flock together. Humans are compelled to affiliate with beings like themselves, beings they admire or beings they aspire to be like. We believe all strong brands must actively create and manage an imagery of their users that invokes and capitalizes on this basic human behavior.

To be smarter with marketing dollars and to stand out from increasingly competitive markets, it's important to have a clear understanding of what your brand stands for and how it uniquely delivers a more compelling benefit to your target audience. So before you embark on any strategic communication project, first ask yourself, will this deliver on our brand promise? Do we have conviction in this idea? Will we tell this brand story consistently over time? Is this an idea that endears our brand to people?

Mallorie Rodak is a Brand Planning Group Head at The Richards Group in Dallas, Texas. She is also an author and a voiceover talent. She holds an MA from the Temerlin Advertising Institute at Southern Methodist University, and two BAs from Drury University in Springfield, Missouri.

Branding is more than gut feelings and emotional connections. All brands have essential elements that create a **brand identity**. These include the name, logo, tagline, colors, typeface, market position and message strategy. Anything that a consumer sees—from advertising to the logo itself—is part of its identity. It is the visual aspect of the brand that connects the product to consumers. Often, companies will create brand identity guides to ensure that their brand identity is communicated correctly. These guides include the exact font, design and colors that must always be used with the brand. For example, Coca-Cola's logo must be in red, but not just any red—Coca-Cola red is number 484 on the Pantone Matching System (PMS), the standard color guide. Target Stores also use red for their brand identity, but Target red is a different shade of red—PMS 186.

Brand Name

Perhaps the most recognizable part of a brand is the name itself. The **brand name** can be spoken and includes letters (ESPN), words (Little Caesar's Pizza) and numbers (7-Eleven). Sometimes, the brand name is the product's only distinguishing characteristic. People will recognize the name and prefer it to another brand that they may not recognize. What's the difference between Del Monte canned green beans and store brand green beans? Other than the brand name, nothing. They are both green beans canned in water. Take the labels off, and you can't tell a difference.

Selecting a brand name is no easy task. The name should suggest the product's uses and qualities and should avoid negative connotations. Chevrolet Nova, which was widely marketed in Mexico, means "doesn't go" in Spanish, is a classic example of choosing a bad brand name for the international market. At the very least, Spanish-speaking consumers were reluctant to buy it. Perhaps that is one reason Chevrolet no longer manufactures the Nova. It is also important that the name is easy for customers to say and spell. When the Korean car brand Hyundai originally came to the United States, they ran radio commercials to teach the automotive-buying public how to say the brand's name. The funny spot told listeners that "Hyundai" rhymes with "Sunday." Otherwise, consumers would pronounce the brand name incorrectly—or not bother trying.

Brand names don't have to be real words—they can be completely made up, like Kodak or Wii. They can be the founder's name, like Campbell's (fruit merchant, Joseph Campbell, founded Campbell's Soup Company in 1869) or not, like McDonald's, which was grown into a multi-billion dollar business when Ray Kroc bought a few hamburger stores from the McDonald's Brothers. Other strategies utilized to create brand names include describing what the company does (Southwest Airlines), describing the experience a consumer has with the product (Jiffy Lube), combining words to make a new word (FedEx), taking a word out of context and repurposing it (Apple), or using an acronym (NASA).

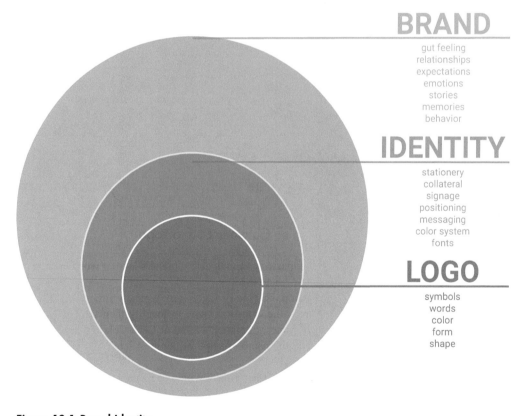

BRAND
gut feeling
relationships
expectations
emotions
stories
memories
behavior

IDENTITY
stationery
collateral
signage
positioning
messaging
color system
fonts

LOGO
symbols
words
color
form
shape

Figure 12.1 **Brand Identity**

The graphic in Figure 12.1 from Stone Soup Creative[5] helps explain the difference between a brand and a logo.

Logos

A **logo** is an element of the brand that cannot be spoken, such as the Nike swoosh or McDonald's Golden Arches. It's the visual representation of the brand. It is a distinctive graphic mark, emblem, word mark or symbol that is used to indicate the product's source or ownership. Think of it as visual shorthand that people can use to recognize a business. Typically, logos are permanent and although they may see a few tweaks and changes over the years, they remain relatively consistent. Take the Apple logo for example. Although the initial logo design was of Isaac Newton under a tree, it was quickly replaced with the iconic image that users all over the world recognize. Over the years, this brand has maintained the same visual elements and only updated the look of the partially eaten apple on their products. When people see the Apple logo, they automatically know the brand and the quality of products that they will be getting (see Figure 12.2).

Back to the future.

Figure 12.2 **Apple Logos Through the Years**
Caption/Permission: "Apple Logos" by bangdoll@flickr is licensed with CC BY-SA 2.0.

Academic Angle

Four Ways That Companies Communicate a Logo

There are four main ways companies communicate a brand's logo: a word mark, a letter mark, a logo design and a brand mark.

Word marks are the most popular type of logo. They typically rely on text and typographic typeface to convey the company name to identify themselves. Think about Google, The New York Times, Campbell's Soup or Coca-Cola—the simplicity and ease of communicating the name of some of the most iconic brands in the world is enough.

Letter marks are also entirely text but typically only use an acronym, or initials. Think of NASA, CNN or FedEx. Your mind automatically knows who these organizations are and what they do—calling them the National Aeronautics and Space

Administration, Cable News Network or Federal Express is a mouthful, a waste of time and not all that memorable. Letter marks are great for companies whose brand can easily be recognized from the acronym.

The NBC Peacock, the Starbucks mermaid and the Nike swoosh are three of the most iconic logo designs. When you see them, you automatically know what the company is. This graphic and image-based type of logo is great for new businesses that want to make a mark in their industry. People recognize it and remember it the best.

Brand marks are combinations of all three. It can use strong graphics, letter marks and word marks in a variety of ways. Often, it is a combination of the company name and an iconic image. The combination of elements is often arranged in different ways so that different parts of an organization can use it for their own needs.

Trademarking the Brand

In addition to the important elements of name and logo, branding is only effectively accomplished when the brand has been trademarked. When the American Trademark Act of 1870 was passed, brands earned legal protection from being copied or used improperly, protecting a company's goodwill and assuring that consumers can properly identify the source of products. A trademark is the legally protected part of the brand, which can include the brand name, the brand's logo (design and colors), tagline (Just Do It), characters (Flo from Progressive), and other aspects of the brand. It is important for companies to protect their trademarks by consistently maintaining how they are used.

Trademark protection typically comes in two ways in the U.S.—through common law protection or federal registration. So, what's the difference? Well, federal registration signifies that the United States Patent and Trademark Office examined, approved and registered a company's trademark. You'll recognize these companies because you'll see the copyright symbol, which indicates that a logo or brand has a registered trademark with the federal government. Common law trademark protection is a bit different. In the course of normal business operations, you can automatically claim a trademark, service mark or even grant creative commons rights. Trademarks are used to protect businesses during normal business practices. Filing for a copyright can become expensive and tedious, so common law trademark protection allows smaller businesses and organizations to protect and claim ownership of goods, brands and images. Similarly, a service mark can be used for any type of unique service that an organization can offer. Creative commons, however, is used to indicate that work is free to copy, distribute, adapt and make commercial. This type of trademark didn't develop until the internet became popular.

Common Trademark Symbols

® = registered copyright
TM = trademark
SM = service mark
cc = creative commons

There are times when a brand can lose its trademark. If a brand name becomes used as a generic term for the entire product category, then a company might lose their trademark. This was the case for linoleum, velcro, jacuzzi and kleenex. If this happens, it's typically because a product has so much awareness in the market that consumers automatically refer to the product name when they need something in the category. For example, if you cut yourself, would you ask for an adhesive bandage? Of course not. You'd ask for a band-aid. This happens more often than you think. When brands become consumer favorites, they often enter our lexicon and begin to become part of our every-day language. Don't believe me? Google it, and you will know why it's important to protect your brand.

Creating Brand Image

Strategic communication plays an important role in creating a positive brand image for a company, product or service. A brand's image is the impression that consumers have about a brand. Brand image is made up of tangible and intangible attributes. Because the brand's image resides in the minds of consumers, everyone may have a slightly different image of the brand. In our minds, we organize our thoughts about brands in a way so that we build relationships with brand, much the same way that we build relationships with other people—through actual experiences. If we have good experiences with a brand, then we become loyal users of that brand, which creates profit and other positive outcomes for the organizations that own and manage the brand.

Tangible and Intangible Attributes

Brands possess both tangible and intangible characteristics. Tangible attributes, also known as functional attributes, of a brand include the design, performance and price. Functional attributes are the characteristics connected to how the product performs. What does the product do? How does it help you? What color is it? How big is it? These functional attributes are all the actual, tangible characteristics of the product.

Intangible attributes, also known as non-functional attributes, are the less tangible experiences that a consumer has with a brand—but are just as important. These include recognition of the brand, its reputation and the trust people have with it, the confidence the consumer has that the brand can serve their needs, the status that the brand might have in the mind of the consumer, the type of store where the product is sold, the level of comfort a consumer has while using the brand and the feelings a consumer has about a brand.

Although experiential or symbolic benefits are not tangible, their impact can be very real. Think about the 2016 U.S. presidential election. Although many voters were supportive of Hillary Clinton as a candidate, many could not identify with her brand. Despite the fact that her resume—functional attributes—may have made her the most qualified candidate, many voters could not get past the negative associations—non-functional attributes—that they had from past experiences (media coverage of her unsecured email server when she was U.S. Secretary of State, for example). Non-functional attributes can create as much loyalty (or disloyalty) as the actual product itself, but these connections are often symbolic and emotional rather than tangible.

The combination of these attributes forms the **brand image**, or the impression that consumers hold in their minds about a brand. Brand image can be likened to the brand's personality, status or reputation compared to other brands in its category. The overall image of the brand depends on tangible attributes—it may be built with advertising in the media, but it is maintained in the mind of the consumer based on their experience. The image of a brand varies from person to person based on the experience the person has with the brand before and after each use. A strong brand image can lead to high awareness about the product, increase demand, allow for premium prices and increase a company's market power.

According to marketing communications guru Don Schultz,[6] consumers create schemas in their minds about brands. These **brand schemas** are a complex network of ideas and objects related to the brand. Because everyone has slightly different experiences, brand schemas vary somewhat from person to person. Brand schemas are formed in the minds of consumers as a result of brand contacts. **Brand contacts** are the planned and unplanned interactions between the consumer and the brand. They might be in the form of direct personal experience with the brand, but also could include hearing about the brand in a news story, from a friend on social media, advertising, signage, store employees and/or promotional items.

Brand Relationships

One important concept related to branding is that consumers do not usually distinguish between types of brand contacts. They don't register the difference between a brand's paid advertisement, owned website or earned media story. Rather, they mentally aggregate all the messages, contacts and product encounters together to create an image of a brand. Whether they read a news story about a brand or notice that a friend liked a brand's Facebook page, they simply combine these contacts in their minds, associate them with other things that they know about the brand and store them away until they receive additional information related to the brand. Strategic communicators need to be aware that all types of brand contact affect the image of the brand and seek to control as many points of contact as possible (see Figure 12.3).

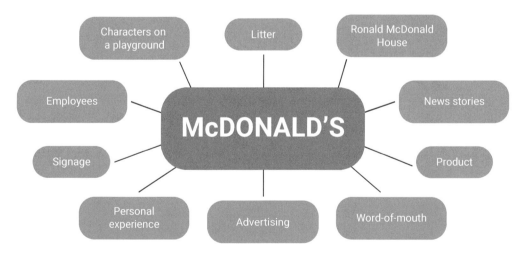

Figure 12.3 McDonald's Consumer Source of Information

All these brand contacts come together to form a brand network in the mind of the consumer. For example, a person's brand network about Disney might include a consumer's wonderful experience from their last vacation at a Disney theme park, along with nostalgic memories from a classic Disney film that they enjoyed as a child, a post on social media about Disney's policy of offering same-sex partner benefits to their employees and a trip to Disney store at the local mall to purchase a princess dress for their daughter. These contacts come together to form this person's brand schema for Disney, which directly shapes their evaluation of the brand and thus the brand's image.

The way a brand communicates with stakeholders helps create brand relationships. Having strong relationships allow the brand to maintain its sales and create **brand loyalty**. Brand loyalty is the tendency that consumers have to buy the same brands repeatedly, sometimes despite the actions of competitor's brands. Do you own an Apple or Android phone? If you own an Apple phone, how many versions of the Apple phone have you purchased? How likely are you to consider an Android phone? In 2011, Samsung launched an advertising campaign that poked fun at how loyal Apple phone consumers are. The ad is an example of brand loyalty taken to extremes and tries to shake iPhone users' mindsets to try a different smartphone brand. When a research firm asked consumers what smartphone people intended to purchase next, brand loyalty figured strongly into their answers. Apple users were overwhelmingly loyal to the brand although a few were willing to switch to Samsung or some other brand. Samsung users also exhibited brand loyalty but to a lesser extent.[7]

Managing the Brand

It's been said that companies make goods and provide services, but, in reality, they sell brands. As products became more similar, the role of brands became more critical. In the early 1990s, Berkeley professor David Aaker wrote one of the first books on branding, called *Managing Brand Equity*.[8] He wrote that brands were a signal to consumers about the source of the product, which protects both the producer and the consumer from competitors who try to provide products that appear similar. In other words, branding tells consumers which product is the real deal and which is a copycat.

Brands and Consumers

The relationship between the consumer and the brand is critical. Brands help buyers in very tangible ways. They help consumers identify what products they do and don't like. They can help consumers evaluate the quality of products and reduce perceived risk of purchase. For example, when people discovered that Lululemon yoga pants were sheer in all the wrong places, sales plummeted in 2014. The brand had to overcome the perceived risks that consumers had in their minds.

Logos, packaging and where a product can be found in a store can have a profound effect on purchasing habits. If brands use bright colors or are placed in the right place on the shopping aisle, they automatically draw the eye and begin to create brand loyalty. Additionally, brands can provide psychological rewards for people owning the product. For example, if a consumer has a product that they find desirable, like a high-end designer purse or the newest laptop computer, a person can feel pleasure while using the brand. Finally, brands can help make repeat purchase decisions easier. They know what their favorite brand looks like in the package, so it is easy to reach for that same package again at the store when their supply is depleted.

The consumer trusts the brand to provide certain attributes and in return allows the maker to command a certain price because the brand consistently delivers on the promise of performance it has with the customer. Therefore, the brand name provides a quick path through the buying process—and these brand names have power. In fact, when 50,000 adults across the nation gave their opinions on which brands were their favorite, certain brands—like Google, Hershey's, Pillsbury and Amazon—reigned supreme in 2018. This has a lot to do with the brand and how it performs, but also how it is communicated to consumers.

According to marketing research firm Morning Consult[9] who asked 6,600 consumers to think of a brand they are loyal to and name the first one that came to mind, these were the results:

Walmart (1,262 mentions)
Amazon (854 mentions)
Target (385 mentions)
Apple (212 mentions)
Kroger (110 mentions)
Costco (102 mentions)
McDonald's (85 mentions)
Coca-Cola (81 mentions)
Nike (78 mentions)
Lowe's (64 mentions).

Brand Equity

Brands have value. They impact the economy and world around them. Whenever your mind recognizes a brand, or you choose one product over another, you can see this impact. Sometimes the brand's value exceeds the actual value of the tangible assets of the brand. **Brand equity** is the added value that results from having a positive brand image. If consumers are aware of a brand and have a positive image of the brand, it becomes more valuable than lesser-known and less well-liked brands. Such as, when a shopper chooses Crest toothpaste and automatically knows which flavor she likes best; or, when a driver selects a red 4-door BMW over a red 4-door Ford because he knows which one will handle the road better at high speeds. Brand awareness, perceived quality, brand loyalty and brand associations all build the brand equity and impressions in stakeholders' minds. It influences purchase habits and that has an economic impact on a brand.

Case Study

United Breaks Guitars

In 2008, musician Dave Carroll and his band, Sons of Maxwell, were on a United flight in from Chicago to Nebraska. A few minutes before take-off, they heard another passenger exclaim, "My God! They're throwing guitars out there!" Concerned, Carroll looked out the window to see his $3,500 Taylor guitar flying. When they arrived in Nebraska, Carroll discovered that his guitar was broken. For the next year, Carroll tried to file a claim with United but was given a firm "No." The reason? He had waited longer than 24 hours to file the claim.

After an unsuccessful year of e-mails, phone calls and pleading, and even asking United to provide the $1,200 cost of the repair in travel vouchers, the songwriter decided to take his complaint to the internet. He released the song "United Breaks Guitars," a catchy tune that used humor to tell his story of his experience with United's customer service. It quickly went viral. One day after it was posted, the video had 150,000 views. When United caught wind of it, they contacted Carroll offering him money to take the video down. Millions of people were watching, laughing at the humorous video and identifying with the pain that Carroll had to deal with—after all, dealing with airlines can be quite the headache. At this point though, Dave Carroll didn't want money. He suggested that the airline donate it to charity and then wrote two more songs about the incident.

It wasn't long before media caught wind of this viral video. Carroll was soon in newspapers, on the local news, on radio shows and talk shows telling the world about how United breaks guitars. In a couple of months, he had been interviewed more than 200 times. It was so ingrained in the public minds, that it was reported that a train full of passengers at Newark began to spontaneously sing it between terminals.

Talk about a PR nightmare for United. The public reaction to a $3,500 problem damaged the brand significantly. Within a month of the video going viral, United's stock dropped in value by $180 million (10% of the overall company value).

Not every brand lost out from the viral video though. Taylor Guitars gave Dave Carroll a new guitar and created their own YouTube video offering their repair services and humorously explaining how to handle a guitar. One pro-tip they offered? Don't throw it.[10]

Brand equity is about the idea that consumers will be more loyal and more likely to purchase a product if they have strong, positive associations with a brand. Research has even indicated that consumers are willing to pay more (up to 30% more) for products that have strong brand equity. Brand equity is the reason that a large Pizza Hut pizza costs $20 or more, while a large pizza with the same quality ingredients from a local mom-and-pop pizza shop can only bring $12. Pizza Hut spent millions of dollars in the media over many decades to convince pizza eaters that their brand of pizza was superior in quality and taste. Consumers trust the Pizza Hut brand and are willing to pay more for it to avoid the risk of buying a pizza from an unknown company.

Consumers can also reject a product when it diverges from the brand, damaging the equity in the market. For example, when the cola wars were raging in the mid-1980s, Coca-Cola decided to change its product to be closer in taste to its main competitor, Pepsi. The company spent more than $4 million developing New Coke, and blind taste tests indicated that people liked the new, sweeter formula over the classic flavor. However, when the company rolled out the new product, consumers rejected it. Although researchers looked at the functional attribute of the new product, they didn't anticipate the emotional attachment to the original brand. Consumers hated New Coke. Coca-Cola was flooded with more than 60,000 phone calls, 40,000 letters of complaint, and loads of bad press—and this was before social media, text and email when it was quite an effort to communicate with a company. Consumers rejected the New Coke product so much that Pepsi saw a 14% jump in sales. After three months, Coca-Cola announced a return to the original formula. The entire misstep cost Coca-Cola millions of dollars in manufacturing and marketing costs, damage to their brand's reputation and a major loss in brand equity.

According to the finance magazine Inc., this brand equity is extremely valuable and adds up. Here are top ten most valuable brands in 2018, according to the firm's rankings:[11]

10. **ICBC**
    Brand value: $59.2 billion
    Percentage change from last year: +24%
    2017 rank: 10
    Since 2008, China's share of global brand value has increased from 3% to 15%, with ICBC (Industrial and Commercial Bank of China) holding its 2017 rank of the 10th most valuable brand in the world.
9. **Walmart**
    Brand value: $61.5 billion
    Percentage change from last year: −1%
    2017 rank: 8
    Walmart is losing value compared to 2017, with the future looking uncertain as the brand started 2018 by closing more than 60 of its Sam's Club stores.
8. **Verizon**
    Brand value: $62.8 billion
    Percentage change from last year: −5%
    2017 rank: 7
    Verizon is down 5% from where it was the previous year, and a big part of that is because it's losing customers to smaller companies like T-mobile.
7. **Microsoft**
    Brand value: $81.2 billion
    Percentage change from last year: +6%
    2017 rank: 5
    Microsoft has had a strong start to 2018, in large part due to its cloud service which is second only to Amazon's. Despite this, it still is significantly less valuable than its top competitors like Apple and Google.
6. **AT&T**
    Brand value: $82.4 billion
    Percentage change from last year: −5%
    2017 rank: 4
    Like Verizon, AT&T net worth fell 5% from 2017 to 2018, and it's likely for the same reasons too. To counter this, it's expanding their entertainment sector.
5. **Facebook**
    Brand value: $89.7 billion
    Percentage change from last year: +45%
    2017 rank: 9
    Facebook is up 45% from last year when it was #9 on the list of most valuable brands. The brand is benefitting from the dominance of digital content, according to the report.
4. **Samsung**
    Brand value: $92.3 billion
    Percentage change from last year: +39%

Last year's rank: 6

Samsung held the #6 spot last year and is climbing the ranks to become one of the most powerful tech companies in the world. In addition to the Galaxy phones, Samsung offers tablets, TVs, home appliances, home security and more.

3. **Google**

   Brand value: $120.9 billion

   Percentage change from last year: +10%

   2017 rank: 1

   Google dropped down from #1 to #3, despite better-than-expected performance in 2017. At the end of the day, Google is struggling to keep up with the #1 brand because, while it champions internet search and cloud technology, it doesn't focus as much of its energy on other sectors, according to the report.

2. **Apple**

   Brand value: $146.3 billion

   Percentage change from last year: +37%

   2017 rank: 2

   Apple defends the #2 ranking when it comes to brand value, rebounding after a 27% drop in 2017. Nearly two-thirds of Apple revenue comes from the iPhone, making it essential for the phones to sell well if Apple wants to hold onto the #2 spot again next year, the report states.

1. **Amazon**

   Brand value: $150.8 billion

   Percentage change from last year: +42%

   2017 year's rank: 3

   Up 47% from its 2017 value, Amazon is the largest online business by market capitalization and revenue. Beyond being an online retailer, it produces cloud infrastructure and electronics and is present in music and video streaming. In addition, the 2017 $13.7 billion Whole Foods acquisition took Amazon from the digital to the physical realm.

Brand Management

In order to maintain the value and equity of the brand, companies must plan and utilize strategic communication initiatives to manage and build the brand. This is known as **brand management**. This will allow brands to create a strong position in the market through strategic messaging. For example, in the 1990s, Lego was struggling. The long-loved toy was not as interesting to kids as the new technologies that were coming out. Video games were king and by 1998 Lego was losing money. When Jørgen Vig Knudstorp stepped in as Lego's CEO in 2004, the brand began expanding its product offering, developed movies and video games, and created a YouTube channel. By examining what was happening in the market and creating a desire for their product again, Lego was able to increase the brand's equity and position. In 2013, Lego became the world's most profitable toymaker. All thanks to a little brand management.

When managing a brand, there are various types of branding strategies that organizations may employ. When a company produces a new product that is related to existing products—such as Frito Lay's Ranch Doritos—this is an example of a brand extension. The new product leverages the brand equity of the original brand and achieves value and awareness almost instantaneously. Co-branding is another unique branding strategy that involves two companies coming together to brand one product, such as A&W Root Beer and Long John Silver's restaurants sharing the same retail space. **Ingredient branding** is another strategy that brands utilize to increase awareness and brand equity. This is the practice of highlighting an ingredient in the primary brand that is from another supplier and making it an important product feature. An example of this would be in the promotion of products such as Microsoft computer ads that feature "Intel Inside," Chevron gas with Techron, or Patagonia products featuring Polartec.

Creating a strong brand strategy is an essential part of communicating with consumers. Without this, companies wouldn't be able to get their brand into the minds and homes of consumers. Creating a strong brand, from the logo to the non-functional attributes develop brand equity, which will bring value to your business.

Summary

Brands are a shortcut device that organizations use to connect with consumers and other stakeholders. Brands are essentially the name of a product or service that are on offer to the public. Strategic communication plays an important role in creating and maintaining brands. It is through strategic communication campaigns that brands derive their meaning with consumers and other stakeholders.

Brands consist of many elements including the brand name, brand symbol or logo, and brand mark. Brands can be legally trademarked, so that other organizations cannot steal the brand symbols and use it on their own products. Trademarks also protect consumers so that they know what they are buying is indeed produced by the company that owns the brand.

Brands are made up of tangible and intangible elements that come together to create a brand's image, which is the impression that stakeholders have in their minds about the brand. It is important to build a relationship with stakeholders and to recognize that a brand's image is different for each stakeholder based on the various contacts that they have had with the brand. Ultimately, the organization hopes to build good relationships and create loyal consumers, who will use their brand on a continuous basis. Brand loyalty creates more value in the brand, which is represented financially as brand equity. Creating and maintaining brand equity is vital for organizations to survive.

Brands surround us and we interact with brands daily. As strategic communication professionals, we must understand how brands work and why they are important to our stakeholders.

Discussion Questions

1   Pretend that you are opening a new fast-food restaurant that specializes in gourmet hot dogs. What would your brand be called? What would the logo look like? How do you develop a brand identity? Why does a company need one?

2   What was the original purpose of a brand?

3   What are the functional and non-functional attributes of a Porsche? How are they different from a Corvette?

4   In the opening vignette you learned about how a nation can be a brand. What might the brand schema for the United States look like? Is it different for U.S. citizens? What about Mexican citizens' schema of Brand USA?

5   What is brand loyalty? Why is it important to companies? What brands are you most loyal? Are there product categories where loyalty is stronger than for others?

Check out the online support material, including chapter summaries, useful links and further reading, at www.routledge.com/9780367426316.

Notes

1   https://www.youtube.com/watch?v=Xn_CPrCS8gs.
2   https://www.thebrandusa.com/about/whoweare.
3   Fullerton, J., Kendrick A., & Rodak, M. (2017). A Propaganda Analysis of the Brand USA Tourism Campaign: Government-sponsored Advertising to International Travelers. In J. Fullerton, & J. Hildreth (Eds.), *Shaping International Public Opinion: A Model for Nation Branding and Public Diplomacy*. New York: Peter Lang.
4   Anholt, S., & Hildreth, J. (2004). *Brand America: The Mother of All Brands*. London: Cyan.
5   https://www.impulsecreative.com/blog/difference-between-logo-design-brand-identity.
6   Schultz, D. E. and Barnes, B. E. (1999). *Strategic Brand Communication Campaigns*. NTC Contemporary Publishing Group.
7   Becker, H. (2014). Apple and Samsung beat all other phone makers in brand loyalty. Brighthand. Com. Retrieved from: http://www.brighthand.com/news/apple-and-samsung-beat-all-other-phone-makers-in-brand-loyalty/.
8   Aaker, David A. (1991). *Managing Brand Equity: Capitalizing on the Value of a Brand Name*. New York: Free Press.
9   https://morningconsult.com/form/most-loyal-brands/.
10 https://www.youtube.com/watch?v=5YGc4zOqozo; Ayres, Chris (July 22, 2009). Revenge is best served cold—on YouTube: How a broken guitar became a smash hit. *The Sunday Times*; https://en.wikipedia.org/wiki/United_Breaks_Guitars, UAL Historical Prices—United Continental Holdings Stock—Yahoo Finance; https://www.youtube.com/watch?v=PGNtQF3n6VY; https://www.youtube.com/watch?v=n12WFZq2__0; https://www.linkedin.com/pulse/united-breaks-guitars-priceline-contracts-bob-james).
11 Tyler, J. (2018). The 10 most valuable brands in 2018. *Inc.com*. Retrieved from: https://www.inc.com/business-insider/amazon-google-most-valuable-brands-brand-finance-2018.html.

Chapter 13

Strategic Communication Campaigns

Learning Outcomes

By the end of this chapter, you should be able to do the following:

- Use the ROPE model to develop a campaign for a client.
- Explain the elements of a campaign plans book and how to construct a campaign.
- Create detailed budgets for the campaign including costs of tactics, contingencies and types of budget that could be used.
- Articulate how different types of timelines can be used to implement a campaign, help team members execute tactics and stay on schedule.
- Know how to use evaluation and measurement tools throughout the campaign process to gauge the effectiveness of the campaign.

Opening Chapter Vignette

A Campaign to Save Lives

When you're on an organ transplant list, time is not your friend. Every minute is a battle wondering what is going to happen next and if you'll somehow get the miracle that might just save your life. Some people wait years for that miracle and some never receive it. Getting people to sign up to be an organ donor is difficult because people often don't want to think about their own mortality.

In Brazil, getting citizens to agree to be an organ donor was especially difficult because of an added stigma with organ donation in Brazil. People who signed up also had to inform their families of their wishes before they could donate, and many families refused to recognize the donation of their loved one after they had died. Brazil had a problem—the lack of donors was close to creating a crisis for those in vital need of a transplant.

Brazilians are avid sports fans. So, in 2012, when Sport Club Recife, one of Brazil's most popular soccer teams, decided to attack the organ donor problem. They hired the global communications firm Ogilvy to create a campaign to solve the problem. For two years, Sport Club Recife and Ogilvy urged fans to become immortal by signing up to be organ donors. The campaign featured people who needed hearts, swearing that their new heart would only beat for Sport Club Recife. People who needed eyes vowed to go to every game with their new vision. The campaign connected with the emotions of their target audiences—donors could become an "immortal fan" and love Sport Club Recife even past death. Thousands of fans signed up at the stadium, through Facebook and by mail. Each new donor received a custom card with their image on it declaring their intention to donate and live beyond death. In turn, these cards started conversations with family members about organ donations and almost single-handedly helped solve Brazil's organ donation crisis in one of its largest cities. In two years, they had more than 66,000 people sign up as donors—almost twice the club's stadium capacity. Organ donation increased 54% in one year, and the waiting list for heart and corneal transplants fell to zero. By measuring the number of new donors and the time on the waiting list, Ogilvy Brazil saw the direct impact of their campaign—lives were saved.[1]

Introduction

Throughout this book, you have learned about various aspects of strategic communication. Now it is time to put it all together into a campaign. A strategic communication campaign is a series of coordinated messages designed to achieve pre-determined goals for the communicative entity. Like a military campaign that is planned and carried out through repeated strategic battles, a communications campaign uses multiple integrated media and message techniques to reach communication objectives. The best campaigns focus on a single, compelling theme that is relevant to the stakeholder and is placed in various media outlets that stakeholder is likely to use. One ad or a single Instagram post does not make a campaign. A campaign relies on repeated messaging of one dominant idea that is carried out over time and space using various media and promotional tactics. Some campaigns last for years while most have a timespan of a few weeks or months.

An election can be a good example of a strategic communication campaign. Think about Donald Trump's campaign for President in 2016. He used one theme throughout the campaign—Make America Great Again. This line was repeated in speeches, at rallies, printed on baseball caps and heard on television commercials. Trump's 2016 presidential campaign cost $398 million[2] and ran for 73 weeks. The campaign's primary goal was to get Donald Trump elected to the presidency of the United States—and it worked.

The Campaign Process

In order to be a successful strategic communication professional, you will be expected to develop campaigns that are effective in meeting the client's goals, within budget and on-time. This chapter will help you understand the campaign process—how to write a campaign plan, how to execute the plan and how to evaluate whether your plan is working. The exact format of your campaign may vary, but the elements of it go back to the foundations of strategic communication that were discussed earlier in this book. If you look at the outline for a campaign plans book below, you will recognize the ROPE concept (Research, Objectives, Programming, Evaluation) that we introduced to you in Chapter 6. Notice that early in the campaign process *research* is conducted and the findings are presented in order to better understand the environment, the client and the stakeholders. Based on the research results, *objectives* are set. *Programming* is the heart of the campaign where each strategy and tactic is explained in detail, along with the time-line and budget. The success of the campaign plan is ultimately gauged by the *evaluation* measures. No matter the complexity of the plan—whether it is 6 or 60 pages—the ROPE model can guide you through the campaign process. You should go through the same four steps with each campaign.

Even though the ROPE model looks simple, planning a campaign is a detailed-oriented task that often requires a devoted team of strategic communication professionals. If you don't take the time to figure out the details, your plan may not come together as you anticipated. Critical to the success of any campaign, you must conceive, plan and ultimately write down how the campaign will progress, what the theme will be, which strategies from the toolbox will be used and how much time and budget you will devote to achieving the campaign's objectives. Finally measuring the outcomes of the campaign are essential in completing the process and deciding if the campaign was a success.

Elements of a Campaign Plans Book

Creating a good strategic communication campaign is a complex and detailed process. You should start by writing the plan in one document called a **campaign plans book**. The campaign plans book is first presented to your client for approval and then used as a blueprint to guide the execution of the campaign. The campaign plan might make perfect sense in your head, but without actually writing it out in an organized manner, you won't be able to communicate the campaign plan to your client effectively, much less instruct your team on how to execute it.

Let's explore what the campaign plans book should include.

Title Page

The cover of your book should be designed to match the aesthetics of your campaign and communicate the client's information, your team (agency) name and the names of individual team members, the title (theme or tagline) of your campaign and the date. This is often the first impression that your client will see, so consider incorporating some sort of attractive visual element into the title page.

Letter to the Client

Immediately after the title page, you should write a one-page letter to the client from your team. In the letter, thank the client for the opportunity to work on their business, explain the inspiration for the campaign and theme, tell the client what they should expect from the campaign and note that you look forward to working with them. Keep the language simple, yet professional. You are building the relationship with the client with this letter and personalizing the work. The account executive should sign it. Or, better yet, have the entire team sign.

Executive Summary

The executive summary is a one-page overview of the key elements of the campaign. The term "executive summary" stems from the busy schedules of executives. You may have a strategic plan that is integrated, detailed and everything the organization could ask for, but when the CEO first gets your proposal, she may not have the time to read every page or detail. Think about it—their company may be considering five or six other proposals, which they must assess along with their other daily tasks. So, this page is your chance to sell them quickly on your plan. Use it to explain the issue, the goal, the primary audience, recap the key points of your plan and what you expect to happen. This will save your client time and prepare them for the upcoming content. This page should include a synthesis of the following items: the campaign theme, summary of key research findings, description of the stakeholder groups, the expected timeframe, budget and a quick overview of the expected results.

Table of Contents

Create an annotated list of the key sections in your book. Label this list with descriptions and page numbers of the corresponding sections within the campaign plans book.

Agency/Consultant Background

On this page, you are introducing the client to your agency and your team. This page personalizes the project and allows the client to recognize faces and names. For this page, either give the history of your agency and/or a quick profile or each member of your team. This page often includes professional headshots of the key players who put the plan together.

Situation Analysis

You will have many sections over several pages for the situation analysis, including an overview of the client's organization, company and/or brand, stakeholder analysis and competitive analysis. Look back at Chapter 7, and review how to construct a situation analysis. This section of the campaign plans book is also where you present the findings of your primary and secondary research and ultimately the SWOT analysis. Remember, the situation analysis section of the plans book provides the background and rationale for your campaign and sets the stage for your recommendations.

Goals and Objectives

This is a small (one-page) section of the plans book, but it may be the most important. It is essential that you state the objectives for the campaign in concrete and measurable terms. The objectives should include the amount of change sought, a defined stakeholder group and a timeframe for achieving the objective. Review the Planning Chapter 7 on how to write good objectives—remember to be SMART.

Big Idea

Next, create a section of the plans book that communicates the core concept or theme of your campaign—sometimes known as the "Big Idea." This is a single, strong message that comes from insights that were gained during the research process. The Big Idea unifies all the concepts within your plan. It's that one thing that catches the attention of your stakeholders and becomes the signature idea of the campaign. Think about "Got Milk?" "Just Do It," "#MeToo" or "Make America Great Again"—they aren't just tag lines, they are the idea that unites the concepts of the campaign.

In the campaign plans book, you must do more than just state the theme or tag line, it is also important to explain the Big Idea conceptually. You should provide the client with a rationale, how the Big Idea was conceived (based on your research findings and stakeholder insights) and why it will work to make the campaign a success.

The Communication Plan

Now you are ready for the core of the campaign—the actual plan. This is the part of the campaign plans book where you consider all the tools in the strategy toolbox and decide which ones will work best for your campaign. In this section, you lay out your recommendations in detail by writing out each strategy along with a rationale and the corresponding tactics that work to achieve each strategy. This is where detail is important. Be sure to include the various elements needed for each tactic—the due date, the cost, who is responsible, how it will be evaluated and any special requirements. This is a great place to utilize the planning matrix (see Chapter 7).

Timeline

This is the calendar section of the campaign plans book. The timing of a campaign and each of its elements is critical to the overall success. The timeline will show the client when each tactic is implemented over the campaign period and later will serve as a schedule to guide the implementation of the campaign. You can present the timeline in a variety of ways—a list of dates, PERT charts or Gantt charts. These calendaring approaches are explained later in this chapter.

Budget

Every campaign has costs associated with it. So, whether the cost is the price of media, the salary for time an employee must work on a project or the cost of production, you need to account for it. In this section, you'll want to present a line-item budget that incorporates the costs for all the elements of campaign (creative, media, promotional, contingency). If you don't have the actual prices from vendors, incorporate estimates. Some guidelines for creating a campaign budget are provided later in this chapter.

Evaluation

The evaluation section is the last, but possibly the most important part of your campaign other than your objectives. In this section, you will show the client how you will know if the campaign is successful or not. Success, of course, is determined by reaching and exceeding the objectives that you presented earlier in the plan. There are multiple metrics to use to measure the success of a campaign, including click-throughs, sales, ROI or attitudinal change—all are explained later in this chapter.

Appendix

The appendix comes at the end of the campaign plans book and is supplemental to the plan. The appendix may include creative concepts, rough drafts of proposed ads, sample press releases and sketches of tactics you are proposing along with any other information you think will help your client understand the campaign. Sometimes these elements are incorporated throughout the campaign plans book when the idea is presented, but you may find it easier to add these to the end of your book. Whichever approach you choose, include references in your plan to the materials included in the appendix.

Work Cited

The citation style is up to you, but you should always provide proper attribution to outside sources that you used in creating your plan. Give credit to sources and people outside the team if you use or were inspired by their work.

Case Study

Best Campaigns of the 21st Century ... So Far[3]

A good strategic communication campaign should grab your attention, make you remember it and get you to respond. A good campaign is unforgettable, it's entertaining and it can determine the failure or success of a brand, idea or organization. Communication campaigns are also a part of popular culture and reflect what's happening in the dynamic world around us. Modern campaigns incorporate technological changes and utilize new channels to distribute the messages.

At the turn of the century, things like podcasts, streaming video and DVRs didn't even exist. Media have changed a lot since then. Because of this rapid evolution, in 2015 Advertising Age magazine selected the ten best advertising campaigns of this short century. Advertising Age asked communication experts to rank campaigns based on three criteria—whether it changed culture, helped a brand become number one in its category and if was it simply unforgettable. Here are what the experts said were the top ten campaigns of the 21st century ... so far:

10 *American Legacy*, "Truth" (2000)—Can you imagine the spectacle of 1,200 body bags dumped in front of Phillip Morris' New York City headquarters? It's a pretty stark image. It's the number of people who die each day from cigarettes, and it's also the first time anyone attempted to take their gloves off and tackle the tobacco industry. The reason, in 1998, the tobacco companies settled with states and gave $1.55 billion to fund anti-smoking activities and advertising. The Truth campaign set out to tell people the facts about what smoking did to you, and the ads were impactful. It's estimated that the campaign prevented 500,000 Americans a year from smoking. The campaign may have been too effective though. Soon after "Body Bags" was aired, Phillip Morris threatened to revoke its billion-dollar payments to the tobacco settlement.

9   *Proctor &Gamble*, "Thank You, Mom" (2009)—We all know we wouldn't be
    where we are today without our moms. They fed us, bathed us, took care of
    us when we were sick and hauled us around to all our after-school activities.
    It doesn't matter if you are an Olympic athlete or not, moms work hard for us.
    When Proctor & Gamble (P&G) had an opportunity to lock up the majority of
    sponsorships for the 2010 Winter Games, they jumped on it. P&G had every brand
    from Pampers to Bounty to Oil of Olay use the idea "Thank you, mom" for their
    Olympic ads, tugging at heartstrings and adding $500 million to P&G sales.

8   *Apple*, "Get a Mac" (2006)—Hello, I'm a Mac. Four words that struck fear in
    the heart of PCs everywhere. With playful humor and clean aesthetics, TWBA
    agency showed Mac (via actor Justin Long) as the good guy of the computing
    world—kindhearted, smart and easy to work with—against arrogant, clueless,
    good-with-numbers PC (via John Hodgman). The commercials were witty,
    delightful and explained to consumers—in way they could understand—how
    Macs were better than PCs. After four years and 66 commercials, Apple more
    than doubled their sales and went from being a David to being a Goliath of the
    computer industry.

7   *American Express*, "Small Business Saturday" (2010)—Black Friday is part
    of American culture, and thanks to the Crispin Porter & Bogusky agency, so
    is Small Business Saturday. In an effort to support their small business clients,
    American Express hired the agency to create a cause marketing campaign. In
    2010, the campaign encouraging people to shop small created a holiday tradi-
    tion. In 2013, it generated $5.7 billion in sales for small businesses and has
    become one of the most successful days of the year for small, local businesses
    around the United States.

6   *Burger King*, "Subservient Chicken" (2004)—If you could tell a person in a
    chicken costume what to do, would you? So would a lot of people. Crispin
    Porter & Bogusky again created this great campaign. It included an interactive
    ad to promote Burger King's chicken tender sandwich, which mimicked a live
    stream webcast. Fans flocked to Burger King's website to tell the man in the
    chicken costume what to do, many of whom didn't realize that the live stream
    wasn't live. Instead, it was a series of 300 videos that were programmed to make
    the subservient chicken do what you said when you said it.

5   *Red Bull*, "Stratos" (2012)—Red Bull may give you wings, but in October of 2012
    they took the world to the edge of our seats and sponsored Austrian sky diver
    Felix Baumgartner's 24-mile live jump from the edge of space. Red Bull planned
    Stratos for years. The energy drink insisted the jump wasn't a stunt or an ad, but a
    scientific endeavor. And, it may have been; the dive broke world records, led the
    first human breaking the speed of sound without the help of an engine, and had
    207 million people in 50 countries seeing the brand front and center. In the six
    months after the dive that entranced the world, sales increased 7%.

4   *Old Spice*, "The Man Your Man Could Smell Like" (2010)—When Wieden +
    Kennedy, an international agency based in Seattle, received a late-in-the-year brief
    from Old Spice for a Super Bowl commercial, they realized they didn't have a
    lot of time to mess around. The chief problem was that men weren't buying body
    wash and Old Spice had to clear inventory. W+K quickly created the idea of The

Man Your Man Could Smell Like after realized that men were just using whatever body wash their wife or girlfriend had on hand. With very little time to produce the Super Bowl commercial, the W+K team dove in and created a spot with a continuous take and very few computer-generated images. It spoke directly to women, was funny and mocked the traditional conventions of advertising. It was so successful that sales jumped an unbelievable 55% the next month.

3   *BMW*, "The Hire" (2000)—Before YouTube was even a thing, the creative team at Fallon convinced BMW to spend $17 million into a campaign that, essentially, made a series of videos that made driving (and destroying) a BMW look really, really sexy. "The Hire," a series of short films about a man transporting people and things in his BMW, was credited as the first big media event of the 21st century. The creative team at Fallon created this *Mission: Impossible* inspired online program, programmed a custom-made web video player so people could have the software to watch, and hired big names, like Ang Lee and Clive Owen, to direct and star in it. The mini-series, which had thousands of people flocking to the BMW website to download and watch it each week, won a Titanium Lion at the Cannes Film Festival and set the tone for advertising in the 21st century. Oh, and if you've ever watched the movie *The Transporter*, then you owe a big thanks to Fallon and BMW—the entire concept is based off "The Hire."

2   *Nike*, "Nike+" (2014)—When R/GA agency partnered with Nike and Apple to introduce Nike+ Running, software that tracked running patterns through an Apple watch and Nike products, they create a whole new market segment—wearable computing, which integrated mobile apps into our daily lives. R/GA didn't just make a cool ad, they worked with both companies to develop new software and a long-term strategy that reshaped the advertising industry. By integrating the tech savvy of Silicon Valley and the creative savvy of Madison Avenue, R/GA invoked envy across the industry and defined an entire market.

1   *Dove*, "Campaign for Real Beauty" (2004)—For more than ten years, Dove worked to change the public's conversation about beauty. By creating ads featuring real women, they allowed people to begin a discussion about how we see ourselves. Dove was so committed to the Ogilvy-developed campaign, that they prioritized selling soap as second to building confidence in men and women, alike. The campaign sparked interest in cause marketing around the world, increased sales from $2.5 billion to $4 billion post-campaign, and created major brand loyalty.

So, what do you think? Were there any campaigns that you recognize? Are there campaigns since 2015 that deserve to be on the list? Which ones would you replace? Did Advertising Age miss any campaigns that you really loved? Why do you think that they selected the ones that they did? Why were they so memorable?

Campaign Budgeting

Every campaign must include a budget. The client may give the agency the budget upfront and ask that they create a campaign within that amount. Sometimes, the client may ask how much it will cost to achieve their stated communication objectives. Often it is a combination of both—they know approximately how much they have to spend, but also want the agency's expertise on how to spend it.

Unfortunately, client budgets and client expectations don't always match, and there's a running joke among agencies about it. Clients want it all—they want their campaigns to change everything, to ignite consumer desires and to inspire their target audience. They want the Mona Lisa of campaigns; unfortunately, they often come to agencies with a Crayola budget.

As a strategic communication professional, you must be aware of how much a communications campaign can cost, including the cost of paid media, promotions, production and agency fees. Remember, communications work has value—it takes time and talent. An agency's employees have trained for years to do what they do, and the client will be paying for the agency's wisdom and expertise. The budget must also cover the basic overhead associated with running the agency—rent on the building, utilities, taxes and insurance. So be aware that time and talent cost money and make sure it is built into the budget.

When an agency presents a campaign plan to a client, it will include a budget. The client needs to know how much the ideas and execution will cost their company. Once the client approves the budget, it is the agency's responsibility not to exceed the stated amount, unless they get prior approval. Strategic communication is a business-to-business transaction. The agency spends money on behalf of the client. Being honest, ethical and transparent with how the client's money will be spent is critical to long-term successful client–agency relationships.

Campaign budgets are typically a detailed accounting of how much it will cost to produce and implement the campaign, as described in the plans book. The agency needs to take all the costs into consideration. One way to think about a campaign budget is to consider five primary expense areas—people, paid media, promotions, production and contingency.

People

How much would it cost to have a team dedicate hours of their time to the client? Agencies are filled with people with different roles and fees. Is a young intern taking on a task to reduce costs? Or, perhaps this project requires the advanced skills of a high-paid executive vice-president? Whoever is assigned to the task, think about the fact that their time has tangible value that must be charged to the client. Most agencies have an hourly fee schedule for the work that they do within the agency for the client's campaign including overall account management, creative ideation, art direction, copywriting, research, and much more.

Paid Media

Usually the largest part of a campaign budget is for media purchases. Advertising isn't free (that's why it is called paid media). If your campaign proposes to run advertising for the client, you need to determine ahead of time how many ads will be needed and what the cost for those ads will be. In addition to the actual cost of the advertising (paid to the media, usually by the agency), the agency adds a commission to cover their time and expertise for placing, monitoring and evaluating the advertising. Traditionally this fee is 15% of the total media budget and is the primary source of agency income. A national campaign's media budget may be millions of dollars. Because of the level of spending, every dollar must be accounted for by the agency.

Promotions

Promotions also cost money. Does the campaign plan include branded giveaways, such as t-shirts? Will the campaign include a sponsored contest or concert? All these expenses must be itemized and included in the budget. Depending on the client, product samples and coupon discounts may also be part of the promotions budget.

Production

Communication materials, such as posters, videos, brochures and radio spots must be produced before they can be placed in the media or used in a promotion. Therefore, the budget must include the cost of production. Often outside production companies are hired by the agency to film, photograph and create materials for the campaign. These costs are passed on to the client (often with a mark-up for agency oversight) and included in the budget.

Possibilities

When planning a campaign, be prepared for every eventuality. That's where the "possibilities" or a contingency budget comes in. A contingency is the backup plan in the event costs are more than expected or a new opportunity arises for the client that you didn't anticipate when you were making the budget. It is important not to go over the total budget of the campaign—rather, incorporate a small contingency for unforeseen possibilities—usually 10% of the total budget.

Line-Item Budgets

Here is a line-item budget for a rally for a political candidate's campaign:

Event location rental	$10,000
Security	$ 5,500
Campaign buttons, hats,	$10,000
Hotel	$ 1,500
Flights	$ 1,000
Subtotal	$28,000
10% Contingency	$ 2,800
Total	**$30,800**

The budget above represents the beginnings of a line-item budget. A line-item budget is the simplest way to determine the costs of your campaign. To create this, simply go through your campaign plan and write down every tactic that might have a cost associated with it. After collecting this list, you need to determine what the cost is for each item and put it in a list. This will allow you to break down the costs by task and objective. Line the numbers up by decimal point and present the subtotal, contingency and grand total of your campaign. Look below for an example from students in a class very similar to the one you are in. The client is PlayScience, a research and consulting firm in the technology and entertainment business.

Table 13.1 Sample Line-Item Budget

Letters to Clients (75 at $0.21)	$15.75
Invitations (75 at $0.17)	$12.75
Black Envelopes (75 at $0.18)	$13.50
Forget Me Not Seed Paper (75 at $1.35)	$101.25
Setup Fee for Seed Paper	$50.00
Business Cards	$22.49
Total Shipping Cost	$22.19
Total Cost for PlayScience Kit	**$237.93**
Gift Bag (250 at $0.55)	$137.50
Setup Fee for Gift Bag	$10.00
Rubiks Cube (250 at $5.09)	$1,272.50
Letters from Alison (250 at $0.21)	$52.50
Envelopes (250 at $0.09)	$22.50
Coupons (250, 10 packs at $2.70 a pack)	$27.00
Notebook (250 at $1.60)	$400.00
Total Shipping Cost	$59.91
Total Cost for PlayScience Think-Kit	**$1,981.91**
Bookmark Pens (500 at $0.69)	$345.00
Setup Fee for Bookmark	$45.00
Total Shipping Cost	$20.23
Total Cost for Book Tour	**$410.23**
Recording Equipment	$37.03
Total Shipping Cost	$8.28
Total Cost for Podcast	**$45.31**
2GB USB Drives (25 at $12.99)	$324.75
Setup Fee and Personalization Charge	$40.95
Postage (6 at $0.44)	$2.64
Total Shipping Cost	$20.64
Total for Media Kit	**$388.84**
Service Learning Scholarship	$2,000.00
Total for Scholarship	**$2,000.00**
Creative Kids Genius Scholarship	$1,500.00
Total for Scholarship	**$1,500.00**
Total for All Communication Efforts	**$6,564.22**
Contingency	**$656.42**
Grand Total	$7,220.64

Campaign Timelines

One of the most important aspects of being a strategic communicator is to be *strategic* with how you communicate. This means thoughtfully planning out when to deliver the messages in the campaign to stakeholders. The best way to explain when the campaign takes place, is with a timeline. A timeline is essentially a calendar. It shows when each of the campaign events and messages will be executed. The timing of communications tactics is an important element for producing an effective campaign, therefore careful thought and planning should go into creating the timeline.

Media Scheduling Patterns

One type of timeline that is very important to a strategic communication campaign is the media schedule. Pre-planning when each message will appear in the media to achieve maximum results is critical to a successful campaign. Scheduling is dependent on how much money is available in the media budget and the levels of communication that are desired to reach the client's goals. Assuming that the client has a set amount of money for the media portion of the campaign, the plan must show how the money is allocated over time.

As you know from Chapter 9, you can't just put a message out there one time and expect it to effectively reach everyone. Research has indicated that a person must see a message at least three times over a month on average before they can even remember it. After they have been exposed 9 or 10 times, that's usually enough—any more is a waste. So, the skilled strategic communicator carefully plans how many and at what time the targeted stakeholder will receive messages.

Typically, there are four patterns that can be applied to messaging: continuity, flighting, pulsing and massing. Which pattern you choose depends on the client and the tactics to be applied. For example, if you were hired by a local arts organization to promote attendance at their fall art festival in early October, you wouldn't create a timeline for the entire year. Doing so would be a waste of resources. Instead, you'd likely start your promotional messages in early September and run them through the end of the event. All your strategies would be grouped together into a short period of time and run consistently throughout that period. This is known as **massing** or a seasonal message frequency.

However, if your client is a casino that is open 24-hours per day all year long and wants to bring customers throughout the year, you'd likely use a continuous message frequency, also known as **continuity scheduling**. In this approach, the message is presented to the audience in a continuous, consistent manner over a long period of time. This type of campaign will definitely reach your target audience; but be aware, running a campaign consistently for 12 months a year can be very costly.

If your client cannot afford a continuous schedule, an alternate timing approach known as **flighting** or bursting may be appropriate. This is a message scheduling that presents the messages in waves—or short bursts (usually three or four weeks throughout the year). During the flights there will be a lot of message frequency in the media for the client, but between flights there will be very little or no messaging (this period is called hiatus). Let's pretend that the client is a jewelry company. They will likely want to reach their potential customers during times of the year when they are most likely to buy jewelry, such as Christmas, Valentine's Day and Mother's Day. Research on the timing of advertising messages for retailers has shown that advertising dollars are best spent when the consumer is likely to buy. So, the jewelry store will not want to spend money for media messages when people aren't thinking about buying jewelry. This is a perfect example for the use of the flighting method—bursts of messaging activity over several weeks leading up to Christmas, Valentine's Day and Mother's Day with relatively quiet periods in-between.

The final message strategy is known as **pulsing**, which is a combination of a continuous message strategy and a flighting message strategy. The idea behind pulsing is that it mimics continuity for a lower cost. By using intermittent short bursts of messaging, the client may be able to reach the target audience for a lower cost than continuously sending messages at the same high level. By using lower (or no) levels of consistent messaging combined with intermittent higher spikes, pulsing will allow a business to maintain sales as well as have spurts of growth. This kind of scheduling is often used for cars, furniture, appliances and charities. You can see examples of how each of these scheduling would look over a period of a year in Figure 13.1.

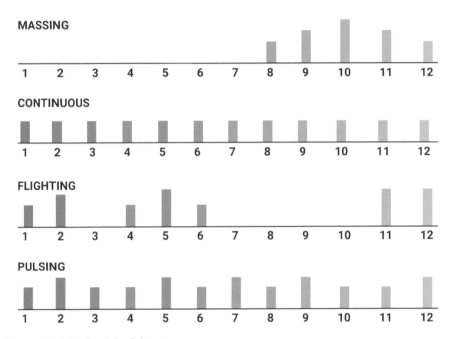

Figure 13.1 **Media Scheduling Patterns**

Implementation Schedule

Another type of timeline that is important to a strategic communication campaign is the **implementation schedule**. This is simply a list of the tasks that you need to accomplish in order to execute the campaign. You start with the date that everything is due and work your way back into the present. Then, you need to determine how long it will take for each tactic to be completed from start to finish. By doing so, you can see how much actual time you have. Let's consider the steps it might take, if you were helping Goodwill promote a digital scavenger hunt on April 21 called "Scavenge for Good":

April 22   Send press release with images from the scavenger hunt to local media
April 21   Monitor digital scavenger hunt, take pictures of participants for the press, declare winners

April 20   Create social media posts for hunt and have them scheduled for posting
April 17   Gauge success of social media promotions and engagement, adjust targeting strategy
April 14   Reach out to local newspaper for article promoting the event
April 10   Finalize list of clues and partners for scavenger hunt
April 9   Write promoted posts to get participants to sign up
April 8   Create a Facebook invite for #ScavengeforGood Campaign
April 4   Develop artwork for digital postings
April 6   Assign manager and team tasks for the scavenger hunt
April 1   Obtain final approval from supervisors, determine budget

Total length of Campaign: 22 days

As you can see, there are lot of small tasks that go into one promotional event. For your campaign to be successful, you need to be able to break down each tactic and figure out the best time frame for each. Once you do that, you can begin to determine what order to do the tasks and which team member is responsible for each.

PERT Chart

Another method of organizing the activities in your campaign is with the Program Evaluation Review Technique, also known as the PERT chart. This tool, developed by the U.S. Navy in the 1950s, helps break larger projects into smaller tasks to determine the best order to execute the project. By doing so, it creates a critical path, or the most effective order for scheduling tasks, and shortens the time it takes to complete the overall project. This is generally used before a project begins to determine the length of time each task will need for completion, which makes the overall campaign more efficient.

To create the PERT chart, identify the major activities in the project. For each one, think about how long it would take to complete. Some tasks may only take a few hours. Other tasks may take several weeks. Once you have determined how long a task would take, lay the different projects out in the timeline to determine what order they should be completed. These are known as nodes. When the nodes are in order, think about what projects are dependent on other projects in order for them to be considered complete. Based off this, create connections between the nodes to determine the critical path. Once this is determined, you can assign projects and start executing the campaign.

Let's look at the example below. Imagine you are working at an agency and have opportunity to win a major client. Once you read the **request for proposal (RFP)**, a document that companies will send out requesting plans agencies might have for their business or brands, you have to come up with the plan to present to the client. To make it to the presentation day, you know you have some major steps to tackle. You have to create campaign strategies, develop and evaluate the visuals, conduct a communications audit, get approvals for the campaign strategy from your boss and then compile and edit all the materials into a campaign plans book before you pitch to the potential client. It's a lot for any agency to tackle in a short time period—especially if you're also managing other clients. By going through the steps and creating a PERT chart, you can see how to efficiently tackle the project. For example, perhaps after creating the chart you noticed that the agency could hire someone outside, such as a freelancer, to complete the communication audit, making the entire project more efficient for the rest of the team.

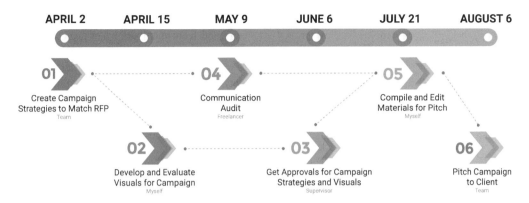

Figure 13.2 **PERT Chart**

Gantt Chart

In World War I, America had to deploy more forces than at any time in its history. They had to cross an ocean, provide millions of American soldiers with food, equipment, medicine, fuel, logistical support and other resources and do it in a timely fashion. It was a daunting task. Fortunately, General William Crozier, the man in charge of executing the deployment, hired a young mechanical engineer named Henry Gantt, to help schedule, manage and execute the deployment. By organizing tasks and breaking down the necessary work to complete them, Gantt created bar charts which helped the military understand the chronological order of tasks to ensure a smooth operation. At the time, these charts were revolutionary and provided a simple visual framework allowing every person involved an opportunity to see when their tasks took precedence. The first published Gantt chart can be seen in Figure 13.3.

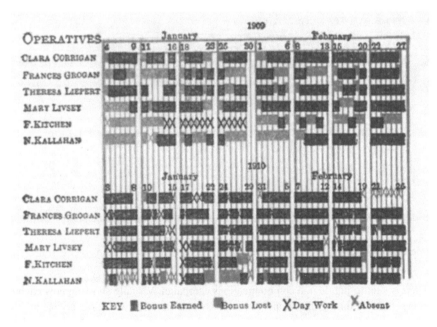

Figure 13.3 **First Published Gantt Chart**[4]

Modern **Gantt charts** are more complex than their initial predecessors. They are still used because they can easily show project managers and team members when projects start, what the tasks are, who is working on them, how long each task is going to take, how they overlap with each other and when everything needs to be completed. Since programs like Microsoft Excel or Project (as well as a variety of other online resources) can help you create your own chart by just plugging dates and tasks, practitioners don't have to schedule everything out by hand like they did a century ago. These tools provide practitioners added benefits which allow them to adjust the project schedule, reprioritize tasks, find the best schedule for the project, track progress and more.

If you've ever seen a media plan, you've probably seen a Gantt chart. A complex media plan will provide a breakdown of the types of media, when it will be run, as well as costs. An example of a media plan from the National Student Advertising Competition for Tai Pei frozen Asian entrees can be seen below. As you can tell, it's very detailed with scheduled items happening on a weekly basis and associated costs and audience impressions for each item.

Gantt charts are also known as flowcharts in some agencies, but they work just the same—thanks to Mr. Gantt!

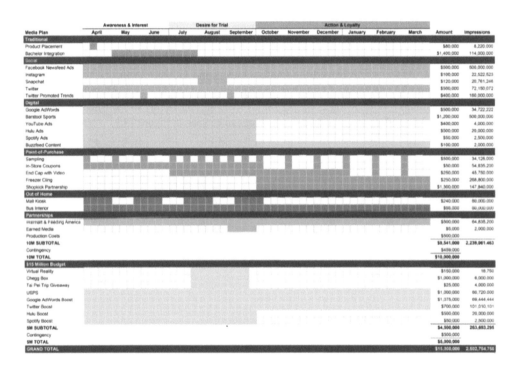

Figure 13.4 **Media Flowchart**

There's a lot to juggle in a communications campaign. Visually showing how each element is scheduled during the campaign is an easy and effective way for everyone involved to know what's next. The campaigns that you plan in school may not be as complex as World War I; however, knowing how to make a Gantt chart—simple or complex—will help the people who read your plan be able to execute it. Here's a simpler, but equally helpful, Gantt chart for a non-profit organization's strategic communication campaign (see Figure 13.5).

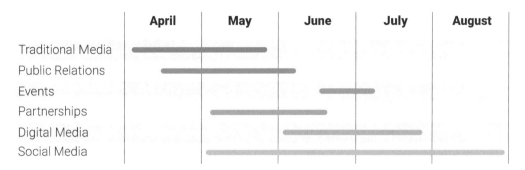

	April	May	June	July	August
Traditional Media					
Public Relations					
Events					
Partnerships					
Digital Media					
Social Media					

Figure 13.5 **Modern Gantt Chart**

Campaign Evaluation

The final step in the strategic communication campaign process is to measure and evaluate your plan. **Campaign evaluation** is a form of research that measures outputs and outcomes to determine if a campaign has accomplished its objectives. The purpose of evaluation is simply to assess the tactics of the campaign during and after they are implemented against the objectives of the campaign. If the evaluation is done in a systematic manner, it will show what is working and what is not. The evaluation phase of your campaign makes you a better strategic communicator.

Evaluation has four distinct, yet interrelated goals: learning, improving performance, informing decision-making and accountability. Through evaluation, you can provide additional recommendations for your plan, refine your strategies and fix issues that may come up. After all, what if the campaign is wasting the client's money? It could spell disaster for the agency.

It is essential to remember that evaluation isn't something that is done only after the campaign is done—it should be done throughout the process. Good campaign evaluation happens before, during and after the campaign.

Stages of Evaluations

The first stage of evaluation occurs before the campaign begins. This evaluation is called **pre-testing**. Pre-testing elements of the campaign before it is launched allows for adjustments upfront that may have affected the quality of the campaign. For example, asking members of the stakeholder group what they think about the message copy and visuals before they are seen by the general public, could help you adjust messaging based on their feedback.

Another form of pre-testing is research that sets your **benchmarks**, or standards by which to measure performance. These benchmarks are based on the client's objectives for the campaign and are therefore determined before the campaign begins. For example, the agency might use focus groups to gauge current attitudes regarding the client or their products. Examining and recording the company's current stock price, determining their market share or a variety of other business metrics might serve as benchmarks for the campaign. Methods for collecting benchmarks can vary, but the object of pre-testing is to establish a starting point so that you can determine later if change occurred as a result of the campaign.

The next stage happens during the campaign. It is called **ongoing campaign evaluation**. This approach monitors the campaign while it is in progress to detect any issues or problems that might pop up, in order to make necessary adjustments. Ongoing evaluation is especially important for campaigns that are 12 months or longer. When a campaign extends for a year or more, it is vital to track the results of the campaign as it progresses. Depending on client's needs, the agency can set measures that evaluate the program weekly, bi-weekly, monthly, quarterly or annually. This monitoring may include measuring weekly click-through rates on the website, ongoing consumer attitudinal change, media impressions, message persuasiveness or any variety of measures. The most important aspect of ongoing evaluation is to understand exactly what you are measuring and do it consistently. You often present these results periodically, in written progress reports to your client. After all, the client probably wants to know what is happening in their campaign and if their money is being spent effectively.

The third stage of evaluation happens after the campaign is completed. At this point, there are two evaluation types that can be used—summative and formative. **Summative evaluation** shows the impact of the completed campaign by comparing final results to the benchmarks stated in the campaign's objectives. How to measure the summative evaluation should be established at the beginning, before the campaign is launched, when you are setting objectives and determining the benchmarks. Whether it was the increase in positive social media mentions, the number of new clients or an uptick in product sales, the client will likely want to see what changed as a result of the campaign.

When the campaign is complete, the agency should present this summative information to the client in a final report. Also, this report will likely contain **formative** evaluations. This is not a summary of what happened in the campaign (i.e. summative evaluation); rather, it is what was learned from the campaign. By presenting this, you can help your client understand what worked, what didn't work and why. The client will be able to look beyond the data and see the bigger picture. The formative evaluation report should provide insights based your expertise and help interpret the campaign through the eyes of a communication professional.

The Barcelona Principles

Over the past decade, technology has caused a massive shift in stakeholder behavior and has affected how we measure the effectiveness of strategic communication. Although traditional strategies can still be used, the emergence of technology to gather data has allowed practitioners to track communication effectiveness in a whole new way.

To address this dramatic shift in communication and technology, strategic communication practitioners from around the world met in Barcelona, Spain, in 2010 to determine new and better ways to measure the effectiveness of strategic communication. For decades, the predominant measure of communication effectiveness included advertising value equivalency (AVE), media reach and frequency and other traditional measures. However, practitioners realized that the strategic communication industry needed better guidelines for measurement, and developed **The Barcelona Principles** to help evaluate more effectively and consistently across the industry. These principles were updated in 2015, and provide a foundation for measurement in strategic communication.

Principle 1. Goal Setting and Measurement Are Fundamental

Creating objectives that are specific, measurable, attainable, relevant, and time specific (or SMART) are fundamental part of campaign planning. At this point in this book, you should know how important it is to make SMART goals and objectives, but if you've forgotten what constitutes SMART goals and objectives, look back now at the chapter on planning (Chapter 7). When the time comes to evaluate your campaign, you will realize how important it is to have SMART objectives. SMART objectives force you to create a baseline for measuring how the plan has impacted the target audience, as well as the client. Without SMART objectives, it would be difficult to tell if the plan has accomplished anything at all. It's fundamental.

Principle 2. Measuring Outcomes Is Recommended Over Just Outputs

In the end, the client wants one thing from their campaign—results. They want to know that the strategies that the agency has implemented and the money they've invested have brought about some sort of positive change. Because of this, strategic communication professionals must be precise about measuring the impact of their work. There are at least three different types of results that can be measured—communication outputs, outcomes and actual business results. Although these sound similar, they actually measure completely different aspects of your campaign. We'll cover business results in the next principle; for now, let's focus on outputs and outcomes.

Outputs are the number of things, products or activities that have been accomplished by the campaign's tactics. This is often the easiest aspect of evaluation for communicators to measure and the easiest for the client to understand. For example, if the agency hosted five events for the National Multiple Sclerosis Society and 150 people came to each event that is 750 people who attended. That's an easy evaluation of the event. It is quantifiable and measurable. The same approach can be used with multiple tactics—the number of click-throughs from banner ads, the number of inquiries from journalists, the tonality of earned media coverage. It's all measurable and can all be used to determine output. Essentially, it is the quantifiable impact that your plan makes on the channels of communication.

However, simply counting people present at the MS event does not reveal the stakeholders' levels of awareness, opinions or attitudes about the disease and if their attendance at the event affected change. These changes are known as **outcomes**, or the direct and indirect impact that campaign strategies have had on your target audience over a period of time. For example, you may have reached 750 people with the Multiple Sclerosis events, but did it change their awareness about MS? Did they learn something new at the event? Will they remember the key messages? Determining outcomes is often more difficult to do, but it is important to strategic communicators in the evaluation process. However, it can often be accomplished with simple surveys or focus groups with the targeted stakeholders, which will gauge whether the communication activities are affecting change.

Evaluation can be complex, so to help evaluate the campaign, apply the logic model below. This model will help you to know what you need to do, what you track and how you plan on doing it. This is different from your campaign planning matrix, so be aware of when and where to use them.

Table 13.2 Evaluation Logic Model

GOAL	TARGET AUDIENCES		
OBJECTIVES			
INPUTS	ACTIVITIES	OUTPUTS	OUTCOMES
This should be a list of external and internal factors that impact campaign success (i.e. staff, budgets, tech or equipment). Ensures it's possible to deliver results of a project.	This should be a list of what you need to do in order to implement the campaign (i.e. conduct community meetings, design campaign materials and collect data to monitor campaign progress).	This should be a list of direct products or things that result from campaign activities. They are usually what the project has achieved in the short term. Think numbers: events, participants, baseline changes, etc.	This should be a list of expected results related to the campaign goal because of campaign activities. Examples include new knowledge, increased skills, changed attitudes, opinions or values, changed policies, or improved efficiency.
			SHORT-TERM 1–3 years / **LONG-TERM** 3 or more years

Principle 3. Measure Business Results Where Possible

The final step of measurement, and arguably the hardest one for communicators to determine, is business results. This is the actual value that the communications campaign has brought to the client's business. Business results could include an increase in revenue for the organization, a larger market share—and increase in stock prices, a decrease in employee turnover and a number of other things. While business results are important, many other aspects of your client's company, beyond communication campaigns, may affect your client's business success, such as leadership, hiring, product quality, etc. Knowing this is true, however, does not mean that the agency shouldn't attempt to track the results and show the impact that the work has on the organization's business.

The client will likely be most interested in two things: cost reduction and revenue generation. They want to know if they got any sort of return on the investment they have made by utilizing the agency's services. Clients often want justification that the money they spent on social media, public relations, advertising and the like has any value. Even if the plan only utilized social media tactics (which the client may think should be free), remember that social media is not free. It takes people, technology, expertise and time—all of which have value—to execute.

Whatever money the client puts into their campaign, they will have the expectation that they will get that money back plus some. This concept is known as **return on investment (ROI)**. ROI is the percentage of how much profit is realized from an activity against its total cost.

To determine ROI, utilize the following formula: First subtract the cost of investment from the gain from the investment, then divide that number by the cost of investment, and multiply that number by 100. This will provide you a return on investment percentage, or the amount that the project gained (or lost).

$$\text{ROI} = [(\text{GAIN FROM INVESTMENT} - \text{COST OF INVESTMENT})/\text{COST OF INVESTMENT}] \times 100$$

OUTPUTS
Impact on media channels

Reach & Content Response - Frequency, attendance, store visits, website hits, click-through rates, tone, message impact, share of voice, media inquiries, social media posts, AVE, etc.

OUTCOMES
Impact on target audience

Perception & Behavioral Levels - Knowledge, opinion, attitudes, awareness, comprehension, recollection, recognition, recommendations, credibility, intention

BUSINESS RESULTS
Impact on Client

Added Value - Revenue, cost reduction, return on investment, contracts closed, brand value, market share, stock price, employee retention, purchasing intention

Figure 13.6 **Three Measurement Types**

When measuring the ROI, remember that you can't determine this through media metrics such as impressions. This is a business result, which is sometimes difficult to determine unless you have access to the client's internal records. However, media metrics and other communication measures can be used to inform ROI. Think about it as a progression of information and data; where one piece informs another, and you can show measurable results to your clients. The investment creates action by the agency, and the campaign creates a reaction with the key stakeholders. After the message causes a reaction, you will start to see non-financial impact, which can eventually lead to financial impact.

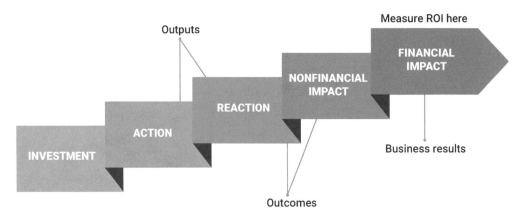

Figure 13.7 **Path to Financial Impact**

Thus, you use the data as way to connect the dots and show the direct line from investment to sales. Let's think about how that idea might work. Often, communicators know the reach of their message. It's easy to know how far the message has spread and can be tracked through a variety of data sources like—Facebook analytics, Google analytics or television ratings. The impact of that reach can be seen through traffic to the client's store or website. By creating benchmarks before the campaign starts, the agency can determine how much the overall campaign and even specific tactics may have directly impacted the client's business. For example, this website traffic or store visits can then be converted to a lead. These leads can then be converted to customers and sales. If interpreted correctly, this sales data can then be used to show the success of your strategic communication campaign.

Granted, that's a complex line of thought. So, it is vital to create objectives for the campaign that communication activities can directly impact. In doing so, make sure that a baseline is established to determine what the client's current situation is and measure changes against it.

Calculating ROI (Return on Investment)

Let's apply the ROI formula. As we mentioned, return on investment can be determined by applying the formula below. Let's utilize this formula and figure out the steps to calculate the ROI for a scenario.

ROI = [(GAIN FROM INVESTMENT − COST OF INVESTMENT)/ COST OF INVESTMENT] × 100

Gigi's Cupcakes spent $3,500 on a communications campaign to bring in new customers and increase sales. In the next month, 257 new customers came to the store, and (amazingly) each purchased three cupcakes at $7.50 per cupcake. If the monthly growth is usually 30 new customers in a month, what is the ROI for this month?

Here are the steps that you'll need to take:

1 **Determine monthly changes**—Figure out how much the campaign impacted the number of people that came into the store. If in a normal month 30 new customers came in, then that is the baseline. You can then determine what the change was by subtracting that from the number of new customers.

   257 − 30 = 227

2 **Determine the income from those changes (i.e. gain from investment)**—To determine how much gain Gigi's made, you need to determine how many more cupcakes were sold to these new customers and how much they are worth. In this case, let's just pretend that every single person bought three cupcakes at $7.50 each. This will show you the gain from investment because it is based off new sales.

   227 × 3 × $7.50 = $5,107.50

3 **Apply formula**—This is where you calculate the ROI based on the formula. Now that the gains from the campaign are known, look at the cost of it. Once you apply it, you'll have a number with a decimal point. ROI can show a loss, so don't be surprised if you have a negative number. If your campaign doesn't meet its objectives, a loss can easily happen.

   ($5,107.50 − $3,500)/$3,500 = .459

4 **Make % by multiplying by 100**—Multiply the ratio number by 100 and you'll have your answer. In this case, the $3,500 communications campaign brought Gigi's Cupcakes a 45.9% return on their investment. So, they are likely quite happy about spending that initial investment.

   .459 × 100 = 45.9% ROI

Measuring ROI can get a lot more complex; but if you know the basic steps, you'll be able to figure out the impact of your campaign.

Principle 4. Evaluation Requires Both Quantitative and Qualitative Methods

Media have changed and so has the way we measure it. Fortunately, we have tools that help us better understand the communication landscape. When conducting campaign evaluation, it is important to remember that there are a variety of methods and measures—both quantitative and qualitative—that can be used to show the results and progress of the campaign.

Evaluation is about more than just results; it is about setting benchmarks and showing change. This can happen through media measurement of online channels, impressions among stakeholders or a variety of other methods. Whatever tool you choose, record the results—good, bad or neutral. Every aspect helps you collect better information to understand what is happening within the campaign.

Earlier in this chapter, we explored how setting goals and objectives can measure output, outcomes and business results. We also mentioned that setting benchmarks is a key component of evaluation. But once the measurement is completed, how do you know if the campaign was a success? How much change is required?

Let's explore how using indicators can help measure the effectiveness of a campaign.

When your objectives are SMART, it should be relatively easy to identify appropriate indicators. But what is an indication of success? As a young practitioner, it may be difficult to gauge what is a good indicator of your objectives. Is a 1.5% increase in sales a good measure? Does an increase of 2,000 donors indicate success? What does increasing awareness by 20% even mean? It can be frustrating. The answer all depends on the size of your campaign and the benchmarks you create to measure change. Benchmarks are the key. Measuring them and knowing the landscape around your campaign before you start can help identify its success. After all, a 1.5% change could show huge movement for an organization or it could show a complete failure. It could be an $100 or $100 million, depending on the scale of the campaign, which is why you need benchmarks. Creating them before the start of the campaign will help determine the indicators and measures needed for success.

If identifying indicators is difficult, you may want to go back and refine the objectives to ensure that they are specific, measurable, attainable, relevant and time-bound (SMART). Define the terms that are being used in the objectives and be sure that there are enough details and benchmarks throughout the campaign. For example, what is meant by changes in attitude or improved knowledge? Have you conducted a pre-test and determined current knowledge levels? You can define what this means through benchmarks and discussions with your client. You just have to be strategic in how you plan on evaluating your success.

Take time with your campaign team to think through SMART objectives to clearly identify your indicators before you begin program planning and implementation. By doing so, you can holistically examine your campaign plans to know whether you are effectively measuring throughout. Don't forget to think about data sources and what is available for you to know. Brainstorm how your measures will be collected and if there are any external factors (i.e. social, political, or environmental) that may impact them.

If your team is struggling with creating good indicators, consider applying the SMART process to indicators as well as objectives.

Specific—Does the indicator measure only one component of your objective? Remember that one objective may have several indicators.

Measurable—Can you actually measure what you want to measure? Can it be observed, counted, analyzed or tested in a way that can be replicated by others with the same findings? It is important to quantify what you mean by "change" (e.g. the number of news stories published).

Attainable—Are your indicators realistic and practical given your resources, knowledge and timeframe?

Relevant—Do your indicators actually measure progress toward your objectives? For example, does an increase in visitors to a science museum indicate an increased desire for STEM knowledge?

Time-bound—Have you identified a specific time frame? Are you interested in immediate change or in long-term changes? When can you expect to see change? A good SMART objective will generally set the time for your indicators.

By applying the SMART process, you may be able to brainstorm on creating strong indicators to evaluate your campaign.

Principle 5. Accurately Measure Earned Media

In the first few decades of public relations practice, practitioners were just as concerned about how to show the value of their work as strategic communication practitioners are today. The Press-Agentry model idea of "any publicity is good publicity" was prevalent; however, few knew how to accurately gauge the value of a good editorial piece. In the 1960s, the practitioners began to evaluate this through the advertising value equivalency (AVE) method, which calculates what the editorial coverage would cost if it were paid advertising space (or time).

However, as the ability to measure more precisely has developed, practitioners have realized that Advertising Value Equivalents (AVEs) do not measure the value of earned media and should not inform future activity. Yes, it can measure the cost of the space and time of a specific effort, but this alone should not indicate the success of a campaign.

If there is no other way to measure besides AVE, consider using the posted advertising rates that are relevant to the client, use a best guess as to how to incorporate negative coverage, and, if only a portion of a story mentions the client, use that portion to gauge the impact. By doing so, it may reduce the over-inflation of the value of AVE and provide a certain measure of legitimacy to it.

Principle 6. Measure Social Media Consistently

Social media is ever-changing—what's hot today may not have existed six months ago. Because of this, being consistent in how you measure social media is extremely important. Measurement for social media is more than just counting the retweets, shares or engagement. You must monitor and respond to trends, stay on top of any issues connected to your organization, and know who the key opinion leaders are for a topic. Social media is often about the community that is connected to a topic. One post by an influencer with a negative connotation can cause untold harm for an organization. On the other hand, a positive post can bring a lot of good coverage. The key is to stay on top of the bad and influence attitudes through relationships. Social media is a constant in our lives and, thus, it must be measured constantly.

Just like any other tool or objective, it is important to create clear goals for measuring social media. Whether you are using online tools like Salesforce, Hootsuite or some other resource to gauge the impact of social media, you should try to create benchmarks, measure the reach of the posts and examine the tone of responses. Although posts are gone in an instant, these online tools provide the opportunity to measure the seen and unseen responses through analytics. They help you see the bigger picture of what people are saying and doing online. Even though social media is merely in its infancy as a tool, it is still extremely powerful and likely an important part of any campaign planning.

Principle 7. Be Transparent, Consistent and Valid in Your Measures

In measurement and evaluation, it is extremely important to ensure that integrity, honesty, openness and ethical practices are employed through the use of valid measures. These concepts are critical to strategic communication, especially as strategic communicators continue to define and refine the best practices of measurement and evaluation. If these principles are lacking, the practitioner is bound to get a bad reputation that just might extend to the entire company; it's better to be wrong with a good reputation than caught presenting fabricated results.

As we have previously discussed, setting goals and objectives are an important aspect of programming, implementing and evaluating your campaign. We've discussed how setting benchmarks—whether it is looking at social or traditional media—can show results that can indicate change in attitude, engagement and action. No matter how it is measured, the principles remain the same—set goals, create indicators, measure consistently, find the change and impact, and report it.

Another important aspect of programming, implementation and evaluation is recording each step to ensure that the work is reliable, replicable and trustworthy. Doing so helps track progress and improves best practices to design better programs in the future. Track progress by recording the source of your success (e.g., Was the content print, broadcast, the internet or some other media?), how it was collected (e.g., Google analytics, Facebook analytics, Hootsuite, etc.), how it was analyzed (e.g., the tone, the reach, the content analysis or survey parameters), the methodology (e.g., the sample size, research type, procedures, screening criteria, the questions, the statistical process), and the results (e.g., how it might impact society on a grander scale, the context, the take-aways). If someone else could go through the same steps following your procedures and get the same results, you know you've done a good job. As a bonus, you can look over your steps at a later time and find ways to improve and grow. Measurement is changing, but so are you—the work you do and your understanding of how to measure will improve with time, if you can reflect upon what you did.

As you conduct your evaluation research, pay attention to potential bias. As the agency of record for the client, it is important to show the success of the campaign and the impact it has had on stakeholder audiences. It might be tempting to fudge the numbers a bit here and there to have research that shines, but don't let your ego get the better of you. People may or may not notice it, but if a fabrication is discovered, it could do untold damage to the reputation of your agency. Instead, opt for consistency and transparency in your reporting. If your campaign didn't do as well as anticipated, explore the reasons behind it—perhaps it was the agency's fault, perhaps it was the client's, or perhaps it was a circumstance outside of anyone's control. Whatever it was, just be honest about it and figure out how to avoid the issue in the future.

Campaign evaluation is complex, tedious but very important. Strategic communicators who can't show the value of their communications efforts, won't survive in the industry. If campaign evaluation is a topic that excites you, then there are many sources of free, cheap and some not so cheap training available to help you become an expert. On the other hand, if this is a topic that you just can't wrap your mind around, then don't worry—you'll have people on your team that will be experts. It is constantly changing, and we will likely see more effort devoted to understanding measurement and evaluation in the future.

Summary

Now that you have finished reading this chapter, you may realize that the campaign process brings together all the aspects of strategic communication that were covered in earlier chapters of this book. By applying the ROPE model, you can build a simple or complex campaign—one that costs millions of dollars or only hundreds. In either case, producing a well written plans book is essential, understanding timing and budgets allow you to execute the campaign efficiently and effectively. Finally, you have learned that evaluating your campaign is essential to keeping your clients happy and improving your work going forward.

Discussion Questions

1   Explain the various elements of a typical campaign plans book for a strategic communication campaign.
2   What makes a great campaign? How do you know?
3   Show how to develop a Gantt chart and a PERT chart.
4   Give an example of each of the various approaches to budgeting.
5   Why is it important to evaluate your campaign before, during and after it runs?
6   Explain why developing SMART objectives are critical to a successful campaign.
7   What is the difference between output measures and outcome measures?
8   How do you know if your campaign was a success?
9   Why is it difficult to connect communication objectives to business results for your client?

Check out the online support material, including chapter summaries, useful links and further reading, at www.routledge.com/9780367426316.

Notes

1   Carneiro, J. (2014, June 1). How thousands of football fans are helping to save lives. *BBC News.* Retrieved online at https://www.bbc.com/news/magazine-27632527
2   Ingraham, C. (2017, April 14). Somebody just put a price tag on the 2016 election. It's a doozy. *The Washington Post.* Retrieved from https://www.washingtonpost.com/news/wonk/wp/2017/04/14/somebody-just-put-a-price-tag-on-the-2016-election-its-a-doozy/.
3   Top ad campaigns of the 21st century. (2015). *Advertising Age, 86*(1), 00–22. https://adage.com/lp/top15.
4   https://rickanderson2managementinfotainer.files.wordpress.com/2014/06/gantt.gif.

Glossary

account management—the management of strategic communication for an organization, its product or service, either in the organization or on behalf of an agency.

active stakeholders—people who are actively seeking out information about an organization and/or its messages.

advertising—a paid form of persuasive communication with an identified sponsor.

affiliate marketing—the process by which a blogger or another publisher earns a commission for marketing another person's or company's products.

agent—a person that acts on behalf of someone else.

aggregation—the process of taking individual data and grouping it into larger meaningful homogeneous segments; opposite of segmentation.

app-based marketing—advertising involving mobile applications.

applied science—putting scientific theory to useful practice.

artificial intelligence (AI)—a constellation of technologies—from machine learning to natural language processing—that allows machines to sense, comprehend, act and learn.

attitudes—a person's overall favorable or unfavorable feelings toward some object.

augmented reality (AR)—technology that overlays digital content into the consumer's real-world featuring transparent optics and a viewable environment, real-time interaction and accurate 3D registration of real and virtual worlds.

aware publics—groups of people that are aware the CE is affecting them but are waiting for an event to trigger them into action.

b-roll footage—additional video footage, still photographs and animation that can be used to enrich the story and give the media outlet flexibility in editing.

benchmarks—standards by which to measure performance.

big data—vast quantities of data collected digitally and made available through algorithms.

billboards—large-format poster displays found in areas of high consumer traffic, such as busy highways and city centers.

boundary spanners—individuals who help the organization and its stakeholders understand each other.

brand—a name, term, symbol or design, or a combination of these elements, that is intended to clearly identify and differentiate a seller's products from a competitor's products.

brand advocates—individuals who feel passionately about a brand and post the brand's content on their social media. Also called brand ambassadors and brand evangelists.

brand contacts—planned and unplanned interactions between the consumer and the brand.

brand equity—the added value that results from having a positive brand image.

brand image—the impression that consumers hold in their minds about a brand.

brand journalism—journalism-style content created by a brand about itself that doesn't read like advertising copy.

brand loyalty—the tendency that consumers have to buy the same brands repeatedly, sometimes despite the actions of competing brands.

brand management—an organizational function that puts a person or team in charge of the planning and development of the brand.

brand name—the part of the brand that can be spoken and includes letters (ESPN), words (Little Caesar's Pizza) and numbers (7-Eleven).

brand schemas—complex network of ideas and objects related to the brand.

branded search campaigns—an online search campaign that targets your brand name.

business results—the actual value that the work has brought to the client's business.

call-to-action (CTA)—a phrase usually at the end of an ad that tells the audience what action to take and how to take it to engage with or buy the advertised product.

campaign evaluation—a form of research that measures outputs and outcomes to determine if a campaign has accomplished its objectives.

campaign plans book—a blueprint to guide the execution of the campaign.

circulation—the number of readers the media vehicle reaches.

click-through rates (CTR)—the number of clicks advertisers receive on their ads.

code of ethics—a document in which an organization or entire profession detail their core values and standards.

cognitive dissonance—psychological uneasiness that consumers sometimes feel after buying a product; buyer's remorse.

communication liaison—a strategic role uniquely focused on the outside-in approach in terms of its emphasis on stakeholder relations and providing the institution with stakeholder perspectives.

communicative entity (CE)—the person or organization that communicates.

constitutive communication—a type of communication whereby understanding and meaning are created through a chaotic interaction between participants in the communication process.

consumer behavior—the study of how individuals or groups select, purchase, use, or dispose of products, and the needs and wants that motivate their behaviors.

consumers—individuals, or groups of individuals, such as companies, governments or organizations, who purchase products and services for personal use.

content marketing—creation and sharing of online material (such as videos, blogs, and social media posts) that does not explicitly promote a brand but is intended to stimulate interest in its products or services, complementary to brand journalism.

continuous media scheduling strategy—a strategy in which media messages are run continually in a consistent manner over a long period of time.

corporate social responsibility (CSR)—a management orientation whereby companies integrate social and environmental concerns with their business operations and their interactions with stakeholders.

covert power—power asserted behind the scenes.

creative—the work associated with creating ideas, artwork, copy and other forms of content for strategic communication campaigns.

cross-cultural communication—refers to how people from different cultures speak and how they perceive the world around them.

cultural interpreter role—the ability to translate local cultural practices for outsiders.

cultural sector—the belief systems, traditions, values and norms, historical interpretation and even traditions of the foods people eat, of hospitality and relaxation of a given culture.

customer lifetime value (CLV)—the total worth of a customer to a business over the whole period of their relationship.

decode—how the receiver receives and understands the message.

deliberate and purposive communication—planned messages and thoughtful, organized responses.

demographics—a common way to describe the attributes of stakeholders such as age, gender, race, profession, socio-economic group or other physical characteristics.

differentiation of labor—the different roles and specific tasks employees must perform.

digital billboards—large, computer-controlled electronic signs.

digital media—content disseminated via the internet, including desktop, mobile, social and gaming media.

digital-native media companies—media companies that began in a digital format, such as Google and Facebook.

division of labor—the different roles and specific tasks employees must perform.

domains of practice—the different fields that require strategic communication.

earned media—messaging about a brand or communicative entity that is not paid for, but run free-of-charge on the media as part of their editorial content, also known as publicity.

economic sector—the kind of economic system a country has, such as a free market system.

effects—the impact phenomena have on society.

emergent strategy—an unplanned strategy that arises in response to unexpected opportunities and challenges.

empiricism—obtaining knowledge through observation and experimentation.

encode—the process by which the sender translates the message into an understandable system.

ethics—the system of morals (a moral code) employed by a person, group or organization that dictates standards of conduct.

ethnocentrism—the view that one's own group is the center of everything and others are scaled and rated with reference to it.

evaluative criteria—features that consumers consider important in making their choices among all of the alternatives in the evoked set.

events—a strategic communication tactic used to develop and enhance brand relationships through face-to-face engagement with stakeholders, such as trade shows or tasting tables in the grocery store.

evoked set—a short-list of products/brands that consumers are favorably considering.

experiential marketing—the creation of experiences that allow stakeholders to interact with a brand; also called engagement marketing.

Facebook pixel—a code placed on a website to collect data that helps track conversions from Facebook ads.

flighting media scheduling strategy—a strategy in which media messages are presented in flights—or short intense bursts (usually three or four weeks)—followed by a period of no advertising, called a hiatus.

frame—to structure a message in a specific way.

frequency—the average number of times a person is exposed to an advertising message.

gamification—the process of using game mechanics and gaming attitudes in order to engage users.

Gantt charts—also known as flowcharts; a visual calendar used to schedule complex projects such as a campaign.

garbage-can decision—random and unpredictable decisions.

geofencing—a location-based service in which an app or other software uses GPS, RFID, Wi-Fi or cellular data to trigger a pre-programmed action when a mobile device or RFID tag enters or exits a virtual boundary set up around a geographical location, known as a geofence.

geographics—location characteristics of a stakeholder group.

geotargeting—mobile advertising that reaches people within designated key geographic areas.

gross rating points (GRPs)—the percentage of an audience exposed to an advertising message including duplication.

group decision-making—employees with different skills sets working together to decide.

guerrilla communication—an attempt to change the rules and norms of communication.

hard skills—skills that are learned such as writing, media production or social media planning.

hierarchy of authority—levels of seniority and power in an organization.

hybrid organization—an organization that makes use of multiple organizational structures at the same time.

hypothesis—a specific prediction about what will happen in a scientific experiment.

implicit bias—subconscious stereotypes all people have of others.

impressions—the total number of exposures to an ad.

influencer marketing—paying individuals who have a fan following or audience to promote a communicative entity's brand or message, usually online.

influencers—people within a stakeholder group that have thoughts and opinions that hold a lot of weight within the group.

ingredient branding—the practice of highlighting an ingredient in the primary brand that is from another supplier and making it an important product feature.

inside-out approach—when the needs of the organization—not stakeholders—are placed front and center.

Instagram Stories—short videos, approximately 15-seconds long on average, and they are only visible 24 hours after they're posted.

integrated marketing communications (IMC)—the coordination of functions relating to marketing and brand communication.

Internet of Things (IoT)—multiple technologies and devices working together to create efficiencies and reduce waste.

interpersonal communication—the (often) spontaneous communication between individuals.

journalism—the practice of reporting and commentary in the public sphere.

key public—the group of stakeholders that has the greatest influential power, urgency or most involvement with the CE.

keywords—the terms that people type into search engines.

latent publics—groups of people who see a situation but don't see it as a problem or are not affected by it.

legacy media—traditional media, like newspapers, also called mainstream media; they are associated with the elite and typically owned by big corporations.

legal sector—the constitution and laws of countries, states or provinces, and cities.

logo—an element of the brand that cannot be spoken—the visual representation of the brand.

macro (societal) level—the larger society in which a communication problem exists.

mass communication—the messages distributed by the mass media.

mass media—communication channels that carry messages long distances to large audiences simultaneously.

massing media scheduling strategy—a strategy in which media messages are grouped together into a short period of time and run consistently throughout that period.

media fragmentation—the splintering of audiences due to plethora of media platforms now available to media users.

media infrastructure—the ability of the general population to have access to media and communication devices.

media kits—professionally packaged materials sent by a communicative entity to media outlets to generate media coverage.

media market—also known as a broadcast market, market region or DMA (designated market area); defined as a geographic region in the United States in which the population receives the same television and radio station offerings.

media/medium—a blanket term for all types of print, broadcast, out-of-home, and interactive/digital communication. The singular noun **medium** refers to a specific type of media.

media planning—selecting, buying and implementing the media to be used in a campaign.

media sector—the different kind of media available to a country's citizens.

media specialist—an expert in understanding all media with the ability to create media content.

mentor—an experienced person who will help you on your career path.

meso (organizational) level—the way the CE organizes itself.

micro (communication) level—the execution of communication tactics.

mission statement—a statement that communicates how the vision will be accomplished.

mobile marketing—advertising on mobile devices, such as tablets and smartphones.

morals—our own personal principles that help us determine right from wrong.

motives—internal forces that move a person toward a goal.

multi-skill—the ability to know and perform more than one task.

multidivisional structures—an organization that has many offices in a country or even globally.

native advertising—media content that looks and reads like editorial but is actually paid advertising intended to promote the advertiser's product or brand. Also called sponsored content.

network organization—an informal organization that is made up of different independent owners.

networking—establishing and nurturing long-term, mutually beneficial relationships with the people you meet.

news conferences—live events used to garner media attention for an announcement. A communicative entity or their representative usually makes an announcement then allows time for reporters to ask questions.

news release—content written with the look and feel of a news story and sent to media outlets to generate interest in an organization or communicative entity.

non-publics—stakeholders who are not affected by the CE and do not interact with it.

objectives—the goals or tasks to be accomplished.

ongoing campaign evaluation—monitoring the campaign while it is in progress to detect any issues or problems that might pop up in order to make necessary adjustments.

organic traffic—online search results that are populated from natural popularity.

organization theory—the study of the factors that shape and affect the success or failure of organizations.

organizational culture—the formal and informal practices of an organization, such as rites, rituals and the display of meaningful artifacts.

outcomes—the direct and indirect impact that campaign strategies have had on the targeted stakeholder group over a period of time.

outputs—the number of things, products or activities that have been accomplished by the campaign's tactics.

outside-in approach—when the needs, attitudes and behaviors of the stakeholders are placed at the front and center of the communication process.

over-the-top (OTT)—the service used to stream digital content to TV.

owned media—sharing of content on a communicative entity's own media, such as their website, catalogues or webinars. Owned media also include store signage, packaging and in-store displays.

paid media—a type of media that involves paying media owners for distribution of messages; also known as advertising.

paid traffic—search engine results from paid Google Ads.

passive stakeholders—people who passively respond to media messages rather than emotionally or intellectually engage with the content.

personal branding—the conscious and intentional effort to create and influence public perception of an individual.

phenomenon—an observable event.

physical sector—the infrastructure of a country such as transport, electricity, and water management systems, and even high-speed internet.

place branding—a strategic communications concept that applies similar techniques used in branding products and services to cities, regions, and countries.

political sector—the political system of a country such a constitutional democracy, a parliamentary system, an autocratic political system or a dictatorship.

practitioners— a person actively engaged in a field of practice, such as professional communicators.

professional practice—the work that trained and educated practitioners do.

proliferation of media—the explosion of the number and types of media.

psychographics—psychological and lifestyle characteristics of stakeholders.

public relations—the practice that establishes and maintains mutually beneficial relationships between an organization and their publics.

public sphere—an area in social life where people come together to identify and discuss societal problems.

publicity—attention given to someone or something by the media.

publics—in public relations, it is a group of people who face a similar problem, recognize the problem and organize themselves to do something about it.

pulsing media scheduling strategy—a strategy in which intermittent short bursts of messaging are implemented over a long period of time; designed to mimic continuity at the lower cost.

qualitative research—collecting data using words, such as a conversation, a written text, or an interview.

quantitative research—collecting data using numerical analysis.

quick response codes—also known as QR codes; a type of barcode that is scanned by users using a smartphone, which directs users to a specific webpage.

rational decision-making—decision-making based on the available data and facts.

reach—the percentage of people in the market that are exposed to an advertising message at least once.

reference groups—groups of people with whom an individual identifies and therefore assumes some of their values; these may be families, church groups or professional organizations.

referral traffic—when users find a website through another website, rather than through a major search engine.

reputation building—the communication practices of an organization that create trust in an organization.

request for proposal (RFP)—a document that companies will send out requesting information about plans you might have for them if they hired you to be the agency of record.

research question—a specific question about specific variables.

return on investment (ROI)—the percentage of how much profit is realized from an activity against its total cost.

roles theory—the study of the roles required in an organization and the skills required to fulfill a role.

ROPE—an acronym that stands for (initial) **R**esearch, **O**bjectives, **P**rogramming, and **E**valuation.

sample—a subset of the population selected for a research study.

search engine optimization (SEO)—the process of maximizing the number of visitors to a website by ensuring that the site appears high on the list of results returned by a search engine.

secondary research—the summary, collation and/or synthesis of existing data.

segmentation—breaking the total population into smaller homogeneous groups.

shared meaning—understanding things in the same way.

shared media—the posting of a communicative entity's content by stakeholders on social media.

situation analysis—a written document to explain the recent history and current situation of an organization. It is used in strategic planning to create a framework for future recommendations.

skippable in-stream ads—digital ads that play before, during or after other videos; the viewers have the option to skip the ad after five seconds, compared to non-skippable instream ads, which don't have the option to skip, giving advertisers a better opportunity to reach viewers.

SMART—an acronym used in developing good objectives that stands for **S**pecific, **M**easurable, **A**ttainable, **R**elevant, and **T**ime-bound.

SMS marketing—capturing a user's phone number and sending them promotional offers via text.

social media influencer—a user on social media who has established credibility in a specific industry, has access to a large audience, and can persuade others by virtue of their reach and authenticity.

social responsibility—an ethical framework which stipulates that organizations and individuals have an obligation to act for the good of the profession and society.

social sector—societal and population trends in terms of income, age, social class, education, geography, gender, and so forth.

soft skills—qualities or traits that impact how you interact with others.

sponsored content—see native advertising.

stakeholders—individuals and groups that can affect or be affected by the messages, actions, goals, and policies of the CE and have a direct or indirect interest in a CE.

statistics—mathematical methods to collect, organize, summarize and analyze data.

stereotypes—a widely held, oversimplified image or idea of a particular type of person or group of people.

stereotyping—a form of categorization that mentally organizes experiences and guides your behavior toward a particular group of people.

strategic communication—the practice of deliberate and purposive communication that a communication agent enacts in the public sphere on behalf of a communicative entity to reach set goals.

strategic communication campaign—a series of coordinated messages designed to achieve pre-determined goals for the communicative entity.

strategic planning—the process by which organizations determine what actions they will take to achieve specific goals.

strategist role—an expert in identifying and solving communication problems.

strategy—a thoughtful, logical and deliberate plan of action.

summative evaluation—evaluation that shows the impact of the completed campaign by comparing final results to the benchmarks stated in the campaign's objectives.

SWOT—an acronym that stands for Strengths, Weaknesses, Opportunities and Threats.

tactics—executional details that relate to the strategy.

target audiences—the intended group of individuals for an advertisement. A segment of the market to which a CE directs its messages.

tasks—the different types of work you must be able to do to perform your role.

technology sector—the technology infrastructure of a country, including the adoption and innovation of technology in society.

theoretical—a way of thinking about a phenomenon.

theory—a complex system of ideas that is intended to explain something.

third-party credibility—the tendency for stakeholders to value the opinion/expertise of a message that is delivered by someone other than the communicative entity.

trademark—the legally protected part of the brand, which can include the brand name, the brand's logo (design and colors), tagline (Just Do It), characters (Flo from Progressive), and other aspects of the brand.

transit advertising—advertising that appears in the public transportation system, including in transit stations, bus shelters and inside taxi cabs.

Transmission Model of Communication—a popular model that demonstrates how a message moves from a sender to a receiver through a medium.

universe—the population size of the group/market being targeted with an advertising message.

value proposition—an attractive statement in an ad that tells the reader why they should click on the ad to learn more about your product.

value system—core values that express the belief system and behavior expected of members.

values—the principles and ideals that a person, organization or culture believes to be important and therefore help guide ethical decision-making.

video news release (VNR)/audio news release (ANR)—a news release in the form of broadcast news story package, complete with video, voice-over, and additional video or audio footage.

virtual organization—an organization where employees telecommute and work in dispersed locations.

virtual reality (VR)—a digital environment that replaces the user's real-world environment.

vision statement—an aspirational and future oriented statement of the reason for the CE's existence.

wokeness—social and political awareness.

word-of-mouth (WOM)—personal communication about a communicative entity.

Index

Entries in *italics* denote figures; entries in **bold** denote tables.

Mill, John Stuart 102
millennials 148–9, 157, 184–5, 237
misinformation ecosystem 219
misrepresentation 104
mission statements 61–4, 72
mobile apps 209, 233, 268–9
mobile marketing 267–9; AR in 272
mobile technology 83
morals 98, 101; *see also* ethics
Motel 6 279
motivations 177
motives 177
MRI (Media Research Institute) 132–3
multi-skilling 31, 33, 49
Mulugeta, Kaleb 207–9, *208*

NAD (National Advertising Division) of BBB
   117
NARB (National Advertising Review Board)
   117–18
NARC (National Advertising Review Council)
   107
Narisetti, Raju 267
NASA 281–2
native advertising 222–4
need recognition 174–5
Netflix 220, 239, 242, 267
network organization 86–8, *87*
networking 37–8, 47, 60, 109
new technology 51; and decision-making
   89–90; and research 122; and stakeholder
   roles 165
New York Times 19, 217, 233–4, 248–50, 282
news conferences 18, 20, 195–6
news media 218; agenda-setting theory 124–5;
   First Amendment protections for 116
News Media Alliance 253
news releases 195
newspapers 233–4; and new technology 248
NFL (National Football League), research by
   122
NGOs (non-governmental organizations) 37
niche media 234–5
Nichols, Cynthia xix, 28, *29*
Nielsen Company 172, 236–7, 239
Nielsen PRIZM 172
Nike 94; brand loyalty to 287; in headlines 205;
   "Nike+" campaign 300; in search ads 258;
   swoosh 282–3
Noddings, Nel 101, 103
non-functional attributes 284
non-profits, career paths in 36–7
non-publics 168
Norenberg, Eric 214
normative stakeholders 164–6
North, Oliver 249
Northam, Ralph 93

Notthaft, Howard 55
NRA (National Rifle Association) 171, 249–50,
   262
NSAC (National Student Advertising
   Competition) 148, 228–30

Obama, Barack 156
objectives: developing in planning process
   146, 150–5; of research 127, 130; strategies
   to achieve 155; verbs appropriate for *153*;
   writing for strategic plan 64–5
observational learning 110
O'Donnell, Victoria 113
office culture 48
Olander, Stefan 270
one-shot designs 137
one-sided messages 197
ongoing evaluation 310
online presence, personal 50
oral report 141
organ donors 293–4
organic posts 256
organic traffic 221, 260
organization theory xvi, *7*, 10
organizational culture 7, 48, 90–2, 94
organizational goals 146, 154
organizational level 22–3, 25, 75; factors at
   85–90; impact of macro level on 75
organizational strategy 155
organizational structures 85–6, 88
OTT (over-the-top) 239
outcomes, measuring 311, *313*, 319
outputs, measuring 311, *313*, 319
outside-in approach 23–5, 72; and macro
   level 75–6; and message strategy 165; to
   planning 149; in public relations 34–5; and
   reputation building 92–3; and stakeholder
   communication 68–9
outstream ads 260
overlap, and choosing a job 48
owned media *204*, 209–10, 226–7, 244; and
   content marketers 220; measuring 227

Page, Max 230
paid media *204*, 205–7, 220–1, 244; in
   campaign budget 301; and earned media 224;
   leveraging 232; measuring 221; sponsored
   content as 223
paid traffic 221
passion 36, 41; and choosing a job 48
passive stakeholders 167–8
Penchansky, Raina 221
people, in campaign budget 301
PepsiCo 61–3, 288–9
Perez, Jacob *128*, 129
personal brand 4, 38–9, 49–50, 53
personal influencers 34